C. Osamaro Ibie

First Edition August, 1986

First Edition on August 1986

2012 Reprint edition by
BTB PUBLISHING
All rights reserved.

ISBN: 978-1-63652-424-5 (paperback)

Distributed online by :
www.bbwlogistics.com

About the Author

Mr. Cromwell Osamaro Ibie was born on 29th September, 1934. He received his elementary and secondary education at Benin City in the Bendel State of Nigeria between 1941 and 1953. He joined the Colonial Civil Service on 1st February, 1954 where he rose to the rank of Executive Officer before proceeding to the United Kingdom for further studies.

During his stay in the United Kingdom he studied at the Universities of London and Strathclyde where he obtained the B.Sc. (Hons) in Economics from the University of London and B.A. (Hons) in Economics from the University of Strathclyde.

He returned to the Nigerian Federal Public Service in September 1963 where he rose to the rank of Permanent Secretary, a position from which he voluntary retired on 1st April, 1980.

Mr. Ibie is currently engaged in private business in Lagos and Benin. He is the Chairman/Chief Executive of several industrial and commercial companies notably:-

    Efehi Ltd, Lagos.
    AEG — Nigeria Ltd.
    Eurotrade Cement Works (Nigeria) Ltd.
    Odin Biscuits Manufacturing Co. Ltd,
    TRW Investments (Nigeria) Ltd.

He is also a member of the Governing Council of the University of Benin.

PREFACE.

This work was embarked upon at the instance of Orunmila, who expressed undisguised anxiety for his followers to know more about him. The works revealed in these books are not just fairy tales contrived to tell interesting stories. They reveal the true account of life both in heaven and on earth. In the first instance, it will only have a meaning to initiates into Ifism, followers of Orunmila, as well as to students who are looking for materials to enrich knowledge of the unfettered ways of life.

The work is not designed to negate the relevance of the Ifa priest. It is only meant to provide a clearer understanding of the significance of whatever the Ifa priest reveals at divination or does, for suffering humanity. This set of books will neither produce an Ifa priest, nor tell all there is to know about Ifism. It will still be necessary to seek the assistance of the Ifa priest.

My gratitude goes to the following Ifa priests who were nominated by Orunmila himself to make their contributions to this work;

(1) Dr. Bayo Ifaniyi of Ode Irele in Ondo State who now resides at 29, Ajaguna Street, Stadium Area, Sango, Agege in Lagos State.
(2) Dr. Idahosa Imasuen who resided in Benin but who unfortunately joined Orunmila in heaven two weeks after completing his revelations. He specialised in the heavenly works of Orunmila, his OLODUS and ODUS.
(3) Chief Omoruyi Edokpayi of Ondo who specialises in the works done on earth by Orunmila and his apostles and disciples.
(4) Chief Adedayo Obalola of Ilesha, who is an all-round specialist on the works of Orunmila both in heaven and on earth. He has lived for over 110 years and is still growing strong.
(5) My father, Chief Thompson Ibie Odin, the Osague of Benin, who prepared the infrastructure for me to embark on this divine assignment.

My gratitude also goes to my expatriate secretary, Mrs. Patricia Mary Bassey, who has developed tremendous interest in this new facet of knowledge and closely assisted in the completion of the work.

I am equally grateful to Mr. Osazuwa Osagie who did the Ifa instrumental drawings as well as to Mr. Sylvester Ohenhen who did the bulk of the typing.

More importantly, my sincere gratitude goes to Orunmila himself who chose to make me the vehicle for imparting this rich and bottomless body of knowledge to mankind. I only hope I have suceeded in conveying his message.

It is hoped that the writer will live long enough to complete the work of preparing all the seventeen books, and that Orunmila will continue to assist in providing the time, health and the means of funding the completion of the work.

C. Osamaro Ibiè,
Efehi Ltd,
P.O. Box 10064,
Lagos, Nigeria.

TABLE OF CONTENTS.

CHAPTER I — Author's Early Association with Orunmila.
The Author's early association with Orunmila.	Pages 4-10
The Divine Invitation.	Pages 10-11

CHAPTER II — Orunmila and Other Divinities.
Orunmila and other Divinities.	Page 12
The Foundation of the World.	Pages 12-13
The Creation of the Divinosphere.	Page 13

CHAPTER III — The First Attempt to Establish A Living on the Earth.
The First Attempt to Establish a Living on the Earth.	Pages 14-16
The other Divinities return to Heaven.	Page 17
The Divinities return to the World.	Page 17
Money comes to the World.	Pages 17-18
The beginning of Physical Conflicts.	Page 18
The beginning of the end of the World.	Pages 18-19
The final destruction of the World.	Page 19

CHAPTER IV — The Second Habitation of the Earth.
The Second habitation of the Earth.	Pages 20-24
The arrival of the other Divinities.	Pages 24-25
The World settles down.	Page 25

CHAPTER V — How mankind comes to the World from Heaven.
How man comes to the World from Heaven.	Page 26
The influence of the Obstacle Divinity on our Destiny.	Pages 26-27
The role of the Guardian Angel.	Pages 27-28
The force of Destiny in our Lives.	Pages 28-29
The place of Divination in our Lives.	Pages 29-30
The origin of the problems experienced by human beings on Earth.	Pages 30-32

CHAPTER VI — Man's Relationship with God.
Man's relationship with God.	Pages 33-36

CHAPTER VII — The Effect of Sacrificial Offerings On Our Lives.
The effect of sacrificial offerings on our lives.	Pages 37-39

CHAPTER VIII — The Place of Esu In The Planetary System.
The place of Esu in the Planetary System.	Pages 40-46
The special significance of the he-goat to Esu.	Page 46

CHAPTER IX — The place of Witches in the Planetary System.
The place of Witches in the Planetary System.	Pages 47-49

CHAPTER X **Orunmila's Code of Conduct.**	
Code of Conduct.	Page 50
Orunmila's Eulogy on Perseverance.	Pages 50-51
Efficacy of patience in Ifism.	Pages 51-55
Ifa's concepts of good and evil.	Pages 56-58
CHAPTER XI **How Does One Come In Contact With Orunmila.**	
How one comes in contact with Orunmila.	Page 59
The role of Guiding Divinities in our lives.	Pages 59-63
The importance of devout fellowship in the Ifa religion.	Pages 63-64
CHAPTER XII **The Ifa Genealogy.**	
The Ifa genealogy.	Pages 65-66
The Order of Seniority.	Pages 67-76
CHAPTER XIII **The Olodus/Apostles of Orunmila Ejiogbe or Ogbe-Meji.**	
Ejiogbe or Ogbe-Meji.	Page 77
The Head as a Divinity.	Pages 77-78
Ejiogbe leaves for Earth.	Page 78
His Birth.	Pages 78-80
His Earthly Works.	Page 80
The Miracle at the Market Place.	Page 80
The Miracle of the Cripple and the Blind.	Page 80
The result of ignoring the advice of Ejiogbe.	Pages 80-82
How Ejiogbe survived the wrath of the Elders.	Page 82
How he got peace of mind.	Page 82
He returns to Heaven for Impeachment.	Pages 82-84
His Marriage.	Pages 84-85
His second Marriage.	Pages 85-86
How he helped a Litigant to win his case.	Page 86
How he made a barren woman to have a child.	Pages 86-87
How he helped the Mountain to resist the onset of his enemies.	Page 87
He saves his Son from the hands of Death.	Pages 87-88
How his Mother saves him from his enemies.	Page 88
How Ejiogbe became the King of the OLODUS (apostles)	Pages 88-91
The contest between Ejiogbe and Olofen.	Pages 91-92
His battle with death.	Page 92
Remarkable features of Ejiogbe.	Pages 92-94
The Puzzle of the Awos.	Page 94
His Poem for Progress and prosperity.	Pages 94-95
CHAPTER XIV **Oyeku-Meji**	
Oyeku-Meji.	Pages 97-98
Other Heavenly Works of Oyeku Meji.	Pages 98-99
How the Fish came to multiply.	Page 99
Oyeku Meji reveals the return of the Divinities to the World.	Pages 99-100
The Birth of Oyeku Meji.	Pages 100-101
God sends his only son Jewesun to Earth.	Pages 101-102
How he came to be called Jewesun.	Page 102
The Earthly Works of Oyeku Meji.	Pages 102-103
Why the Children of Oyeku Meji do not wear caps.	Page 103

How Eji-Oye solved the problem of Death.	Pages 103-104
How Oyeku Meji won favours and gifts.	Page 104
How he became King of the Night.	Pages 104-105
How he named a child Adenimi.	Pages 105-106

CHAPTER XV   Iwori-Meji

Iwori-Meji.	Page 107
Iwori-Meji's works in Heaven.	Page 107
Ejikoko Iwori makes Divination for the Sun, Moon and Darkness.	Page 107
Iwori-Meji makes Divination for Akun (the coral Bead).	Pages 107-108
He also makes Divination for the Lead.	Page 108
Ejikoko Iwori makes Divination for the Lion, the Cow and the Buffalo.	Pages 109-110
Iwori-Meji leaves Heaven for Earth.	Pages 110-111
His Birth.	Page 111
He contests for Seniority on Earth.	Pages 111-112
How he eventually excelled his Brothers.	Pages 112-114
How he became a strong Ifa priest.	Page 114
The later works of Iwori-Meji.	Pages 114-115
He made divination for an only child	Pages 115-116
He made divination for Orare	Pages 116-117
He made divination for Kiniun	Page 117
Advice to the sons of Iwori-Meji.	Pages 117-118

CHAPTER XVI   Edi-Meji.

Edi Meji.	Page 119
Idi-Meji helps Ode (outside) to regain prosperity.	Page 119
How the Groundnut came to multiply.	Pages 119-120
Idimeji makes Divination for the male sperm and the female menstruation.	Page 120
Idi-Meji as a prominent fighter.	Pages 120-123
He leaves for the Earth.	Pages 123-125
He cures the Cripple and the Blind Man.	Pages 125-126
The healing of the Blind and the Hernia afflicted.	Pages 126-127

CHAPTER XVII   Obara-Meji.

Obara-Meji.	Page 128
The rough passage of Prosperity to the World.	Pages 128-134
Obara-Meji's encounter with enemies.	Pages 134-135
He turns black into white.	Pages 135-136
He shows ingratitude to the Mother.	Pages 136-137
He wins a Chieftancy title.	Pages 137-138
He endures in his prosperity.	Page 138
The last major miracle performed by Obara-Meji.	Pages 138-139

CHAPTER XVIII   Okonron-Meji.

Okonron-Meji.	Page 140
He makes Divination for the Ant.	Page 140
He makes Divination for the tree family.	Page 141
He leaves Heaven for the World.	Pages 141-143
He becomes the Head Chief of Ilaye Oko.	Page 143
He makes Divination for Akpon to be able to bring peace to Ife.	Pages 143-144
The Salvation of Akeriwaye.	Page 144
The ill — fated coronation of Adeguoye	Page 144

CHAPTER XIX   Irosun-Meji.

Irosun-Meji.	Page 145
He makes Divination for all the Divinities before they left Heaven for the Earth.	Pages 145-146
He makes Divination for the Crocodile.	Page 146
He makes Divination for the Fish and the Rat for them to multiply.	Page 146
He comes to the World.	Pages 146-148
He makes Divination for the Earthworm.	Pages 148-149
He begins a new life on Earth.	Pages 149-150
The benevolence of Irosun-Meji.	Pages 150-151
He makes Divination for Airowosebo and Queen Mother of the Benin throne.	Pages 151-152
How he got popularity with kingship.	Page 152
He makes Divination for Olowu of Owu.	Pages 152-153
He makes Divination for the Eko and Akara sellers of Odere.	Page 153
Ifa-alaaye takes the crown of Odere.	Pages 153-154
The last test for Irosun-Meji.	Page 154

CHAPTER XX   Owanrin-Meji.

Owanrin Meji	Page 155
He prepares to come to the World.	Pages 155-156
He ties the hands of his enemies.	Pages 156-158
His experience as a Trader.	Page 158
He tries his hands at Farming.	Pages 158-160
He takes a new wife.	Pages 160-161
He checkmates the machinations of his enemies.	Page 161
Owanrin-Meji on the threshold of Prosperity.	Pages 161-162
He becomes famous through his Son.	Pages 162-163
The last major work of Owanrin-Meji — he saves the favourite wife of Olofen from the evil machinations of her mates.	Pages 163-164
He makes Divination for two wives of the same husband.	Pages 164-165

CHAPTER XXI   Ogunda-Meji.

Ogunda-Meji.	Pages 166-169
The Heavenly Works of Ogunda-Meji.	Pages 169-170
He makes Divination for the Boa.	Pages 170-172
He makes Divination for ODE.	Page 172
Eji-oko seduces the wife of Death.	Pages 172-174
Eji-oko's second wife.	Pages 174-176
He escapes from Heaven to the Earth.	Page 176
He makes Divination for Oyi.	Pages 176-177
He settles down on Earth.	Pages 177-179
Ogunda-Meji cures the barreness of Olofen's wives.	Pages 179-184
He makes Divination for Aguofenla (the trench hunter.)	Pages 184-185
He makes Divination for 2 fish catchers.	
How Ogunda-Meji got the sobriquet of Ogunda-Ja-Meji.	Page 185
His surrogates take over Divination for the crown prince of Benin Kingdom.	Pages 185-186
He helps the people of Oyo in their war with Ilesha.	Pages 186-187
Ogunda-Meji leaves for Heaven.	Pages 187-190

CHAPTER XXII   Osameji.

Osa-Meji.	Page 191
He makes Divination for the cotton plant.	Pages 191-192
Osameji prepares to come to the World.	Pages 192-193
His Birth.	Pages 193-194
Esu finally gets his he-goat from Osameji.	Pages 194-195
The Witches discover the Truth.	Pages 195-196
Osameji makes Divination for sixteen Obas.	Page 196
He is accused of being a Witch.	Pages 196-197
He discovers the cause of his problems.	Page 197
He finally settles his score with Witchcraft with a concordat.	Pages 197-200

CHAPTER XXIII   Etura-Meji.

Etura-Meji.	Page 201
He makes Divination for the Groundnut.	Pages 201-202
He makes Divination for the Whiteman when he was anxious to know how to manufacture a live human being.	Page 202
He makes Divination for Truth and Falsehood.	Pages 202-203
Otumeji leaves Heaven for the World.	Pages 203-205
He opens the way for Wealth to come to the World.	Pages 205-206
The origin of Coup d'etat against seniority.	Pages 206-207
He goes to Imodina to help the Imoles.	Pages 207-209
He goes to Imeka.	Pages 209-211

CHAPTER XXIV   Irete-Meji.

Irete-Meji.	Page 212
Eji Elemere reveals how Orunmila fought the battle for prosperity on behalf of his followers.	Pages 212-213
Eji Elemere comes to the World.	Pages 213-220
How Success evoked emnity for Eji Elemere.	Pages 220-221
How the he-goat became the staple food of Esu.	Pages 221-222
The Divination for (Yeye Olomo Mefa) the Mother of six children.	Pages 222-223

CHAPTER XXV   Eka-Meji.

Eka-Meji.	Page 224
He makes Divination for the Cat.	Page 224
He prepares to come to the World.	Pages 224-225
He leaves for the Earth.	Page 225
He wins a crown.	Pages 225-226
Poem for correcting the difficult features of Ekameji.	Pages 226-227

CHAPTER XXVI   Ologbon-Meji.

Ologbon–Meji.	Page 228
He makes Divination for Ekun and Ifaa (the Tiger and the Bush Cat.)	Pages 228-229
He makes Divination for Egherun the most beautiful bird in heaven as well as Ugun or Vulture.	Pages 229-230
He makes divination for the hunter with a stubborn wife.	Pages 230-231
Ologbon-meji leaves heaven for earth.	Page 231
He seduces the wife of Ogun.	Pages 231-232
How Orunmila left the World.	Pages 232-233

CHAPTER XXVII   Ose-Meji.
Ose-Meji. — Pages 234-235
His activities in Heaven. — Pages 235-237
He leaves for the Earth. — Pages 237-240
He takes to Ifa art and practice. — Pages 240-241
He makes Divination for Akinyele of Iwere. — Page 241
The hard luck story of Olokose. — Pages 241-242
The Divination for the Olubadan of Ibadan. — Pages 242-243
He makes Divination for Olokun. — Page 243
The personal experience of Osemeji. — Pages 243-244
He lives longer than any other Olodu. — Page 244

CHAPTER XXVIII   Ofun-Meji.
Ofun-Meji. — Page 245
Ofunmeji reveals how long it took for God to complete his creative works. — Pages 245-246
How the Parrott became a symbol of nobility. — Page 246
Orunmila converts the authority of all the other Divinities to himself. — Pages 246-247
Ofunmeji leaves for the Earth. — Pages 247-248
His Birth. — Page 248
He returns to Heaven. — Pages 248-249
The origin of the Secret fraternity. — Page 250
Ofunmeji's second coming to the Earth. — Page 250
The Divination for Orangun and Akogun. — Pages 250-251
Divination for Aganbi, the barren woman of Ife. — Page 251

THE COMPLETE WORKS OF ORUNMILA — THE DIVINITY OF WISDOM

INTRODUCTION

Ifa philosophy is one of the oldest forms of knowledge revealed to mankind. Unfortunately, the revelations of Orunmila have since the beginning of time, been shrouded in utter secrecy and those who could afford the time and leisure to acquire it, had no means of leaving any records behind them. Whatever we know of Ifa today has been handed down from generation to generation. A lot of what people know about Ifa is also revealed, even to this day, by Orunmila himself because he constantly appears to his adherents in dreams, to teach them what they ought to know about him and his works. Knowledge of Ifa has mainly survived by oral tradition from one Ifa priest to another. No conscious effort has ever been made to record the complete works of Orunmila for public consumption. Even the Ifa priests themselves are often reluctant to part with their knowledge for fear that if the knowledge becomes public property, the mythical facade behind which they operate will be destroyed. This is not entirely their fault because it takes at least 21 years of indentured servitude to produce a proficient Ifa priest.

But for the fact that this work was directly inspired by Orunmila himself, it would not have been easy for anyone to afford the cost in time, effort and money, to embark on such an endless adventure. That is to say that the body of knowledge called Ifa is endless, ageless and eternal. It will be seen from his revelations that Orunmila, although the youngest of all the divinities created by God, was actually God's own witness when he began to create other organic and inorganic substances. That is why he is referred to as Eleri Upin. He alone knows the true nature and origin of all animate and inanimate objects created by God.

This knowledge has given him such unparalleled powers that make him the most effective of all the divinities, who were the first creatures of God. His followers who are able to acquire some of the knowledge therefore wield tremendous powers which have often baffled many into calling it magic or juju.

On the other hand, the expression "Ifa" encompasses the revelations, way of life, and religion taught by Orunmila. That is why it is often said that Orunmila is the divinity but Ifa is his word.

The Ifa priest is the mouth-piece of Orunmila and until relatively recently, he was the axis around which daily life revolved in the community. In those days, it was respectable to go to him openly to seek solutions to the problems of living. In recent times, it has become fashionable to consult the Ifa priest in absolute secrecy and stealth. Three factors have been responsible for this spectacular change in attitude.

The first is the advent of modern civilization and the education it brought in its wake. The second is the over-bearing influence of later-day religions which were used by mankind as weapons of conquest not only of mortal minds but also for manifestly territorial ambitions. The third is the aggregate impact of the first two forces. The children of Ifa priests no longer wish to be associated with the religion and way of life of their parents, which they dismiss as superstitious paganism.

Many Ifa priests endowed with brilliant knowledge of the theory and practice of Ifa or Ifism have since died leaving no records of their wealth of knowledge and experience. The volumes of books which I am about to embark upon, are therefore an attempt to leave a historical account of the great works of Orunmila. They are meant to provoke debate for the enrichment of knowledge so that upcoming generations will know about Orunmila and his approach to religion, and in time, be proud to be associated with it.

This work is also designed to assist students of Ifa philosophy in acquiring more in-depth knowledge of Ifism, as well as to generate greater interest in it. It will also provide assistance to those who have been initiated into the Ifa religion, but who continue to doubt the veracity of the entire concept of Orunmila. All too often when people go to an Ifa priest, he chants away to his clients, the incantations of the particular ODU that has appeared to him. Thereafter, he prescribes the sacrifices to be made without bothering to tell the enquirer the history underlying the sacrifice he is required to make. Ifa priests do so because they believe that the uninitiated mind will not understand it. The client begins to wonder whether or not the sacrifice is relevant. Whether or not he does the sacrifice becomes contigent on the reputation of the Ifa Priest and not on his conviction of the necessity for it. More importantly, it is an attempt to make the religion of Ifa (or Ifism) rank paripassu with much younger religions like Judaism, Christianity, Buddism and Islam. These other religions had the advantage of earlier documentation. Otherwise we shall see that Ifa is a much richer and an older body of knowledge.

It is important to note however that this work lays no claim whatsoever to a complete account of the Ifa religion. It is said that no one can know in full the complete works of Orunmila. This work is therefore a beginning and the research will continue through out the life of the writer. It is hoped that it will be updated from time to time in the light of the out-come of further researches and revelations.

On the other hand, the writer hopes with these volumes of seventeen books in all, to de-mystify the philosopy of Ifa religion. Contrary to all outward appearances there is nothing magical about Ifa. The art is analogous to the work of Astrology. An astrologer tells a man's future by reading the behaviour of the stars that were in the sky at the time the person was born. In the same way, when a child is born and Ifa's principal divination instruments are used to touch its head and sounded, the instrument will declare the name of the ODU that is his guiding star. The Ifa priest will then reveal the life history of the ODU that has appeared to him and can proclaim with 100% certainty that the life of the child will take the same path like that of the appearing ODU. It is the same thing that happens when a particular ODU appears at divination when a person is being initiated into the Ifa religion at the secret conclave (Ugbodu).

For example, if at a naming ceremony or during Ifa initiation, Ejiogbe is the ODU that appears, the person can conveniently be told that his life story will follow the path of Ejiogbe's life. If for instance, the initiate is dark complexioned and of average height, he can be told that if he is able to follow the ethos and taboos of Ejiogbe, he will surely prosper in life and will spend most of his life in the service of humanity. If on the other hand the person is fair in complexion or short, he can be told that he is not likely to be exceedingly prosperous unless he assists his Ifa through special sacrifices to remove the obstacles that Ejiogbe had in similar circumstances. In his case, Ejiogbe had to return to heaven to regenerate himself before fortune smiled on him on earth.

In the same way, if any particular ODU appears at divination the Ifa priest is going to advise the enquirer to perform the same sacrifice performed by that ODU or which he advised his clients to do in the same circumstances when he was practising in the world. If divination reveals that death is imminent for a person, the Ifa priest will merely tell the person to do the same sacrifice that Orunmila did or was told to do and which he advised others to do, to avoid the danger of untimely death, in similar circumstances.

It is reasonable to imagine from the foregoing analysis that far from being a magician, the Ifa priest is only a skilful interpreter. As long as he can develop a retentive memory, since most of them cannot read and write, he has only to relate the problems of a client to a corresponding situation that occurred thousands or millions of years ago to reveal the problems besetting an enquirer of today and put them in the proper frame. These accounts of the work of Orunmila are an attempt therefore to assist non-initiates as well as neophytes to be able to translate Ifa revelations for themselves in order to appreciate what the priest tries to do in the course of his Ifa art and practice.

It is important to appreciate from the outset that Orunmila does not go about looking for converts. This is religion for the individual, which does not rely on the weight of numbers for survival. Infact, Orunmila teaches that the best way of knowing and appreciating his teachings is through the efficacy of his work and not by the melody of his music.

CHAPTER 1
AUTHOR'S EARLY ASSOCIATION WITH ORUNMILA

For a man who was born into a Christian Family, baptised with the name of Clement, and confirmed with the name of Joseph in the Catholic Faith, and who at an earlier stage in life even contemplated a sojourn into the priesthood, it is difficult to imagine how the writer came about a "primitive" religion like IFA, or Ifism. That perhaps goes to indicate the strength of the traditional pull that the Ifa religion has on the minds of its followers.

My father retired as a civil servant at the age of 48 in 1951 after which he took to farming and politics. But the Ifa pull became so strong that he eventually gave up farming for an indepth study of the Ifa religious corpus. At eighty three today, he is a practising Ifa priest. I had always argued with him that it bordered on laziness for him to take to such "fetish idolatry". He would always respond by ridiculing me with the remark that in time I would change my mind. Nonetheless, each time I saw people coming to thank him for saving their lives, those of their children or other members of their families or for helping them to avert what to them was a near catastrophe, I began to wonder whether there was actually something miraculous about this seemingly mundane religion. I have seen ardent Christians and Muslims coming to him and his colleagues for succour. I have seen people coming to see him from places far and near because they were told that unless they did so and so in an Ifa shrine, they would not be free from their afflictions. I have also seen such people return days, weeks, or months later to express profound gratitude.

Although I was still too much of a practising Christian to give any positive thought to these contemporary developments, there is no gainsaying the fact that I was beginning to ask myself certain questions. When I therefore retired from the civil service in 1980, I decided to find out more about this religion in an irresistible quest for answers to the many questions that man has tried to answer over the ages. What is the actual relationship between man and God? What is the relationship between heaven and earth and what is the relationship between man and the divinities.

I wish however to narrate a spectacular development soon after my retirement from the public service in 1980. There was this Yoruba man in his nineties who had been associating with my father since my childhood but who I had not seen for over eleven years. His name is Chief Obalola, himself a practising Ifa priest all his life.

One day, I was buying materials for renovation work in my house at Benin when this old man walked up to me and I knelt down to greet him. He asked after my father and I told him he was very well. He then asked me whether I was still in Lagos and I told him that although I had retired from the public service, I was nonetheless still very much in Lagos. Curiously, he asked whether I already understood the Yoruba Language and I confirmed that although I had lived in Ibadan and Lagos since 1959 I still could not speak a sentence in Yoruba.

He shook his head and remarked that he sympathised with me. I told him that I did not think I needed sympathy since I was not missing much from my non-understanding of the Yoruba Language and that in any case I had a Yoruba wife who could always fill in the gaps. After a deep reflection, he told me that ever since I was a child, he had told my father that Orunmila had a special assignment for me and that he was only lamenting on that day because Orunmila had told him that if I had understood his language

(Yoruba) he would have done great things through me. I asked what in this world would Orunmila hope to do through me when I did not even believe in him. As he was leaving, he told me to look out carefully so that I would not have to be between the devil and deep blue sea, before appreciating the place of Orunmila in my life.

When I got home, I told my father what Chief Obalola told me and he confirmed that they had discussed the matter ever since I was eight days old when they did my naming ceremony through Ifa religion.

When I retired voluntarily in March 1980 at the age of 45, I discovered soon afterwards that I did not have much to do to keep me busy, so I decided to write a book on the Economic History of Nigeria between 1960 and 1980. I had scarcely gone one fifth of the way in writing the book when the Ifa pull became too strong for me to ignore. I do not believe in mysteries and miracles, but I must confess that by 1981 I did not think of any other thing except how to make other people know about the secrets of the Ifa religion.

I have however since discovered that there are no mysteries in the Ifa religion. It is just that its knowlege has down the ages been left in the brains of illiterate old men, who having spent scores of years learning about Ifa are not too keen to part with the knowledge except to those who are prepared to subject themselves to the apprenticeship process that they too went through. I have since discovered that to become an Ifa priest, the student has virtually to become an indentured servant to an Ifa priest, for anything between twenty and thirty years.

In the first place, there was a Mr. Bayo Ifaniyi, an Ikale man from Ode Irele in Ondo State whom I met in 1967 when a relation brought him to my house to help him secure a menial factory job to do. I subsequently introduced him to Enpee Industries Ltd at Ilupeju, Lagos, where he was employed as a machine operator. He did that job for about 2 years after which he gave it up but I did not know at the time why he gave up the job. About seven years later, he visited me in the company of the relation who brought him to me in the first instance. I gave them kolanut which he split and began to say sooth through the kolanut. In a mood of impatience with his unsolicited fortune telling I told him to eat his kolanut and drink the beer I gave him and go away. He however said one or two things — I did not quite listen to him — but which manifested within a matter of days. A week later, I told my cousin to invite him. It was at that stage I was told that he had given up his factory work because Orunmila wanted him to take to the practice of Ifa on a full time basis. He was therefore the first person I invited to tell me more about Orunmila when the call came to me in 1981.

I also recall another young man who I met in 1969. He is Mr. Idahosa Imasuen of Benin. I got to know later that my father prepared my own Ifa for me in 1944 when I was in Primary II in the elementary school. All I can remember of that incident is that I suddenly became crippled and could no longer stand on my two feet. For about six weeks I was a cripple, crawling all over the place on my knees. My father got a paper from his office and took me to see a white Medical Officer at the General Hospital in Benin City. I think his name was Dr. Stevenson, who examined me and suggested I should be taken to Lagos for proper medical examination. My mother would not buy the idea of my going to Lagos for treatment for fear of having my legs amputated.

I had become very irritable because I loved my classroom life and my role as a mass server in the Catholic Church. I was also too fond of my Catechism lessons under the late Brothers James and Pius. I was missing all those exhilirating chores, for, since I could neither walk to school nor to church, I was not in a position to participate in any educational or Christian activities.

I have vague recollections of what happened after I had been ill for exactly six weeks. My father had invited some old men who came to his house to prepare some black kernels which they placed in a calabash full of oil and I was called into that room. I cannot quite remember what happened thereafter nor do I know whatever it had to do with me. But I do remember that later that night, I was able to stand on my feet again to walk outside the house to urinate. I was however not quite awake and so I did not raise any alarm about the change in my physical condition. The following morning I woke up normally and walked to my father's room to offer him the traditional morning greetings. He was surprised to see me back on my feet. He muttered something which I could not quite comprehend, but I was able to go back to school that morning and there has been no relapse ever since.

However, in 1955, I had left secondary school and was working at Warri, still a practising Catholic. In August of that year, I had an attack of malaria. I was treated with Mepacrine Tablets, the popular anti-malarial tablets available at that time. It was a Doctor Ezekwe who treated me. The Malaria persisted for quite sometime and when it became serious, I was put on three days sick leave.

I was at the time living alone as a young bachelor at No.4, Ginuwa Road in Warri. One afternoon, my guardian in Warri, a Mr. Wilfred O. Osunde, himself a Nursing superintendent cum Radiographer at the Warri General Hospital, visited me and found me in a pretty bad shape. He asked whether I had been taking the medications given to me at the hospital and I answered affirmatively. He administered four tablets to me on the spot and left.

Soon after he took leave of me, I began to perspire profusely and soon felt well. My temperature went down and the fever had ostensibly gone. It was a Saturday, and I was able to light my stove to prepare a meal. My late friend and next door neighbour at No.4, Ginuwa Road, Warri, Mr. Joseph Okuofu had planned to go to Benin when he returned from his UAC job that afternoon. At about 1p.m, he came into my room to find out how I was faring. Seeing that I was virtually well, he suggested that I should accompany him to Benin for the week-end since I had not been home for weeks. Since I felt strong enough for the journey, I readily agreed to go with him.

At that time, the Ologbo river between Sapele and Benin was flooded and the stretch of the road between Koko junction and Ologbo town had become unmotorable. People travelling from Warri and Sapele to Benin at the time had to disembark at the Koko junction to ferry across the river by canoes, to take motor transport from Ologbo to Benin. I still remember that we travelled with Joseph's girl-friend, Elizabeth, an Urhobo girl. When the Armel's lorry took us from Warri to Koko junction, we all dismounted and the three of us walked down the slope to board a canoe to Ologbo town. I was beginning to feel dizzy by the time we boarded another motor vehicle at Ologbo. I must admit that to this day, I have no memory of what happened between Ologbo and Benin.

I was later told that I was rather passive in my reactions during the rest of the journey to Benin, not talking to anyone and not replying when spoken to. On getting to Benin, Joseph and his girl friend bade me good night and went away. I must have hovered around a bit and took the direction of the first road I saw. I did not regain consciousness until about

10p.m that night when I suddenly found myself in the middle of no where. When I saw a young man on push bicycle coming along the road, I stopped him and asked him to show me the way to No.4 Edo College Road, my father's residence in Benin City. The young man alighted from his bicycle and asked what was wrong with me. I told him I was coming from Warri but was not altogether feeling fine, when I left Warri for Benin.

In an exclamation of sympathy he told me that I was five miles away from Benin at a village called OKA. He then offered to take me to Benin with his bicycle. Since he did not know Edo College Road, he stopped as soon as he got to the town to ask for directions and he eventually landed me in my father's house at about 11.15p.m. When he narrated how he found me at Oka village to my parents, my mother burst into tears. They compensated the young man after he told them to take good care of me.

I slept soundly that night, although I had renewed bouts of hallucinations the following day. It was now clear that I was suffering from spasmodic paranoid psychosis. Since I was on three days sick leave which had expired the previous Friday, I had to return to Warri on Sunday and to the Doctor. My mother accompanied me to Warri on Sunday. The following morning, my mother accompanied me to the hospital where she made a passionate plea to place me on a week's sick leave to enable her take me back to Benin for adequate care. The Doctor felt insulted and instructed that I should immediately be hospitalised for observation and treatment.

I was given a bed at the General Hospital and my blood samples were taken by the late Pathologist Ikomi. He diagnosed what was later called "Mepacrine Psychosis". For the next three weeks, I was receiving treatment at the hospital with very little or no change in my condition. My cousin and guardian Mr. W. O. Osunde then made a special appeal to the Doctor to discharge me for traditional treatment at home. Reluctantly, Dr. Ezekwe agreed to put me on two weeks sick leave and told me to report back at the end of that period.

My mother and I travelled back to Benin immediately. On getting home, my father told me that we had to complete my Ifa ceremony immediately because Orunmila was said to be complaining that he had remained for too long inside the oil — eleven years (1944 to 1955). I must confess that I had no idea of what he was talking about. During my hospitalization he had once again invited the old men who prepared the initial stages of the Ifa ceremony. He disclosed to me that the old men had told him that Orunmila followed me to the world because of the hydra-headed problems I was destined to come across on earth and that I did not recognise his importance in my life. My father told me that all was set and that the ceremony was to commence at once.

All that was Greek to me because I remember telling him that if he wanted to eat meat, I would buy a goat for him to kill but should not tell me anything about some black kernel juju which had remained for too long inside a calabash of oil. In any case, I soon lost my memory again and by the time I regained consciouness, my hair had been clean shaven as part of the ceremony. The Old men who I recognised later to be Ifa priests, were gathered in my father's sitting room and they began to tell me about my past, present and future. They mentioned the name of my Orunmila and told me that my life would go according to the life of that Orunmila. It was from that moment that I began to follow the rest of the ceremony, and exactly seven days after I came from Warri, I was well enough to go back to work.

When I returned alone this time to Dr. Ezekwe, I was able to discuss intelligently and flawlessly with him once more. He laughed and later told my cousin that traditional medicine had worked wonders. I was back to work soon afterwards and have had no more hallucinations ever since.

I got married in 1959 and had a daughter by that marriage. I married my wife with the blessings of the Catholic Faith because I still could not have anything to do with this Orunmila, which my father kept with him. Throughout my course of studies in the UK, I remained a practising Catholic with my wife, who is also from a Catholic family. While in Glasgow, I was such a devout Catholic that the Chaplain of Glasgow Universtiy, Reverend Father Matthew Dooley and even Bishop Ward of Glasgow virtually became my parents-in-Christ. I spent all my leisures at the chaplaincy, and was always a mass-server in the chaplaincy. At one stage, I even gave serious thought to the idea of priesthood. The only factor that checkmated my admiration for the priesthood was that I wanted my wife to have a boy in addition to my daughter. But providence did not chance us to have any other child.

I returned home in 1963 and remained a practising Catholic, attending St.Anthony's Church at Surulere and later St.Dominic's Church at Yaba. My wife still did not have another child and my parents were really beginning to mount pressure on me to take a second wife, which was for me, out of the question, true to the tenets of the Catholic faith.

The crunch came in 1969 when out of frustration at not having any more children coupled with temporary impotence, I almost took my life on a Saturday night in August, 1969. The Ifa priests had warned me during the final Ifa initiation ceremony in 1955 that If I did not take to the Ifa religion, Ifa would not be in a position to help in abating the danger to my life by an incident of temporary sexual impotence, which was bound to occur at one stage in my life. My father kept reminding me that he was told when I was eight days old that I was destined to have many children, but that Orunmila would not be able to usher them in if I did not take to the ways of Ifa. On the other hand, I preferred to die rather than abandon my Christian ways.

I was only miraculously saved from taking my life on that fateful Saturday night in August, 1969 at about 3.00a.m at the back of my 2 Elmes Road residence at the Medical compound in Yaba. As soon as my attempted suicide was foiled by divine intervention, I wept for the rest of the night without having any sleep.

The following morning, which was a Sunday, I went as usual to St. Dominics Catholic church at Yaba. On my return from the Church, I met a man at the entrance to my residence dressed in the regalia of a Bini chief. I asked him what his mission was and he replied that he was asking for the address of the late Dr. Idehen, when he was directed from the Yaba roundabout to the house of a Bini man inside the medical compound, who might direct him to Dr. Idehen's residence. He introduced himself as Chief Igbinovia of No.8 Nekpenekpen Street in Benin City.

I took him to my sitting room and entertained him to the traditional kolanuts and drinks. When he split the kolanut in the traditional way, he threw it on the plate on which it was presented and he muttered something to himself. Meanwhile, I telephoned Dr. Idehen who regretted that he could not see that man immediately because he had a job to do at the State House. He asked me to tell the man to see him later that day, between 5 and 6p.m.

Coming back to Chief Igbinovia, he asked me whether I had Orunmila, and I told him that although my father was supposed to have prepared one for me several years before, I was nonetheless a Christian, as he could see that I was just returning from the church with prayer books and a

Rosary in hand. To my utter amazement, he brought out his Ifa chain (OKPELE) and inquired whether it was my house Orunmila sent him to visit in Lagos. With all I had heard about the ways of these "quack native doctors", I began to wonder whether he was looking for an opportunity of making a few pounds on me. After he threw down his Okpele three times, he turned to me and said that whether or not I believed what he was going to tell me, he was in duty bound to give me the divine message all the same. He then disclosed that he was sleeping in his house the previous night, when at about 3a.m Orunmila woke him up and told him that one of his children was between life and death in Lagos and that he should go at once to tell him to return home to where his Ifa was prepared for him, and feast it with a goat, so that he, (Orunmila) could disclose the cause and cure of the man's problems.

In view of the fact that the time of 3a.m at which he supposedly had his dream in Benin coincided with the time I had attempted to take my life the previous night in Lagos, I became more interested in his exposé and began to listen to him with rapt attention. Without disclosing to him what happened to me the previous night, he told me that whatever problems I had were not bereft of solutions, provided I went home to make the sacrifice prescribed by Orunmila. The only question I asked him was whether Orunmila was the cause of my problems because I had refused to tread his path. He replied that Orunmila was not given to punishing or blackmailing those who refused to follow him. He added that the reason why Orunmila insists on being recognised by those who he accompanies to this earth, is to be put him in a position to help them thwart the evil machinations of their enemies. He also disclosed that my temporary sexual problems, preceded by ten years of childlessness was caused by enemies who contrived them as a way of bringing an abrupt end to an otherwise long and eventful life. I promised him that I was going to do the sacrifice and he left. He refused to accept any money from me except his transport fare of £2. I never saw him again until ten years later in 1979, at a relation's house, nor have I seen him again since then.

The following Monday, I successfully applied for my annual vacation leave and immediately travelled to Benin. For about three weeks before my attempted suicide, I had been totally impotent and absolutely incapable of having sex, both extra-murally and intramurally. On getting home I told my father what happened and once again he invited some of the Ifa priests who were still alive to help in offering the sacrifice to my Orunmila. After serving it, the priests were assembled five days later to sound Ifa as they call it — that is, to ask him what revellation he had to make. What I can disclose of what they told me on that day is that I should keep my Orunmila shrine with me wherever I chose to live and since I was living in Lagos, I should go to Lagos with it.

Incidentally, Chief Obalola who was once again available, asked me pointedly whether I was still a complete man as I was standing before him. I could not help but answer negatively, although I had not discussed that aspect of my problems previously with anyone at home. He also asked me whether I had tried to take my life and I answered in the affirmative. He re-assured me that having survived those two pre-destined ordeals, that was going to be the turning point in my life, provided I stopped neglecting my Orunmila. He predicted that any woman I would have an affair with from then on would become pregnant, but I should not decline responsibility or get scared. I was not to take any medicine for my condition and the surprising aspect was that he asked whether my wife was around and I told him she was not around. He told me that if I had any girl friend in

Benin, I should invite her that night to sleep with me. He reassured me that Orunmila told him I would regain my potency from that night. Suffice it to say that everything he said came true as he predicted.

I have come to have several children between 1970 and the present time, and my life has been a success story since then. One of the Ifa priests present on that day was Mr. Idahosa Imasuen, who is a major contributor to the subject of this book.

I met the third of my Ifa teachers soon after my retirement in 1980. He is Chief Omoruyi Edokpayi, who lives in Ondo. He visited me on the 21st of May, 1980 at my new residence in Ajao Estate at Oshodi on the precincts of Lagos. He came in the company of a relation of mine. Once again, in accordance with the Bini tradition, I gave him kolanut and when he split it and threw it on the plate he looked at me with astonishment. I became baffled again, because I had seen many of such ominous looks in the past. He told me that Orunmila had asked him to tell me that people were going to be sent to come and kill me unless I made sacrifice to Ifa immediately. He told me that if I made the sacrifice I would escape death but would be the victim of some theft, to atone for my life.

He called one of my wives and told her to make sacrifice to Orunmila with a sword to avoid being killed or injured with a sword. She, being the daughter of a Bishop, never used to give much attention to such things, so she did not do the sacrifice although I added a sword to the materials with which I made the sacrifice.

Exactly seven days after I made the sacrifice, which was on the 1st of June 1980, forty armed Robbers attacked my Lagos house at 2a.m. They broke every door in my house and removed everything of value in the house. But by the Grace of God, no life was lost even though the head of the robbers did at one stage of the nearly two hours operation, order the three men pointing guns at me, to shoot. I do not know how I was saved from them. They were probably dazzled by the items of value which they took away.

One of them tried to rape my wife who was told to make sacrifice with a sword. As the rapist tried again to tear up the girdle she was wearing, the sword also injured her thigh. She was saved by the timely orders of their commander to move when time was running out on them.

It was during the cause of reflecting on these spectacular events in my life that I began to wonder whether a prima facie case was not already established for researching in-depth into the mysteries of Ifa. When Chief Edokpayi interpreted the life history of my own Orunmila, he told me that everything that happened to me since I was born, coincided with the life history of my own Orunmila.

This book is therefore an attempt to find out the correlation co-efficient between the life of Orunmila and the lives of Ordinary mortals, who suddenly find themselves more by accident than design, becoming the followers of Orunmila.

The Divine invitation:

I did not know that the voice which stopped me from taking my life on the 23rd of August, 1969 was that of Orunmila. I only recognised it on the 3rd June, 1979 when the voice spoke to me again in Hamburg, Western Germany. I had been to Germany for medical check-up, at which I was given an untidy bill of health. The Doctors had told me to go easy in whatever job I was doing and I had been contemplating a strategy for giving myself a more liveable schedule of work.

I went to bed very early that evening and at about 1a.m, a man dressed in a white robe with a horse tail in hand, woke me up. He also wore blue beads on his right wrist. He introduced himself as the Eleri Ukpin and the servant of God. He asked me whether I had forgotten that he accompanied me to the world. He told me that I had promised in heaven when I was leaving for the earth that I would only serve humanity up to the age of 45 after which I was to begin to serve the divinities. He told me that I should not allow the first anniversary of his appearance to me, to meet me in the service of the public.

He also told me that if I allowed the attractions of office to becloud my vision, I would pay for it with my personal freedom. Before departing, he reiterated that I should not allow the middle of the following year to meet me still doing the work that I had been doing for the past 25 years. I was quite confused. I did not know whether it was an apparition or a dream, but I was wide awake and did not sleep much for the rest of that night.

I flew back to Lagos soon afterwards and went straight to Benin to seek my father's advice on the significance of that strange experience. When I disclosed to my father how the man appeared to me and what he called himself, he told me that it was Orunmila that appeared to me. He advised that notwithstanding the fact that I was not ready for retirement, he thought it best to put in my notice of retirement right away. When I returned to Lagos the following day, I quickly called my secretary and dictated my notice of retirement.

Once again in January, 1980, the same voice ordered me to wake up and see the board he had positioned in front of me. In that single night, he taught me the names of the sixteen apostles (OLODUS) of Orunmila and how to mark them on the Ifa tray. He promised to let me know subsequently how to construct the names of his 240 disciples (ODUS). With that he again disappeared from view and I got up quickly to jot down the sixteen names and their markings.

He appeared subsequently to me to teach me the names of the 240 ODUS and I wrote all of them down on a big chart which I have to this day. Three days before my notice of retirement was to expire, he appeared once more to tell me that he wanted me to let the world know about his role in the planetary system. He also taught me how to recognise and read the divination instrument called Okpele. Before leaving, he told me that since I did not understand his language (Yoruba), I should look for a man called Bayo Ifaniyi to tell me what to do. I had not seen Bayo for almost seven years. I then quickly sent for him and told him that Orunmila asked me to consult him. That was the beginning of my long sojourn into the endless work of Orunmila and the Ifa philosophy which form the basis of this book.

I wish to end this chapter by paying tribute to Orunmila for giving me a timely warning to leave the public service in 1980. I did hesitate for a long time, because I wondered whether it was reasonable to live at the beck and call of a voice from the unknown. It was not easy to give up the lofty post of Permanent Secretary in the Federal Public Service; a position which I had occupied for five years. When I however realised that it was the same voice that stopped me from Harakiri in 1969, I reassured myself that I would not lose anything by heeding the advice of the voice.

It is significant to mention that if I had disobeyed the instruction, there is no way I would have totally escaped the unpleasant events that occurred in Nigeria between 1983 and 1985. In a negative way, I also thank the last Minister I worked with, whose intractability and intransigence helped to firm up my decision to retire from the public service.

CHAPTER II
ORUNMILA AND OTHER DIVINITIES

No one should confuse the world by trying to equate the divinities with God. Orunmila has clearly revealed that all the lower divinities were created by God to assist him in the management of the planetary system and that without exception, they all owe total allegiance to Him. The divinities regard themselves as servants of God sent by God to the world to help Him make the world a more liveable place for lay mortals, so that through them, man may be able to appreciate how God loves his creatures. When for instance a priestess of the water Divinity (OLOKUN) gets possessed, she starts off by singing in praise of God and appreciating the supremacy of God over all that exists. When Ogun (the Engineering Divinity) priest is possessed, he too, starts by paying tributes to God Almighty and thanking Him for making it possible for him (Ogun) to tell mortals what they would not otherwise know about themselves. The same is true of the Electricity Divinity, Sango, and indeed of each of the 200 divinities created by the God Almighty. They are said to be the members of the Divine Council of God.

In the same way, the Ifa priest begins his operation by acknowledging God as the repository of all knowledge and wisdom. Let no man therefore think that service through any of the divinities is a substitute for service to God.

Orunmila has revealed to his followers that the first creations of God were the lower divinities. They were the first inhabitants of heaven, and they all lived normal lives in heaven each in the image which took after God's own. Death is one of the favourite creatives of God, and he it was who fetched the clay with which man's image was moulded after those of the divinities. After casting the human image in clay, it was time to give it the breath of life, so, God told all the divinities who were present to close their eyes. All of them closed their eyes except Orunmila who merely covered his face with his fingers without closing his eyes. As God was breathing the breath of life into man He discovered that Orunmila was watching Him. As Orunmila tried to close his eyes after being caught spying, God beckoned to him to keep his eyes opened since nothing spectacular was ever done without a living witness. That is why Orunmila is called Eleri Ukpin or Eleri Orisa (God's own witness).

Following the creation of man, it was time for God to carve out the earth to be inhabited. But man was still too young and inexperienced in the ways of heaven to be exposed to the task of founding a new abode on his own discretion. God therefore chose to send the Divinities to earth to found it with their own knowledge, experience and discretion.

THE FOUNDATION OF THE WORLD

When God sends any one a message, He does not give him detailed terms of reference. He expects the messenger to use his own common sense or discretion to carry out the assignment. God only expects positive results and it is left with the messenger to make four of two and two.

The first inhabitants of this earth were the 200 divinities. The earth was then called DIVINOSPHERE, at a time when the Divinities, as it is today, were the only ones with the Spiritual Capabilities to communicate between heaven and earth. They are able to know at once what is happening on earth and in heaven with their extra-visionary powers.

The heavens were becoming over-populated, and God Himself, who could at the time, like the Omnipotent Father that He is, attend physically to the complaints of all His children in Heaven, found the task becoming over-bearing for Him. He therefore decided to found a new Firmament for Divinities and Humans alike to dwell in, as a means of depopulating the heavens. Infact, what He did not disclose to his creatures was that he was going to transfigure into thin air, so that thereafter he could only be communicated with in Spirit.

THE CREATION OF THE DIVINOSPHERE:

This work is not going to challenge all the other accounts of "the Creation" which have previously been given by earlier seers and prophets. It is merely going to narrate Orunmila's account of how the geographical phenomenon now referred to as the earth, came to be a part of the planetary system.

At one of the weekly meetings of the Divine Council, God asked the divinities which of them was prepared to go to the earth to found a new habitation. God told them that whoever volunteered to go was going to operate within a Divine Council injunction to establish on earth, the natural laws which made heaven such a beautiful place to live in. He told them that the same rules should operate on earth. There were only two broad body of rules he gave them.

1. No one should take undue advantage of His (God's) physical absence to arrogate to himself His role as Father of all the Universe. They should all give his due respect to Him as the creator of all, that is, they should always begin their works on earth by paying due respects to Him as their everlasting Father; and
2. No one should do to the other what he would not like others to do to Him — which is popularly known as the golden rule. This meant that they were not to kill without due judgement by all the Divinities. They were not to steal one another's property since in heaven, the punishment for stealing was death. They were not to lie against one another, seduce one another's wife, or do any other thing to one another that could result in pain. They were to resist the urge to take vengeance against one another since all mutual dis-agreements were to be resolved through the communal judgement at the Council of Divinities. Above all they were to respect his divine rule that whatever anyone did to wrong his fellow divinity, the retribution would come to the offender ten-fold. Finally, He told them the secret of success was to listen always to the silent voice of the divinity called Perseverance.

CHAPTER III
THE FIRST ATTEMPT TO ESTABLISH A LIVING ON EARTH

Against the background of this set of rules and regulations, God evolved a plan for dispatching all the divinities to earth simultaneously but without any advance warning. One fine morning therefore, God called on his maid ARUGBA to invite each of the Divinities from their respective homes to appear at the Heavenly Palace the following morning for a special assignment.

ARUGBA set out very early that morning. However before then, God had prepared a special Chamber completely equipped with various implements with which He expected the divinities to carry out their assignments on earth. Arugba's message to each of the Divinities was clear. "My Father has sent me to invite you to prepare for a special assignment tomorrow morning. You are to get your self prepared to set out for the assignment as soon as the Divine message is given to you. You are not to return to your house before embarking on the mission".

Most of all the Divinities took the message literally and did not bother to enquire from their own counsellors or guardians on how to set about the assignment that God had in store for them. Arugba visited the houses of the divinities in order of seniority, which meant that Orunmila, the most junior of the divinities, was the last to be visited.

Meanwhile, Orunmila who was in the habit of making a situation divination every morning, was advised by Ifa to make a feast on that particular day in anticipation of all callers to his residence. At the time that Arugba got to Orunmila's house, it was already very late in the evening. Not having taken any meal since morning, Arugba was already very hungry when she got to Orunmila's house. Before allowing her to deliver the divine message, Orunmila persuaded her to have a meal. She ate to her satisfaction and then told Orunmila that God wanted him to report to His Palace the next day, together with the other Divinities for a special errand.

In appreciation of Orunmila's hospitality, she confided further in him by disclosing the details of the errand that God had in store for them. She advised him to ask for three special favours from God in addition to whatever instruments he would collect from God's inner-chamber for his mission. He was to ask for the CAMELION, (Alagemo in Yoruba and Omaenerokhi in Bini) the multi-coloured hen in God's household, and God's own special bag (Akpominijekun in Yoruba and Agbavboko in Bini). We shall see the significance of these special requests later. In a final aside, Arugba told Orunmila that if he so desired he could also persuade God to let her accompany him on his mission. With these words of advice Arugba left for home, having completed her assignment.

The following morning, one after the other, all the divinities reported at the Divine Palace of God. As soon as they got there, God ordered each of them to proceed on the journey to earth without returning to their respective homes. One after the other they came and got the marching orders to leave for earth. The first divinities to get to the earth soon discovered that there was no ground there to tread upon. The whole place was still water-logged. There was only one palm-tree which stood in the middle of the water with its roots in heaven, which was the gateway from heaven. As they were coming in, they had no where else to stay except on the branches of the Palm-tree. It was a very hard time indeed.

Before leaving heaven, each of the divinities collected from God's inner Chamber all the materials and instruments of their choice. It is the same instruments that initiates to the cults of each divinity use for initiation to this day.

By the time Orunmila came to the Palace of God, all the others had gone. When he reported to the Almighty Father, he too got the marching orders to proceed at once to earth. He was told like the others, to collect whatever instruments he found in the inner Chamber. However, all the available instruments had at that time been collected by the others and since there was only one empty Snail's shell left, he had no choice but to hold on to it. He then appealed to God that since he had nothing to collect from the inner Chamber, he should be given:—

(a) The Camelion — the oldest creature in the house of God to advise him on how to tackle the teething problems of terrestrial habitation;

(b) The benefit of going to earth with the multi-coloured hen in the divine household of God;

(c) The Almighty Father's own Divine Bag, to collect the things he was going with; and

(d) The privilege of going to earth with Arugba, to remind them of the rules of heaven.

His four wishes were granted. As he was leaving, he collected four different plants, which Ifa priests use for all their preparations to this day. He also collected a sample of the plants and animals that he could lay hands upon.

He kept all his collections inside the bag which God gave to him. The Divine bag had the mysterious capacity of accommodating anything no matter the size and also of producing whatever was required from it.

When Orunmila reached the gate-way to the earth, he found all the other divinities hanging on to the palm-tree branches. He too had no option but to join them.

After Orunmila had been sitting or standing on the palm-tree branch for some time, Arugba advised him from within the Divine Bag where she was kept, to turn the mouth of the snail's shell downwards into the water below because it contained the foundation soil of the earth which would make the ground hard for treading on. Orunmila who had collected the empty snail's shell from the inner chamber of God did not know its contents. It is also obvious that he only met the snail's shell inside God's inner Chamber because all the others had ignored it. None of them except ARUGBA knew that it contained the Secret of the Earth.

As Orunmila turned the snail's shell face downward, the scanty sand content dropped into the water below and the water began to bubble. Within a very short time, heaps of sand had started piling up around the foot of the palm-tree. After so many heaps had formed, ARUGBA once again spoke to Orunmila from within the bag, this time, advising him to drop the hen down to the heaps of sand. As it scattered the heaps, the area of the ground began to spread. It is the same operation that the hen is still performing to this day. Wherever the hen is found, it is seen to be using its feet to scatter the sand on the ground.

After the grounds had been extended over a large area, the other divinities who were now amazed at the mysterious performance of Orunmila ordered him to go down and tread on the ground to verify whether it could support them.

Once again, ARUGBA advised Orunmila from within the bag, to drop the Camelion to tread first on the ground. The Camelion walked about stealthily on the ground, for fear it would collapse under its feet. But the ground held together, and it is that same cautious walking process to which the Camelion became accustomed, to this day. That is why the Camelion treads softly on the ground.

As soon as Orunmila was sure that the ground was strong enough, he came down to earth from the palm-tree branch and his first task was to transplant the plants he brought from heaven. Thereafter, all the other divinities came down to earth one after the other.

That is why the palm-tree, the first creation of which had its roots from heaven, is respected by all the divinities. It is the root of their genealogy. All the divinities spread out from the palm-tree to establish their various abodes in different parts of the earth.

Orunmila, being the youngest of all the divinities, stayed with and served each of the more elderly ones in turn. He served OGUN, SANGO, OLOKUN, EZIZA ETC. In the course of his servitude, one of the divinities seized ARUGBA from him. He was thus deprived of his Chief Counsel and confidant.

It is significant at this stage to mention that the process of initiation into Orunmila's religion of Ifism is an attempt to commemorate this process of leaving heaven and coming to the world to settle through the palm tree. The woman who carries the IKEN on her head to UGBODU is called ARUGBA. In view of the fact that Orunmila never married Arugba, it is also not advisable for any IFA initiate to marry the woman who followed him to UGBODU. By the same token it is not advisable to use one's wife for the ceremony, lest the woman will surely be seduced from one sometime later after the ceremony, either by death or by others.

The presence of Arugba as the only woman around created a host of problems for the divinities. One after the other, they fought to retain her. The struggle for Arugba soon brought out the worst in the divinities. The more ferocious ones, namely, Sango, Sankpana, Ogun etc., fought one another with all the weapons at their disposal. There was complete confusion which led to acrimony among them. This time, Orunmila was the first to return to heaven to make a report to God. The guardian role of Arugba became lost to the divinities because she had been deprived of the company of Orunmila with whom she came to the world.

All the other divinities had established themselves with the instruments they collected from God's inner Chamber. On his part, Orunmila had lost the use of all the things he brought including even the Divine Bag which without the advice of Arugba, he did not know how to use. After living a life of deprivation and penury, he decided to go back to heaven to ask God why life on earth was so painfully different from life in heaven. Even the four plants he brought from heaven did not help him although they are the ones used during IFA initiation to this day, and they are also used for any medicinal preparation done by Orunmila.

When it was time for Orunmila to return to heaven, he went to the foot of the palm tree and climbed up to its branches. From there he transfigured into heaven. Back in heaven, he was one of the few divinities to see the last of God's own physical existence. The Almighty God who was never known to lose his temper was obviously annoyed at the sight of Orunmila. He apologized to God for seeing the remains of his corporeal, from the neck upwards, but explained the difficulties he had experienced on earth in the hands of his brother-divinites. He complained that surprisingly, the rules of heaven were not being adhered to on earth.

After hearing out Orunmila's report, God cleared him to remain briefly in heaven but sent Obstacle, the most powerful of all the divinities, (Elenini in Yoruba and Idoboo in Bini) to go and verify Orunmila's report. When Elenini got to earth, he watched the performance of the remaining divinities at close quarters. He was not only satisfied that Orunmila's account was correct, he became afraid that with the deprivation prevalent on earth, the divinities would end up warring against one another.

Other Divinities return to Heaven

As soon as Orunmila left for heaven, the other Divinities refused to co-operate with one another. Their youngest brother who used to serve all of them had left and none of the rest was prepared to serve anyone else. Life became intolerable especially as there was no medium of commercial exchange. The need for money had become very evident. One after the other, they all trooped back to heaven to report mission impossible. They also decided that they were going to request God to give them Divine authority (ASE) with which they could cause things to happen, for mortal servants to serve them and for money with which to do business with one another.

On getting to heaven, they asked for these favours and God gave it to all of them, but promised to despatch money after they returned to earth. All of them including Orunmila were ordered to return to earth to complete the mission they had started. This time, since the grounds had been formed on earth, it was possible to return by the land route to earth.

One by one, the divinities began to troop back to earth with their human followers. As they were leaving none of them bothered to find out the mysterious factors responsible for the difficulties, they had encountered on earth. Esu, the Evil divinity, had vowed to create problems for any divinity who failed to enlist his support before returning to earth. Oyeku Meji will later reveal how Esu unlocked the rain pipes of heaven to cause a three year rainfall which prevented the divinities from getting to their destination on time. Before leaving however, Orunmila sought the advice of his counsellor who told him not to be in a hurry to get hold of the money which God had promised to send to the world, and to offer sacrifice to Esu before leaving heaven. Orunmila did as he was told.

Divinities return to the earth

Before departing from heaven, Orunmila had been advised by God to return to the foot of the palm tree from which the divinities alighted in the first instance because it was the foundation of their existence on earth. As soon as the divinities set out on their return journey to earth, a heavy rain began to fall. The rain continued for several days and nights. But Orunmila had been advised not to seek shelter from the rain before getting back to earth. In defiance of the rain he moved straight on to build a hut at the foot of the palm tree. All the others did not find their way until after the rain stopped, that is, one thousand days and one thousand nights later. Following the abatement of the rain, they met a road side sooth-sayer called Okiti kpuke who advised them that they could only settle down properly after paying homage to the seat of their foundation which is the foot of the palm tree.

It took them time to trace the location of the palm tree where Orunmila had meanwhile established a viable habitation. Since he was the keeper of the palm tree, he reaped the benefits of all the sacrifices made by each of the divinities at the foot of the palm tree.

Money comes to the World

After they were all reasonably settled down, the parrot was the first to discover the heap of cowries which decended from the sky to the ground by the side of the expanse of water separating heaven from earth. The parrot alerted the divinities, who, without adequate preparations proceeded to extract money from the heap. We shall see later how those who tried to extract it, were all perished under its avalanche. Esu was still at his game of destroying all the divinities who refused to acknowledge his influence and authority. When Orunmila saw that all the other divinities who ran after money failed to return home he decided to go and find out what was happening to them. He subsequently discovered that they had all perished under the avalanche of money. He therefore decided to sound his guardian angel on what was responsible for the mass destruction.

He was told that any one who approached money with greed and avarice was bound to be destroyed by it because money was always a hungry phenomenon. Anyone who desired to enjoy the benefit of money had first to feed it. He was told what to do to feed money and how to extract it. He did as he was told and he became the only divinity who succeeded in making money his servant. That is why an Ifa shrine seats on money and cowries to this day.

The beginning of Physical Conflicts

The success with which Orunmila discovered the secret of money earned him the wrath of the remaining divinities, who resorted to open aggression to destroy him. By special sacrifice revealed by Ejiogbe, Orunmila made his enemies to be fighting among themselves. There was complete pandemonium on earth over the sharing of the money. Meanwhile news was getting to heaven that there was general commotion on earth. God sent Death to go and bring those responsible for the conflict back to heaven, but he tried and failed. He only succeeded in removing the followers of the divinities but not the divinities themselves. With their followers destroyed by death, they discovered that they could not achieve much without the help of their auxiliaries.

The beginning of the end of the World

Death and Money had succeeded in breaking the backbone of the divinities because they had totally ignored the laws of heaven when they got to the world. It was the turn of the strongest divinity (Misfortune or Obstacle) to come and finish them up. He left the palace of God with clear instructions to come back to heaven with the rest of the divinities. He left with his Akpo-minijekun to collect all of them and bring them back to heaven.

Meanwhile, Orunmila made his daily divination one morning and saw that catastrophe was approaching. He was advised by Ifa to prepare an elaborate feast for a powerful visitor that was coming from heaven. He was told that he would have a sign appearing on the horizon three days before the arrival of the visitor. On the day of the visitor's arrival he was to collect all his followers and dance in procession from his house to the town hall where they would dance and sing in praise of the "August" visitor. From the town hall, he was to invite the visitor to his house for a feast. That was the only way he could save himself from the imminent catastrophe.

He did as he was told. About seven days later, he saw a red star appearing on the sky and he realised that the visitor was on his way. He made the preparation he had been advised to make and was in a maximum state of preparedness. Unknown to him, the visitor was already in the world. Misfortune Divinity, the most powerful of them all, was around.

His first port of call was at the home of Ogun. He met Ogun in his workshop and quickly turned him into a leaf and pocketed him. He did the same thing with all the other divinities over the next three days. On the third day he had imprisoned all of them inside his bag and it was time to go to Orunmila.

As he was heading for Orunmila's place he met a long procession of praise singers and dancers. They gave him kola to eat and water to drink calling him the father of them all and the closest divinity to the Almighty God. For the first time since getting to the world, Misfortune smiled. Orunmila then came out and told him that he suspected that he must be hungry and had prepared a feast for him. He followed them home at the head of the procession amidst singing and dancing. On getting to Orunmila's house, the heavenly visitor was elaborately feasted with all his staple foods and he was exceedingly happy. At the end of the feast, he remarked that if all the other divinities were as magnanimous as Orunmila, heaven would not have been replete with news of internescine atrocities on earth. He told Orunmila and his followers that God did not design the world to be an antonym but as a synonym to heaven. He reported that God was determined to destroy the world rather than allow it to continue as an embarrassment to the goodness of God's image and reflection.

He wondered if Orunmila with his wisdom could make it a better place. He replied that the task was not easy but that he would continue to do his best. With that, Misfortune gave him the bag containing all the other divinites, and proclaimed that from then on, he was to have authority over all of them. That explains why the only diviners who succeed in the ways of heaven are those who have the support and co-operation of Orunmila to this day. Be it an Ogun priest, Olokun priest, Sango priest etc, unless they have their own Ifa, they do not have the blessing of heaven. Otherwise they become the victims of all kinds of obstacles.

The Final Destruction of the World

No sooner did the divinities regain their freedom than they went back to their fratricidal feuds. They were particularly angered by the realisation that it was Orunmila who brought about their salvation from the cold hands of Misfortune.

News of their atrocities continued to go to heaven. God had been told that Orunmila was the only divinity who was abiding by the laws of heaven on earth. God then invited the palm tree to go to earth to provide a platform for Orunmila to return to heaven with his followers. One night, Orunmila was invited by his guardian angel to arrange to climb up a palm tree which had suddenly grown in front of his house. He was given three days to prepare. He climbed up the palm tree and asked all his followers to climb after him. As they got to the top of the palm tree, they were all absorbed into heaven. As soon as they were all safely in heaven, God, released the dyke holding rain in the sky and the ensuing downpour of rain flooded up and consumed the world.

That was the end of the divinosphere and of the first attempt to found a habitation on earth. It can be seen from the foregoing analysis that the devil played very little or no part in the destruction of the world.

CHAPTER IV
THE SECOND HABITATION OF THE EARTH

Orunmila reveals that seven generations had passed in heaven before God decided to embark on a second experiment for the habitation of the earth. The divinities had argued that the first attempt failed because there were too many cooks preparing the soup. God yielded to the suggestions of the divinities and decided to give each of them a chance to exhaust his capabilities. It was Elenini the Misfortune divinity who prosposed that Ogun, the Engineer should be given the first attempt. Ogun accepted the challenge and decided without delay to set out for the mission. That is why he is regarded as the path finder of the universe.

Alagbede (Ogun) the Metal/Iron Divinity was then sent by God to prepare the way for the others. As the Iron-monger of the divinosphere (the world of the divinities) he was to lay the infrastructure for others to build on in the world. He was sent with 200 human beings (men and women) to inhabit the world. Ogun was however so egocentric that he did not see any point in consulting anyone else in heaven for advice before setting out with his followers on his mission. He left for earth with his 200 followers without bothering to make adequate preparations for feeding his followers on earth. He thought that founding a habitation in a virgin environment was like going to war. Ogun is also the warrior divinity. When he goes to war, he goes without making any provision for feeding. He feeds his army from the plundering he does along the war path. He left for earth on the same assumption.

As soon as they crossed the last of the seven hills before the boundry of heaven, they came to the grey zone between heaven and earth. The grey zone is called Hades, which is the home of the faes, (Abiku in Yoruba and Igbakhuan in Bini). From then on they moved to the dark zone of the boundry, where there is no sunshine. It is called Erebus. Many travellers used to get lost in that zone at the time when people travelled freely between heaven and earth. It now approximates to the darkness of the female womb for travellers coming to the world.

On getting to earth, he set his men to work without any delay, preparing temporary abodes and roads. The following morning, his 200 mortal followers asked him what they were to eat. Since there was no food around, he told them to cut sticks from the surrounding bush to eat. They ate sticks to their hearts' content but it only whetted the appetite of their alimentary canals. Within 14 days he had lost more than half of his mortal followers to starvation. He was left with no option but to retreat to heaven with the feeble remnants to tell God that he had no food with which to feed his followers. That was how Ogun gave up his mission and returned to heaven.

Next, God invited the water divinity (Olokun) to go to the world, to found an auxiliary habitation there. He too was given 200 persons to accompany him to the world. Like Ogun before him, Olokun also set out without making adequate preparations for the trip. On getting to earth, the followers of the water divinity also asked him what they were to feed on and he gave them water to drink, which failed to give them any nutritional satisfaction. As his followers were getting depopulated by starvation, Olokun, like Ogun before him, returned to heaven to report the failure of his mission.

God invited a number of other divinities for the assignment, but they politely declined to go since they doubted whether they stood any chance of success in a mission which had defied the efforts of their elders, Ogun and Olokun. Determined to found a habitation in the world, God finally invited Orunmila (the wisdom divinity) to have a try. Orunmila immediately sought counsel from the heavenly elders who advised him to seek the assistance of Esu (the trickster divinity). He made sacrifice to Esu who advised him to come to the world with a luggage comprising samples of all the foodstuffs, birds, reptiles, animals etc. available in heaven. He collected all these items in his divination bag called (Akpo-minijekun in Yoruba and Agbavboko in Bini) and got his followers to carry them with him to the world. This mysterious bag has two spectacular features. It takes whatever is put into it weightlessly, and it produces whatever is demanded of it.

Orunmia made the initial mistake of not seeking advice from his senior colleagues Ogun and Olokun, who had earlier made abortive attempts to found the world. As he left on his journey from heaven, Esu went to ridicule Ogun and Olokun that Orunmila had sought and obtained clearance from him before leaving for the world and that he was going to succeed where they had failed. He disclosed to them that their failure was their punishment for not seeking and enlisting his support before going to the earth. He reminded them of the heavenly saying that the dog only follows those who treat it benevolently.

Out of envy and anger, Ogun caused a thick forest to block the path he had earlier made to the world. On getting to that point, Orunmila and his followers could not proceed because they lacked the instruments for clearing their way through the thick forest. While waiting, the Mouse volunteered to trace the path-way to the earth. He actually traced the pathway but being a smallish animal, the path he cleared was not wide and high enough to provide adequate thorough-fare for the human figure. It was at that stage that Orunmila sent for Ogun to assist him. Ogun appeared and rebuked Orunmila for not telling him before leaving for the world. Orunmila instantly apologised to Ogun and explained that far from ignoring him, he had in fact sent Esu to inform him (Ogun) of his impending journey to earth. When Ogun remembered that Esu actually came to inform him, he piped down and agreed to clear the route he had blocked. He however warned Orunmila that while on earth, he should feed his followers with the same food (sticks) with which he (Ogun) had fed his followers during his brief stay on earth. With that, the forest cleared and Orunmila continued on his journey with his followers.

Before they got to Erebus the boundary of heaven and earth, Olokun also caused a big river to intercept the path-way earlier constructed by Ogun to the world. When Orunmila and his followers got to the bank of the river, they could not proceed on their journey. After wandering for sometime, Olokun appeared and queried Orunmila for daring to leave for the world without telling him. Once again Orunmila apologised to Olokun and explained that he had in fact sent Esu to tell him of his proposed journey to earth before setting out. Remembering that Esu had in fact told him, Olokun forgave Orunmila and instantly dried up the river for Orunmila and his party to proceed to the world. Before leaving however, Olokun ordered Orunmila to do what he did by feeding his followers with water when he got to the world. With these injunctions Orunmila entered the world.

The point at which they entered the world was a thick forest, so he quickly got his followers to build make-shift dwellings for themselves while he was busy planting the crops he brought from heaven. As they were being planted, Esu intervened and made them grow and bear fruits the same day. By the following morning, the crops were all ready for harvesting. These included maize, plantains, yams, cocoyams etc. and a variety of fruits. The birds and animals they brought also multiplied overnight through the machinations of Esu and they were ready for slaughtering at dawn.

In the morning, Orunmila's followers gathered to ask for their food. In deference to the undertaking he gave to Ogun in heaven to feed his followers as he did, Orunmila gave sticks to all his followers to eat. Next, he also respected the wishes of Olokun by giving them water to drink. This is very symbolic, because from then on, the tradition became established that human beings begin their day by chewing sticks to clean their teeth. This is followed by the use of water to rinse their mouths. This tradition has subsisted to this day albeit with slight modifications with the use of brushes and toothpastes — which still approximate to the chewing stick. After brushing the teeth, water is still used to rinse the mouth.

After giving his followers sticks and water, they were still asking for more food. He told them to go to the farm which had then blossomed and harvest foodstuff to eat. They had a field day and began to eat all descriptions of food to their hearts' content. The animals and birds were also available in abundance to provide meat for all of them. Thereafter they happily stayed on earth as its first inhabitants.

Orunmila later travelled to heaven to report his success to God, and all the other divinities began to come to the world one after the other with their retinue of followers. We shall see in the ensuing chapters and volumes that Orunmila's achievements evoked enemity for him from other divinities. This is the never-ending envy in the world today between doers and loafers, excellence and indolence, success and failure and all other positive and negative forces affecting human lives. It explains why those who strive to succeed incur the displeasure of those who tried and failed or those who refused to try at all.

It is significant at this stage to remember, that whatever we do that benefits us in life is a function of the guiding divinity accompanied to the world by our original ancestors who established human habitation on earth. The adherents of Ifa today are decendants of the first set of human beings who followed Orunmila to the World. The same is true of Ogun and his followers Sango and his followers, Olokun and his followers, Sankpana and his followers, etc. etc.

Meanwhile, Orunmila went back to heaven to report the success of his efforts to the Almighty Father. On getting back to heaven, Orunmila reported the success of his mission first to God and finally to the Council of Divinities. The news of his success was greeted with murmurs of envy and it marked the beginning of the end of the close affinity which previously existed among the divinities.

In this connection, contrary to the commonly held belief that Esu, or the devil, is the most wicked divinity in the planetary system, there are more aggressive ones. The only reason for which Esu is blamed for every mishap is because he is the embodiment of evil. We shall see later that although he has no creative powers, he has the ability to mutilate anything and anyone created by God, which is to be expected, because God appeared to eliminate the forces of darkness which Esu represents. On his part, Esu has ensured that far from being eliminated, the force of evil which he represents, continues to flourish. This struggle has continued to express itself in the preponderance of evil over good on earth, to the present time. We shall see more of this argument when we come to examine the influence of Esu on the firmament.

At the head of the more ruthless divinities, is the Divinity of Death, who is responsible for the demise of all beings created by God. Infact, we shall see that he is the only divinity who feeds directly on human beings and who was the happiest among all the divinities when man was created by God. He exclaimed at the creation of man, "at last God has created a staple food for me". He gets at his victims through four of the most aggressive divinities. The first of them' is Ogun who is responsible for all destructions resulting from strife, fire, wars and accidents. He kills by the mass. There is Sango, who also destroys albeit only when his victim contravenes natural laws. There is Sanpana, who destroys indiscriminately through epidemics, and the sickness divinity, who is the wife of Death and who destroys by euthanasia. There is also the Night Divinity who destroys innocent beings by the mass. These are all divinities created by God and given their destructive powers by God. We shall see that the most powerful of all the divinities created by God is Misfortune or Obstacle. He is the closest divinity to God because he is the keeper of the Divine palace of God.

Most of these divinities immediately assumed an aggressive stance the moment they knew that Orunmila had stolen the show from them. They immediately vowed to go and destroy the world established by Orunmila. On his part, he quickly approached Esu for help who told him not to worry. Esu assured Orunmila that the bellicose divinities would destroy themselves before destroying the world created by him. Orunmila also went to the Obstacle Divinity (Elenini in Yoruba and Idoboo in Bini) and feasted him elaborately to enlist his support and co-operation.

Meanwhile, all these divinities began to make arrangements for their trip to the earth. Oyekumeji will later reveal to us how they all left for the world and how it took them three years to get there.

Orunmila had been advised at Divination to make sure that he was the last to leave for earth. He was also warned that there was going to be a very heavy rain on earth which would last for 1,000 days and nights. He was to defy the rain and not take any shelter before getting to his destination.

One after the other all the divinities left for earth. On getting to the boundry of heaven and earth, they discovered that they had to cross the last river in heaven with a tiny rope bridge which could only accommodate one passenger at a time. It took them quite a while to cross to the earthly side of the river. On getting to Erebus, the land of continuous darkness, they discovered that it was raining and they all began to seek shelter where ever they could find one. All their designs for world destruction had evaporated into thin air as a result of the difficulties they encountered on the way, which were contrived by Esu.

Among the friendly divinities who were on the side of Orunmila were Ule (House) and Igede (Incantation). The House who does not move, told Orunmila to carry him in his Divination bag. Incantation, who has no limbs told Orunmila that the battle that awaited him on earth was going to be very stiff. He therefore advised Orunmila to take him along by swallowing him up so that whatever he said would come to pass. Orunmila agreed to the two requests.

As advised, he waited for all the aggressive divinities to leave for earth before he left. When he got to the bank of the river, he met only one divinity left. It was the Queen of witchcraft (called Iyami Osoronga in Yoruba and Iyenigheekpe in Bini). She was too weak to cross the bridge. She had beseeched all other divinities to help her cross the bridge, but they all refused, because they were traditionally afraid of her. When she saw Orunmila coming, she begged him to help her but he replied by saying that the bridge could only take one occupant at a time. She then proposed that Orunmila should open his mouth for her to fly inside promising to come out at the end of the bridge. With that, Orunmila agreed to oblige. He had ignored the fact that she was one of the divinities that vowed to destroy him on earth. At the earth's bridge head, Orunmila told her to come out but she refused on the grounds that his stomach was a suitable abode for her. He bluffed that she would starve inside his stomach, but she called off his bluff by taking a bite at his intestines telling him that all her staple foods (heart, liver, intestines etc.) were abundant inside him.

Realising the risk he had taken on, he quickly used his divination instrument to seek a solution. He pulled out a goat from his bag, slaughtered and cooked it. Having cooked it ready, he invited her to come out to eat but she said that she could only eat in private. He got out a white cloth and made a makeshift tent with it. She then came out and concealed herself inside the tent and fed on the goat meat.

While she was enjoying her meal Orunmila disappeared into the darkness of Erebus, braving the rain, and without looking back, continued non-stop on his journey.

He met all the divinities taking shelter at one spot or the other by the road side. In consonance with the advice he was given in heaven, he continued on his journey under the rain until he got to his destination. He was happily received by his followers who were beginning to wonder why he had kept so long in returning.

On getting home, he told Igede and Ule to come down. Ule came down but died instantly, while Igede told him that he would be more effective inside his stomach. That explains why Orunmila is regarded as the patron of incantations, and the only divinity capable of conjurring with the spoken word.

He told his followers to prepare a fitting grave for Ule. As he lay in state awaiting burial, the most wonderful occurrence since the establishment of the world occurred. Rows of houses suddenly began to spring up all over the settlement, similar to the type of houses they have in heaven. That was the beginning of the architectural foundation of the world. In place of the huts previously built by the followers of Orunmila, palacial buildings began to spring up all around.

The Arrival of the other Divinities

Those who took shelter from the rain camped permanently in all kinds of squalid locations for the long duration of the rain. By the time the rain subsided, they had become so used to their make-shift accommodations that they saw no point in moving out of them. That is why divinities like Ogun, Sango, Olokun, Ovia, Ake, Sanpana, Uwen, Ora, Leron, etc. have their shrines outside the house to this day. Orunmila, being the only one who came straight home in defiance of the rain is the only divinity, (apart from Orisa Nla who came later) being located and served in the home.

It will be recalled that the aggressive divinities who came with Orunmila to the world did so with one determination, to come and destroy the world he had built. Unfortunately for them, they were ill-prepared for the trip because they obtained no formal clearance from God before leaving heaven. On getting to the world, they soon discovered that without God's own authority, they could not accomplish their mission. They then got together and decided to return to heaven to obtain proper clearance from God. Led by Ogun, the most senior of them all, they left for heaven.

On getting to the palace of God, they asked for the Divine authority (ASE) with which to make and unmake. Since God does not refuse any request, he gave them and they all surrendered their own ASE to Ogun to take custody of them. Anyone who wanted to make use of his own ASE went to Ogun to collect it, and to return it after making use of it.

With these instruments of authority, they began to create all sorts of problems for Orunmila and his followers, who in turn began to make all kinds of sacrifices to defend themselves against the evil designs of the aggressive divinities. When it came to the point at which Orunmila and his followers were using all their money to make sacrifices to dispel the wicked machinations of the divinities, he decided to ask his guardian angel what to do about it. He was advised to prepare a special charm now referred to as Gbetugbetu in Yoruba, or Ataighi mua in Bini. After preparing it, he was to use it to visit Ogun and to order him to surrender all the ASEs he had in his custody, to him. With that charm it is possible to conjure anyone to behave as directed by the user.

He accordingly prepared the charm as directed and he paid a visit to Ogun. On getting to Ogun's house Orunmila told him that he came to collect all the ASEs with him. Without any hesitation whatsoever, Ogun went to his treasury and brought them all out and surrendered them to Orunmila. With the ASEs in his hands, Orunmila left for home. On getting home, he swallowed all of them up.

Five days later, Ogun wanted to use his own ASE and went to his treasury to fetch it. To his amazement, he discovered that not only was his own nowhere to be found, the whole lot belonging to the other divinities, had also disappeared. He tried to remember who visited him during the last five days, but since his memory had failed him, he decided to check on the divinities. He went first to Orunmila to ask whether he was the one who came to collect the ASEs from him. Orunmila denied ever visiting him let alone to collect the ASEs from him. With the ASEs of the Divinities gone, Orunmila and his followers had some respite and they began to live happily and peacefully.

The World settles down

As soon as a firm foundation was established for permanent habitation on earth; more inhabitants of heaven began to make frequent visits to the earth. Those who found Heaven unbearable to live in, escaped to the world. Others came out of curiousity. The vast majority of those who followed the divinities to the world, were their followers in heaven. This book will however be limited to the Orunmila kindred and those who followed him to the world.

Initially, it was for a long time possible to walk on one's feet from heaven to this world and back. It was the appeal made by the feminine gender to Esu that ended the physical passage between heaven and earth. Previously, it was possible to leave heaven and to get to the world with clear recollections of whatever one wished to accomplish on earth. It was Esu and Elenini who blocked that memory passage.

When the divinities left for heaven one after the other, they left their followers and decendants to keep life afloat on earth. We have already seen the conflict which characterized the earthly cohabitation of the divinities. As they returned to heaven one after the other, the conflicts became even more ferocious among the lay mortals. That explains the fights, wars, treacheries, commotions and mutual destruction that subsists among the inhabitants of this earth to this day. It was so from the beginning and so shall it remain to the end of time. It is not entirely the fault of men. It is a reflection of the never ending conflict between good and evil.

CHAPTER V
HOW MAN COMES TO THE WORLD FROM HEAVEN

There is always a tendency to see man strictly from a biological perspective. A man and a woman mate and a child is born to them and the new child is seen as an independent entity. We have already seen that at the beginning of terrestrial habitation, human beings travelled to this world under the leadership of one or the other of the divinities. We shall see from the up-coming chapters that a man's sojourn to the world is merely a continuation of his activities in heaven. We have already seen that before man came to live in the world, the inhabitants of heaven travelled on their feet to and from earth, completed their assignments on earth, and returned to heaven. It was Esu who blocked the free passage between heaven and earth and made the female womb the passage way between the two places. Before then, the pelvis in all animals, like in plants, was on the forehead and it was neither recognised nor respected, both in animals and human beings. The pelvis which was a living organism in heaven went for divination and was advised to make sacrifice with a black he-goat to Esu and it did. Thereafter, Esu asked the female to open her legs and extracted the pelvis out of her forehead and positioned it between her legs. He then extracted a part of the skin from the body of the black he-goat with which the pelvis made sacrifice to him, and Esu used it to cover the pelvis up in its new abode between the female legs.

Thereafter, Esu went to the boundary of heaven and earth and blocked it forever with total darkness. That part of the planetary system approximates to what in Greek mythology is called Erebus. It was Esu who blocked it permanently and ordained that rather than keeping the gates of heaven permanently busy by travellers coming from earth to ask for children in heaven, from then on, any one, animals and humans alike, who wanted to have children should appeal to the pelvis, and the womb of all females was made to symbolise the darkness and mysteries of Erebus. The gestation period it takes for a female to bring forth a young one also approximates to the time it used to take for different species of the animal family to travel to and from heaven for a child.

We shall also see how the mutual attraction between the productive organs of males and females came to characterize the basis of their total existence. We will also discover from later chapters how the penis and the pelvis on the one hand and the ovum and the spermatozoa on the other, made sacrifices to make it possible for them to co-operate to bring forth a child from heaven.

Before coming to the world, all human beings make their own wishes at the divine palace of God. Some merely choose to make flying visits to the world and to return to heaven as quickly as they came. Others prefer to return at the prime of life — middle age, while others prefer to return at a ripe old age. When we make our wishes at the divine altar in the palace of God, the favourite servant of God called MISFORTUNE, the most powerful of all the divinities, is the only one present. The Yorubas call him Elenini while the Binis call him IDO-BOO. This is the only force capable of standing in the way of realising our destiny on earth because he is there present when we are making our life wishes. Those who are painstaking enough to pay homage to him before leaving heaven are given a free hand to go about their business on earth without let or hinderance.

THE INFLUENCE OF THE OBSTACLE DIVINITY ON OUR DESTINY

Iworibogbe, one of the senior ODUS (disciples) of Orunmila will later reveal the influence on our lives, of the Misfortune Divinity. Elenini (Idoboo) is the keeper of the inner chamber of God's divine palace where we all go on our knees to make the wishes for our sojourn to the world.

Once we have completed our departure arrangements, we are led by our guardian angel to the inner chamber where we make our own wishes. God does not tell us what should or should not happen to us or give us any special assignments. Whatever we say we wish to do or become, He merely blesses by saying — So be it my child.

When Iworibogbe was leaving for earth, he made a wish that he wanted to change the face of the earth by eliminating all wicked and vicious elements. To be able to accomplish his task, he requested from God a special power over life and death. God replied that his wish was granted. Overwhelmed by the power bestowed on him by God, he set out quickly for his journey to earth. His guardian angel reminded him of the need to underwrite his wishes with Elenini and the more powerful divinities, but he told his guardian angel that there was no force greater than God and that since he had obtained divine clearance he saw no justification for appealing to any lower authority.

As soon as he left the divine palace Elenini introverted the wishes of Iworibogbe. On getting to earth, he discovered that contrary to his wishes, he was running into difficulties. It transpired that the opposite of whatever he wished was always manifesting. When he prayed for people to live, they would die, while those he wished dead, lived. He became most disillusioned, because no one dared go to him for divination or assistance, since those who did, paid dearly for it. After starving in frustration for sometime, he decided to return to heaven.

On getting to heaven he went to his guardian angel who reminded him of the advice given to him before leaving heaven. It was at that point that he agreed to go for divination where he was told to make elaborate sacrifices to Elenini and the more senior divinities. He did the sacrifice and returned subsequently to earth for a more prolific and fulfilling life.

THE ROLE OF THE GUARDIAN ANGEL

The principal architect of our fortunes both in heaven and on earth is our guardian angel. He tells us what to do before leaving heaven for the world. Anyone who follows the directions and instructions of his guardian angel never goes astray. The Yorubas call him Eleeda and Binis call him Ehi. Those who are meticulous enough go for divination in heaven before coming to the world, and do whatever they are advised at divination to do, stand a better than even chance of a reasonably smooth sojourn on earth. Those who refuse to abide by the prescriptions or do so half-heartedly encounter all kinds of problems both in their journey to, and their life in the world.

All animate creatures of God have their individual guardian angels. The lower divinities and humans alike are known to have their guardian angels. These angels reside in heaven and keep close vigil over our activities on earth. It is believed in mythology that an individual's shadow is the image of his guardian angel. It follows us wherever we go. Occasionally, when we are asleep, we dream of up-coming events and some people are actually advised through dreams. Our guardian angels are believed to be the ones mirroring these events to us through dreams. These books are going to be replete with instances in which the guardian angels of various people appeared to them in dreams to guide them in their activities on earth. This happens mostly when an individual is veering away from the path of his destiny and he is not given to going for divination. It is in such instances that the guardian angels resort to the use of dreams or advice through close friends and relations, to forewarn us about impending events. When a guardian angel discovers that his ward does not believe in dreams, he can even speak to him through other diviners. There are many instances in which some strange seer will come along to a person along the road, in his place of work or his house to warn him of impending dangers and what he can do to ward them off. All such instances are master-minded by our guardian angels.

For those who believe in divination and sacrifice, they are often advised to make sacrifices to their guardian angels. We shall discover from these books that the materials for such sacrifices are used by the guardian angels to entertain higher powers in order to enlist their support in achieving our various objectives in life. The most important role of the guardian angel is to use the sacrifice made by his ward in heaven to feast all the divinities likely to play a role in his daily activities on earth. Those who fail to make such sacrifices in heaven are the ones who become paupers on earth. The sacrifices we make through our guardian angels before departing from heaven approximate to the seeds we sow, which like the night follows the day, produce the benefit which we reap later in the world. It is a travesty of divine justice to eulogize a life of perpetual deprivation and penury as a rectitude. Poverty is not synonymous with virtue, because no one given the option to choose between affluence and penury, will choose the latter.

The simple truth is that no one reaps what he did not sow. No one goes to collect his pay packet from where he did not work. No one goes to collect money from a bank in which he has no deposit or goodwill. No one expects to collect dividends from a company in which he has no investment. And no one, expects to collect a certificate or diploma for a course of study he has not successfully undertaken. In the same way, no one can expect a good life on earth, if he did not make sacrifice for it before setting off from heaven.

THE FORCE OF DESTINY IN OUR LIVES

As already indicated, the length of our stay on earth, the type of work we do, and the degree of our success or failure in life are all functions of our own chosen destinies. We shall see for instance from the works of Iworibogbe, that if a person chooses to pay a flying visit to the world, there is virtually nothing anyone can do to prolong the life of such a person on earth, except in rare instances, where his guiding divinity can change the subject's destiny. This class of people who are called fays (Imere in Yoruba, and Igbakhuan in Bini) come to the world for a few hours, days, weeks, months or years and die when their chosen time is up. It is only Orunmila who discovered the secret of how to prolong the lives of such persons on earth, that is only if the parents of the child are able to discover from divination, well in advance, that the in-coming child is a fay.

For instance, a person leaves heaven with a determination to become a farmer on earth. Depending on the type of clearance he got from the heavenly forces, he could take to farming as soon as he grows up in the world and thrive in it immensely. If on the other hand he failed to obtain clearance from the higher powers in heaven, he might take to a completely different profession in which he would never be able to make ends meet, having strayed away from his chosen vocation or profession.

A significant point to bear in mind is that no one ever remembers his wishes in heaven on getting to earth. Esu uses the waiting period in Erebus and the process of childhood to obliterate all memories of what we were in heaven and what we planned to do on earth. No one ever leaves heaven except the fays with bad wishes for themselves. Everyone desires to succeed in whatever he does, but his success depends largely on the amount of clearance he got from the higher divinities before leaving heaven.

Some people do run away from heaven without obtaining clearance from anyone. These are the people who wander about in the world for want of a settled life. Almost invariably a tranquil life eludes them throughout, since they did not programme for it. Such people come to the world to blame God, their guardian angel, or their heads, and fellow human beings, for their misfortunes and failures. But they only have themselves to blame. It is like some one leaving for a new farm without a matchet to work with, nor food to eat.

On getting to the world, a number of people are fortunate to have good parents who go for one kind of divination or the other. If the parents are able to discover in time the type of child they have, they can embark early enough on the task of preparing the child's feet on the right path of his destiny.

One very important aspect of a person's destiny is the ruling divinity of his life. As earlier indicated, man's forebears came to this world under the leadership of one divinity or the other. It is a person who came under the ruling star of Orunmila that will be required to thrive by serving Orunmila in the world. The same is true of all the other divinities, like Ogun, Sango, Osun, Olokun, Oya etc. In the same way, it is the person who came under the guiding star of Orisa Nla (God's personal representative) that will thrive by following the path of modern religion. The tragedy of human existence is that when a follower of one divinity, sees the followers of other divinities, happy and contented in their own sect, he believes that he will thrive equally by giving up the service of his own divinity for the service of another. These are the people who either fall from the frying pan to the fire or live through life as if they are engaged in a never-ending search for a base.

The advice to such people is to go for any form of divination they are used to in order to discover their ruling divinity. As soon as they discover their base, a sizeable proportion of their problems will have been solved.

THE PLACE OF DIVINATION IN OUR LIVES

Divination is defined as the faculty of foreseeing. It comes from the Latin word Divinatus, Divinare — to foresee. The art and practice of foretelling future events or the unknown by occult or oracle means. A prophesy, prediction or augury.

Divination is the art of having an insight into one's fortunes, misfortunes and future. It can be done either by prayer through Christian seers or through the Ifa priest, or any other divine priest, or through any other form of oracle. The Ogun, Sango, Olokun etc. priest who foretells the future when possessed is a diviner. With particular reference to the Ifa divination, it is done in one of four ways by the Ifa priest.

It can be done with a four-piece kolanut thrown on the floor, and interpreting the proclamation of the Odu appearing through the pieces of kolanut. The range of divination through the four-place kolanut is limited and only highly proficient Ifa priests see and say much from it.

Divination is more often done with Okpele, which is capable of translating the entire range of the Ifa oracle. We shall see later that there are 256 ODUS in the Ifa corpus. The principal ones called OLODUS are sixteen in number. The remaining 240 are simply called ODUS. All of them are however addressed by their individual names. When the Okpele is thrown on the floor, the priest reads out the Odu that has come out to speak to the enquirer. As soon as the Odu's name is known, the priest immediately recalls the work of that Odu relevant to the question asked.

Let us assume that a man preparing to leave heaven for earth goes to an Ifa priest in heaven for divination and the priest decides to use Okpele. Let us further assume that after throwing down his Okpele, Ogbe-Oligun comes out. The Ifa priest will merely recall the sacrifice which Ogbe-Oligun did before he left heaven for earth at the beginning of time. If on the other hand Ogbe-Oligun comes out in an earthly divination for a man who wants to proceed on a journey, the Ifa priest will also recall the experience of Ogbe-Oligun in a similar situation when he was in the world. The Odu coming out from this kind of divination is similar to the star which astrologers read when a person is born. The highly knowledgeable Ifa priest has a reasonable knowledge of what each Odu did in heaven and during his life on earth. If one therefore goes for divination and a particular Odu appears, the priest has only to recall the particular event in the life and works of that ODU, relevant to the subject of the enquiry and tell the enquirer to do what Orunmila did in similar circumstances. If he recommends sacrifice and it is accordingly done, the enquirer will certainly obtain the kind of relief that Orunmila had in a similar situation.

The third form of divination is the Ikin or (Iken in Bini). This is made up of 16 Ifa kernel nuts shifted between the two palms of the hand. The Ifa priest gets the enquirer to touch his head with the sixteen nuts and the Ifa priest starts off by shuffling the nuts between his two palms. Using the left palm as the base of the sixteen nuts, he tries to remove all of them with the right palm. If for instance he removes all of them leaving two seeds on the left palm, he then marks one stroke on the Ifa tray laden with Iye-rosun or divination powder. He also marks two stokes if only one seed is left on the left palm. He goes through this process eight times until a full Odu appears on the Ifa tray. It is this first ODU that appears on the Ifa tray which will provide the information that the priest will interpret later.

After marking the first Odu, the priest goes on to seek confirmation through the same process to obtain a second ODU. To complete the process he finally asks whether there are any obstacles on the subject of the enquiry. If it is disclosed from the third marking on the tray that there are obstacles, the priest will proceed to ask for the cause and type of obstacle there is, before finding out what has to be done about it. The details of these processes will be explained later in the books.

The fourth and most important form of divination is the one that takes place when a person is preparing his own Orunmila — or when he is initiated into Ifism. That is when he goes to Ugbodu. The process takes the same form as the last one, but this time, the first Odu that comes out at Ugbodu becomes the name of the initiate's Orunmila. The life history of that Orunmila is narrated to the initiate and his life will experience the same problems and prospects like those of the Orunmila.

THE ORIGIN OF THE PROBLEMS EXPERIENCED BY HUMAN BEINGS ON EARTH

If the guardian angel realises that the number of enemies who are determined to destroy his son or daughter or frustrate his or her fortunes in life, are too many, he approaches one or the other divinity to follow his son or daughter to the world to protect him against the machinations of such enemies. On getting to earth, if the person is fortunate to come across the guiding divinity early enough in life, he is able to live a comfortable life. If on the other hand the person misses his way and chooses say a religion that will keep him or her at arms length from the guiding divinity, he or she becomes the victim of all the difficulties created by sworn enemies.

That is why our fore-fathers devised the practice of naming ceremonies as a means of discovering the prospects and problems awaiting a newly born child in order to begin early to remove the obstacles in his way.

Those who have lived a reasonably inoffensive life in heaven may come to the world without plenty of problems. These are the people who are seen to succeed without many difficulties in life. Such instances are however few and far between.

Normally, we grow up in the world to find ourselves having difficulties with our parents, brothers, sisters, colleagues, contemporaries, associates, marital partners etc., etc. without knowing exactly why. People get disliked by others at first sight for no visibly justifiable cause. At the same time, just when all hopes seem lost, someone comes out of the blue to offer succour. Those who understand the secrets of life are not often surprised at these developments, because the design was made in heaven.

No one comes to the world with a bad destiny. Contrary to the commonly held view that God ordains whatever fate befalls us on earth, the Almighty Father only confirms whatever we wish for ourselves when we appear at the Divine altar to make our wishes for our sojourn on earth. It is unrealistic to imagine that the all merciful and loving God will discriminate by ordaining some to become successful and others to become failures on earth. Everyone coming to the earth wishes for success and prosperity. A practical illustration will explain this phenomenon.

As already demonstrated in the chapter on destiny, our life on earth is a continuation of our life in heaven. We had as many enemies and friends in heaven as we have on earth. When a person therefore goes before the Divine altar to make his wishes for his journey to the earth, he prays for all the good things of life. When he completes his wishes, God stamps his mace of authority on it and says, "so be it for you". Almost immediately, a detractor in heaven comes before the altar of God to say that as soon as the first person starts climbing the ladder of success he or she will drag him down. Again God stamps his mace of authority on the wishes of the enemy of the first wisher. A friend of the first person comes along to wish that whenever the enemy sets out to strike the first wisher, he or she will defend the wisher. God will also confirm the wish of the third person. The chain of wishers continues in this manner without anyone of them knowing what the last person's wishes are for or against him or her. They all leave for the world and they can be born as children of the same or different parents. As they grow up in life, they can meet as brothers, sisters, friends, schoolmates, workmates, members of the same club, lovers, husbands and wives or wives of the same husband.

Efosa was having a lot of problems in heaven, and he understood from travellers returning from earth, that it is an interesting place to live in. He decided to end his problems in heaven by travelling to earth. He went before the divine palace and made several wishes for prosperity and longevity on earth. The Almighty Father blessed his wishes and he was convinced that that was all he needed. As soon as Odioma heard that Efosa was leaving for the world, he too vowed to follow him to earth to settle his score with him. Odioma went before the Divine altar to wish for success in getting Efosa to repay his debt of 30k on earth. Madam Akaruosa who stood surety for Efosa on his indebtedness to Odioma also went to the Divine altar to wish that she too was coming to the world to get Efosa to relieve her from her bond. Her wishes also received the blessing of God.

The heavenly guardian of Efosa, being an angel who operates in spirit, knew what Odioma and Akaruosa had in store for his ward on earth. Before setting out for the earth, Efosa's guardian angel advised him not to leave heaven without repaying his debt. He replied that if he had enough money, he would not be leaving for earth. Without making any sacrifice of any kind, Efosa left for earth. Nonetheless, his guardian angel went to Ogun and appealed to him to lead Efosa to the world. Ogun agreed.

Efosa was subsequently born on earth into a polygamous family. He was the fourth son of the senior wife of the family. A sister of Efosa's father, also gave birth to Odioma, while the mate of Efosa's mother gave birth to Akaruosa. As the children grew up, they lived in the same locality, but they were always fighting and arguing among themselves. One day as Efosa was returning from his father's farm, he saw a trap set by Odioma which had caught a grass-cutter. He released the grass-cutter and brought it home as the catch of his own trap.

On getting home he got his sister Akaruosa to sell the grass-cutter for him in the market. The grass-cutter was sold for 30k. Meanwhile, Odioma went to the farm and saw all the indications that his trap had been tampered with. On a closer examination of the trap, he discovered all the signs that his trap had caught a grass-cutter because all the hooks of the animal's skin were still on the ground. He was not aware that Efosa had brought a grass-cutter home.

When he got home he narrated his misgivings to his mother, who knew that Akaruosa had brought a grass-cutter to the market for sale the previous day. The woman paid a visit to Efosa's home and probed Akaruosa on the origin of the grass-cutter she sold in the market the previous day. She replied that it belonged to Efosa.

On getting home the woman narrated her findings to her son Odioma, who became convinced that Efosa was the culprit who removed his grass-cutter. In the ensuing confrontation with him, Efosa had no option but to confess that he removed the animal but intended to surrender the money to Odioma. Asked to produce the money, he said he had spent it.

That debt of 30k dragged on until the elders of the night intervened. Efosa became ill and died subsequently. Akaruosa was also taken ill, just before she was to be given out in marriage and she too died. It was the turn of Efosa's mother to appeal to the divinities to destroy whoever was responsible for the death of her son. Odioma was eventually taken ill and he too died.

The triple tragedy provoked a meeting of the village elders, who ordered that the deaths should be investigated. An Ifa priest was invited who after divination, revealed that they all settled the score that took them from heaven to the earth. He revealed that the tragedy could only have been averted if their parents instead of appealing to the elders of the night, had made the necessary sacrifices, which the trio had failed to make in heaven.

CHAPTER VI
MAN'S RELATIONSHIP WITH GOD

This question has engaged the attention of thinkers through the ages. Some philosophers argue that the relationship between man and God is like the relationship between a dead father and his surviving offsprings. Others have argued that God once lived but died several millenia ago and that it is his spirit that continues to direct the affairs of the planetary system just as some believe that the souls of one's departed ancestors continue to play a leading role in one's affairs.

Orunmila's revelations confirm that God's existence cannot and should never be a subject for debate. The way he has ordered the design of heaven and earth and the retributive justice for those who contravene the laws of nature are unquestionable testimonies to the interventionary role of God in our lives.

It is my considered view that the concept of a personalised and personified God who is constantly watching over the affairs of all his creatures wherever he may be, might on closer examination, be defective. The idea of an unforgiving Almighty Father who condemns offenders to ever lasting hell fire is simply atrocious and untenable. If an ordinary mortal cannot be unforgiving enough to condemn a bad child to the wolves or into a burning fire, why should anyone think of the Almighty Father as being even more heartless and ruthless. The punishments for contravening any of the natural laws are laid down. They are not based on the will of God. We shall not sketch for God therefore, the picture of a disciplinarian who sits in judgement over any and every offence committed by his creatures. The penal sanctions for offending the laws of nature are retributively automatic. They are similar to the application of terrestrial laws. The law enforcement agencies will carry out the dictates of the law on any offender whether or not he is the son of one of those who made the law — that is under normal circumstances. It goes without saying therefore that God cannot harm humanity, the way he is adjudged to do, to those who offend natural laws. After all, any harm done by God to man is a harm done to himself, since humanity is an embodiment of His own being.

God is equal to all that is and exists, and that includes both organic and inorganic creatures. We all play one role or the other to make His whole body work more effectively. The forces of good and evil co-exist within his physiological make-up just as they exist within our microscopic bodies. The relationship between God and ourselves is analogous to the relationship between ourselves and the living organisms operating inside our bodies. To perform and live as human beings we have millions of cells operating within our bodies each of which performs a distinct role.

There is no means through which we can directly influence the way these cells perform their individual functions except through our general behaviour. For instance, when one hits one's hand on the table to make a point, one has destroyed or injured hundreds of thousands of living cells inside one's body and these are cells which may have been praying inside one's body for some form of deliverance.

In the same way, what excitement can it give to God to kill hundreds of thousands of his creatures, made up of mankind, plants and animals, in an earthquake? Nor does it give him pleasure when the world destroys itself in wars. Wars are intra-fratricidal conflicts within the body of God, since conflicts are part of the living process.

We have no means of knowing the wishes and aspirations of the living organisms inside our bodies except that their conditions reflect on our own out-look and health. If they are hail and hearty they perform their jobs well and we also feel healthy. In the same way, God is happy when all the tiny little cells inside his body, plants, animals, water, fire, sun and moon, men and women are all performing their functions happily and satisfactorily.

Orunmila on the other hand reveals that God once had a physical existence and that it was often possible for his closest aids, the divinities and living beings to interact with him like we openly interact with our parents. As the planetary system expanded in size and population, the task of listening to everybody coming to him became cumbersome. It was at that point that He decided to evaporate into thin air. Before doing so however, he appointed the 200 divinities to assume the responsibility of adjudicating and intervening in the affairs of heaven and earth. It is therefore not an accident of history that each of the various divinities has his own retinue of adherents. The worshipers of Ogun, Osun (Osonyin in Yoruba) Olokun, Orisa Nla, Sango, Christ, witchcraft, Budda, Judaism, Orunmila, Asukporu etc have no justification for claiming superiority in their modes of worship over others, because according to the revelations of Orunmila each of these agencies came to different parts of the world to assist the forces of good to become preponderant over the forces of evil. The common dominator between all of them is that they advise their followers not to do any evil and not to destroy their fellow beings, because it is against the laws of nature so to do.

They are all subject to the natural laws, that their followers should do to others what they also wish for themselves. Those who contravene this golden rule get their due reward in punishment here on earth.

In the light of the foregoing, it is clear that the relationship between God and man is likened to the father who dispatches his children to leave home to pursue different vocations for the total advancement of the whole family. The father leaves each of his children the discretion to determine how best to carry out their assignments. He is only interested in the end result of his children's efforts.

God creates us with hands, feet, intelligence and discretion to enable us fend for ourselves within the broad rules of the body of ethics called Natural Laws.

God does not stop anyone from doing good or evil, because it is ordained in the divine laws that like the night follows the day, whoever does good shall have good coming his way and he who does evil will surely reap the fruits of evil.

Orunmila reveals that God only laughs in two circumstances, when a wicked person who plots evil against his fellow men, goes on his knees to beg God for a favour, God laughs hilariously at him. On the other hand, when people are plotting against a person with a clean heart, and they pray to God to bless their evil plans to manifest, God laughs at them.

If you sow corn, you can only expect a corn harvest. No one can justifiably expect the serpent to give birth to a fowl. These are against the divine laws of the universe. That is why the divinities can only listen to the voice of the righteous. Those who resort to the use of diabolical medicines for giving manifestation to their evil intentions, do so because they could not enlist the support of the divinities. Neither God nor any of his servants will cooperate with anyone who prays for help to destroy or harm his friends, relations or neighbours. To engage in wicked behaviour against one's fellow men in the hope that praying round the clock can save one from the long arm of retributive justice, is to put the efficacy of prayer in doubt. One can only wish for success if one also appreciates or encourages success in others. One cannot constantly obstruct the cause of justice and expect the higher powers to do justice to one's cause. That is the law of retributive justice.

Several messengers from heaven have through the ages tried to teach the world how to serve God. They have all emphasised that we do not serve God by flocking into a house of prayer to praise and flatter Him or to pray for selfish favours. They have all emphasised without exception that the only true way of serving God is by doing good to our friends, relations, neighbours and even enemies.

What favour can a man expect from God when he refused to use his car to convey the neighbour's wife to the hospital when she was in labour. The man who sped his car past a dying victim of a motor accident without helping to take him to the hospital, may call for the help of God sixteen times a day, it will never come to him because he did not sow for it. If he had obliged the needy in his critical moment, God would also send help through any source to him when he was in difficulties. Can prayers bring deliverance to the man who refused to oblige a jobless relation with N2.00 to feed his family, when in fact he had over N300.00 in his cupboard at that material time. We do not have to pray for what we have not earned. We could only earn the benevolence of the divinities if we did not hesitate to assist those who needed our help on any previous occasion.

Here lies the similarity between prayer and sacrifice. For prayer to manifest there must be evidence that the offerer had previously sacrificed his effort, time or money to assist the needy. This approximates very closely to the physical sacrifice often made to divinities when we desire their assistance.

That is why Qrunmila advises his followers never to refuse assistance to needy friends, relations and neighbours. We shall see how the forces of the night punished the man who concealed the deer which he killed in the bush, to look like a human corpse merely because he did not want any member of his community to share out of it. He lost two of his children before he was able to determine the causal relationship between his treachery and the children's deaths. In fact Orunmila advises his followers to always have food at home so that chance or hungry callers may have something to eat. He assures that anyone who behaves in this manner will never be denied the means of funding his hospitality. As long as we are behaving the way God ordains us to do, we shall remain happy because one is only truly happy by making others happy. There are many ungrateful persons in the world, but the victim of ingratitude always lives longer and happier than the ingrate.

The story of how God sent Nene to fetch snails for sacrifice to soften the heat of heaven will illustrate how we are expected to use our discretion to chart the course of our lives. Nene, a maid in the Divine Palace was sent by God to fetch snails for sacrifice. Without asking any questions, she left for the assignment. God called her back to collect four gifts for the journey; one kolanut, one aligator pepper, one piece of white chalk and a piece of white cloth.

She knew that at that time, snails were not available in heaven, but she was determined to comb the length and breadth of heaven and earth to get the snails. After wandering in the bush for sometime, Esu, the evil divinity, transfigured on four different occasions to tempt her. First, an elderly woman appeared to her who cried for chalk to do some work for her daughter who was in labour. Nene obliged with the piece of chalk that

God gave to her. Next, an elderly man appeared to her crying for a piece of white cloth to bring relief to his grand child who was suffering from convulsion. In a gesture of genuine concern and sympathy, Nene parted with the only piece of white cloth given to her by God.

Not long afterwards, a woman emerged with a child crying on her back. The child was hungry. As soon as Nene heard the cry of the child, she ran to the mother to find out what was happening. She explained that she had been in the forest all day without any food to give the child. Kolanut is the staple food in heaven. Nene gave the only kolanut she had to the woman who was very happy.

Finally, a hunter came along to ask her for an aligator pepper which she also willingly parted with. With that, she had done favour with all the materials given to her by God. As soon as she gave the aligator pepper to the hunter, he moved a little distance forward and returned to meet her.

He asked her what she was doing in the forest. When she explained that she was sent by God to fetch snails, the hunter told her to wait. He opened the aligator pepper and threw the seeds into the bush. He then told her to enter the bush in the direction to which he threw the seeds of aligator pepper. She went into the bush and saw a countless number of snails. It will be noted that it was only by parting with what Nene had that she was able to obtain what she was looking for. If she had sat at home or knelt down in the forest to pray for the snails to come to her, she would have failed in her mission. It should also be noted that God did not tell her what to do with the gifts given to her. She was left to use her own discretion.

CHAPTER VII
THE EFFECT OF SACRIFICIAL OFFERINGS ON OUR LIVES

The ordinary dictionary definition of sacrifice is the offering of anything to a deity. A giving up or foregoing of some valued thing for the sake of something of greater value or having more pressing claim. Thus said Addison. "If thou preserveth my life, thy sacrifice shall be ...." Whatever a person desires to have in heaven or on earth involves some sacrifice or giving up of something. Life does not thrive with taking alone. It also involves giving, hence it is said that life is a process of giving and taking. The simplest sacrifice one makes for anything is time. One sacrifices time and effort for whatever is worth having. Even the relatively simple task of begging, involves the sacrifice of one's human pride and independence. How many things does one get from one's fellow man without begging for it, bribing for it or making some prior atonement or gratification even if it has to be promised in advance.

When it comes therefore to benefits desired or won from the divinities, a greater sacrifice is required. It is not enough to merely beg for such benefits or favours. It must involve physical sacrifice. There are sacrifices involving the offering of animate or inanimate objects. When one desires any form of progress or gain, it must involve some sort of investment. A farmer sacrifices part of his seeds for planting in the following year in order to reap a harvest at the end of the year. A trader invests his savings or borrowed funds in his business in order to realise the profit that will discharge his recurrent commitments.

In the same way, when one deals in the sphere of the divinities, one must give them what they want in order to beseech them to come to one's aid. Hence, the sheet anchor of the Ifa religion is the making of sacrifice. Orunmila says, sacrifice is deliverance. No matter what problems one may have at any time, if one promptly makes the sacrifice prescribed at divination, there must surely be a relief. Orunmila reveals that before anyone leaves heaven for the world, he is advised to obtain clearance from the guiding deities. If he abides by the advice given to make sacrifice he will find the world an easy abode. But if he refuses to make sacrifice before setting out from heaven, unless he makes the sacrifice, after getting to the world, he is bound to have problems on earth.

We shall discover from the lives of the 256 OLODUS and ODUS of Orunmila that virtually all of them were advised to make sacrifices before they left heaven. We shall also see what happened to those who made sacrifices as well as to those who failed to make sacrifices. All these sacrifices involve the offering of one or more he-goats to Esu, who can be very helpful to those who make offerings to him and disruptive to the fortunes of those who refuse to make offerings to him. That is why some people refer to Esu as the bribery divinity, because he does not help any one ex-gratia.

The fundamental difference between Orunmila and the other divinities is that right from the time they were created by God, he was the only one who recognised the disruptive powers of Esu and devised a strategy for having a rapport with him. That strategy was sacrifice. He realised that Esu was only interested in recognition and food. Esu has often told Orunmila, "my friend is the one who respects and feeds me, while my enemies are those who dispise and starve me. I neither have a farm nor a trade of my own. My farm is the entire universe and my wares are the creatures of God".

We shall see later that he was able to infiltrate and mutilate everything created by God. It is for this singular recognition of the power of Esu and how he has put it to his own advantage, that God named Orunmila, "The wise one". Oyekumeji will later reveal how the life of a man called ODO Agutan (the heavenly shepherd) or (Jewesun as Ifa calls him) was short-lived on earth on account of his refusal to make offerings to Esu before he left heaven. After giving him more than an even chance of changing his mind, Esu eventually infiltrated his flock and ended his life. This is in spite of the fact that when Jewesun went before God to make his wishes for the earth, he promised to live physically in this world for one thousand years. He vowed that during that period he was going to wipe out any trace of evil and the hand of Esu from the face of the earth. He was however advised to offer sacrifice to Esu, which he indomitably refused to do because he could not imagine the logic of making sacrifice to a scoundrel that he was going out to destroy. The rest of the story is history and the forces of evil continue to thrive on the face of the earth. It is not enough to condemn Esu as the "devil" who does no good. He can be a dispenser of good tidings depending on one's attitude to him.

In the same way, on getting to the world, man is required to make even more sacrifices for whatever he desires to have. We shall see that no problem in life can defy the efficacy of sacrifice provided it is made promptly. We shall also see the lives of people who after refusing to make sacrifices initially were required to make doubled sacrifices when they were between the devil and the deep blue sea.

There is often a tendency to think that an Ifa priest who recommends sacrifice with animals like goat, ram or he-goat simply wants an excuse for having meat to eat at the expense of a helpless enquirer. Far from it. Any Ifa priest who recommends more sacrifice than is ordained for any purpose will pay for it ten-fold. In the same way, Orunmila even advises Ifa priests to use their own money to fund sacrifices for demonstrably destitute enquirers. He proclaims that such priests will be recompensed ten-fold. We shall see from Ofun-Ogbe, how Orunmila used his own materials and money to make sacrifice for Orisa Nla and how he was eventually compensated 200-fold.

There are two major sacrifices which should not be delayed. These are sacrifices to Esu and Ogun. The writer has seen people who were advised to make sacrifice so Esu but refused and only a few days later ran into major difficulties. One young man was advised to give a he-goat to Esu in order to avoid being apprehended for an offence he did not commit. He did not refuse to do it but promised the Ifa priest that he would perform the sacrifice when he received his salary at the end of the month.

The priest warned the young man that the danger foreseen at divination was too imminent for the sacrifice to wait. The young man who was also an Aladura man told me in an aside that his church had seen the same vision for him, but that he had been advised to offer special fasting and prayers. The Ifa Priest, a very old man in his nineties, told him that if he had money, he would have done it for him, so he could repay him at the end of the month. The writer also offered to help, but like the proud man that the enquirer is, he preferred to wait until he got his next salary.

Exactly three days later, a team of gun-totting policemen raided the house in which the young man lived, in search of a wanted Armed Robber. Everyone knew that the young man had no track record of criminal behaviour. But he was inadvertently arrested by the policemen and taken away. He was in detention for 23 days. As soon as the writer was informed of the incident, he travelled to Benin to inform the victim's mother about the sacrifice he had been told to make. The writer eventually funded it and the sacrifice was quickly made. Three days after the sacrifice was made, the young man was released after the actual culprit had been apprehended. A sharp coincidence one would imagine?

There is also the case of another man who was advised by an Ifa priest to offer a cock and a dog to Ogun at a divination, he made on a Saturday morning. He had been told not to travel anywhere before making the sacrifice. He gave money to his wife to buy the sacrificial materials and went out to visit a friend. In the friend's house, they got a report that his friend's mother was seriously ill in a village called Iguosodin, about sixteen kilometers away from Benin. Forgetting the advice he had been given, and before making the sacrifice, he decided to drive his friend in his own car to the mother's village. On their way to the village, they met a burial procession and he drove into the crowd killing two of the funeral celebrants. His car was not only burnt, he was instantly lynched to death. These are very bitter memories because the unfortunate victim was a dear friend.

Of equal importance is sacrifice to one's own guardian angel (ELEEDA OR EHI). One's own guardian angel is a little more patient and accommodating. None-the-less whatever sacrifice one is told at divination to make to One's guardian angel should be made even if it involves borrowing money to do it. The guardian angel does not ask for sacrifice unless he has cause to use such sacrifice to appease other deities to which his ward may not have easy access. For one to starve one's guardian angel of prescribed sacrifices amounts to starvation of one's self. The guardian angel is one's solicitor and advocate in the divinosphere.

CHAPTER VIII
THE PLACE OF ESU IN THE PLANETARY SYSTEM

Esu is commonly referred to as the "Devil". We have been told by other religions that he was the angel of God who fell from Grace and was subsequently banished out of paradise. At best Esu can be described as the magic deity. He is often dismissed as the Chief of evil forces in the divinosphere although there are more deadly deities than himself. The King of Death destroys massively. Ogun, Sango and Sankpana do not forgive when they are offended, and they destroy ruthlessly. They are divinities in their own rights and not agents of Esu. The penalty of offending them is death. On the other hand, Esu would create obstacles in one's way to give his victim a chance to recognise him after which he could transform misfortune to fortune. He is a trickster alright but only to those who belittle him. He is the divinity of confusion and obscurantism.

There has been a conscious effort to approximate Esu the divinity of evil with the biblical Lucifer, who is said to have fallen from grace in heaven. We shall see that the difference between them is that one existed autonomously side by side with God whilst the other was created by God and infiltrated by Esu.

We shall see from Ejiogbe how Esu came to be. It is revealed that darkness existed before Light. Darkness, that is whatever we cannot see through, or comprehend readily, represents the force of Evil, which heralded the existence of Esu. Just as Darkness heralded the advent of Esu, that is how Light heralded the advent of God. Light represents truth, goodness, objectivity, honesty and positivism. Good and Evil exist side by side and are in constant and never-ending competition. One is not a creation of the other because good cannot beget evil just as evil cannot beget goodness.

In the light of the foregoing, the divinity called Esu which we shall be referring to in this book is an entity that should be seen as independent of God. He came to be at about the same time as God. The superiority of God lies in the fact that Esu cannot create, whereas God is the only authority that can create. But he can multilate, transform and damage, when he likes and he can also be constructive and even objective, when he is persuaded to do so. God is the only agency that can be good and dispense the objective good from the beginning to the end. He does not have to be bribed to dispense favours on his creatures. On the other hand, Esu is always taking every opportunity to demonstrate that if one does not recognise his authority, he will compel one to do so, by deliberately creating problems for one.

We shall also discover that Esu in his capacity as the dispenser of evil, can conquer the greatest minds, take them over and manipulate them. It was this Esu, who took over the mind of Lucifer and turned him against God. He was also the one who took over the mind of Judas Iscariot and turned him against Jesus Christ. It is the same Esu who turns a son against his father, who turns a wife against her husband, who turns friends against friends, brothers against brothers, men against men, nations against nations, earth against heaven, etc., etc.

It has been argued that he has the greatest amount of followership among any community of living creatures. There is nothing that God creates which he cannot manipulate. Beginning with the divinities that God created first to assist him in the administration of the universe, Esu created so much problems for them that he uses them at will. When the divinities perpetrate evil, either against one another or against defenceless mortals, they are doing so under the influence of Esu and not as servants of God. Some of the divinities often think they can ignore Esu and get away with it.

As already disclosed in the preceding Chapter on the creation of the world, God sent the favoured 200 divinities to the world, but Esu came with them as the 201st divinity. All the others came with instruments they collected from God's inner chamber except Esu, who is an independent phenomenon. The instruments and paraphenalia which the favoured divinities brought to the world constitute the materials with which their followers get initiated to the priesthood of their various faiths and orders, to this day. The difference between the other divinities and Esu is that Esu has no religion of his own and no one gets initiated to his cult. Apart from the stone procured from a moving river which is used to prepare his shrine and his favourite he-goat, there is no other instrument with which Esu can be associated. His shrine is often prepared only by those who prefer to enlist his support rather than his antagonism, and not that he is served in any discernible manner.

The truth of the place of Esu in the divinosphere is that he is about the most treacherous of them all. We shall discover later in these books that soon after he came with the other divinities to the earth, they all ostracized him. They refused to recognise his power and authority. We shall also see what problems he created for the whole lot of them as a means of compelling them to recognise his powers. We shall discover later that when all the divinities decided on getting to the earth to contest for seniority, they agreed that each should in turn feast all the others in their individual homes in order of seniority. Orisa Nla was told to start the feasting, since he was God's chosen representative on earth. Esu however warned them that no one could claim to be senior to him because he was around before any one else came into existence. He was told by all the others to keep his mouth shut.

Orisa Nla then proceeded to organise his own feast. On the day of the feast, as soon as the table was laid for the eating and drinking to commence, Esu blinked his eyes to two of Orisa Nla's children and they were instantly afflicted with convulsion. As the feast was about to begin, shouts were heard from the direction of Orisa Nla's harem and everybody abandoned the dining table to find out what was happening. Before anyone could do anything about it, the two afflicted children died.

The same incident in varying degrees occurred when it came to the turn of all the other divinities. In the end they all agreed to let Esu start with the feasting. Thereafter all the others made their feasts without let or hinderance.

This incident clearly illustrates that no one can win in any contest with Esu. Even God Himself, who is supposed to have the power to eliminate Esu from the face of the planetary system, left him to dwell freely among lay and helpless mortals. Orunmila is the only one of the divinities who knew how to handle Esu to this day. We shall see from Ogbe Idi, how Esu became a close associate of Orunmila. He is the only Deity who knows how to placate Esu and get the best out of him. That is why Orunmila, knowing that Esu is the architect of misfortune often advises his followers to make frequent sacrifices to him. Anyone who wishes to succeed in farming, trading, hunting, etc., is advised by Orunmila to begin by giving he-goat to Esu. We shall see later from Ogbe-Okonron how a stranger who wanted to farm was asked by his host to farm on the swamps, when they knew only too well that during the rains any crops planted on the swamps would normally be destroyed by floods. Orunmila asked the farmer to give a he-goat to

Esu, who reacted by holding up the rains for that year. Since all the other indigenes of the town made their farms on the hilltop and on the valley, their crops got burnt for want of rain water. All the other citizens of the town had to buy food items from the stranger-farmer that year because his farm on the swamps was the only one that bore a rich harvest.

The following year, the stranger-farmer was told by the elders of the town to make his farm on the hills, while all the natives made their farms on the swamps. The visitor-farmer again went to Orunmila who once more advised him to give another he-goat to Esu. After making the offering to Esu, the farmer proceeded to make his farm on the hill-top as directed by his hosts. Having accepted his offering, Esu went once more to unlock the plug with which he stopped the rain pipe from heaven during the previous year. It began to rain so heavily that only the stranger's farm on the hill-top flourished immensely. All the other farms made on the swamps were destroyed by flood. Once more the entire town had to buy foodstuff from the stranger-farmer throughout the following year. These two incidents made him easily the wealthiest man in the town. We shall read more of this story on how the man was later crowned the Oba of the whole area, when we come to consider the works of Ogbe-Konron, one of the odus of Eji-Ogbe.

At this stage, this story is only meant to illustrate that Esu can be helpful if one does not under-estimate or undermine him. That is why I had earlier described him as the divinity of reason — or the interplay of good and evil. He operates in a variety of ways. He can influence the mind of a judge adjudicating in a case to make or mar a judgement affecting people depending on whether or not the person offers sacrifice to him. We shall see later how Esu punished the conceited Army general who was sent to conquer an enemy town by the king. Before leaving for the war-front, he went for divination where he was advised to give he-goat to Esu. He was so sure of his ability that he did not consider it necessary to make any sacrifice. He then proceeded to war, but was warned by the diviner to beware of misfortune after his battle exploits.

He was actually victorious in battle, and when he came back to the king to report on his success, Esu influenced one of the king's counsellors to say that it was not enough to narrate how he beheaded the king of the vanquished town, but that the General should be told to demonstrate how he actually did it. As he was dancing and demonstrating with his sword, Esu jettisoned the sword from the General's hand and it fell from his hand and hit the king, who immediately fell down unconscious.

The General was immediately apprehended and bound in chains awaiting trial and execution. It was while in custody that the general remembered the sacrifice he had been advised to make in order to avoid disaster after his victory in battle. He then sent words to his wife to immediately offer a he-goat to Esu. Having got what he wanted, Esu went in spirit to Orunmila, who was also the king's physician advising him to use a particular leaf to revive the king. Orunmila instantly left for the palace to heal the king. As soon as he used the leaves prescribed to him by Esu, the king regained consciousness. Once again, Esu took over the mind of the king's counsellor who earlier made the suggestion culminating in the General's catastrophic sword demonstration and made compassionate auto-suggestion to him. The same man then appealed to the king to remember all the good works of the General in the past by recalling the saying that "a loyal servant cannot be condemned on the basis of a single fortuitous and unintentional error." His suggestion was readily accepted by the king and the General was pardoned and ultimately praised for his victory.

This story, as we shall see later, clearly illustrates what Orunmila has told his followers, that no one can win a battle against Esu, because he has the power to influence all of God's creatures and can manipulate them at will. Esu is capable of twisting man round his fingers. Man can only therefore strive to avoid the wrath of Esu by feeding or placating him from time to time without necessarily submitting to him. Esu is capable of turning parents against children, wives against husbands, friends against friends, the innocent to become guilty, witches against man and fortune to misfortune, depending on whether or not one courts his support or incurs his displeasure.

The role of Esu as the divinity of good and evil will be clearly illustrated in the revelations of Irosun Irete, who will be telling us later how a priest called Okpini was advised by Ifa never to leave his house on divination missions, without first giving roasted yam to Esu early in the morning for seven days.

He carried out the spirit and letter of the advice for six consecutive days. On the seventh day, he was summoned very early in the morning to the royal palace because the king wanted him for an urgent assignment. Without waiting to give roasted yam to Esu, he left hurriedly for the palace although he had the intention of doing it after returning from the palace. Esu was annoyed and decided to make him pay for deferring more to the King than to himself.

Okpini got to the palace and he was told that things were not going well with the king. He was told that subjects were no longer paying regular homage and that the fortunes of the palace were flagging. The King wanted him to find out what was responsible and how to improve the situation.

After divination, Okpini told the King to make sacrifice so that the situation might show signs of improvement from that very day. He predicted that after the sacrifice, hunters would bring to the palace on that day; a boa constrictor, a live deer and news from two hunters that they had shot a buffalo and an elephant.

The king quickly made the prescribed sacrifice and waited for Okpini's predictions to manifest. After divination, Okpini left for home. All his predictions would have come true, but Esu was determined to thwart their manifestation.

Meanwhile, Esu transfigured into an elder citizen and took position on the town's gateway (Ubode in Yoruba and Ughee in Bini). When the man with the boa constrictor came by, the elderly man told him not to proceed to the palace in his own interest, because the king was performing some sacrifices in the palace and that the Ifa priests had told the king that any hunter who came to the palace with any animal or to report the shooting of any animal (it was the tradition in those days for anyone shooting big games to report and surrender them to the King) should himself (the hunter) be used in performing the on-going sacrifice in the palace on that day.

As soon as the man bringing the boa constrictor heard the bad news he thanked the old man and sat there to wait at Ubode. The man with the live deer, the man who shot a buffalo and the man who shot the elephant also took temporary refuge at the same venue. All of them spent the night there, neither daring to enter the town, nor proceeding to the palace.

After waiting in vain for Okpini's forcasts to come true, the King became annoyed and on the next morning, he sent for Okpini once more. By this time, Okpini had given the roasted yam to Esu, albeit belatedly.

On getting to the palace, the Oba accused him of lack of proficiency and of being a liar and a cheat. He was thoroughly disgraced. Dejected, Okpini returned to his house, bundled up his Ifa and threw it into the river Oshun for deceiving him in his predictions.

However, as soon as he left the palace, Esu, having got his roasted yam, went to tell the hunters waiting at Ubode that the palace sacrifices had been completed and the way was clear for them to proceed to the palace. All of them got to the palace at the same time and surrendered their games to the king.

The king however wondered why they all had to arrive in the palace at the same time. He asked them whether they all went to the same place for their hunting expedition. In reply, they explained how they had, out of fright, spent the night at Ubode, otherwise they would actually have arrived severally the previous day.

At that point, the king realised that Okpini's predictions manifested after all, but for the evil machinations of the unknown tale bearer, who scared the hunters away. The king quickly sent for Okpini once more and apologized for embarrassing him earlier in the morning. He told him that all his predictions had in fact come true. He compensated him elaborately and conferred a higher title on him. Okpini later returned home at the head of a triumphal dance procession.

As soon as he got home he went right back to river Oshun to retrieve his Ifa, and on getting home, appeased it with the goat given to him by the king. Readers can imagine how, failure to give ordinary roasted yam to Esu, gave rise to so much upheaval. That is why in Ifism, people are often advised to offer sacrifices prescribed for Esu without any delay.

A final example is given by Irosun-Osa, of the royal barber who was advised to make sacrifice to Esu in order to avoid doing things in half measure. He refused to make the sacrifice.

Meanwhile, the King sent for the barber to come and give him a haircut. When he realised that the barber had refused to make sacrifice to him, Esu turned into an elder citizen of the town and went to the barber for a hair-cut just as he was about to leave for the palace. The old man prevailed on the barber to give him a hair-cut quickly before leaving home. Try as he would to convince the old man to come later because he was going to answer a royal call, the barber could not shake him off.

In the end he decided for the price of 5 kobo to cut the old man's hair. But it turned out that as he shaved the hair it was always growing instantly, so much so that he spent the whole day on the old man's hair without a single hair dropping to the ground.

At the end of the day, the old man accused the barber of inefficiency and refused to pay him because his hair was even more bushy that it was before he came for a hair-cut. It was at that stage that the barber having disappointed the King for that day, realised that he had to make the prescribed sacrifice.

The point to note from these analyses is that like all other divinities, Esu is invisible and can influence situations and events in diverse ways. It is wrong to assume that God expects us ordinary mortals to antagonise Esu, because we cannot even see him for open combat. He operates in spirit and more often than not, by proxy. The rule in Ifism is to give to Esu whatever it takes to please Esu, and unto other divinities, whatever they desire, so that one may have the chance to reach the goals of one's destiny.

As we go through life, we have no means of confronting the unseen forces which have good or evil influences on our lives. True enough, as long as we keep to the golden rules, doing to other children of God what we expect them to do to us, we are squarely in the service of God. But that does not mean that we are not going to be vulnerable to other evil forces who are envious of our virtue and who are determined to wipe out the attributes of goodness from the face of the earth. Orunmila reveals that the way God expects us to react to the forces of evil is not to do evil ourselves, but to defend ourselves against them.

The question therefore is how many human beings who complain about the evil acts of others against them, can themselves claim total absolution from evil practices?

The boss in an office who insists that his subordinates must give him bribes before promoting them, male bosses who insist that their female subordinates whether or nor married, should go to bed with them before they recommend them for routine rights and privileges, the worker who demands a bribe from a concessionaire before granting statutory and civic dispensations, the policeman who takes a bribe on a case in order to alter the cause of justice, the bank employee who causes untold sufferings to the public by selling foreign exchange in the black market, thus depriving them from being used for discharging more legitimate national obligations, those who use physical and diabolical (which comes from the Latin word Diabolus or the Greek word Diabolicus both meaning devil) to procure the death of anybody adjudged by him to be standing in his way of gain, profit, promotion or contest, anybody who falsifies any situation at the expense of others for his personal gains, any person who participates in rigging any position or appointment to the detriment of others for his selfish ends, anyone who steals overtly or covertly from his neighour, and any public officer who inflates the cost of projects and contracts because of his own kick-back, cannot expect to invoke the grace of God, no matter how hard he prays. It is a fundamental principle in the rules of the divinosphere that those who seek the blessing of the divinities must do so with reasonably clean hands. No man, can, with any justification, expect better justice from the higher powers, by casting aspersions on the intergrity of others when they are themselves guilty of similar offences. When we engage in any unwholesome practice, we are operating as agents of evil and not as the servants of God. If such a person is praying or wishing for anything and expects God and the divinities to hear his prayers he is merely expecting water to come out from a stone.

It is therefore reasonable to conclude that since not many people can serve God the right way, it is only logical that we should go for the second best alternative of reaching God through his agents, the divinities and hence appeasing the forces of evil from which we are not ourselves free. In other words, those who are truly clean at heart, and they are few and far between, can afford to ignore Esu and get away with it. But as long as we swim, bath and drink from the stream of evil, we are in no position to condemn Esu. It is only through absolute good that we can fight and ward off Esu. That is why in the New Testament when the crowd wanted to stone Mary Magdalene to death for prostitution, as was the custom of the Jews in those days, Jesus Christ asked any member of the crowd who considered himself as abiding fully by the commandments of God, to be the first to stone her. No one did.

In the same way, we have no legitimate right to cast Esu aside if we are not sufficiently clean, that is, if we do not truly obey the commandments of God with all our hearts, and if we do not love our fellow human beings enough to protect and serve their interests as much as we do our own.

That is why Orunmila, the Wisdom Divinity, tells us that the best approach to Esu is to appease him so that he might not obstruct our paths in life, because we are neither physically nor spiritually strong enough to engage him in any combat.

THE SPECIAL SIGNIFICANCE OF THE HE-GOAT TO ESU

Readers will find out later in this book that the he-goat is the staple offering to Esu. We shall see later that, the he-goat together with the dog used to be the domestic servants of Orunmila in heaven. It was the disloyalty of the he-goat that turned him into a sacrificial victim for Esu. More importantly however, the he-goat became the staple offering to Esu because of the debt which Orunmila's son owed to the King of Death. Irosun Irete will later reveal how the son of an ODU of Orunmila called Imonton (Irenfoo in Bini) or "Know all" annoyed the King of Death. To test whether he actually had all knowledge as his name implied, the King of Death gave him a he-goat to rear for him, ordering him to bring the kids delivered by the he-goat to him every year. Although Orunmila had thought of buying a female goat to live with the he-goat, Esu warned him that that approach was not going to be acceptable to the King of Death. Esu told Orunmila to give him the he-goat to eat and that he would know what to do when the time came.

Four years later, the King of Death sent a message to Orunmila's son to bring him his he-goat and its off-springs. At that point, Esu asked Orunmila to buy him another he-goat which he also killed and ate leaving one of its limbs and the head. He used the foot to mark foot-prints on the ground to feign the movement of a large herd of goats. Esu also prepared ropes supposedly used for tying plenty of he-goats. Esu next accompanied Orunmila to answer the riddle of the King of Death. On getting there Esu explained that when they were coming with the kids born by the he-goat, a group of armed bandits attacked them, stealing the he-goat and its children. To substantiate his explanation, Esu showed the king of Death the ropes used to tie all the goats. He added that they had killed the original he-goat and that is why they brought him the hand and the head.

The king of Death then turned to Esu saying that he would have to pay for the he-goat in perpetuity. Esu in turn, assembled the 200 divinities and told them that from then on, if they wanted peace and prosperity, they should always offer him he-goats to repay his debt to the King of Death. That is the he-goat we all pay to Esu to this day. As far as the writer can verify, all known divinities often advise their followers to offer he-goats for sacrifice to Esu from time to time.

CHAPTER IX
THE PLACE OF WITHCHES IN THE PLANETARY SYSTEM

Witches are commonly referred to as the evil spirits operating in the night to bring hardship and sufferings to human beings. Like the devil, we are supposed to dread witches and run away from them. In the course of my research, I have come to discover that they belong to a cosmogonic sphere, which has earned them the name of the elders and owners of the night. We shall see from Osameji how they came to settle down in the world and how they became so powerful that no other divinity can subdue them. They can thwart the efforts of all other divinities that fail to give them their due regard.

I have also come to discover that they are not as evil as they are often painted to be. Like all other collections of celestial and terrestrial bodies, there are good or white witches and there are bad or black and red witches. They probably operate the most equitable system of justice. They do not condemn without a proper and fair trial. If anybody approaches them with an indictment against anyone, they will consider all sides before reaching a decision. Ose-Osa and Osameji, will tell us how witches came to the world and how they over-powered all the other divinities. Orunmila tells us why he does not kill anybody unless the person has traversed the oath taken between Orisa-Nla, Orunmila, and witches. The witches do not kill any man who truly operates according to the ethoes and taboos proclaimed by the Almighty God.

We shall also see how Orunmila revealed that witches were originally more considerate than lay mortals. It was human beings that first offended them by killing their only child. It so happened that the witches and the laity (Ogbori in Yoruba and Ogboi in Bini) came as sisters to the world at the same time. The laity had ten children while the witch had only one child. One day, the laity was going to the only market available at the time called Oja Ajigbomekon Akola (Eki Adagbon Aderinmwin in Bini). It was situated at the boundry between heaven and earth. The inhabitants of heaven and earth used to trade in common.

As the laity was going to the market she asked the witch to look after her ten children during her absence. The witch took great care of laity's ten children and nothing happened to any of them. Then it was the turn of the witch to go to the market. Her actual name was Iyami Osoronga in Yoruba and Iyenuroho in Bini. As she left for the market, she also asked her sister to look after her only child during her absence. While she was away, the ten children of the laity became interested in killing a bird to eat. Ogbori told her children that if they wanted a bird meat she would go to the bush to catch birds for them to eat, but that they should not touch the witch's only child.

While their mother was away to the bush, her ten children got together and killed the witch's only child and roasted his meat to eat. As Ogbori's ten children were killing the witch's son, the latter's supernatural power gave her a sign that all was not well at home. She quickly abandoned her trip to the market and returned home only to discover that her son had been killed. She was understandably annoyed because when her sister was away to the market, she succeeded in looking after her ten children without any hitch, but when it was her turn to go to the market, her sister could not take care of her only child. She wept bitterly and decided to pack out of the house where she lived with her sister.

They had a brother with whom they came to the world at the same time but who preferred living in the middle of the forest because he did not wish to be disturbed by anyone. That was the Iroko. When Iroko heard the witch crying, he invited her to find out what was happening, and she explained how the children of their sister Ogbori killed her only child, without their mother being able to stop them.

Iroko pacified her and assured her that from then on, they were to feed on the children of Ogbori. It was from that day that, with the assistance of Iroko, the witch began to pick the children of the laity one after the other. We shall also see how Orunmila intervened to stop the witch from destroying all the children of the laity and why the feud has continued to this day. It was Orunmila who appealed to Iroko and the witch and asked for what they would accept in order to stop killing the children of lay mortals.

That is how Orunmila introduced the sacrifice of (Etutu) the offering to the night, which involves a rabbit, eggs, plently of oil and other eatable items.

Like Esu, we cannot antagonise the witches without adequate backbone. We only try to find out through divination what we can give them to enlist their support and the moment they are given what they ask for, they often get off one's back. Those who do not understand this aspect of human existence are the ones that fall easy victims to witchcraft.

We shall also see from Ogbe-rukusa how the men of Ife once decided to antagonise their witches, as a result of which the witches withdrew to the town of Ilu Omuo or Ilu Eleye on the outskirts of Ife. From their new abode, the witches resolved to depopulate Ife by killing its inhabitants one after the other. After Ife had lost many of its sons and daughters, the elders decided to wage war on the town of Eleye. All the armies sent to fight them never returned alive. All the other divinities were approached to save the situation but their efforts were neutralized by the superior prowess of the witches of Omuo.

Finally, Orunmila was adjudged by public divination to be the only one capable of engaging the women. As soon as he was approached for the assignment, he made the necessary sacrifices and instead of going to Ilu Omuo with an army, he went with a dance procession which danced right into the town. When the women saw a long procession of gorgeously dressed men and women dancing in the town with melodious music, they realised that it was time to return home to Ife. Before they knew what was happening, they were all back in Ife and there was general reconciliation and jubilation.

This incident again clearly illustrates that it is not easy to overcome the forces of witchcraft through aggression, without resort to a superior authority. The easiest way of dealing with them is through appeasement.

Orunmila does not solve any problem through confrontation unless all available means of conciliation have failed. Even then, he often seeks the aid of the more aggressive divinities to do the dirty jobs for him. He is a very patient divinity. He says that he can only react after being offended thirty times and even then it takes him at least three years to be offended after giving the offender ample opportunity of repenting.

The only force that can overcome the strength of witchcraft is the ground/earth. We are told by Ose-Osa (Osemolura) how God himself proclaimed that the ground (Oto or Ale) should be the only force that would destroy any witch or divinity who transgresses any of the natural laws. This decree was proclaimed at the time when a powerful Witch Doctor from heaven called Eye to yu Oke To yu Orun was engaged in the destruction of the earthly divinities because of their wicked behaviour on earth. Osemolura, who ferried the mother of witches to the world, because no one else agreed to do it, will also tell us that the oath which Orisa Nla made witches to take was the ground. The oath was taken against unjustifiable destruction of human lives. It tells us why the witches have no power to destroy the true children of God as well as devout followers of Orunmila.

We shall also see that the strong power wielded by the elders of the night was given to them by the Almighty God at the time when God lived freely and physically with the divinities. The witches were given the exclusive power to keep vigil whenever God was having his bath just before the crowing of the cock. It was forbidden to see God in the nude. The witch divinity was the only one given that authority. The witch divinity often gave signal to the cock that God had taken his bath, after which the cock crew for the first time in the morning.

God did not however leave the rest of creation helplessly at the mercy of the elders of the night. Through Osa-Ose, Orunmila will reveal how God expected us to protect ourselves against the powers of witchcraft. There was a beautiful girl at the palace of God who was ripe for marriage. Ogun, Osonyin (Osun), and Orunmila were interested in the girl. God agreed to give the girl in marriage to any admirer who proved himself worthy of her hand. The task to be performed as proof of eligibility for the girl's hand was to harvest a yam tuber from the Divine farm without breaking it, a seemingly simple task.

Ogun was the first to volunteer to perform the task. He went to the farm and up-rooted the yam tuber. As he pulled it up, it got broken, which clearly dismissed his candidature.

Osun was the next to try his luck. He too ended up with the same experience. It was Orunmila's turn to go to the farm. He did not move directly to the farm. He decided to find out why those who tried before him, failed, and what to do to succeed. He went for divination, during which he was told that unknown to all of them, God had appointed the elders of the night to watch over the divine farm. They were therefore responsible for conjurring yams up-rooted at the farm to break. He was told to feast them with akara, eko, and all items of edible food stuff, and a big rabbit, and to deposit the feast at the farm in the night. He accordingly performed the sacrifice in the night. That night all the custodians of the divine farm feasted on the food. In the same night, Orunmila had a dream in which the witches sent someone to tell him not to come to the farm on the next day. He was to come on the following day. Next day, the witches caused the rain to fall heavily in order to soften the ground.

Thereafter all the witches took a solemn oath not to conjure Orunmila's yam to break. The third day, Orunmila went to the farm and up-rooted the yam successfully and brought it to God, who instantly gave the girl to him in marriage.

It will be observed that God did not tell any of the girl's admirers the odds awaiting them at the farm. He also did not tell them how to attack the problem he knew they were going to face. He expected them to use their discretion. It was only Orunmila, who never leaps before looking deeply, that knew that it was only by appeasing the witches that he could get what he wanted.

CHAPTER X
ORUNMILA'S CODE OF CONDUCT

Interestingly enough, all the divinities have similar ethoes and taboos. Subject to their varying degrees of aggressiveness, they all accept the immutability of natural laws, which theologians and theosophists have codified into the ten commandments of God. This is not to say that some divinities do not kill when they believe they have strong justification for doing so, just as terrestrial and celestial codes allow for capital punishment to be meted out to convicted capital offenders. Without exception, all the divinities also accept the supremacy of the Almighty God. In the case of Orunmila, he makes a point of reminding all his apostles, disciples, priests and followers that he is only a servant of God, and at best God's own witness, which is why he is generally called Ajiborisa kpeero and Eleri Ukpin. Ajiborisa kpeero means the one only divinity who wakes up in the morning to go and greet God in the court of destiny while Eleri Ukpin means the divinity who sat as God's witness in the court of destiny when the destiny of every creature was being designed. We shall see later in this book how Orunmila was appointed as God's witness when the Almighty father began his creative work. Ogunda-meji will reveal to us later in this book why God ordered all the divinities to return to heaven after founding the earth. When the earth was in a state of turmoil, he sent Elenini to capture all the divinities and return them to heaven. Eji-Ogbe, the most senior apostle of Orunmila, will, in this connection, reveal how he returned to the world under the name of Omoonighorogbo to teach the people of the world how to behave in accordance with the wishes of God. He demonstrated by precepts, examples and deeds how to live and operate in accordance with natural laws, and how to live at peace with God. He also demonstrates that true happiness only comes when one devotes one's time to the selfless service of others. He also illustrates the virtue of love for one's fellow men. It goes without saying that if one loves one's fellow man, one cannot seduce his wife, kill him, bear withness against him, steal his property and cheat him.

As a practical philosopher therefore, Orunmila appreciates that much as one may extend all the love to one's neighbours, the good turn is not often reciprocated. Nonetheless, he strongly advises against retaliation and vengeance because the divinities will always intervene on the side of the righteous. A man's first obligation to himself is to preserve himself through divination and sacrifice. If a stronger person is waging any overt or covert war on someone who lacks the power to fight unseen forces, Orunmila advises resort to divination when in doubt and to make any sacrifice prescribed for the higher powers. Once sacrifice is made, the recipient of the sacrifice will almost immediately assist in thwarting the evil machinations of known and unknown enemies.

Orunmila advises his followers not to engage in destructive medicinal preparations because they can lead to self immolation. There are however some disciples of Orunmila whose stock in trade is the preparation of medicines, but only for constructive purposes, salvation and deliverance. Orunmila is the best teacher of the effectiveness or efficacy of perseverance. He teaches that while there may be medicines that are not efficacious, there is no patience that fails to overcome all difficulties — because the divinities will in the end come to the succour of those who persevere.

ORUNMILA'S EULOGY ON PERSEVERANCE

Orunmila advises perseverance in all that his followers do. They should not on their own volition avenge any wrong done to them by others. He does not want his followers to get involved in diabolical acts especially those aimed at the destruction of other persons. He advises in a poem that those who take the souls of others will also pay with their own souls or with those of their children and grandchildren. He insists that he is in a better position to protect his children if they do not take the laws of nature into their own hands. Orunmila maintains that if anyone plots death against his children, he will make sure that the conspirators do not succeed. But if his children however retaliate by also scheming the death or downfall of those who offend them, he (Orunmila) is denied the justification of arguing the cases of such children when the divinities sit in judgement over the matter. No matter is settled without being determined by the divinities.

The divinities on their part, do not condemn anyone without a fair trial. But if anyone preempts divine judgement by returning tit for tat, he has lost the justice of his cause. Orunmila advises that if his followers know of anyone who is planning evil against them, their first reaction must be to go for divination to find out whether the person will succeed. More often than not, if the balance of guilt is against the other person, one will be told that the enemy will not succeed. If on the other hand the balance of guilt tilts slightly against you, you will be advised during divination on the sacrifice which you must make so that the person plotting evil against you might not succeed. Instead of making sacrifice, some people prefer more revengeful acts by going to local witch doctors to prepare deadly medicines with which to fight the enemy. In some cases, if Orunmila sees that the medicine his son is preparing against his enemy will do him harm and earn him painful repercussions in the end, he will neutralise the force of the medicine and render it ineffective. In that case, the person might begin to wonder whether the witch doctor deceived him. He did not. Orunmila has merely demonstrated to his son that to destroy one's enemy is to destroy one's self. If you point one finger at your enemy, the remaining four which are more in number, and symbolising repercussion, are pointed at you. Orunmila will illustrate that anyone digging the grave of his enemy is at the same time digging his own grave. That is why the common prayer of Orunmila is for the good of friends, enemies, witches, divinities, brothers and sisters, but that those who therefore wish him evil may not succeed.

He advocates that it is even more rewarding for you to pray for an enemy who is planning evil against you so that when the divinities gather to determine the case, the balance of righteousness will be on your side. It is better to have the support of the divinities in such a situation than to incur their condemnation.

THE EFFICACY OF PATIENCE IN IFISM

Orunmila says that when he is in a hurry, his speed of action is not as fast as the pace at which the smallest ant or the fastest snail moves. He says that even when he is moving and a tree falls to obstruct his advance, he stays by the fallen tree, until it rots away before continuing on his journey. If on the other hand a stone blocks his movement he will wait until shedded foliage heaps up to the height of the stone before crossing with the bridge provided by the heap of leaves. Even when he decides to react he does not do so directly. He appeals to one of the more aggressive divinities like Esu, Ogun, Sankpana or Sango, by making sacrifices to them and exhorting them to act on his behalf.

Orunmila says that if he reacts too soon, he will do so in three years and only when his patience has been exhausted. But when he finally decides to react, he does so ruthlessly. Ogbe Suru provides the clearest illustration of how Orunmila operates in this connection.

Once upon a time, a princess lived at Iwo whose beauty was so captivating that all the men of Iwo were not considered eligible enough for her. Her father, the Oba of Iwo had been told not to betroth her to anyone except to a man chosen by herself. When the people of Ife heard of her fame and beauty, they decided to contest for her hand in marriage. Ogun was the first to make an attempt. Ogun went to Iwo and the sight of the princess completely un-nerved him and he vowed to stop at nothing to win her for himself.

When Ogun professed love to her she accepted him without any hesitation. She however insisted that she had to live with her suitor in her father's house, in which suggestion Ogun readily acquiesced. She entertained Ogun elaborately for the first seven days. On the third day of his arrival at Iwo, she asked Ogun to tell her what he forbade in order to narrow down the margin of friction between them. Before Ogun left Ife for Iwo, he had been warned to make sacrifice to his guardian angel and to Esu in order to return home alive from his mission. Ogun boasted that since no battle had ever defied his strength and valour he did not see the justification in making any sacrificial preparations when he was going to meet a woman. He did not do the sacrifice.

In reply to the princess's question Ogun told her that he forbade palm kernel oil (Adin or Uden) and menstruation. In other words he is forbidden to see any woman's menstrual pad or discharge. As soon as the seven days of hospitality were over, the princess saw her menstruation. She then prepared a meal with palm kernel oil for Ogun to eat. When she passed the food for Ogun to eat, she deliberately sat on his shrine without padding her menstrual discharge.

When Ogun settled down to enjoy the meal he discovered that the soup was prepared with palm kernel oil. When he raised up his head in fury to query her he saw that there was also menstrual discharge on his shrine. In fury Ogun rose up to strike her and she quickly ran into her father's apartment for succour. When her father saw Ogun pursuing his daughter, the Oba used his ASE to conjure him to stop and quickly commanded Ogun to transfigure into the sledge hammer used by blacksmiths, which he is to this day. That was the end of Ogun's attempt to win the princess of Iwo for his wife.

After waiting in vain for Ogun to return with the princess to Ife, his junior brother Osonyin (Osun in Bini) decided to proceed to Iwo for the dual mission of searching for Ogun and if possible, of winning the princess for himself. Before going to Iwo, he too was advised to make sacrifice to his guardian angel and to offer a he-goat to Esu. He also boasted that as the owner of all the diabolical medicines that existed, it would be degrading for him to make any sacrifice to any other divinity. He then set out for Iwo.

On getting to Iwo, he was quickly introduced to the princess who extended to him the initial reception and hospitality to which she previously treated Ogun. On the third day of Osonyin's arrival, she also beseeched him to disclose to her what he forbade in order to minimise the risk of friction. In reply, Osonyin wanted to know if she had previously met Ogun. She confirmed that she did, but that in view of the shabby reception she gave to Ogun, he felt too embarrassed to return home and decided to seek a new abode far away from Ife and Iwo. In a mood of flattery designed to elate Osonyin she told him that Ogun's eyes were too frightful for her liking and that the soft-spoken Osonyin was her kind of man. With that, Osonyin was disarmed and proceeded to disclose to her that he forbade palm oil and menstruation. She re-assured Osonyin, like she did Ogun before him, that she merely asked the question in order to obviate the risk of any misunderstanding between them.

Shortly after the expiry of the honeymoon the princess began her menstruation. She then prepared a pottage with fine palm oil for Osonyin to eat. She also went to his bed to stain it with her menstrual discharge. When Osonyin was about to start his favourite pottage meal, he discovered that it was prepared with palm oil. He then abandoned the food, reminding her that he forbade palm oil in his food. She apologised to him by embracing him and cajoling him into his bedroom for romance. But as soon as he was about to lie down on the bed, he saw menstrual discharge and accused her of trying to kill him.

When he brought out his wand to curse the princess, she again ran into her father's apartment and the father stopped Osonyin with his ASE. The Oba commanded Osonyin to transfigure into a pot of water, which is what he is, to this day. Once again, that marked the end of Osonyin's attempt to win the princess for himself.

After waiting in vain for Ogun and Osonyin to return home, the people of Ife enjoined Orunmila to go in search of them. He then invited his Awos for divination and they told him that Ogun and Osonyin were no more. He was advised that before going to Iwo, he should make sacrifice to his Ifa and give he-goat to Esu. He was warned that very shabby treatment awaited him at Iwo, unless he made up his mind never to exhaust his patience until the very end. He made the sacrifice and then left for Iwo, after resolving to forebear whatever he experienced.

On getting there, he began to dance at the gateway to the town, and people gathered to welcome him. Subsequently, the princess came along and professed love to him. He returned her love and agreed to live with her in her father's house. She extended the usual hospitality to Orunmila, and ended up by asking him what he forbade. Before agreeing to answer her question, he asked for the whereabouts of his elder brothers, who came earlier to Iwo to seek her hands in marriage. She told Orunmila that the first one was too aggressive for her liking, while the second one was much too diabolical for her comfort. That was why she turned down their overtures and as a result of their disappointments, they decided never again to visit Ife or set foot on the land of Iwo. She presumed that they had gone to found new homes in other towns. Orunmila did not believe the story; but it was enough to put him on guard.

Finally, he revealed to her that he forbade rat, fish, hen, goat, bush goat (Oguonziran in Bini and Edu in Yoruba), palm oil, palm wine and women's menstruation. Incidentally, apart from the last item, all others happened to be the staple food of Orunmila.

A few days later, the woman started her menstruation and she prepared food with rat for Orunmila and sat squarely on his Ifa shrine. When Orunmila saw the rat in his food, he asked her why she gave him what he forbade. She explained that it was because there was no meat at home. After a deep reflection, Orunmila said to her; the essence of marriage is the sharing of mutual pains and pleasures. It is on account of one's loved one that one eats what one forbids. Why should I be afraid of death, when I have the queen of beauty by my side. With those amorous remarks, he embraced the woman and decided to eat the rat to please her. After he had eaten, as she got up from where she sat on his shrine, to collect the plates, Orunmila saw that the white cloth adorning his shrine, had been soiled with menstrual discharge. Once again, she apologised to him on the grounds that the discharge came unexpectedly. He forgave her readily and went out to wash the soiled cloth by himself. The princess was puzzled.

One after the other, the woman gave him, each of what Orunmila told her that he forbade, but he refused to lose his temper. After exhausting the list of Orunmila's forbidden foodstuffs, and he did not lose his temper, the princess of Iwo decided on a completely new act of provocation. She invited a lover from outside to come and visit them under the guise of being a relation of her's. In the night, the lover made love to her before the very eyes of Orunmila. That was exactly three years after Orunmila had been living with her.

The following morning, Orunmila fetched water for the lover to have his bath. As he was about to leave, Orunmila suggested that he would join the woman to escort him. It was time for him to react.

As soon as they were out of the town, he invoked Esu to intervene. Esu used his own head to constitute a stumbling stone, on the pathway, and the lover who was in front, hit his foot on it, and he fell. At the same time, Orunmila pointed his Uranke at him and he transfigured into a snail, which he quickly broke and used to annoint the woman's body for the pollution she got from the intruder.

When they got back home, the princess, who became very frightened at the prowess of this endlessly patient suitor, went to her father to proclaim that she had found the husband she would agree to marry. Her father quickly invited Orunmila and his daughter and they both professed that they were willing to become man and wife. The following month, she became pregnant.

It was at that stage that Orunmila sought the permission of his father-in-law to return to his home town of Ife with his wife. He readily agreed. On getting home to Ife, he introduced the wife as Iya ile Iwo — meaning the product of my sufferings at Iwo. That is the origin of the Yoruba word "Iyawo" which means a wife.

Orunmila then composed a special song in praise of perseverance, and made a feast of jubilation for the success of his over-three years mission to Iwo.

This experience also went to confirm a fundamental Ifa philosophy that if a man reveals what he forbids to his wife, it is exactly what she is going to do to him when she plans to undo him. The person who does not forbid anything only prolongs his life. That is why Orunmila does not forbid anything. We shall soon see how Ejiogbe's mother gave his father palm wine to drink because she knew he forbade it.

Under Osa-Etura, Orunmila will teach us the virtues of prosperity without vanity and strength without arrogance. This is how Orunmila teaches us to be modest. He likened modesty to the slow but graceful movement of the milipede who has 200 limbs. Normally, a creature with that number of limbs should run faster than anyone else. On the contrary, the milipede moves very slowly but gracefully.

When one finds oneself in a state of prosperity, one should use it not to the detriment of others, but for promoting the overall welfare of humanity. Anyone who uses his power or prosperity to suppress the rights and interests of his fellow men will have destruction awaiting him at the pinnacle of his success. To be able to harness one's strength and prosperity judiciously, Orunmila says that one should always appeal to the inner head not to destroy the outer head. He describes the mind as the head in the stomach and the main head as the outside head. It is the mind that directs the fate of the head and it is therefore the director that must always be persuaded to monitor the direction to which the head moves.

In fact Orunmila says that he respects three sets of human beings:
(1) a beautiful woman or a handsome man who does not flirt;
(2) a wealthy person who is humble and unassuming; and
(3) a powerful functionary who is liberal and equitable in the exercise of his or her authority.

IFA'S CONCEPTS OF GOOD AND EVIL

Orunmila is a strong advocate of the objectivity of Truth. He is however realistic enough to say that truth is bitter and that people strive a great deal to avoid or circumvent it. In spite of the difficulties, trials and tribulations associated with the defence of truth, and the exigency and cheap popularity of falsehood, he advocates that in the final analysis, Truth is more rewarding than falsehood.

Orunmila illustrates quite clearly the problems associated with the defence of the objective good. Right at the outset of the work of the first of Orunmila's apostles to come to earth, we shall see from Ejiogbe, who was in heaven called Omonighorogbo (Odolevbo in Bin) (one who stands for liberalism and objectivity) that he came to the world to improve the quality and standards of human behaviour. He got himself deeply involved in humanitarian gestures to mankind, without expecting or demanding any reward in return for his gratuitous services. One would have thought that his behaviour would not only be appreciated but also serve as a shining example to others. On the contrary, those who were in the world before him were so disapproving of his actions, that they began to send incessant messages to God in heaven, that Omonighorogbo, rather than improve the condition of the world, was in fact damaging the code of conduct he met in the world, so much that he was making life unliveable for others.

These reports became so prevalent and persistent that God, who never condemns without verification, sent a heavenly constable to the world to invite Omonighorogbo back to heaven, after investigating his performance on the spot. The policeman, after concealing his own identity, got to Omonighorogbo's house early in the morning and offered to serve him as an auxiliary. From that very morning until dusk, the policeman saw that Omonighorogbo spent so much time in the service of others, delivering pregnant women, healing the sick, making divination for the distressed, settling quarrels between people etc., all without any gratification of any kind, that he did not even have time to take his breakfast.

After watching his performance throughout the day, the heavenly policeman, subsequently revealed his identity and disclosed-that God wanted him in heaven. Almost immediately, he dressed up for the return journey to heaven. On getting to heaven, God rebuked him for going to damage virtues in the world. Before Omonighorogbo had time to explain, it was the policeman who spoke on his behalf. He explained that those who came to complain against him were those who could not be at ease with his benevolence, because it posed a threat to their own extortionate behaviour. He added that the vast majority of people would miss his invaluable role on earth, if he was to remain permanently in heaven.

With that testimony, God ordered him to return to earth to continue his good works, but that in order to survive the evil machinations of his enemies he should henceforth charge reasonable fees for his services to human beings. That was how the Ifa priests obtained God's clearance to charge fees for whatever they did. It will be remembered that Ejiogbe was the first of Orunmila's apostles to come back to the world.

This experience of Ejiogbe clearly illustrates that those who work in defence of the objective good, court the risk of envy and open aggression from others less endowed with benevolence and magnanimity. Those who insist on doing things the right way, incur the displeasure and wrath of those who stand to benefit from chaos, cheating and confusion. Those who do their work without expecting any extra-curricular benefits in return get called all kinds of discreditable names.In fact false stories are even invented against them because the selfishness of human nature does not allow people to concede to others more credit that they are able to admit to themselves. For their own peace of mind, the less righteous must of necessity surround their consciences with a facade of false assumptions and justification. They must assume that others must be doing what they themselves are doing. If they demand bribes and kickbacks before doing the jobs for which they are otherwise paid handsomely, they must assume that everybody else is doing it. If they suddenly discover variations to their assumed norms, their immediate reaction is to move to the offensive. That is why those who live by, and in defence of, the objectivity of truth, stand to suffer tremendous hostility and deprivation. However, their consolation, like God advised Omonighorogbo in heaven, is to continue on their chosen path in defence of truth. After all, there is eternal satisfaction and candour in being different. If every one else loses his head and one is able to keep one's own, the ultimate and inevitable vindication that comes to those who stand by the truth, is more rewarding than all the transient attractions that money can buy.

The question which one must ask therefore is, what are the material benefits deriving from ethical objectivity. It is fashionable to measure material satisfaction in terms not of man's immediate requirements, but of avarice. The man who steals from the public coffers to be able to acquire a private jet in an environment, where people cannot even get jobs to provide for respectable living, must be avaricious, when there are commercial air lines to take him to where ever he wants to travel. The public officer who doubles the logical or functional cost of a project because of the kickback he expects to receive has committed an unforgiveable crime against humanity, because the aggregate cost of his disloyalty to society would have provided additional opportunities and benefits to the suffering masses of people.

When the righteous looks at the unscrupulous in society and sees that they are ostensibly more prosperous, there is a tendency to wonder whether there is virtue in selfless objectivity. Orunmila tells us that the benefits of cheating are purely transient. The cheat may be seen to prosper ostensibly but if one came close enough to him, one might discover that his material contentment was hollow and that he was not what he seemed to be. And if he gets away with his greediness, the punishment will be handed to his children and grand children until he atones in full for what he has undeservedly extracted from society.

In this connection, we shall see how Orunmila postulates the spiritual satisfaction deriving from living one's life in accordance with divine laws, and the spiritual poverty of those who believe they can make it by cheating throughout life. Although instances abound in the works of Orumila in which sacrifices were made for evil doers in order to succeed in their nefarious designs, nonetheless, Orunmila makes it quite clear that such success is only ephemeral.

As soon as God appeared through light to conquer darkness and the forces of evil, Esu vowed that he would put up a fierce battle to gain ascendancy over God's creatures.

The prosperous man is the one who derives final contentment from what he has and what he is, and the poor man is the one who although materially wealthy, goes insatiably in quest for endless material acquisition at the expense of others. For, what is the difference between a common thief and a gentleman if they both seek monetary goals at the expense of integrity. There is no eternal justification for mortgaging one's conscience in quest of wealth to bequeath to one's children, whilst denying his children the pride of inheritting his good name, because the best legacy a man can bequeath to his children are his principles, and his identity. The children can be proud of his good name, but not of his wealth if everybody knew he acquired it unscrupulously.

CHAPTER XI
HOW DOES ONE COME IN CONTACT WITH ORUNMILA

Ifism is not meant to be a universal religion in terms of fishing out for adherents and converts. The hard-core of Ifism is made up of the re-incarnates and off-springs of the original followers of Orunmila and his OLODUS and ODUS, all the way from heaven. It is not everybody who can become a follower of Orunmila unless they are specifically chosen. Orunmila does not seek to convince anyone to belong to his flock. In fact, many people come to him when they are having difficult problems, and he often demonstrates that such problems are not insurmountable. If a person is fortunate, he will have an early means of knowing that he was destined to be a follower of Orumila. Once a person is chosen as a follower, he should endeavour to follow him fervently, because half-hearted followership used to pose lots of problems, not necessarily caused by Orunmila, but because half-hearted service will not put him in a position to tackle his followers' problems effectively. There are a variety of ways in which one may come into association with Orunmila.

In the past, the significance of naming ceremonies for newly born children was to enable parents to know which path the child should follow in life. Eight days after a child is born, Ifa priests and other seers, who specialise in the astrology of newly born children are invited to read the life of the child. In some parts of Africa, the ODU which appears for the child at the naming ceremony is later prepared for him as his own Ifa. It is from that ceremony that Orunmila tells the parents the type of child they have. If it is a Fay (Imere or Elegbe) who is making a short trip to earth only to desert the parents soon after endearing himself to them, Orunmila will tell the parents what to do to prevent the child from returning to heaven prematurely. Amost invariably, Ifa is prepared for that kind of child very early in life, as a counterpoise against untimely death.

On the other hand, some people run into serious problems in the course of their lives. If a person is a potential Ifist from heaven, Orunmila can appear to him in a dream or cause his guardian angel to reveal to him in a dream, that he is experiencing difficulties because he has not discovered the divinity that accompanied him to the earth. If such a person is experienced enough in the ways of life he then goes for divination where it will be confirmed to him that he should arrange to obtain his own Ifa. There are many people who come to this point of realisation only when they are between life and death.

Out of ignorance, some neophytes who obtain relief from their problems soon after their initiation into Ifism, are tempted to conclude that Orunmila recruits followers by creating problems for them. That will most certainly be an act of ingratitude because Orunmila does not create problems for his followers. It is only when a person's guardian angel discovers in heaven that his ward is going to experience certain problems in life that he (the guardian angel) appeals for the support of Orunmila in order to be at hand to assist when those problems occur.

The Role of Guiding Divinities in our lives:

At this point I should like to illustrate the part that a ruling divinity plays in the lives of mortals. Amayo decided in heaven to come to the world. He went for divination on what to do in order to have a successful stay on earth. At divination he was told that he was going to succeed in

whatever he did on earth. His star would shine brightly but enemies would try to extinguish it. They would not succeed provided:—
   (i)   He succeeded in persuading Ogun and Orunmila to follow him as patron-divinities to the world;
   (ii) He did not marry a light-complexioned woman while on earth, because a light complexioned woman had sworn in heaven to shorten his life on earth; and
   (iii) He did not neglect his patron divinities while on earth.

He was then advised to pay homage to all three divinities which he did in heaven with the aid of his guardian angel.

He was subsequently born into an average family on earth. He completed his education up to University level. While in the University, he met Ayo, a light complexioned damsel. Since no one remembers on earth the do's and dont's of his destiny, he fell head over heels in love with Ayo who was studying medicine.

When Amayo was leaving the University as a history graduate he got married to Ayo who finished her education two years after their marriage. Ayo became pregnant as she was leaving the University. They soon had a baby boy and the couple lived a reasonably happy life. They both came from Christian families where no one knew anything about the higher divinities.

One night when Amayo had a fever, he had a dream and someone looking like him (apparently his guardian angel) told him that he had forgotten the pledge he made in heaven. The voice talking to him in the dream told him to proceed without delay to his uncle at Udo. He was told to abide by whatever advice his uncle gave him.

When he woke up, he mentioned the dream to his mother who insisted that they should both go to Udo to see his uncle. His uncle happened to be an Ogun priest. He refused to go to Udo but sent his driver to take his mother there. On getting to Udo, the mother met the uncle who, possessed by the Ogun divinity, was telling the people present about their future.

As soon as the possessed uncle saw his brother's wife, he inivted her to come to him and to kneel down. She did as she was told. The priest then told her that it was the son's guardian angel that instructed him to come. Asked why he did not come, she explained that her son was indisposed. The priest told her that the sickness was going to be prolonged and serious and that it was going to be a turning point in his life. The priest then revealed that Amayo should immediatley arrange to have his Ogun and Orunmila and since he could not advise him to divorce his wife, he should not insist on keeping her if she chose to leave him. The priest warned the woman not to allow the son to ignore his advice, lest the next story she would bring to him would be to report his demise.

The woman quickly went home and told the son about the revelation. On his part, he preferred to die rather than get involved in fettish idolatry. The mother went to report the matter to Amayo's father who also could not persuade his son to change his mind. Meanwhile, the Doctor diagnosed that he had hypertension and he was being treated accordingly.

One night, he had a mild stroke which did not do much physical damage to him but affected his speech. He was then moved to the doctor's private clinic for bed rest. He stayed there for five weeks. Subsequently, his uncle at Udo sent another message that if he did not carry out the pledge he entered into in heaven he would not live to see the new moon.

At that stage, the mother came to seek the advice of a prominent Ifa priest who told her to arrange to prepare Orunmila for her son not later than the following day because the son's life was about to extinguish. Poor woman, she wept bitterly and went to the market to buy all the prescribed materials. By the time she saw the son the next morning at the hospital, he was already unconscious.

Nonetheless, the woman went ahead with the ceremony of preparing Orunmila for the son. At the same time, the father invited the brother from Udo to come and prepare Ogun for his son. The ceremonies were completed on the same day and the parts that required to be used to touch Amayo's head were sent to his sick bed in hospital.

That night, Amayo was heard crying in his dream that he could not accompany someone on a journey to which he was being invited. When he woke up he asked for his eighteen months old son, who was instantly brought to the hospital. He then began to regain consciousness. A week later he was discharged from the hospital.

It was not until a month later that close friends and relations knew that the sickness had left an indelible scar on his system. He was sexually impotent.

His wife now began to infer an association between the "juju" that his relation forced him to do, and his impotence. The argument became so stiff that the wife, herself a medical doctor, decided to leave the house. Obviously, Amayo loved his wife and was not prepared to see her go. But the wife told him that the only condition for her return to him was a written promise not to have anything to do with the "juju" prepared for him. At that stage his father intervened that Amayo should choose between his wife and the rest of the family. Remembering what the uncle in-law's Ogun told her at Udo, the mother appealed to Amayo not to forsake his family for a woman who chose to desert him at the darkest moment of his life. With that, the wife was allowed to leave the house with her only child for Amayo.

Not long afterwards, Amayo became fully well and is now happily married again to another graduate who already has four children by him. He is also doing very well in his job, and has built his own house and has also completed his Ogun and Orunmila ceremonies.

The problem Amayo had was the delay in discovering the true path of his life. Happily, he had a good mother who would not take "No" for an answer. It is believed that many people run into similar difficulties without being able to do the right things about them.

It goes without saying therefore that far from creating problems for their wards, the ruling divinities only expect us to keep them by our side, against the contingency of the inevitable problems, we are destined to encounter in the course of our lives. The divinities do not come to us because they do not need anything from us. It is our guardian angels that go to them to solicit their support in seeing us through life. We shall see later that the sacrifices we make to the divinities with the solitary exception of Esu, are used as feasts to bribe the forces of evil to get off our backs.

On the other hand, those who have developed the habit of going for divination, or their friends and relations, may be told during routine consultations that if they are to avoid imminent problems, they must have their own Orunmila without any delay. Many people have ignored such advice at divination because not many people are interested in subjecting their freedom to the beck and call of any divinity. In most cases, such people come round to it again when the problems foretold actually manifest. I know of a specific instance of a man who was told in 1968 to have his own Orunmila in order to avoid being put in chains (that is, going to prison or detention) later in life. This man was reasonably successful in life. He had a University Education overseas and rose rapidly in his employment to the position of a head of his department. When his parents told him of the revelation that he was required to get initiated into the Ifa religion, by having his own Orunmila, he reacted by telling his parents to mind their own business because he was satisfied with his Christian Faith.

Seven years later, there was a national calamity which landed this man in all kinds of problems inter alios. First, he lost his lofty job and next he was put in chains and spent several months in detention. It was during his detention that he remembered what he was told seven years earlier and he told his parents to prepare for the ceremony.

He was tried along with others subsequently and eventually regained his freedom.

I am aware of another case of a man who was always spending his time in and out of prison, on stealing charges. He was not the dare-devil type of robber. He was often caught stealing trivial things like a fowl, yams, goats, etc. by the road side or in farms. He never broke in to people's homes. Once again he was jailed for petty larceny, and when the situation became embarrasing to his relations, they decided to find out why he could not have a settled life. They were advised that Orunmila was the only divinity who could save him and he should therefore have his own. When he came out of prison his relations gathered together and contributed to fund the expenses of having his own Orunmila. Soon after the ceremony, he decided on his own, but influenced by the advice of Ifa, to start his own farm. He soon made enough money from farming to build his own house, marry two wives and to raise several children. He is today a highly respected citizen. He has not been to prison or been arrested for any mis-demeanour during the last fifteen years.

In the cause of having one's own Orunmila, one is often advised to do or not to do certain things, the adherence or otherwise, to which accounts for one's subsequent performance in life. A person might be told to give up a particular habit because it is repugnant to his own Orunmila or his Guardian Angel. Some are told to give up certain professions or vocations for other callings. Some others are even told to divorce their wives or husbands. Others are advised to perform additional ceremonies in order to have an antedote against up-coming problems in life. One can only ignore such warnings and advice at one's peril.

I know of a man now late, who as soon as he got his own Ifa was told that he should give up drinking of alcohol in order to avoid an incurable stomach trouble later in life. This man was a very lively person but try as he would, he could not give up drinking. Later, he developed stomach ulcer, and even after having the ulcer, he continued to drink. I still have very clear memories of how he died in 1957. He attended a New Year eve's dance a few houses away from my father's, where he again had a lot to drink. At about 3.00a.m. he had a severe attack of stomach griping. Subsequently, he began to vomit blood. He was then rushed to the hospital, but died before he got to the hospital.

I am also aware of another successful man who also died because he could not abide by the advice he was given during his Ifa initiation ceremony. When he was preparing his own Orunmila, he was told that he would succeed tremendously in life but that if he wanted to live long, he should do away with his wife. He was so infuriated by the advice that he even disclosed it to his wife, who from then on, held the priest who prepared the Ifa for him, at arms length. He became very successful in his job by getting very close to the apex of his career pyramid. He had plenty of assets and was living in affluence. At the height of his success, his wife began to create lots of problems for him. They soon got separated and he subsequently became so ill that he got hospitalised for over one year, during which time his wife could not as much as call on him in hospital.

I still clearly remember him in his state of unconsciousness crying out in his sleep at night and calling on his wife to spare his life, even by taking all that he had. He died soon afterwards and today his widow is the beneficiary of his legacy.

The Ifa religion is not all about hard luck stories. There are more interesting stories of those who followed the advice and guidelines enunciated by their Orunmila and have survived in peace and prosperity.

I know of a top rate business tycoon, unfortunately now late, who was an ardent Ifa follower. He rose to the pinnacle of success in both moral and material excellence. He was even named after Ifa. Still alive is another Octo-generian who is an industrial pioneer in Nigeria. He is the son of Oyeku-Meji whose life in terms of moral integrity, intellectual dignity, and material dexterity, has been a source of inspiration to many generations.

The point to stress is that like Equity, those who follow Orunmila must do so with clean hands. Ifa cannot guarantee one's individual success in one's endeavours and aspirations if one is in the habit of either hindering the progress or procuring the downfall and death of others. In fact those who spend their lives plotting evil against others may succeed for some time. In the end all their evil designs for others are eventually visited upon them and their off-springs.

The importance of devout followship in the Ifa religion

There is no need to worship Orunmila in the same way that we worship God Himself. All that Orumila demands of his followers is to bring all their problems to him. He will advise through divination or dreams what sacrifices are to be made from time to time. Like in all other religions, there are many people who think that Orunmila is a Magic Divinity, who can double money for them, or who can avenge injuries caused by others. He does these things in his own subtle way and at his own pace. Some followers are in a hurry to realise their objectives and when they are late in coming forth, they caste the Orunmila shrine aside and look for something else to accelerate the manifestation of their desires. That is a most unfortunate thing to do because all those who have thrown their Ifa shrines into the river or bush out of frustration have almost invariably been worse off for it. Others abandon their shrines after being initiated into the Ifa religion and expect miracles to happen. The centre-piece of Ifa art and practice is sacrifice. If one takes Orunmila and keeps it inside the cupboard or abandons it in a place where it is not cared for, it will not be in a position to protect the life and interests of the follower.

As soon as one completes the Ifa ceremony the next task is to find out what problems his own Orumila encountered both in heaven and on earth during his time. One should then set about trying to resolve such problems or anticipate them by making the requisite precautionary sacrifices and ceremonies. Whatever problem one has, should be referred to Orunmila through divination by inviting experienced Ifa priests to sound him on appropriate occasions.

A follower of Orunmila should not lose faith in his ability to solve problems provided one bothers him through divination and sacrifice with those problems from time to time. The purpose of this book is partly to educate followers of Orunmila on the ways of Orunmila so that they might not lose faith. There are good and bad patron-Orunmilas. Those who are unfortunate to come to the world under the patronage of unfortunate Odu-Ifas should not despair. There is a way to improve their lots, by approaching Ifa priests, because Orunmila can turn misfortune to fortune, hard luck to good luck and a bad head to a good head. In fact he says that the more difficult a problem is, the happier he is to solve it.

CHAPTER XII
THE IFA GENEALOGY

There are sixteen principal apostles (OLODUS) of Orunmila. They are in order of seniority as follows:—

ORDER OF SENIORITY ACCORDING TO THE IFE SCHOOL.	ORDER OF SENIORITY ACCORDING TO THE OYO, ONDO AND BINI SCHOOLS.	
1. Eji-Ogbe	Eji-Ogbe	(1)
2. Oyeku-Meji	Oyeku-Meji	(2)
3. Iwori-Meji	Iwori-Meji	(3)
4. Idi-Meji	Idi-Meji	(4)
5. Obara-Meji	Obara-Meji	(5)
6. Okonron-Meji	Okonron-Meji	(6)
7. Irosun-Meji	Irosun-Meji	(7)
8. Owanrin-Meji	Owanrin-Meji	(8)
9. Ogunda-Meji	Ogunda-Meji	(9)
10. Osa-Meji	Osa-Meji	(10)
11. Etura-Meji	Irete-Meji	(11)
12. Irete-Meji	Etura-Meji	(12)
13. Eka-Meji	Eturukpon-Meji	(13)
14. Eturukpon-Meji	Ose-Meji	(14)
15. Ose-Meji	Ofun-Meji	(15)
16. Ofun-Meji	Eka-Meji	(16)

The difference is really as between the places of Etura and Irete and Eka and Ofun. Each school of thought has very cogent reasons for its own order of seniority. The difference between them is only a matter of tradition. The effect will become clear later when we examine the place of seniority in the Ifa kindred for purposes of divination. They are nonetheless agreed on the name and number of Odus in the Ifa family tree.

At this juncture it is nonetheless necessary to mention briefly Orunmila's explanation for the difference between the two schools. That reason partly explains why it is forbidden to expose the Ifa divination tray (Akpako) to the open air. It is often covered with a piece of white cloth or paper when it is being carried from one place to another, when it involves exposure to the open air.

Long after the town of Oyo was founded by Oronmiyan, whose name was actually Jegbe, the senior son of Olofen, the Ododuwa of Ife, the people of Oyo decided to meet Ogbe-Alara, a disciple of Orunmila at Ife to teach them the markings of the sixteen Olodus of Ifa. Ogbe-Alara marked out the sixteen Olodus for them on the Ifa tray and they decided to carry the tray back to Oyo with the markings of the Olodus on it.

On their way home, there was a gale force wind which upset some of the markings. On getting home they tried to recast the markings from memory. They recalled the names and numbers all right, but missed the sequence after the tenth Odu. Ogbe-Alara returned to heaven before they could meet him again, and that is why the people of Oyo have held on to their sequence ever since. On account of the special relationship between Oyo and Benin kingdoms, the Binis learnt Ifa art (Not Oguega — the Bini equivalent of Ifa art) from the Awos of Oyo.

Each apostle (OLODU) of Orunmila has fifteen disciples (ODUS). It means in effect that there are sixteen OLODUS and 240 Odus in the Ifa kindred. The order of seniority of the 256 apostles and disciples is listed out in the table to this Chapter. This book is going to be arranged in such a way that there will be seventeen volumes on the whole.

The first volume will be devoted to the life and works of the sixteen OLODUS (apostles). The remaining sixteen volumes will deal with the work of the fifteen ODUS of each OLODU. Every effort will be made to reflect the life history of each apostle and disciple right from heaven to this world. The heavenly account will reflect what the particular Odu did or did not do in heaven before he came to the world. The earthly account will reflect what each of them did for themselves and for others, and what was done for them while on earth. Each of them will be referred to in the book as Orunmila, in consonance with tradition.

This is very important because it will be seen that if a person gets initiated into Ifism, and one of the disciples or apostles comes out at Ugbodu — (which is the secret conclave in which one finds out the name of one's ruling ODU) — it must follow as the night follows the day, that one's life story will take the same course as that of the patron ODU.

This book will therefore be of immense benefit to those who have their own Orunmila and who may otherwise not have the opportunity of knowing the history of their patron-Odu and ipso facto their own. The book will also contain the names of the Ifa priests who revealed these historical accounts in case anyone is interested in probing them further on the details of the broad revelations embodied in the various volumes.

The second volume will start with the details of the Ifa oracle, and the science of divination.

IFA GENEALOGY
ORDER OF SENIORITY

(ORUNMILA FAMILY TREE)

1. EJI-OGBE
2. OYEKU-MEJI
3. IWORI-MEJI
4. IDI-MEJI
5. OBARA-MEJI
6. OKONRON-MEJI
7. IROSUN-MEJI
8. OWANRIN-MEJI
9. OGUNDA-MEJI
10. OSA-MEJI
11. ETURA-MEJI
12. IRETE-MEJI
13. EKA-MEJI
14. ETURUKPON-MEJI
15. OSE-MEJI
16. OFUN-MEJI
17. OGBE-OYEKU
18. OGBE-IWORI
19. OGBE-IDI
20. OGBE-OBARA
21. OGBE-OKONRON

22. OGBE-IROSUN
23. OGBE-OWANRIN
24. OGBE-OGUNDA
25. OGBE-OSA
26. OGBE-ETURA
27. OGBE-IRETE
28. OGBE-EKA
29. OGBE-ETURUKPON
30. OGBE-OSE
31. OGBE-OFUN
32. OYEKU-LO-OGBE
33. OYEKU-BI-IWORI
34. OYEKU-IDI
35. OYEKU-OBARA
36. OYEKU-OKONRON
37. OYEKU-IROSUN
38. OYEKU-OWANRIN
39. OYEKU-OGUNDA
40. OYEKU-OSA
41. OYEKU-ETURA
42. OYEKU-IRETE
43. OYEKU-ETURUKPON
44. OYEKU-BE-EKA
45. OYEKU-OSE
46. OYEKU-OFUN
47. IWORI-BO-OGBE
48. IWORI-OYEKU

49. IWORI-IDI
50. IWORI-OBARA
51. IWORI-OKONRON
52. IWORI-IROSUN
53. IWORI-OWANRIN
54. IWORI-OGUNDA
55. IWORI-OSA
56. IWORI-ETURA
57. IWORI-IRETE
58. IWORI-EKA
59. IWORI-ETURUKPON
60. IWORI-OSE
61. IWORI-OFUN
62. IDI-OGBE
63. IDI-OYEKU
64. IDI-IWORI
65. IDI-OBARA
66. IDI-OKONRON
67. IDI-IROSUN
68. IDI-OWANRIN
69. IDI-OGUNDA
70. IDI-OSA
71. IDI-ETURA
72. IDI-IRETE
73. IDI-ETURUKPON
74. IDI-EKA
75. IDI-OSE

76. IDI-OFUN
77. OBARA-OGBE
78. OBARA-OYEKU
79. OBARA-IWORI
80. OBARA-IDI
81. OBARA-OKONRON
82. OBARA-IROSUN
83. OBARA-OWANRIN
84. OBARA-OGUNDA
85. OBARA-OSA
86. OBARA-ETURA
87. OBARA-IRETE
88. OBARA-EKA
89. OBARA-ETURUKPON
90. OBARA-OSE
91. OBARA-OFUN
92. OKONRON-OGBE
93. OKONRON-OYEKU
94. OKONRON-IWORI
95. OKONRON-IDI
96. OKONRON-OBARA
97. OKONRON-IROSUN
98. OKONRON-OWANRIN
99. OKONRON-OGUNDA
100. OKONRON-OSA
101. OKONRON-ETURA
102. OKONRON-IRETE

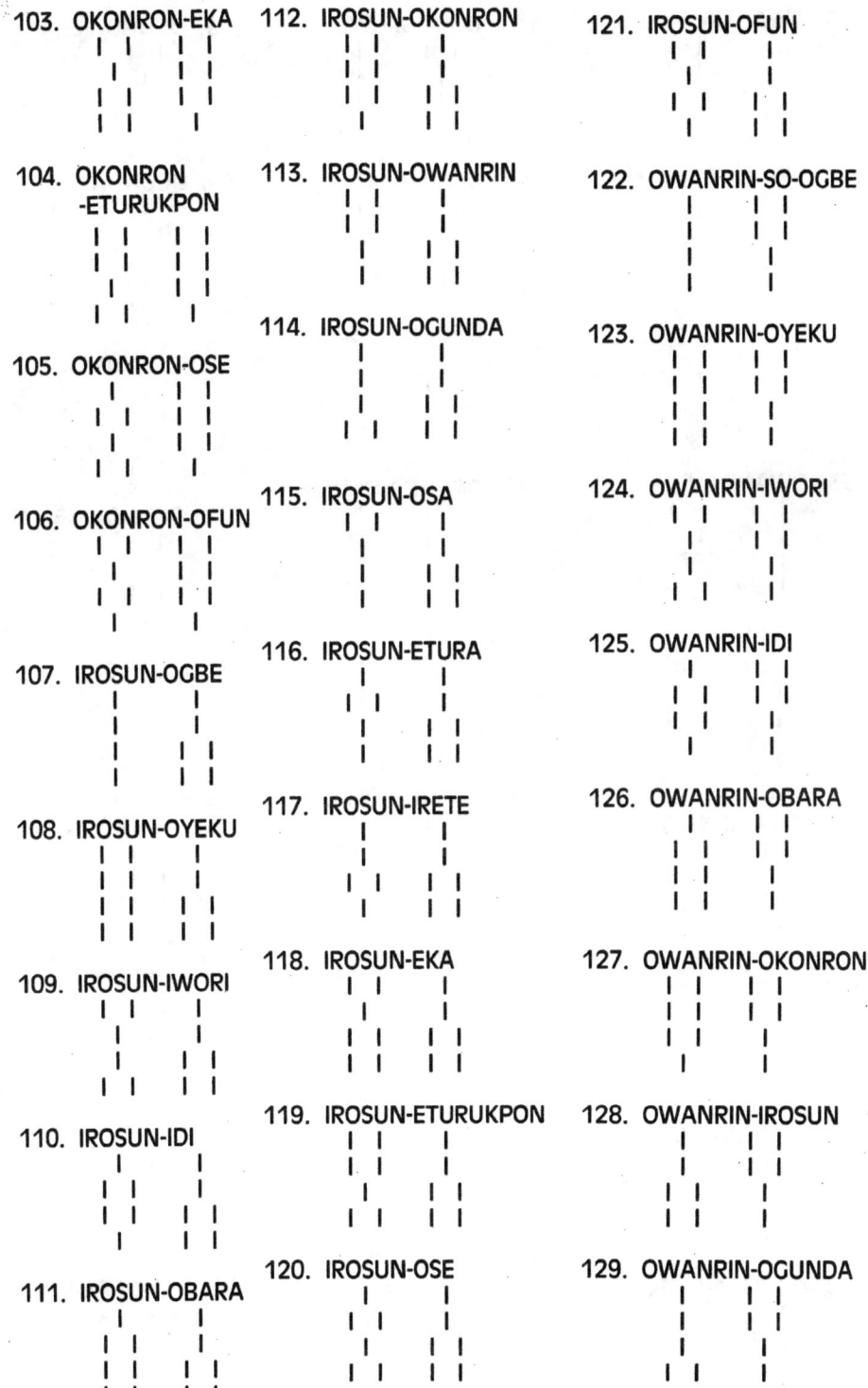

130. OWANRIN-OSA
```
I I    I I
I      I I
I      I
I      I
```

131. OWANRIN-ETURA
```
I      I I
I I    I I
I      I
I      I
```

132. OWANRIN-IRETE
```
I      I I
I      I I
I I    I
I      I
```

133. OWANRIN-EKA
```
I I    I I
I      I I
I I    I I
```

134. OWANRIN-ETURUKPON
```
I I    I I
I I    I I
I      I
I I    I
```

135. OWANRIN-OSE
```
I      I I
I I    I I
I      I
I I    I
```

136. OWANRIN-OFUN
```
I I    I I
I      I I
I I    I
I      I
```

137. OGUNDA-OGBE
```
I      I
I      I
I      I
I      I I
```

138. OGUNDA-OYEKU
```
I I    I
I I    I
I I    I
I I    I I
```

139. OGUNDA-IWORI
```
I I    I
I      I
I      I
I I    I I
```

140. OGUNDA-IDI
```
I      I
I I    I
I I    I
I      I I
```

141. OGUNDA-OBARA
```
I      I
I I    I
I I    I
I I    I I
```

142. OGUNDA-OKONRON
```
I I    I
I I    I
I I    I
I      I I
```

143. OGUNDA-IROSUN
```
I      I
I I    I
I I    I
I I    I I
```

144. OGUNDA-OWANRIN
```
I I    I
I I    I
I      I
I      I I
```

145. OGUNDA-OSA
```
I I    I
I      I
I      I
I      I I
```

146. OGUNDA-ETURA
```
I I    I
I      I
I      I
I      I I
```

147. OGUNDA-IRETE
```
I      I
I      I
I I    I
I      I I
```

148. OGUNDA-EKA
```
I I    I
I      I
I      I
I I    I I
```

149. OGUNDA-ETURUKPON
```
I I    I
I I    I
I      I
I I    I I
```

150. OGUNDA-OSE
```
I      I
I      I
I      I
I I    I I
```

151. OGUNDA-OFUN
```
I I    I
I      I
I I    I
I      I I
```

152. OSA-OGBE
```
I      I I
I      I
I      I
I      I
```

153. OSA-OYEKU
```
I I    I I
I I    I
I I    I
I I    I
```

154. OSA-IWORI
```
I I    I I
I      I
I      I
I I    I
```

155. OSA-IDI
```
I      I I
I I    I
I I    I
I      I
```

156. OSA-OBARA
```
I      I I
I I    I
I I    I
I I    I
```

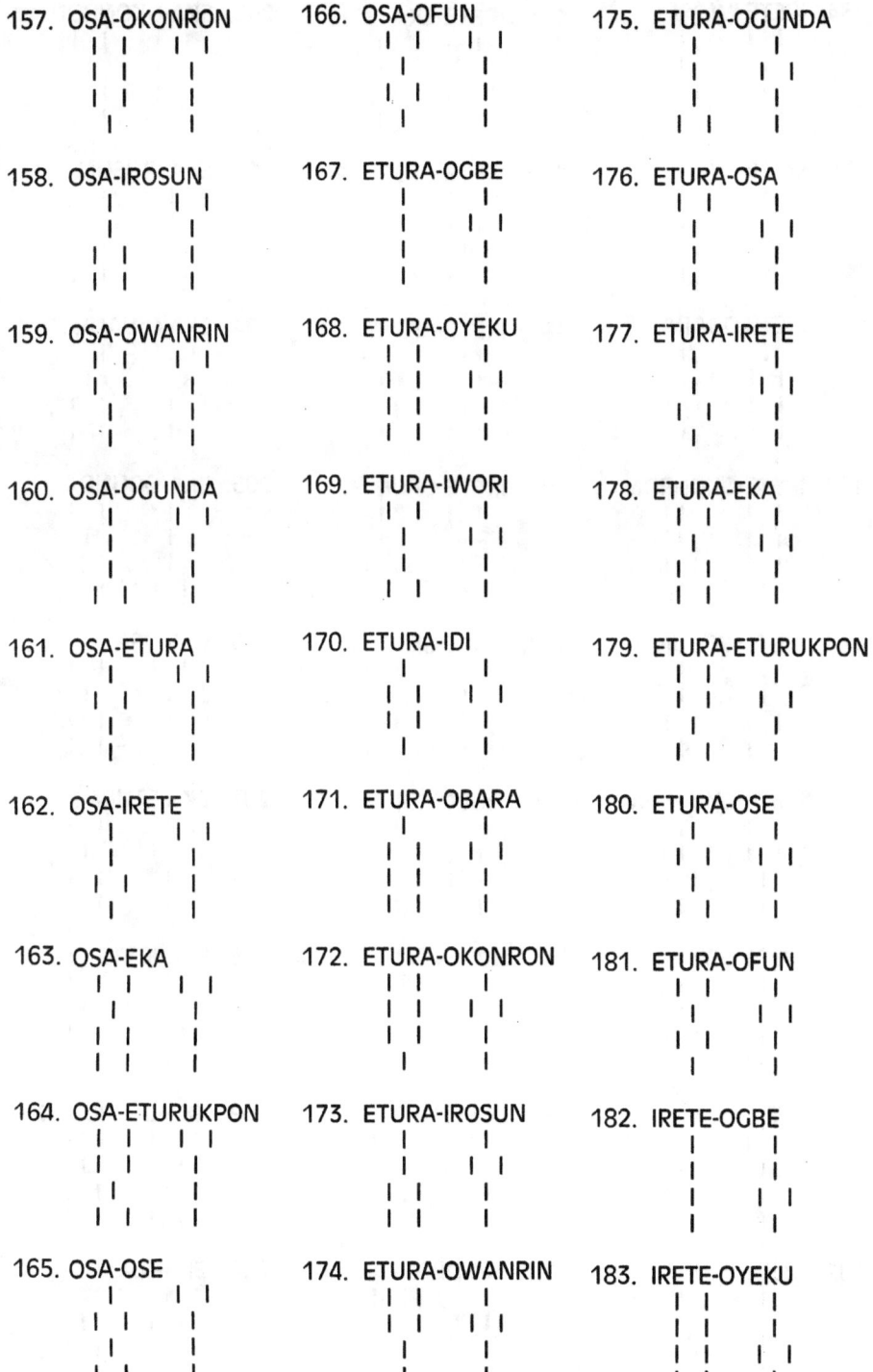

184. IRETE-IWORI
```
I I   I
 I    I
 I   I I
I I   I
```

185. IRETE-IDI
```
 I    I
I I   I
I I  I I
 I    I
```

186. IRETE-OBARA
```
 I    I
I I   I
I I  I I
I I   I
```

187. IRETE-OKONRON
```
I I   I
I I   I
I I  I I
 I    I
```

188. IRETE-IROSUN
```
 I    I
 I    I
I I  I I
I I   I
```

189. IRETE-OWANRIN
```
I I   I
I I   I
 I   I I
 I    I
```

190. IRETE-OGUNDA
```
 I    I
 I    I
 I   I I
I I   I
```

191. IRETE-OSA
```
I I   I
 I    I
 I   I I
 I    I
```

192. IRETE-ETURA
```
 I    I
I I   I
 I   I I
 I    I
```

193. IRETE-EKA
```
I I   I
 I    I
I I  I I
I I   I
```

194. IRETE-ETURUKPON
```
I I   I
I I   I
 I   I I
I I   I
```

195. IRETE-OSE
```
 I    I
I I   I
 I   I I
I I   I
```

196. IRETE-OFUN
```
I I   I
 I    I
I I  I I
 I    I
```

197. EKA-OGBE
```
 I   I I
 I    I
 I   I I
 I   I I
```

198. EKA-OYEKU
```
I I  I I
I I   I
I I  I I
I I  I I
```

199. EKA-IWORI
```
I I  I I
 I    I
 I   I I
I I  I I
```

200. EKA-IDI
```
 I   I I
I I   I
I I  I I
 I   I I
```

201. EKA-OBARA
```
 I   I I
I I   I
I I  I I
I I  I I
```

202. EKA-OKONRON
```
I I  I I
I I   I
I I  I I
 I   I I
```

203. EKA-IROSUN
```
 I   I I
 I    I
I I  I I
I I  I I
```

204. EKA-OWANRIN
```
I I  I I
I I   I
 I   I I
 I   I I
```

205. EKA-OGUNDA
```
 I   I I
 I    I
 I   I I
I I  I I
```

206. EKA-OSA
```
I I  I I
 I    I
 I   I I
 I   I I
```

207. EKA-ETURA
```
 I   I I
I I   I
 I   I I
 I   I I
```

208. EKA-IRETE
```
 I   I I
 I    I
I I  I I
 I   I I
```

209. EKA-ETURUKPON
```
I I  I I
I I   I
 I   I I
I I  I I
```

210. EKA-OSE
```
 I   I I
I I   I
 I   I I
I I  I I
```

211. EKA-OFUN

212. ETURUKPON-OGBE

213. ETURUKPON-OYEKU

214. ETURUKPON-IWORI

215. ETURUKPON-IDI

216. ETURUKPON-OBARA

217. ETURUKPON -OKONRON

218. ETURUKPON-IROSUN

219. ETURUKPON -OWANRIN

220. ETURUKPON-OGUNDA

221. ETURUKPON-OSA

222. ETURUKPON-ETURA

223. ETURUKPON-IRETE

224. ETURUKPON-EKA

225. ETURUKPON-OSE

226. ETURUKPON-OFUN

227. OSE-OGBE

228. OSE-OYEKU

229. OSE-IWORI

230. OSE-IDI

231. OSE-OBARA

232. OSE-OKONRON

233. OSE-IROSUN

234. OSE-OWANRIN

235. OSE-OGUNDA

236. OSE-OSA

237. OSE-ETURA

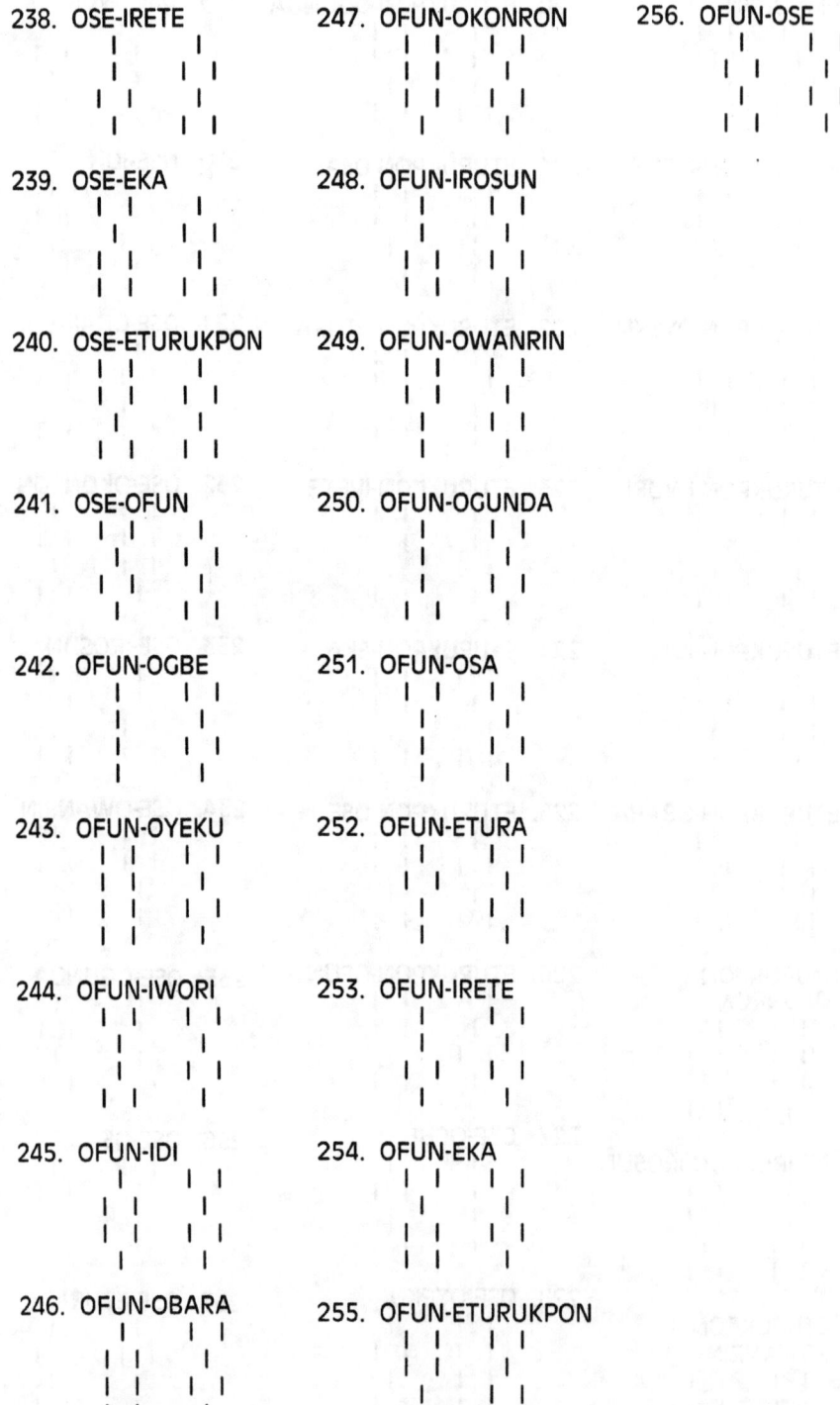

CHAPTER XIII
THE OLODUS/APOSTLES OF ORUNMILA
EJIOGBE or OGBE-MEJI

```
I    I
I    I
I    I
I    I
```

The most remarkable work of Ejiogbe in heaven is his revelation of how the Head, which was itself a Divinity, came to have a permanent abode on the body. The Divinities were originally created without the Head as it is today, because the Head itself was one of the divinities.

The Head as a Divinity

The Awo who made divination for the Head, Ori-omo Atete Ni Iron (hereafter called ORI) was called Amure, awo eba ono, who lived in heaven.

Orunmila invited Amure to make divination for him on how to have a complete physical feature, because none of them (divinities) had a head at the time. The Awo told Orunmila to rub both palms upwards and pray To have a head (Dumusori in Yoruba or uhunmwun arabona in Bini). He was told to make sacrifice with four kolanuts, clay bowl, sponge and soap. He was told to keep the kolanuts on his Ifa shrine without splitting them because an inconsequential visitor would later come to break them.

ORI (Head) also invited Amure for divination and he was told to serve his guardian angel with four kolanuts, which he could not afford to buy, although he was told that he would only begin to prosper after making the sacrifice.

After making his own sacrifice, Orunmila left the four kolanuts on his Ifa shrine as he was advised to do. Thereafter Esu announced in heaven that Orunmila had four beautiful kolanuts at his shrine and was looking for a suitable divinity to break them.

Led by Ogun, all the divinities visited Orunmila one after the other, but he told each of them that they were not strong enough to break the kolanuts. They felt slighted and left him in annoyance.

Even Orisa Nla (God the Son) himself visited Orunmila, but he entertained him with different and better kolanuts, remarking that the controversial kolanuts were not meant for him to break. Since God is never known to lose his temper, he accepted the fresh kolanuts given to him by Orunmila and left.

Finally, ORI decided to visit Orunmila, since he was the only divinity who had not tried to break the mysterious kolanuts, especially as he could not even afford to buy the ones with which he was required to serve his guardian angel. He then rolled up to Orunmila's house.

As soon as Orunmila saw ORI rolling down to his house, he met him and carried him up inside the house. Orunmila immediately got the clay bowl, filled it with water and used the sponge and the soap to wash ORI, clean. After towelling him, Orunmila carried ORI to his shrine, and requested him to break the kolanuts because they had for long been kept for him.

After thanking Orunmila for his honorific gesture, ORI prayed for Orunmila with the kolanuts that whatever he did should have fulfilment and manifestation. Next ORI used the kolanuts to pray for himself to have a permanent abode and plenty of followers. ORI then rolled backwards and charged against the kolanuts and they broke up with a very loud explosion which echoed throughout the length and breadth of heaven.

On hearing the sound of the explosion, all the other divinities immediately realised that the kolanuts at Orunmila's shrine had finally been split and they were all curious to know who succeeded in breaking the kolanuts that had defied everyone including God. When Esu subsequently announced that the kolanuts had been split by ORI, all the divinities agreed that the "Head" was the right divinity to do it.

Almost immediately afterwards, the hand, feet, body, stomach, chest, neck etc., each of which before then had distinct identities, all assembled and decided to go and live with the head, not having previously realised that he was so important. Together, they all carried the Head high above them and right there at the shrine of Orunmila, the Head was crowned the king of the body. It is on account of the role played by Orunmila in his fortune that the head touches the ground to defer and rever to Orunmila to this day. That is also why in spite of being the youngest of all the divinities, Orunmila is more important and more popular than all of them.

For the son of Ejiogbe to live long on earth, he must look for knowledgeable Awos to prepare a special bathing soap for him on the skull of any animal. Ejiogbe is the patron divinity of the head because it was he in heaven, that performed the sacrifice that made the Head the king of the body.

Ejiogbe has turned out to be the most senior Olodu or Apostle of Orunmila on earth although he was originally one of the most junior. He belongs to the second generation of the prophets who volunteered to come to this world in order, through examples, to make it a better place for those living in it. He was a very benevolent apostle of Orunmila both when he was in heaven and when he came to this world.

EJIOGBE leaves for Earth

Meanwhile, Orisa Nla was already in the world and was married to a woman called Afin, who, unknown to him was not too keen on having a child. But Orisa Nla desperately wanted to have a child on earth. At the same time in heaven, Omonighorogbo had gone to the altar of God to wish to come to the world as the child of Afin and Orisa Nla. He was also determined to show the world what it takes to be benevolent and kind hearted. His wishes were granted by the Almighty Father. After obtaining clearance from his guardian angel, he left for earth.

The Birth of Ejiogbe

Meanwhile, Afin, the wife of Orisa Nla became pregnant on earth. Traditionally, Orisa Nla forbade palmwine, while his wife Afin forbade salt. Orisa koi mu emo. Afin koi je iyo. The pregnancy of Afin did not altogether defuse the tension that existed between the couple. The woman became even more pugnacious as her pregnancy advanced in months.

Nine months later — a male child was born. Soon after delivery, Orisa Nla realised that there was no food in the house for feeding the nursing mother. He quickly left for the farm to fetch yams, okro and vegetables. He was a bit late in returning from the farm, which infuriated the wife. She began to complain that the husband had left her to starve on the very day she delivered, and remarked that it was a confirmation that he had no love for her. She thought it was time to terminate the marriage by ending his life. Knowing that Orisa Nla forbade palm wine and that drinking it could end his life, she proceeded to add palm wine to his drinking water pot. As soon as she did that, she left the day-old child on the bed and went out to visit her neighbours.

Meanwhile, Orisa Nla returned from the farm and proceeded to prepare food for the wife. While the yam was cooking on the fire, he went to the room to fetch water with his traditional cup, a snail's shell, from the poisoned water pot. As he was about to drink the water, the day-old son lying on the bed spoke to him, "Father, do not drink that water because my mother added palm wine to it." Surprised at the ability of a day-old child to speak, he nonetheless heeded the advice.

Orisa Nla however completed the cooking but in a gesture of retaliation, he added salt to the soup knowing that it was his wife's poison. After keeping the food for the wife, he went out to play Ayo game with his friends. Meanwhile, the wife returned and made for where her food was kept. As she took the food out to eat, the son again said to her — "Mother, do not eat that food because my father added salt to the soup."

Almost immediately after hearing out the son, she became hysterical and shouted on neighbours to come and save her from a husband who was trying to kill her for bearing him a child. Her screams attracted spectators from the neighbouring houses. Soon afterwards, a meeting of the divinities was convened in Orisa Nla's house. Orisa Nla was invited from where he was playing Ayo and he stayed calm throughout, even as his wife gripped him and was tearing away at him.

Ogun was the one who took the chair at the conference, since Orisa Nla, the traditional Chairman was himself in the dock this time. Ogun invited Afin to state what happened and she narrated how the husband added salt to her food which he knew she forbade. Asked how she knew that salt was added to the soup, and that it was the husband who did it, she explained that she was informed by her day old infant child. The divinities thought she was mad because no one could appreciate how a day old child was capable of speaking to the mother.

Orisa Nla was invited to defend himself against the accusations and contrary to expectation, he confirmed that he actually added salt to his wife's soup. He explained however that he did it to avenge a similar treatment meted to him by his wife earlier on the same day. He accused the wife of adding palm wine to his drinking water pot when everyone including herself knew that he forbade it. Asked how he knew about the wife's alleged action, he again explained that it was his day old child that warned him not to drink from his traditional water pot because his mother had added palm wine to it.

All eyes then turned to the child who was already being looked upon as a mysterious creature. Without being asked in so many words, he volunteered the missing pieces of the puzzle by saying, "Eji mogbe mi ogbe enikon. The translation meant that he came to the world to save the lives of his two parents and that was why he gave each of them the warning that saved them from mutual destruction. It was no small wonder therefore that when the child was to be named seven days later, his parents decided to call him EJIOGBE or Double Salvation.

It is on account of this first earthly work of Ejiogbe that when it comes out during initiation ceremony at Ugbodu, all the sacrificial materials are required to be produced in doubles — 2 goats, 2 hens, 2 snails, 2 fishes, 2 rats, etc. When Ejiogbe comes out at Ugbodu, salt and palm wine are always added to the initiation materials in commemoration of the events that transpired on the day Ejiogbe was born.

The Earthly Works of Ejiogbe

The wonder boy did a lot of mysterious things when he was growing up but the first major miracle he performed was at the age of fifteen when his mother took him to Oja-Ajigbomekon, the only market existing at the time and in which traders from heaven and earth transacted all kinds of businesses, from sale of goods to divination. Everyone having any kind of goods, skill, art, technology etc., for sale, came to that market to trade in them.

The Miracle at the Market

On their way to the market, he met a woman. He stopped the woman and told her that she had a problem. As she was about to speak, he told her not to bother because he knew her problems better than she herself. Ejiogbe told the woman that she had been pregnant for three years, but that it had not developed. He told her to make sacrifice with 16 snails, one hen, one pigeon, five "laughing" kolanuts and honey. He also told her to use a he-goat, Akara (bean buns) and Eko to make sacrifice to Esu.

The woman brought the materials for the sacrifice and after performing it, Ejiogbe assured her that her problems were over. He however told her that after she had delivered safely, she should bring a small boa, a serpent of the constrictor family called Oka in Yoruba and Arumwoto in Bini to offer thanksgiving to Orunmila. He told her to add snail and whatever else she could afford. The woman did the sacrifice and went her way.

The Miracle of the Cripple and the Blind

The next person Ejiogbe met on his way to the market was a cripple called Aro. Like he said earlier to the pregnant woman, he told Aro that he had a problem, but the cripple replied that he had no problem and that it was the young boy (Ejiogbe) who had a problem. Ejiogbe brought out his Uroke (divination wand) and pointed it at the cripple's hands and legs. Instantly, the cripple got up to walk. It was at that stage that Aro realised that far from dealing with a boy, he was dealing with a priest. Aro went on his knees to thank Ejiogbe for curing him of a deformity that he was born with. Ejiogbe however advised him to go and be serving Orunmila but should in future refrain from concealing his problems because he would never know when God would respond to his prayers. Ejiogbe remarked that if anyone concealed his ailment, the ailment would bury him inside the ground.

Next, Ejiogbe met a blind man and asked him if he had a problem. The blind man replied that he had no problem whatsoever. Once again, Ejiogbe stretched out his Uroke towards the man's eyes and he instantly regained his sight. The man was overwhelmed with joy but Ejiogbe advised him to arrange to become a follower of Orunmila in order to minimise his difficulties with mankind. He also told him to serve his head with a cock on getting home. With that Ejiogbe got to the market.

Ejiogbe performed the foregoing miracles without asking for any reward from the beneficiaries.

The Result of Ignoring the advice of Ejiogbe

On their way home from the market, his mother left him behind. Ejiogbe came across a squirrel by the side of the road. He advised the squirrel to make sacrifice to Esu with a he-goat so that the words spoken from his mouth might not bring him destruction. The squirrel retorted that if the young man wanted meat to eat, he could not get it from him. The squirrel is called OTAN in Bini and Okere in Yoruba.

Just near-by, he also saw the boa called Okaa in Yoruba and Aru in Bini. He told him that death was lurking around and that it would be brought to him by a loquacious neighbour. To avoid the calamity, he advised the serpent to serve his head at a secret place with a snail. He was not to allow anyone to encore Amen to his prayers when serving his head.

Finally, he met the thick bush (Eti in Bini and Illo in Yoruba) and advised him to offer he-goat to Esu in order to avoid unwarranted trouble. He also met the palm tree who he advised to give hegoat to Esu so that someone else's problem might not break his neck. The palm tree did the sacrifice without delay, Illo did not.

After that performance, Ejiogbe went home. The journey to and from Oja Ajigbomekon normally took about three months. As soon as he got home, he received a message that the woman he met on his way to the market was in labour. He quickly ran to the woman's house and delivered her with the use of an incantation which Ifa tradition does not permit to be reproduced in this book. That is one of the incantations with which Ifa priests deliver pregnant women to this day. She gave birth to a male child.

As soon as the woman put to bed, the husband took his hunting boomerang, (Ekpede in Bini and Egion in Yoruba) and left for the forest in search of the boa as well as the meat with which to feed his wife.

When the boa heard that the woman who had been pregnant for three years brought forth a child, he realised that her husband would soon come in search of him as he was told that Ejiogbe had directed. Rather belatedly, he ran into the house of Illo (the thickest part of the bush) to serve his head privately there. Illo gave him permission to serve his head in his house.

As soon as the Okaa sat down to pray to his head, Okere came into Illo's house. As Okaa said his prayers, Okere encored ASE, ASE (Amen) Okaa retorted by warning Okere that he did not require Amen from anyone to his prayers. He then ran farther into Illo's house. At the same time. Okere changed his tune and began to sing; Okaa, Jokoo Kpekpe re kpe.

At that point, the man with the boomerang who was searching for Okaa heard the squirrel shouting and began to trail his position. As the squirrel continued to shout hysterically, Okaa shot him and he died. The man then cut a fork-stick to clear the thick bush (Illo). While he was cutting and clearing Illo, he saw the boa on the ground and killed him. At the same time he saw by the side of the Okaa, the dead squirrel and the snail that the boa was going to serve his head with. He collected all of them and went home.

The thick weeds that the hunter cut with a fork stick were on the body of tall palm tree. The palm tree rejoiced and had a new lease of life as soon as the shrubs disrupting fresh air from reaching his body were cut off. That is because he was the only one of the lot that made sacrifice at the right time. To this day, it is the mouth of the squirrel that kills it. It is also the squirrel that tells people where the boa is hiding, and invariably attracts death to it.

This also explains why the appearance of Ejiogbe for a tall dark complexioned man at Ugbodu, signifies assured prosperity for the person, because of the height of the palm tree who alone made sacrifice. If on the other hand it comes out for a smallish fair complexioned man, unless he makes sacrifice he will not make it in life. That is the significance of the failure of the short but dark Illo and the fair complexioned squirrel and boa to make the prescribed sacrifices.

How Ejiogbe survived the wrath of the Elders

The benevolence of the young Ejiogbe made him so popular that his house was streaming with callers night and day. He healed the sick, made sacrifice for paupers to become rich, helped the barren to have children and safely delivered all pregnant women who demanded his assistance. These activities earned him admiration from the beneficiaries of his magnanimity, but incurred him the enimity of the more elderly Awos who could not match his altruism and benevolence. He soon became restless and one night, he had a dream in which his guardian angel told him that some elders were plotting against him. When he woke up in the morning, he was so confused that he decided to go for divination.

How Ejiogbe got peace of mind

He went to the following Ifa priests for divination:—
Ajogodole efo ni mo kpe Ifa mi.
Osigi sigi le ekpo
Usee mi oojagba igbo
Abu kele kon lo obe ide.
They advised him to make sacrifice to his Ifa with a basket of snails. Since he did not even have money to buy snails, all the people he had helped previously brought all the required snails to him. The snails were broken up and the liquid from them was collected. The Awos collected Ero leaves and mashed them in the snails' liquid for Ejiogbe to bath with.

After the sacrifice he began to live a peaceful life. That is why when Ejiogbe appears during divination, the person is advised to offer snails to Ifa. When it comes out at Ugbodu the goat for the ceremony should not be offered on that day until five days later. What are to be offered on that Ugbodu day are snails, dried rat and dried fish. When peace of mind returned to Ejiogbe after the ceremony, he rejoiced singing: Uroko iro, Erero lu uroko iro Erero.

Ejiogbe returns to Heaven for Impeachment

Before he made the sacrifice, the elders, who felt that he had blocked their means of livelihood by performing miracles for gratis, were going to heaven one after the other to report to God. They accused him of spoiling the world and of introducing a new code of behaviour which was totally alien to the ethos on earth.

On his part, Ejiogbe had no life of his own because he spent all his time in the service of others. When children had convulsion he was called upon to heal them, which he did with incantations. He delivered pregnant women, settled disputes for people and went to the rescue of the oppressed. Little did he know that these humanitarian activities had annoyed the traditionally extortionate priests to the point of even plotting to kill him.

At that stage, Olodumare, (Osalobua in Bini) the Father in heaven, sent for Ejiogbe. He sent a Knight of Heaven to fetch him. The knight used his discretion to decide on a strategy for arresting Ejiogbe to heaven. Before he got to Ejiogbe's house, he removed his Knightly uniform and kept it in his bag and feigned an unemployed applicant looking for a job. On getting to Ejiogbe very early in the morning, he begged to be given a menial job to enable him earn a living. Ejiogbe told him that he had no jobs to offer because his own occupation was to give free service to the people of the world. He was about to have his breakfast when the visitor arrived. He invited the visitor to eat with him, but the man explained that he did not qualify to eat on the same plate with Ejiogbe. The visitor insisted he would eat whatever remained after Ejiogbe had eaten.

While this argument was going on, some new callers came in crying for help. They complained that an only child of the parents had convulsion and wanted Ejiogbe to go and revive the child. Without eating the food, he set out, followed by the Knight from Heaven. He got to the house, put his left knee on the ground and repeated an incantation after which he called the child's name three times and he answered. The child then sneezed, opened his eyes, and asked for food.

As he was completing that healing operation, other callers accosted and beseeched him to help them deliver a pregnant woman who had been in painful labour all night. He went straight to the woman who was almost taking her last breath when he arrived. When he got there, he made a quick divination and assured the people that the woman would deliver safely. He gave her Iyerosun (divination powder) and water to swallow it. As she was swallowing the water he repeated an incantation and the child together with the placenta all came out at the same time. There was general rejoicing in the house, and as usual, he left without demanding any compensation.

Ejiogbe and his visitor then left for home. This time, it was well past mid-day and he had still not had his breakfast. As they were getting home, he met a large crowd waiting. The people had a dispute which they wanted him to settle for them. One after the other he settled all the disputes for them and the people trooped back to their respective houses happily and reconciled. By the time he became free enough to eat his meal, the sun was almost setting. He settled down to eat the food prepared for him and once more invited the visitor who insisted on eating after him. As he was beginning to eat, the visitor went into the room and put on his knightly garment.

The sight of the visitor in the heavenly dress told Ejiogbe that he was a divine messenger from heaven. He quickly stopped eating and asked the celestial knight what message he had for him. The man at that point told him that God wanted him to come to heaven at once. He quickly dressed up and left for heaven with the man.

As soon as they were out of the town, the Knight embraced him and almost instantaneously, they were both in the palace of God. As soon as they arrived, the voice of God asked for Omonighorogbo (Ejiogbe's heavenly name before leaving for the world) to give an explanation for creating so much confusion in the world that he had upset the other divinities on earth. Omonighorogbo went on his knees to offer an explanation, but before he could say a word, the messenger sent to fetch him, volunteered to explain on his behalf. The Knight explained that the Almighty Father Himself could not have done what Omonighorogbo was doing on earth. He illustrated that since morning Omonighorogbo had not even had time to eat a proper meal because he was in the yeoman service of mankind, without receiving any reward whatsoever. The messenger explained that it was his attempt to behave on earth as they did in heaven that annoyed the money-loving divinities on earth.

On hearing the details of the observations of the messenger, God ordered Omonighorogbo to rise from his kneeling position, since it was clear that all the representations made previously against him were borne out of envy and jealously. God then ordained him to return to the world to continue his good works, but that from then on, he should charge reasonable fees for his services, but should continue to help the needy. He then received God's blessing and left the palace of God.

Before returning to the world, he decided to meet his heavenly Awos who made divination for him before he left heaven in the first instance. He went to:—
(1) Eduwe koko mejinja won sarawon kpelenje kpelenje.
(2) Ejo-Mejinja, won sarawon loroku loroku. Meaning —
  (1) When two cocoyam leaves are quarrelling, the wind carries them about.
  (2) When two snakes are fighting, they embrace each other.

They advised him to offer another he-goat to Esu. They told him that he would come across a fair complexioned woman on earth whom he should marry. After marrying her he was to give a big he-goat once more to Esu so that the woman might not leave him. He was assured that his marriage to the woman would bring him strength and prosperity, but that if he allowed her to leave, he would return to penury. He made the sacrifice to Esu in heaven and then returned to earth. As soon as he closed his eyes, as he was told by the heavenly Knight, he was just waking up from his sleep on earth. Callers were beginning to wonder why Ejiogbe slept for so long that morning.

The Marriage of Ejiogbe

When he woke up eventually, the first person he met that morning was a fair skinned woman called Eji-Alo. He fell in love with her as soon as he set his eyes on her and the woman also told him that she came to offer herself to him in marriage. After marrying the woman he forgot to give a big he-goat to Esu as he was directed in heaven to do. Eji-Alo was the daughter of a very wealthy chief at Ife. She soon became pregnant and gave birth to a male child who was crippled from the womb. The father who was able to heal other cripples could not heal his own child. That is how the saying came that a "doctor" can heal others but not himself.

Eji-Alo was so frustrated over the birth of the cripple that she refused to stay with Ejiogbe to look after him. Eventually she packed out of Ejiogbe's house leaving the child behind. Subsequently, Esu, Ogun and Obalifon met Ejiogbe to ask him why he had not been seen out side for sometime. He replied that Eji-Alo had left him with a crippled child to look after. Esu then volunteered to approach an awo in heaven. The two awos turned out to be Eduwe Koko meji and Ejo mejinja, who coincidentally were the two Awos who made divination for Ejiogbe during his last spiritual trip to heaven. They reminded Ejiogbe of the big he-goat they told him to give to Esu after marrying on earth so that his wife might not desert him.

The two awos prepared medicine to wash the child's legs and life instantly returned to his limbs. That was after giving the he-goat to Esu. Inspite of the sacrifice and the healing of the child, Eji-Alo did not come back to Ejiogbe because she had meanwhile married Oluweri. Nonetheless, a portion of the medicine used to cure Ejiogbe's child was prepared into an ASE for him to use to command the wife to return to him if he so desired.

Since he realised that she was already married to another man, Ejiogbe preferred to use it to call Eji-Alo to meet him at a venue far removed from Ife's environs. He also used the ASE to command Oluweri, who seduced his wife, to meet him at the same venue.

As soon as the couple appeared before him he conjured them to fall down and he fused them into one body and to move forward forever never to look back any more. With that, Eji-Alo and Oluweri turned into a flowing river, which is the river now called Oluweri in Ondo State of Nigeria.

When Ejiogbe comes out of divination for a woman who is thinking of leaving her husband, she should be advised not to do so because the consequence will surely lead to death, especially if the woman is the wife of an Ifa priest.

The Second Marriage of Ejiogbe

The first wife of a true son of Ejiogbe will never stay long with him, unless she is fair in complexion. The next woman Ejiogbe met was called Iwere were who was a witch. No matter however much they may avoid it, Ejiogbe's children (that is those for whom Ejiogbe appeared during Ifa initiation or Ugbodu) are, more often than not, marrying women who belong to the world of witchcraft. If he has three wives, at least two of them must be witches.

Ejiogbe was still very poor when he remarried and they were always living below the starvation line. Whenever they killed a rat, Orunmila would give the head to the wife. The same thing happened with a fish, a hen and even a goat. By the time they were able to afford a goat it was clear that their fortunes were beginning to improve. Eventually they became sufficiently well-off to build their own house, raise children and marry other wives. At that point he decided to offer thanksgiving to his Ifa. He then bought a cow for a big feast, to which he invited other priests who were the members of his family.

During the feast, when the meat was being shared among the invitees, the senior wife expected as usual to be given the head of the cow. After waiting in vain to be given the cow's head, the senior wife drew it to herself. Almost instantly, some of the more vindictive priests rebuked her on the ground that the head was not the right part of a cow to give to a woman. The cow's head was then taken away from her. She paused for some time to allow the husband to intervene to redress the situation. When no positive reaction was forthcoming from him she retired from the feast chamber to her room.

Three days later, she collected her belongings out of Ejiogbe's house and went to live with her brother called Iroko who gave her sanctuary soon afterwards. With the thanksgiving ceremonies over, Ejiogbe went out in search of her. After combing everywhere in vain he went to her brother who confirmed that he gave her refuge.

On seeing Iwere were, Ejiogbe asked her why she left him so unceremoniously. With tears in her eyes she reminded him that when they were poor he often gave her the head of whatever animal they could afford to slaughter for food and no priest or member of his family showed up at that time. She went on to ask why it was, that it was only when they were well-off enough to feast with a cow that they came to deny her the privilege of keeping its head. Why did any member of his family not come to demand the heads of the rat, fish, hen, etc? In a poetic incantation she exclaimed:—

What man can boast of being bigger than the elephant?
Who can claim to be bigger than the buffalo?

Who can boast of being more influential than the king?
No head-tie can be wider than those used by the elders of the night!
No rope can be as long as the one used by the witches!
No hat can be more famous than a crown;
In width or in breadth, the hand cannot be taller than the head;
The palm frond is often taller than the palm leaves on the head of a palm tree;
Wherever there is a musical performance it is the sound of the bell that sounds louder than all other instruments; and
The palm tree is more influential than all other trees in the forest.

As soon as Ejiogbe heard this poem he too was in tears and apologised to the wife to forgive him. The wife then took pity on him and agreed to return with him to the house on the condition that he would agree to appease her with a piece of white cloth, some money and to serve her head with a goat.

This explains why whoever is born by Ejiogbe at Ugbodu is required to serve the head of his senior wife at the height of his prosperity, with a goat.

When it comes out of divination for a person who was born by Ejiogbe he should be asked whether he has already served his wife's head with a goat. He should be told that his senior wife, if yellow, is a benevolent witch who would help him to prosper in life provided he could refrain from despising her.

If, on the other hand, it comes out of divination for a man whose senior wife has left his house, he should be advised to go and beg her to return to him without any delay lest he would return to penury.

How Ejiogbe helped a Litigant to win his case

As soon as he became prosperous, he was able to afford to invite other awos to work for him. When therefore Baba jagba Loorun came to him when he had a case, Ejiogbe invited another awo called: Ajagba, Agbagba, Ajagba jagba, ni ira. Toon difa fun Baba jagba jagba lo orun.

The awo told the litigant to make sacrifice in order to be free from the case. He was told to make sacrifice with 2 hens. hand spun thread and plenty of ginger (Unien in Bini and Eruru in Yoruba). He produced all the materials and the awo prepared the sacrifice for him. The feathers of the hen and the ginger seeds were sewn with the thread into a necklace worn round his neck, and it was removed with Uroke at the shrine of Esu. When the case eventually came up for trial and judgement, Babajagba won the case.

When Ejiogbe therefore appears at divination for a person who has a case pending, he should be advised to make the above sacrifice, which has however to be done for him by an Awo who knows how to do it.

How Ejiogbe made A Barren woman to have a Child.

Ebiti okpale Ligbe
Oowo le kuuru ku
Adifa fun olomo Agbuti.

These were the names of other Awos invited by Ejiogbe when he made divination for Elerimoju when she came to Ejiogbe because she could not have children. Ejiogbe told her to make sacrifice with a hen, a guinea fowl and a goat. She made the sacrifice without any delay. After preparing the sacrifice, Ejiogbe told her to carry the offering to a running water drain

(Agbara in Yoruba and Orogho in Bini). She did so accordingly.

Esu was however annoyed because he got no share of the sacrifice, but Eleri-Moju otherwise called Olomo Agbuti replied that she had previously made plenty of sacrifices to Esu to no avail. Esu then invoked rain to fall in order to stop the drain from enjoying the sacrifice. The rain fell so heavily that the flood going through the drain carried the sacrifice right up to the river (Olokun), the water divinity who in turn carried the sacrifice to heaven.

Meanwhile in heaven, the son of Olodumare was ill and the heavenly Awos had been invited to cure him. While the awos were performing divination on the illness of the child, they asked Olodumare to go to the back of his house to bring one sacrifice that was coming from earth for them to use to heal the child.

When Olodumare got to the back of the house, he saw the sacrifice of Eleri Moju. He took the sacrifice to the awos, who added Iyerosun (divination powder) to it after which they touched the sick child's head with it. Almost immediatley afterwards, the child became well.

As soon as the child became well, Olodumare invited Olokun to ask him what he was looking for that made him to perform the sacrifice that saved his son.

Olokun explained that he did not know from where Agbara or Orogho (drain) brought the sacrifice. Olokun invited the drain (Orogho or Agabara) to explain where he got the sacrifice from and he dislosed that is was Eleri Moju who performed it. Her guardian angel in heaven was then invited and she explained that her ward was advised by Orunmila to make the sacrifice because she had remained barren since getting to the world. The guardian angel explained that Eleri Moju even lamented that the sons of her contemporaries with whom she went to the world at the same time, were even growing up to woo her for love.

Olodumare then brought out his mace of authority and proclaimed that Eleri Moju would have a child and before her eyes were closed, her children and grandchildren would also have children before her own eyes.

Before the following morning, Eleri Moju saw her menstruation. When she became whole and clean again, she mated with her husband and became pregnant. After nine months, she gave birth to a child who was named Adeyoriju. She had several other children, grand children and great-grandchildren before she returned to heaven.

When Ejiogbe therefore appears at divination for a woman who is anxious to have a child, she should be advised by the Awo to make the foregoing sacrifice and she would unfailingly have plenty of children.

How Ejiogbe helped the Mountain to resist the Onset of his enemies.

Aja kulu mo, Ajaa kuulu mo.
Adifa fun Oke, Ota le lu run okoo.
Ebo oke shoota, ota legbeje Adaa.
Ebo oke shoota.

Oke, or mountain, was advised to make sacrifice and he did, because of the evil plans of his enemies. Plotting to destroy him were the Hoe and the cutlass. After the mountain had made the sacrifice, the hoe and the cutlass left to destroy him, but they could not even scratch his body. He even got bigger. He then rejoiced and offered thanksgiving to his diviner.

Ejiogbe saves his Son from the hands of Death.

Ono gbooro miti fewa — was the Ifa priest who made divination for Abati, the son of Ejiogbe when Death planned to take him away in seven days time. Abati was told to make sacrifice with one cock, one hen and snails and to give a he-goat to Esu. Death made three vain attempts to remove Abati from this earth after which he left him to complete his sojourn on earth. He then sang the following poem:—

Uku gbemi, otimi;
Tiri Abati, Abati tiri;
Arun gbemi, Otimi;
Tiri Abati, Abata tiri.
Death held me and left me.
Sickness tried me and left me.
No one eats tortoise along with its shell.
No one eats a Ram together with its horns.
The shell of the snail is kept after eating its meat.
I have survived the evil plans of my enemies.

How Ejiogbe's mother saved him from his enemies.

Efifi nii shoju omo teeree te
Okpa Teere be ejo leyin
Oshudi Eereke
Oshudi Ereeke.

These are the names of the awos who made divination for Olayori, the mother of Ejiogbe, when people were making sarcastic remarks against his good works. She made sacrifice with 4 pigeons and 4 bags of salt. After the sacrifice, the same people who were despising his works began to make favourable comments about him. This is so because no one puts salt in the mouth and makes bad comments about its taste. As soon as the hen comes to roost on it eggs, it will change its voice.

How Ejiogbe became the King of the OLODUS (apostles)

After all the sixteen OLODUS had come to the world, it was time to appoint a head among them. Ejiogbe was not the first Olodu to come to the world. Many others had come before him. Before them, Oyeku Meji who was the king of the Night had been claiming seniority. The lot fell on Orisa Nla (God the son, or God's representative on earth) to appoint a king of the Olodus.

Orisa Nla invited all of them and gave them a rat to share between themselves. Oyeku-Meji took one leg, Iwori-Meji took the second leg, Idi-Meji took one hand and Obara-meji took the remaining hand. The other parts were shared in the order of conventional seniority. Ejiogbe being very junior was given the head of the Rat.

In order of sequence, God subsequently gave them a fish, a hen, a pigeon, a guinea fowl and finally a goat — which were all shared in accordance with the order established with the the rat. In each case, Ejiogbe was given the head of each of the slaughtered animals.

Finally, God invited them to come to him for a decision after three days. On getting home, Ejiogbe made divination and he was told to give a he-goat to Esu. After eating his he-goat, Esu told him that on the appointed day, he should roast a tuber of yam and keep it in his bag together with a gourd of water. Esu also advised him to go late to the meeting of the Olodus in God's palace.

On the appointed day, the Olodus came to invite him to the

conference but he told them he was roasting yam on the fire to eat before leaving for the meeting.

After they had left him, he got out the yam, peeled it and kept it inside his bag with a gourd of water. On the way to the conference, he met an old woman just as Esu predicted and in consonance with the advice given to him by Esu, he relieved the old woman of the burden of fire wood she was carrying, because she was already so tired that she could scarcely walk.

After gratefully accepting the offer, she complained that she was terribly hungry. Instantly, Ejiogbe brought out the yam inside his bag and gave her to eat. After eating the yam she asked for water and he gave her the gourd of water inside his bag. With the refreshment over he carried the fire wood while the old lady walked along with him. He did not realise that the woman was the mother of God the son.

Meanwhile, as he seemed to be in a hurry, the old woman asked him where he was in a hurry to get to. He replied that he was already late to the conference at which Orisa Nla (God) was going to appoint a king from among the Olodus. He said he was taking his time anyway since he was nonetheless too junior to aspire to the kingship of the sixteen apostles of Orunmila.

In her reaction, the old woman assured him that he was going to be made king of the apostles. When they got to the woman's house, he was told to deposit the wood at the back of the house. It was on identifying it as Orisa Nla's house that he realised that the woman he had been helping was no other person than the mother of God the son. He then heaved a sigh of relief. The woman told him to follow her inside her apartment. On getting there she brought out two pieces of white cloth, tied one on his right shoulder and the other on his left shoulder. She then inserted a red parrot's feather on Ejiogbe's head and a white chalk on his right palm. She next showed him the 1,460 (ota legbeje) stones outside the front of Orisa Nla's house and directed him to go and stand on top of the white stone at the middle. In his new outfit, he went to stand there while the others waited in God's outer chamber.

After some time, God asked the others who they were still waiting for and they all replied that they were waiting for Ejiogbe. Orisa Nla then asked them for the name of the man who was standing outside. They could not even recognize him as Ejiogbe. Orisa Nla directed them to go and pay respects to the man. One after the other they went to prostrate and touch the ground with their heads at the foot of where Ejiogbe stood. Thereafter, God formally proclaimed Ejiogbe as the king of the Olodus of the Orunmila kindred.

Almost unanimously, all the other Olodus grumbled in annoyance and did not diguise their disapproval at the appointment of a junior Olodu to be head amongst them all. At that point God asked them how they shared the animals he had been giving to them over the seven days trial period. They explained how they shared them. He asked them who was taking the head of each of these animals and they confirmed that they were giving the heads in each case to Ejiogbe. Orisa Nla then exclaimed that they were the ones who unwittingly appointed Ejiogbe to be their king because when the head is out of the body, the rest has no life in it. On that note, they all dispersed.

When they left Orisa Nla's place, they all decided to keep Ejiogbe at arms length. Not only did they all resolve not to recognise him, they also decided neither to serve him nor to visit him. Before dispersing Ejiogbe composed a poem which he used as an incantation.

Oja Nii ki owo won jaa

Owuwu oni koo wo won wuu.
Ikpe Akiko kiiga akika deenu
Ikpe orire kii gun orire deenu
Etuu kii olo tu won ni mo
Inu lo otin ire efo ebire waa

With that special incantation, he expected to neutralise all the evil machinations against him. He used special leaves for that purpose.

After that incident, they told him that before they could accept him as their king, he would have to feast all of them with:—

200 calabashes of pounded yam
200 pots of soup prepared with different kinds of meat
200 gourds of wine.
200 baskets of kolanuts
Etc., etc.

giving him seven days to arrange for the feast.

Needless to say that it seemed an impossible task because they knew that Ejiogbe could not afford to finance a feast of that magnitude. Ejiogbe sat down lamenting over his poverty, and the prospect of remaining a sheperd without a flock.

Meanwhile Esu came to him to find out the cause of his melancholy and he explained that he had no money to fund the elaborate feast demanded by the Olodus before they could agree to submit to him. Esu retorted that the problem could be solved if Ejiogbe would give him another he-goat. Ejiogbe lost no time in giving another he-goat to Esu. After eating the he-goat, Esu advised him to prepare only one each of all the things demanded for the feast and to produce 199 additional empty containers of each item and line them out at the feast chamber on the appointed day. Ejogbe followed the advice of Esu accordingly. In the meantime, each of the Olodus had been making jest of him since they knew that there was no way Ejiogbe could afford the feast.

On the seventh day, they began to visit him one by one to ask whether he was ready with the feast. Since they did not hear the sound of a pestle on mortar from the direction of his kitchen, they knew there was going to be no feast after all. Meanwhile, having lined out the empty containers, Esu went to the feast chamber and commanded the single preparation to multiply into the empty containers. Instantly, all the calabashes, soup pots, gourds, baskets, etc., were filled up with fresh preparations and the feast was ready.

As soon as Oyeku Meji got to the feast chamber to find out what was happening, he was atonished to see that the feast was ready after all. Without waiting for any formal invitation, he sat down to help himself to the food. He was followed accordingly by Iwori-Meji Idi Meji, Obara Meji, Okonron-Meji, Irosun Meji, Owanrin-Meji, Ogunda-Meji, Osa-Meji, Otuu Meji, Irete-Meji, Eka Meji, Eturukpon Meji, Ose Meji and Ofun Meji. Before they realised what was happening, they had all dined and wined to their hearts' content.

After the feast, they all carried Ejiogbe high above their heads and began to dance in a procession singing:—

Agbee geege.
Agbee Babaa.
Agbee Geege.
Agbe Babaa.

They danced in the procession right through the town. When they got to the bank of the sea, Ejiogbe told them to put him down and he sang in praise of the awos who made divination for him and of the sacrifice he made. With that he was formally crowned the head of the apostles of Orunmila with the title of Akoko-Olokun.

At that spot, he slaughtered four snails on the banks of the sea and it was the last sacrifice he made before he became prosperous — and the throne began to flourish.

Contest between Ejiogbe and Olofen

In his position as the king of the Olodus, Ejiogbe became very famous and wealthy. Uneasy over the presence of a powerful king in his domain, Olofen, the traditional ruler of Ife, assembled an army to fight Ejiogbe. Meanwhile, Ejiogbe had a dream in which he saw that an attack on him was imminent. He then invited an awo called OOLE JAGIDA, OLUPE KPEROJA (An easy compromise ends up in hostility) to make divination for him. He was told to fetch a porcupine (Okhaen in Bini, Urere in Yoruba), which was used to prepare a meal but he was told not to eat out of it. All others present feasted on it. Thereafter the plot against him came to naught.

Not long after-wards, when Olofen saw that Ejiogbe was still around and was becoming even more popular than himself, he raised another team of night elders to fight him. He went once more to the same awo who advised him to fetch a hedgehog (Akika in Yoruba and Ekhui in Bini) for another sacrifice. The Ifa priest added the revelant leaves and used it to prepare yet another feast, advising Ejiogbe once more not to eat out of it. After the feast, those appointed by the Olofen to fight him diabolically became too shy to face Ejiogbe. After each feast, the awo had collected the head, skins and bones of the two animals.

When Olofen discovered that Ejiogbe was still in town and as popular as ever, he invited people to openly expel him from the town. Once again, Ejiogbe invited the priest who advised him to produce a he-goat and a whole antelope for a special sacrifice to Esu. Ejiogbe got the two animals and they were both used to make sacrifice to Esu. The Awo used the meat to make another feast out of which Ejiogbe was told not to eat. Even after enjoying the feast, the people insisted that they would have to expel Ejiogbe from Ife. Try as they would, it did not materialise.

At this point, Olofen decided on a new strategy altogether. He invited Ejiogbe for a meeting in his own palace, in three days time. On the appointed day, Olofen requested his royal executioners or assassins to lay in ambush for Ejiogbe and to murder him during his journey to or from the palace.

Before leaving home for Olofen's palace, Ejiogbe went to the shrine of Esu with a kolanut, a spoonful of palm oil, and a snail to invoke Esu with an incantation to escort him to and from the invitation since he did not know what plot awaited him this time. Before actually setting out, he made his own sign on the ground and repeated another incantation. He walked past all the ambushes without any incident and got safely into the palace. Olofen was surprised to see him and since he had nothing tangible to discuss, the meeting ended as it started. Olofen was sure that the ambush would strike when Ejiogbe was returning home.

As the assassins waited to deal the fatal blow on him it was time for Esu to intervene. As soon as Ejiogbe was approaching the ambush, Esu called on the antelope with which Ejiogbe had earlier made sacrifice to become whole again and it jumped out of the midst of the assassins in the ambush. Almost immediately, they all abandoned their vigil and pursued the antelope until they got to Olofen's palace. As the antelope entered

Olofen's palace there was general pandemonium and communal fighting in the town of Ife. While the commotion was going on, Ejiogbe quietly walked back peacefully to his house without any molestation whatsoever.

On his part, Olofen accused the assassins he sent to waylay Ejiogbe of failing to carry out his instructions and they were all locked up. It was Ejiogbe who later came to the palace to quell the confusion that had been created by the mysterious antelope. He used his divination tray and another incantation to return peace and tranquility once more to Ife. Thereafter, Ejiogbe invited all the Ifa priests, chiefs and elders of the town for a feast prepared with a cow, goats, and hens for thanksgiving to Orunmila, the divinity of wisdom. After the feast, he resolved never to fraternise with Olofen anymore. He then sang in praise of the awo who saw him through the molestation of Olofen and of Esu who used the antelope with which he made sacrifice to scatter his enemies.

It is for this reason that all the Ugbodu children of Ejiogbe forbid porcupine hedge-hog and antelope to this day because they were the animals he used to fight off the evil plans of Olofen against him. It also explains why the children of Ejiogbe do not get on very well with any Oba or King in their domain.

Ejiogbe's Battle with Death

It is now clear that Ejiogbe suffered in the hands of all imaginable enemies because he stood out to defend the objective good. He had survived problems from the laity and priests alike, from his household, from fellow divinities and from the king. It was the turn of Death to take him up in combat.

The name of the Awo who made divination for him on this occasion was Iku kii ja nille olodumare. Aron kii ja nille olodumare.

(Death and sickness do not wage war on the House of God.) Ejiogbe was told that he would die before the end of that year, unless he made sacrifice with 200 bells and a he-goat to Esu. The bell will always ring because it does not die. The bell was prepared by the two Awos for him to be ringing every morning. With that he was able to survive to the end of the year and beyond. This is the kind of sacrifice that is made when Ejiogbe appears at divination and predicts death to the enquirer.

When Death saw that Ejiogbe had survived him that year, he made yet another proximate plan to take the breathe out of him within seven days. As soon as Death firmed up his morbid strategy, Ejiogbe had a dream that night and saw Death hovering round him. He quickly invited one of his surrogates to make divination for him. The Awo, called Una Oke, rororo moota, told him that Death had slated him for slaughter in seven days time. He was advised to make sacrifice with a he-goat, a cock and 20 kolanuts. The he-goat and the cock were given to Esu and he was to be breaking each of the 20 kolanuts for Ifa over a 20 day period. He was to pinch the broken kolanuts on Ifa seeds (Ikin) and to say as he did so:

Let me live to break kolanut for Ifa the next day;
Whoever pinches kolanuts for Ikin never dies.
In the end he lived for the next fifty years.

Remarkable Features of Ejiogbe

In a special poem, Ejiogbe reveals that if he appears at Ugbodu for a person who is very fair in complexion, the fatherhood of the person must be thoroughly examined because there may be some misgiving about it.

He emphasizes that if the truth about the parentage of the neophyte is not examined, the risk of premature death is very real. He says that no one should blame Orunmila over the untimely death of the initiate if the truth is not told about the duplicity of his fatherhood. He insists that there is no way the person, especially if he is short, will ever prosper in life.

On the other hand, he proclaims emphatically that if he appears at Ugbodu for a person who is dark complexioned and tall, he must be the true son of Ejiogbe. He will not only prosper but will be famous and popular. The person will surely be conferred with a state or traditional title later in life provided he clears the way for Ifa to assist him. The person will not be given to playing dirty tricks or to ambivalence.

He says that it is the short and light complexioned initiate of Ejiogbe who takes to treachery and double dealing. On the whole, the children of Ejiogbe have a lot of difficult hurdles to cross before seeing the limelight.

All children of Ejiogbe should however refrain from eating the meat of the following animals:— Antelope, hedge-hog (Ekhui in Bini and Akika in Yoruba), porcupine (Okhaen in Bini and Ururee in Yoruba).

The children of Ejiogbe should also try to avoid eating plantain and red yam in order to obviate the risk of stomach ache.

When Ejiogbe assists anyone, he does so whole-heartedly. If on the other hand he is provoked into aggression, he destroys irreparably. Children of Ejiogbe are otherwise very persevering and forgiving.

All the same he is quite capable of changing fortunes because Orunmila does not believe in impossibilities as can be seen from the following poem composed by Ejiogbe:—

Serious minded people do not listen to the bird singing the songs of woe;
Difficulties and problems bring out the best in man;
Patience and sacrifice make the impossible to become possible;
Give me a difficult problem to solve that doubters may believe;
give me a war to wage that mortals may appreciate the strength of divinities;
To learn from past misfortunes is to be wise;
Not to learn from previous mistakes is folly;
The person who fails to make sacrifice vindicates the diviner;
Just as the one who ignores advice turns the adviser to a seer.

The man who learns from quarrels and the man who does not learn from quarrels (Ajaagbon, Aagabon) were the two surrogates of Ejiogbe who made divination for the land of Quarrels. They advised the people to make sacrifice with 7 dogs, 7 tortoises and 7 snails so that they might be rid of incessant quarrels. They got together and made the sacrifice. Two each of the sacrificial materials were offered to Ogun, who with Osonyin were always fermenting quarrels for the town. Two each of the sacrifical victims excluding the snails (Osonyin forbids snails) were given to Osonyin. four snails were offered to the ground divinity. The three remaining dogs were prepared and left to wander about in the town. It is on account of this sacrifice that some children of Ejiogbe are advised to rear dogs.

The dogs soon began to produce and multiply. Any time Ogun was bringing trouble to the town, the dogs would all start barking at him. In anger, Ogun would pursue and kill one of the dogs to eat, thus abandoning his mission.

On his part, any time Osonyin approached the town to cause chaos, the ground would release plenty of snails to line his path. The sight of the snails would always annoy him and he would run away.

That was how peace and concord replaced turmoil and discord in the town. This explains why dogs bark at Ogun priests to this day.

Normally, when Ejiogbe appears at Ugbodu during an initiation ceremony, before the ceremony is completed, there is bound to be a heavy rain. The Ifa priest who made this disclosure intimated that he had a personal experience. He recalls that during his own initiation ceremony in 1953, there had been no rain for over five months in Ondo. Even the Osemawe of Ondo had invited rain makers to induce rain, but no heavy rain fell.

When the sacrifice to his Ifa, which happened to be Ejiogbe, was being prepared, the Awos told him that before the sacrifice was completed, there was going to be a very heavy rain. At that moment, the heat of the sun was so intense that he just dismissed their prediction as trash.

Before the sacrifice was half way through the weather had changed. By the time he was told to deliver the sacrifice at the shrine of Esu, the rain became so heavy that he could not reach the shrine because of the consequential flood. According to the priest, Awo Omoruyi Edokpayi, that was the first wonder that Orunmila did to him. He has experienced several other instances since then.

The Puzzle of the Awos.

After hearing so much about the activities of Orunmila in the days of Ejiogbe the king of Ife decided to test him along with the other awos in the hope of denting or dwarfing his growing popularity. The King got a calabash and inserted in it, the sponge and soap used by a newly wedded bride. He also added can wood and black woven calico (Asho Etu) and tied up the calabash with a piece of cloth. The King then kept it on his Ifa shrine after which he invited the Awos to come and reveal the contents of the calabash. All the other Awos tried and failed until it was the turn of an awo called Adaro eeku, ashawo kookuta, oke olobitun ofiyi she okpe. Ogbo ogbo ogbo, one of the surrogates of Ejiogbe. As soon as he was seated, he sounded his divination wand (Uroke) on the divination tray (Akpako) and Ejiogbe appeared. He then named the materials to be used to make sacrifice as sponge and soap used for bathing a bride, can wood and black calico. The king had got the answer he wanted and he was quite satisfied. He then compensated the Awo with a chieftaincy title and four wives, 2 dark complexioned and 2 fair in complexion.

EJIOGBE'S Poem for Progress and prosperity

ENI — Shee inoo ni moo
EJI — Jiji le ekpon agbo oji — eejaa.
ETA — Maa taaku nu, Maa Taarun daanu.
ERIN — Bi a baarin, adife ooye la agbo.
ERUn — Maarun Kaasha, maada mi.
EFA — Efa ule, efa ono ouniti erukoo.
EJE — Bi aghoro ba tii shoro, aakiije.
EJo - Uwaami aajo, eyin mi aajo.
ESOn — Uwaami aasuon, Eyinmi aasuon.
ENO — Inoo wale ayo, Kuroiita.
OKONLA — Elereni eleno diiro
        Alara, Eleno diiro Ajero, eleno odiro
        Oba ado, Ooni Oka siru Eleno diiru re.
        Osemowe aamu udu ghaaran
        eleno diirure, Orunmila ome kikan

IFA PRIEST

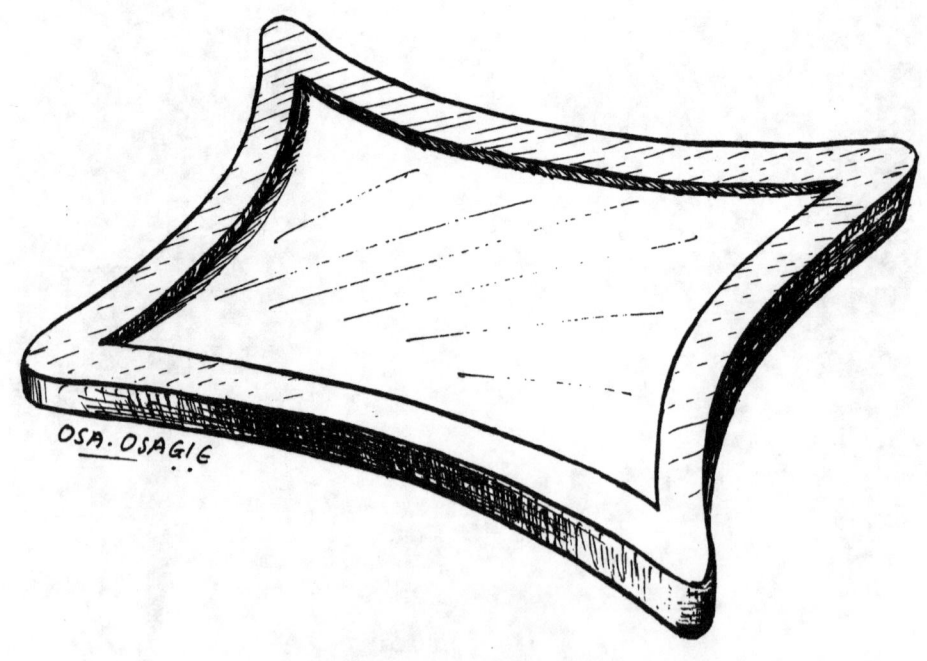

ATE-IFA (Akpako)
(Divination Tray)

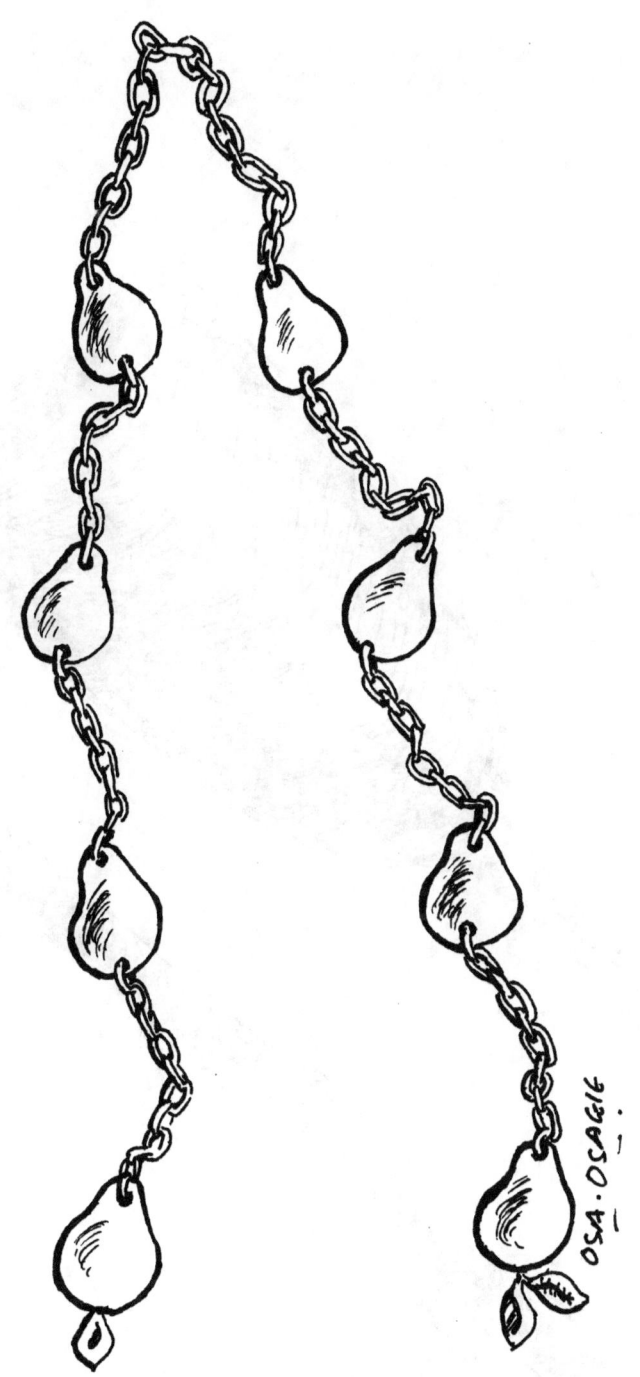

OKPELE
(Principal divination instrument)

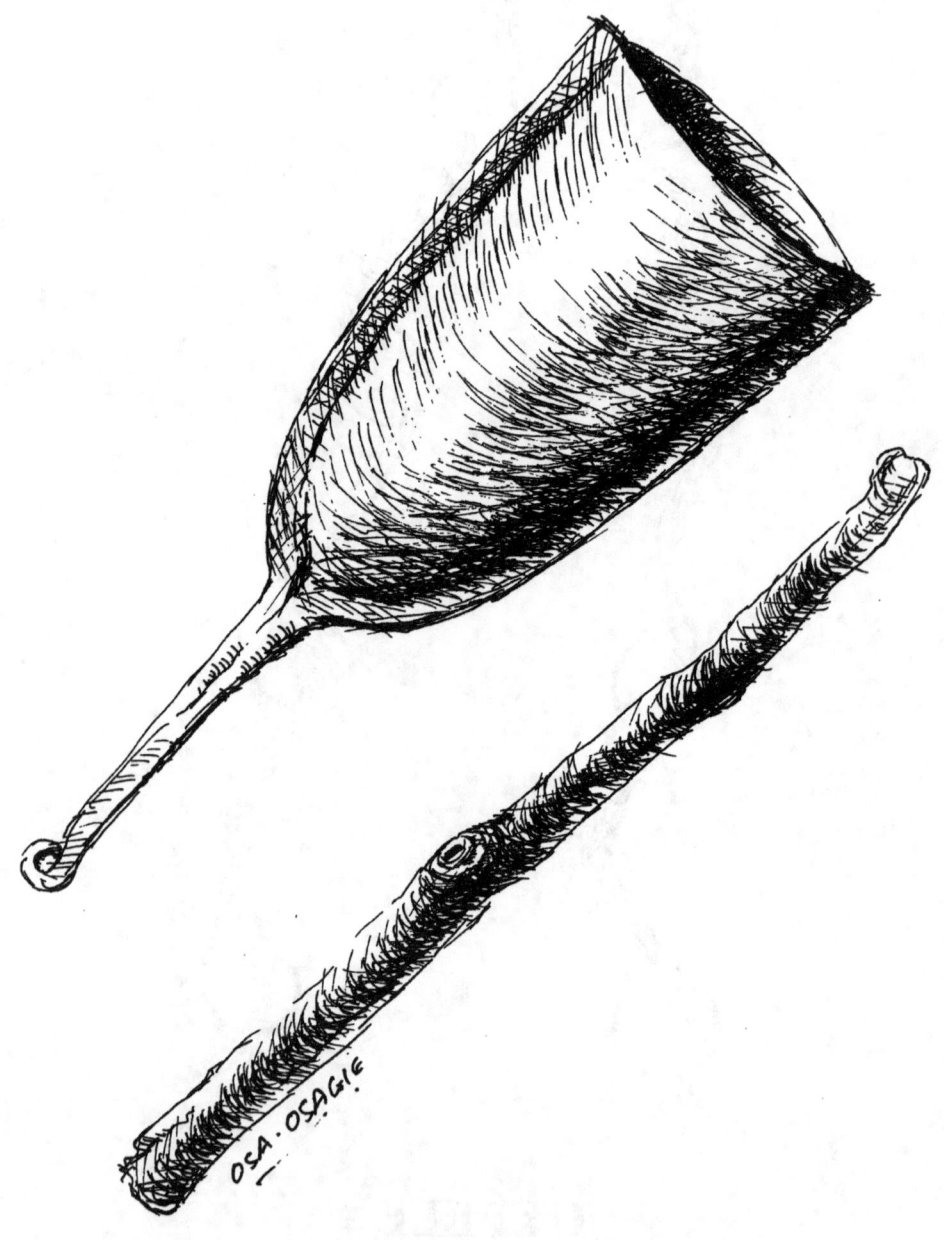

AGOGO (Gong)

AJA (knife)

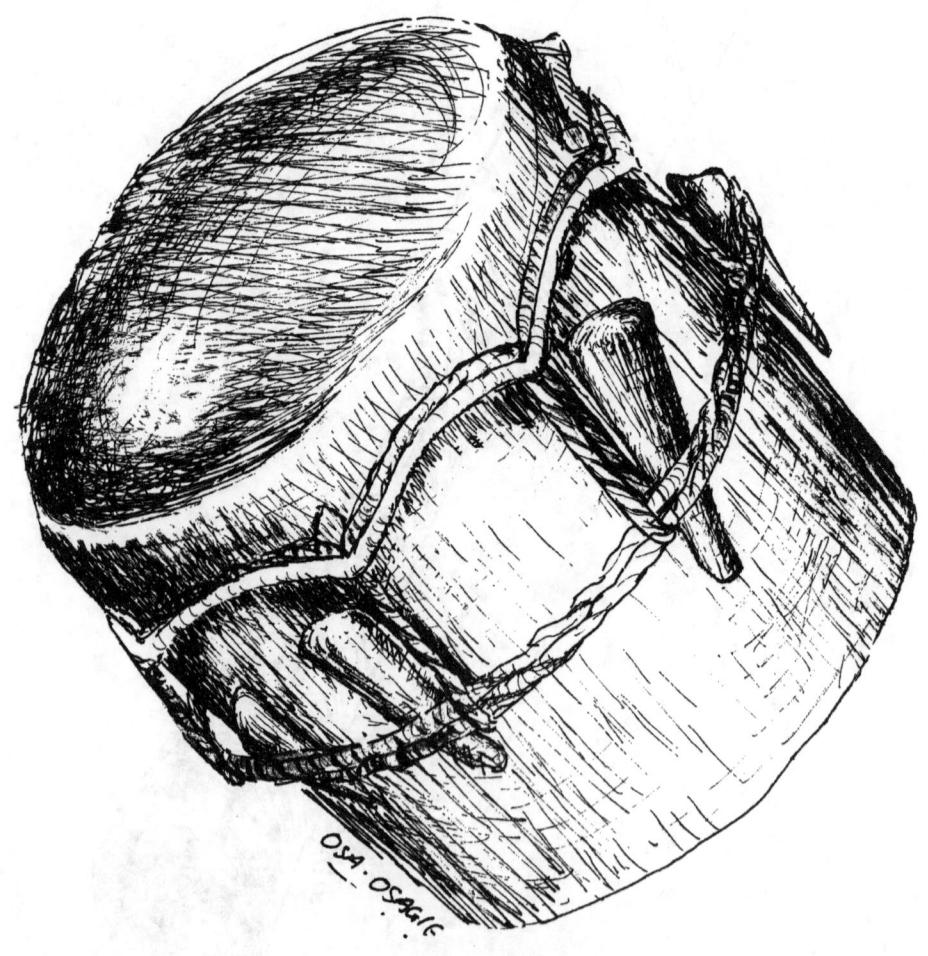

ILU (Drum)

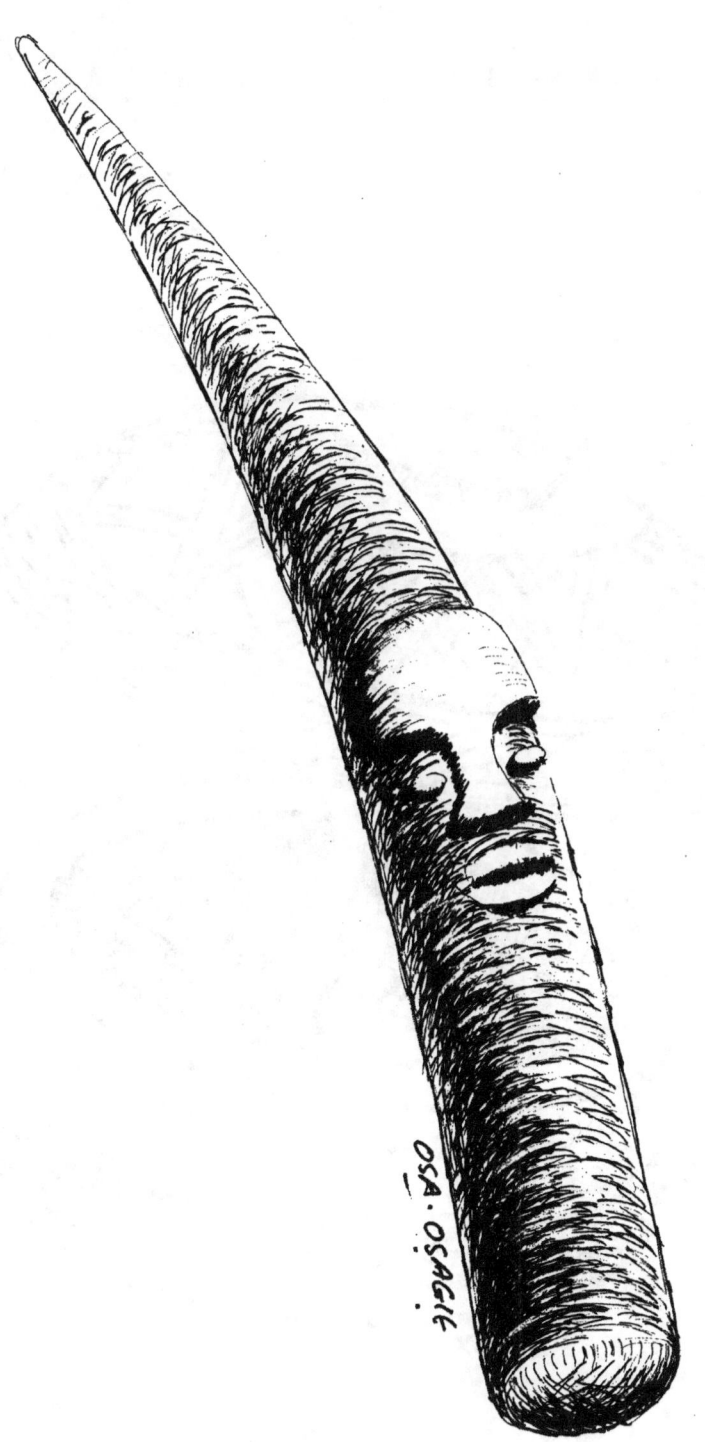

OROFA
(Divination staff)

OKPON-IFA
(Ifa seeds container)

URANKE
(Horse Tail)

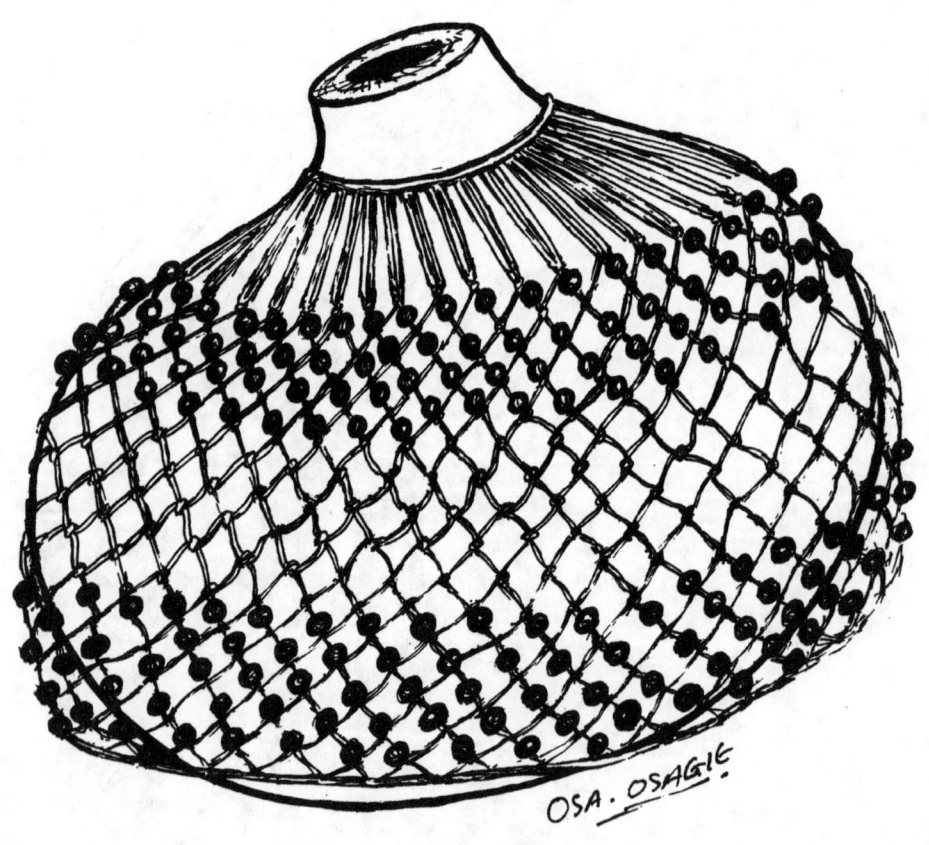

AKESHE
(Musical Instrument)

eekekun ro rabe eleno diiru re.
Ta ago, Teeru niiso ni ile oloja
Gbelemi soomi eeton ni nuule Alade
Aasofun oluware yi aalesio.

English Translation

ONE — A person adds to what he already has.
TWO — No matter how much the testicles of a ram shakes, it does not sever from its body.
THREE — I will survive the cold hands of death.
FOUR — A long discussion takes one as far as Ife.
FIVE — When I eat fire, I will swallow it.
SIX — The hoe drags home gifts from inside and outside the house.
SEVEN — When a priest serves his divinity, it lasts 7 days.
EIGHT — I will prosper in life as well as beyond.
NINE — I will succeed in life and hereafter.
TEN — Ayo can only be played on its container.
ELEVEN — Only respectable gift parcels are presented to the Kings of Ara, Ijero and Benin. Gifts to the Ooni of Ife, Osemawe of Ondo and orunmila are also presented in multiples. The nails of a tiger are not used like knife to scratch human body. The gift carrier discharges his luggage in front of the elderly recipient to which it is consigned. Loading and unloading as well as going and coming never end in the home of the ants/termites.

The person should be told after the special ceremony that goes with this poem that progress and achievements would always remain with him. It takes a lot of persuasion before Awos can agree to perform this special ceremony for the children of Ejiogbe.

Akpetebi annoys Ejiogbe

Ejiogbe was known to be particularly patient and tolerant. One day, one of his wives irratated him so much that he decided to leave the house in anger.

On the way, he met the following agents of destruction, one after the other, Esu, Witchcraft, Fays, Sickness and Death, each asking him where he was going with such fume and fury. In reply he told them that he was leaving home for his wife who was not allowing him to have peace of mind. Each of them promised to return home with him to deal with the offending wife.

On the night Ejiogbe left home, the offending wife had a dream which scared her so much that she decided to go for divination the following morning. She was told that misfortune, sickness and sudden death were on her trail because Orunmila had reported her to the higher powers. She was told to sweep and clean the house, wash his clothes, and prepare a feast in five multiples of soup, pounded yam, meats, wine, kolanuts, water etc against the husband's return, and to present the feast on her knees to him as soon as he returned to the house.

Ejiogbe was away for five days. As he returned on the fifth day, all the five divinities followed him home. As they got to the main entrance to his house, he told them to wait and he went in through the back entrance. In tears, the offending wife went on her knees to embrace him and to beg for forgiveness. She gave him the multiple feast, one for everyday he was away.

Being the soft hearted man than he was, Ejiogbe collected the feast and gave them to the five divinities waiting outside. After eating, they moved to attack the woman, but Ejiogbe told them that she had atoned for her transgressions because she was the one who prepared the feast they had just enjoyed. He reminded them of the divine rule that one does not kill the person who feeds one. That was how he saved his wife from destruction.

When Ejiogbe therefore comes out of divination for a married woman, she should be asked to prepare the above-mentioned feast in multiples of five because she has offended her husband so much that the destructive divinities have taken a hand in the anger.

CHAPTER XIV
OYEKU-MEJI

```
I I    I I
I I    I I
I I    I I
I I    I I
```

It was Oyeku meji who revealed how Orunmila taught mankind how to ward off the menace of premature death. When man was created, Death saw the new creature as the best staple food for him to feed on. Death was thus the only divinity who rejoiced at God's creation of man. While other divinities saw man as a lower being created to serve them, Death saw man as feedstock. He however waited for man to multiply and thereafter went at will to their abode to pick them up for use as food. Lacking in the means of self-defence, let alone of fighting back, man resigned himself to the fate of incessant onslaught by Death. They had no one to appeal to, because the logic was that just as man saw the lower animals as food for him to feed on, that was how Death regarded man as meat to feed on.

As long as we understand the over-riding philosophy of the existence of plants and animals, who were created to serve a purpose in the planetary system; we should not be unduly disturbed at the inevitability of death. Just as we use the lower plants and animals to satisfy our routine and staple desires, we are also at the mercy of the more powerful divinities. Having given us a role to perform in the planetary system, which includes, provision of food for the higher powers, God has given us the intellect to defend ourselves as best as we can, either by appeasement or by diversion. This is clearly illustrated in the following revelations of Oyeku Meji.

Uku yee
Iruku Yee
Eku meji Looruwe
Eja meji Ajoko Loore
Olule Adiye
Ideregbe Aaba murede
Agboghaka,Eji Laba odumeta
Ako Elila toun to oshukaare.

Death rejoiced at man's creation,
He plundered humans at will to eat,
Two Rats were playing on land,
Two fishes were playing in water,
The hen had laid its eggs and gone to roost,
The goat had delivered many kids,
The strong three year old Ram,
The fat male Cow endowed with beefy flesh,
were all created to appease Death,
This assemblage of livestock
Gave Death neither appeasement no satisfaction,
Death continued to focus,
His gaze on the human flesh.

When man eventually approached Orunmila for divination on how to check the menace of Death, he told them that no sacrifice could ever divert Death's attention from man. His flesh constituted the only meat, that could satisfy his divine appetite. All others, rats, fish, fowl, goat, Ram and even Cow, were the staple food of the priests of the divinities. He asked them whether anything could stop them from feeding on their own staple food. He however told them that the best way to ward off an evil divinity was to make sacrifice to him with what he forbade. Orunmila in his capacity as Eleri Ukpin (God's own witness at creation) is the only one who knows what each of the other divinities forbids.

He then advised them to prepare scrambled or mashed yam (obobo in Bini and Ewo or Elo in Yoruba) to be laden with small pebbles. He also advised them to fetch a small live chicken. They collected the materials and all the men assembled at the conference hall where Death used to pick them up one after the other. Orunmila advised them to eat the mashed yam, but throw the pebbles away. They were also to tie up the chicken at the entrance to the house of Esu, without killing it.

As Death approached the conference Chamber for yet another attack, he found the pebbles that the men were discarding from their meals. When he put the pebbles in his mouth to taste the food men were eating, he could not chew it. He then wondered that those who were able to eat such strong objects must be terrifying creatures, who could fight back if over-provoked. As Death was contemplating what to do next, the chicken at the entrance to the house of Esu began to cry uku yee. On hearing the cry of the chicken, Death ran away because he forbids the sound of a chicken. Death then left the men in peace and they rejoiced, thanking Orunmila for demonstrating to them the secret of Death. It was since that time that death devised other ways through proxies of getting at man.

From then on, Death could not kill man directly because he is otherwise a chicken-hearted divinity. He has since been relying on his more aggressive and vindictive brothers like; Ogun, the Iron divinity who kills by fatal accidents, Sango, the thunder divinity who kills through lightening, Sankpana, who kills through epidemics like small-pox, chicken-pox and measles, the Night divinity who kills through witchcraft etc. Where these deadly divinities are slow to fetch food for Death, the King of Death uses Sickness who is his wife to fetch food for the family. But that was after man had learnt the secret of how to scare Death away. Before then, Death used to prey on man by himself.

When Oyeku meji therefore appears during divination, the person can be told that Death is lurking around him, but that he should make sacrifice to Esu with mashed yams mixed with salt and palm oil and laden with pebbles. He is also to tie a live chicken on the shrine of Esu to scare Death away.

When Oyeku meji however comes out at divination for a newly born child, the parents should be told to make similar sacrifices like Rain made before coming to the world so that the child might tower over the several powerful enemies he is bound to have during his life time. This kind of sacrifice requires special incantations which can only be made by adepts of Ifism.

Other Heavenly Works of Oyeku Meji

With the nickname of Edidu kpere kpere ojumuna, he made divination for Rain in heaven before he came to the world. Rain was called Ojogidigidi Tiinshe omo Okurin Orun. He advised Rain to make sacrifice because he was going to come out in the midst of enemies on earth. Rain was told to make sacrifice with a he-goat, black cloth, and a bundle of cudgels. Rain made the sacrifice before leaving for the earth.

As he was about to be born his more aggressive elders were already on earth. These are: the sunshine, brightness and drought. Before the arrival of rain, they had all vowed that there was not going to be a place for Rain on earth. Meanwhile, the Rain began to threaten. Since he had already made sacrifice to Esu, he set out on his journey to earth. Esu then brought out the dark cloth with which Rain made sacrifice and spread it out to form a thick layer of cloud over the sky. There was total darkness on earth. Esu then gave Rain multiples of the cudgels he used to make sacrifice and advised him to use them to beat any one who dared to stand in his way. Those cudgels are the showers which the rain uses to beat both kings and slaves, high and low alike, to this day. Thus, he was able to subdue the dews, drought, heat, dust, trees etc. all of which were his enemies.

How the Fish came to multiply

Iwo oye
Emi oye
Oye ontoke bo
Oshebi oju loomo

Oyeku meji made divination for the Fish when she was coming from heaven. The Fish was the daughter of the River in heaven. He advised fish to make sacrifice in order to be able to have plenty of children on earth.

She was told to make sacrifice with a goat, hen and pigeon. She did the sacrifice and came to the world where she began to have children in multiples of hundreds at a time.

Oyeku Meji reveals the return of the Divinities to the world

Uji odo Nimo gbu uji odo
Ibi ono meewa mo gbu ji edun
Akeke ge igi nu ugbo
Agboun re gegerege
Iyoyo Agbo ni rin konre konre
Olule oje gbrironmu romu oja tontonton
Olule eti gbironmu
Ronmu oja titi ronronron
Adifa fun Orunmila ni igba to ti ko
Run bowa kole aye.

The sound of the mortar echoes from the spot where it sits;
I stood on the pathway and heard the axe felling the tree; The axe was felling a tree in the forest and the sound echoed several miles away;
As the ram moves, its hood oscillates from left to right;
The man living in a house near the market hears the noise of the market place.

These are the names of the awos who made divination in heaven for Oyeku meji when he was coming to the world. They advised him to make sacrifice with a he-goat to Esu, and to offer goat, cock, pigeon, white cloth and cowries to Olokun, the water divinity. He did the sacrifices.

The 200 divinities (Ugba run mole in Yoruba and Ihenuri in Bini) decided to visit the earth to find out how its inhabitants were faring. When they got to the boundary of heaven and earth at Oja Ajibomekon, they met two women called Oja and Aje. These women personified money and prosperity. As we shall see later, nearly all the 200 divinities made no sacrifice before leaving heaven nor did they bother to obtain clearance from Esu, who they all dispised as an obscurantist.

No sooner did they leave heaven than Esu unlocked the rain cord from heaven. The rain soon began to fall heavily, and all the other divinities took shelter at one point or the other. Orunmila, who had been advised by his diviner not to stop on the way until he got to earth, no matter how heavily it rained, proceeded on the journey alone, in the company of the two women. When they reached the earth, his children gave them clothes to change into. They were given white apparels to wear.

The rain fell continously for three years. Meanwhile, Orunmila lived in marriage with the two women Aje and Oja and they had produced children, but the other divinities had still not arrived.

After waiting in vain for the other divinities to arrive, their children and followers on earth decided to go and search for them. When citizens of earth met the divinities and persuaded them to follow them home, they declined the offer on the ground that they were quite comfortable in their new abodes and environments.

On his part, Orunmila had been practising the Ifa art successfully on earth and had recruited several new converts. He also took to trading with the assistance of Aje and Oja, who had become his wives. They both made him exceedingly wealthy.

This revelation explains why the shrines of most other divinities are kept outside the house to this day, except Orunmila, together with Aje and Oja (Olokun) who followed Orunmila to the world. The others are kept at the various locations where they took shelter from the rain when they were coming to the world. The reason why Olokun and Orunmila are served with white apparels to this day, is because that was the cloth, they changed into upon arrival on earth after being drenched by the rain during their journey.

The revelation also explains why the children of Oyeku-meji are not expected to use umbrellas, because their patron divinity did not take shelter from the rain that soaked him during his journey from heaven. If the Ono ifa (Odiha) is carefully prepared for the children of Oyeku meji (that is, those for whom he comes out at ugbodu) they will be very rich and prosperous in life, provided they are able to forbid the use of umbrellas and never to allow the rain to stop them from proceeding with whatever they are contemplating to do. Their prosperity is often influenced by wives if they are fortunate to marry the right woman early in life.

The best profession for the children of Oyeku meji is livestock farming or trading. This was the advice given to Oyeku-meji before he left heaven that he should trade in sheep or live stock, fowl, pigs, goats, cows or whatever. It will give them a good start in life although they will from there graduate into the higher reaches of economic endeavour.

The Birth of Oyeku Meji

The father of Oyeku meji was as patient as the rubbish dump (otiton in Yoruba and Otiku in Bini) while his mother was as strong as the three-road junction. In other words, the father was a layman while the mother was a witch who used to transfigure into the astral or psychic world to hold meetings with the elders of the night.

When the powers of the wife became too over-bearing for him, he went for divination and he was told to make sacrifice with a boa (okaa in Yoruba and Arumwoto in Bini). He did the sacrifice and the wife soon became pregnant.

On the night she was to deliver, she again transfigured into the witch world. When she woke up, Esu had positioned the boa serpent with which the husband made sacrifice, at the back of their house. Meanwhile, she felt like easing herself. She then went through the back of the house to the toilet, which was traditionally far removed from the house. On her way from the toilet, she saw the snake and ran off in fright beyond the house until she got to a three-road junction. It was there she developed instant labour and delivered a male child unaided.

She was so happy at the double salvation and joy she had in one night, that the child was named OYE KU MEJI. She had escaped death by surviving the attack of the boa, and at the same time, got a child she had been longing for in years.

When Oyeku meji comes out at divination for a woman who is longing for a child, she should be told that she is responsible for her barreness because she is not only stronger but also sees farther than the husband. She should be advised to submit to the authority of the husband if she truly wants to have a child.

If it comes out at divination for a man who is anxious for the wife to have a child, he should be told that his wife is not as desirous as himself for a child. In order to get the wife to have a child, he should use a boa to make sacrifice to his Ifa if he has one, or he should make arrangements to have his own Ifa, in order to contain the superior diabolical powers of his wife.

The Coming of Jewesun to Earth

It was also Oyeku meji who revealed how Jewesun came to this world. The awo who made divination for him before he left heaven was called:
Bi aba kpe oku ni kponkpo
Alayiye, looma Daun
Odifa fun Odo agutan
tiinshe okonbi omo olodumare
Obe laa arinrin igbatema omo araye
Meaning:—
when death is called at a distance,
it is a living being that will answer the call.

The son of God who was called Jewesun in heaven was told to make sacrifice with a sheep and red cloth in order to survive the plot that was going to be hatched by human beings against him on earth. He was told also to give a he-goat to Esu which he bluntly refused to do because he had vowed to come to the world to destroy the forces of evil represented by Esu.

He however agreed to make sacrifice with the sheep and red cloth. The awo told him that if he did not make the sacrifice to Esu, it was the agents of Esu that would kill him and shorten the span of his life and missionary works on earth. Since he had however made sacrifice with the sheep, he would wake up after three days and his fame would outlive him, after returning to heaven.

When he got to the world, as he was about to begin his work of preaching the objectivity of truth, the way people live in heaven and the love of God for his creatures, Esu appeared to him in a dream and warned him that not even God himself had succeeded in eliminating his (Esu's) influence from the entire planetary system. Esu told him in the dream that if he did not give him a he-goat he would have himself to blame because he would infiltrate his followership to destroy him. Jewesun once again refused to serve Esu on the ground that goodness could never surrender to evil.

Jewesun was actually killed three years after he began his work on earth.

How did he come to be called Jewesun

His mother had secretly gone to Orunmila on the eve of Odo agutan's departure for earth and persuaded him to make the sacrifice to Esu, which her son had refused to do. She came to Orunmila's place with the he-goat just after sunset. Orunmila told her that he would have to pluck 201 different leaves in the bush with which to wash the head of her son on the shrine of Esu. Since it was not possible to wash anyone's head in absentia, there was no way of performing the sacrifice to Esu. When the woman inisted that Orunmila should improvise some arrangement, he replied by saying that the leaves in the forest were already asleep and should not be disturbed. That expression in Yoruba means "Jewesun", which Orunmila said should be the name of Odo Agutan, tiinshe okonbi omo Olodumare, when he got to earth. Since Jewesun was due to leave for earth the following morning, there was no opportunity of making the sacrifice to Esu,, and it was never made.

When this ODU comes out of divination for a conceived child, the parents should be told that the child is coming to the world as a reformer, but that unless the special sacrifice is made for him, like Odo Agutan was told to make in heaven, he would not live to accomplish his task and that his popularity would only blossom after his death.

The earthly Works of Oyeku Meji
He made divination for (OLOBA) Fire:

Aamu Eku, Eja, Adiye, kpelu ewure
Amushe a ye oloba,
Aye Oloba ku dududu.
Won lo bere lowo Eji oye;
Kini laama mu shaye Oloba
K'aye re adide.
Oloba (Fire) was sick and dying
The rat, fish and hen were offered as sacrifice;
The goat was later used to make sacrifice to revive Fire,
Inspite of these sacrifices;
His illness became even more serious.

Orunmila was then asked what could be done to revitalise Fire (oloba). After divination, Orunmila revealed that the only way of bringing fire back to life was by using palm oil, 3 dried pieces of kolanut, dried palm leaves and a cock to prepare special sacrifice for him to bath with. After the sacrifice was prepared, Orunmila took him to a road junction and washed him up. After the bath, Oloba was taken back to the house. The three-piece kolanut, the palm leaves and the oil were ground together and marked on the head of Oloba.

Shortly afterwards, Sango released lightening from heaven, which invoked Oloba back to life and it ignited fire and he quickly unleashed a conflagration.

That is why Orunmila is praised with the song/poem which says that he was the only divinity that brought life back to Fire when he was so ill and feeble that he could neither burn anything nor anyone.

But Orumila told him that he should never repay him with ingratitude and should always remember what he did for him. That is why, to this day, when fire enters a house where Orunmila is, if it consumes at all, it will at least not touch the shrine of Orunmila. It would always make a circle around the shrine. The poem/song is the incantation used by Ifa priests for putting out burning fire when it is threatening to do any havoc.

Why the Children of Oyeku Meji do not Wear Caps

Ligbo Lere Ligbo
Ligbo naa re eri
Ligbo naa tieri Elede Ule
Ligba naa ri awori
Airi eron ekon jeun modun modun
There is virtue in valour,
It is vigour that multiplies;
That enables domestic pigs to multiply unmolested.
It is vigour that makes guinea fowls congregate in large flocks.
It is also vigour that multiplies.
The sheep when they get to a town.

These are the names of the awos who made divination for Oyekua meji. They advised him to make sacrifice so that he might multiply. He was told to make sacrifice with the meats of bush and domestic pigs, guinea fowl, and two sheep, so that his kindred might multiply. He made the sacrifice.

The priests prepared one of the sheep with medicines, adding the appropriate leaves and the Iyerosun of Oyekumeji. Thereafter, they took the sheep to the foot of the palm tree, where it was bathed with the prepared leaves. Oyekua-Meji himself was also told to have his bath with the leaves at the foot of the same palm tree. It was a young palm tree which had just started growing.

After the bath, the pot and its contents was turned mouth downwards to cover the young palm tree. The young palm tree was expected to cast the pot aside as it grew. That is how Oyeku-Meji flourished after casting aside the hat of poverty at the foot of the palm tree. That is why the children of Oyeku-meji are not supposed to wear hats on their heads.

Oyeku Meji then brought home the bathed sheep. The second sheep and the remaining animals/meat were prepared and buried on the floor of his house. That was how Oyeku-Meji's head became strong. He left the sheep to wander about in the town, while taking good care of it. As the sheep gradually began to multiply, Oyeku meji also began to multiply. He had several wives and children.

When Oyeku meji comes out during an initiation at Ugbodu the person should be told that his head is not strong. He should therefore be taken to a road junction by a knowledgeable priest who knows the appropriate Ono ifa (Odiha) with a cock, 3-piece kolanut and dried palm leaves and bathed there. He should also be told that he is a fay and that he was to be washed by awos at a road junction. If he is able to make sacrifice he will flourish on earth. He should be advised to start life with the rearing of sheep or pigs, which would develop into wider dimensions.

How Eji-Oye solved the problem of Death

As soon as Oyeku-Meji began to prosper, death was on his trail because it is often said that death does not kill a goat that has no settled existence.

In the same way, Death scarcely goes for paupers and vagrants. It is when a person begins to climb the tree of prosperity that Death goes after him. That is why Orunmila says that the path to prosperity is often very tortuous and rugged. This time, Oyeku-Meji began to have horrifying dreams. He then invited some of his surrogates to make divination for him.

The Awos he invited were called:
Okpa gboungbo ounshiwaju du ona.
Ese mejeji onjija du ona.

They told him to make sacrifice with 4 hens, 4 rats and 4 fishes in order to survive the evil machination of Death against him. He did the sacrifice and Eji-oye lived to a ripe old age. It is revealed that he did not actually die. He walked back to heaven.

How oyeku-meji won favours and gifts

To be able to enjoy the fruits of his labour without molestation and the risk of return to penury, Oyeku-Meji had to make another sacrifice. After offering one rat and one fish to ward off death and illness, he was told to offer one pig to Ifa and a second goat to his head. He did the sacrifices and he became so wealthy that he could himself not believe that he alone owned his possessions. The children of Oyeku Meji are often very prosperous, because of the sacrifice made by him at the beginning of time.

The awos who made that divination for him were called Eroke ile aaberu gegere and Eroke ile abidi birikpe. He also gave he-goat to Esu, cock to Ogun and Tortoise to Osonyin. Thus he had bought prosperity from all the principal divinities.

Oyeku Meji becomes King of the Night

The divinities are in the habit of holding meetings every five days. At one of their meetings, they carried a motion that each of the divinities should demonstrate his prowess for the others to see. On his part, Oyeku-Meji boasted that he was the only one who knew how to prevent worms from entering a rotten object, and how to make a dead animal more famous than its live equivalent. He was told to demonstrate these avowed capabilities at the next meeting.

The following day, Oyeku-Meji went to the market and bought a goat, which he walked round the town with a rope tied to its neck. Throughout the walk, the goat only made the usual innocuous sounds of which no one took any notice. The next day Oyeku-Meji slaughtered the goat and removed the skin to dry it up. As soon as it was dry enough, he made a drum out of the skin. After preparing the drum , he began to beat it and its sound was heard all over the town so much that people began to wonder what he was up to.

On the appointed day, he went to the meeting with his drum dubbed with a prepared black soap, which was specially prepared for expelling witches from one's environment. He was then called upon to prove the points he made at the previous meeting. He responded by asking whether anyone heard the sound of the live goat he paraded round the town recently. A few of the members confirmed that they heard the cry of the goat, but many others said they did not hear the sound. He again asked whether anyone heard the sound of the drum he had been beating during the last two days. Everybody confirmed hearing the sound of the drum, but they wondered how that proved his point.

He then explained that the messy soap on the face of the drum was the rotten animal that had no worms while the drum represented the dead animal that sounded louder than a living animal. All the members then comprehended the points and he was instantly made the king of the Night.

If Oyeku-Meji comes out of Ikin divination for a man, he should be told to offer a dead goat to Ifa — by killing the goat before serving Ifa with it. It is a special offering because Orunmila wishes to make a secret revelation to the man.

If it comes out for a woman, she is very likely to be pregnant or is having her menstruation. If the two probabilities are not applicable, she should be advised to offer a cock to Ogun to prevent any incident likely to lead to her spilling blood within the next three to five days. She should be told that there is an old woman close to her who is troubling her with witchcraft. She should then offer a hen and nine eggs to the night to neutralise the evil machinations of the old woman. He or She should also be told that if she or he has not already lost some money, it would soon happen, but she should not be unduly bothered about it, because the loss is meant to atone for more grievous calamities.

How Oyeku-Meji named a child Adenimi

Liimko, Miimiiko le rinmikoo.
Mi ejiogbe yio she teere kaari.
Limiko miimiko erimiko.
Mi iworimeji yio shabe firiyan.
Liimiiko miimiiko, ierimiikoo.
Mi edimeji yio gbiku tuei tuei.
Limiko mimiko, ierimiko,
Mi obarameji yio shori te bele
Limiko mimiko, ierimiko.
Mi okonromeji yio shose gberege
Limiko mimiko, ierimiko
Moje wo o bon wooda shoromi
Memo tii miiko ia fi owun
Oyeku meji yio owun nukon mimiaye kobem bem
Omo tounba ti bi ni wa kati teun a ankpe ladenimi

When it come out of divination for a pregnant woman, the child will surely be a girl, who shall be name Adenimi. Oyeku asked his followers:
Who has a plump and stout physique.
They replied, Is it Ejiogbe? He answered, Ejiogbe is tall but thin.
The dialogue continued on four other Olodus,
For each one, Oyeku replied:
Iwori has big head and fat legs but tiny abdomen.
Idi has small head and tiny legs but pot belly.
Obara has a small head, but big abdomen, and legs.
Okonron has big head and big stomach but tiny and disproportionate legs.
Oyeku Meji then boasted that there was no other Olodu with symetrical physique from head to foot.
It is he alone Oyeku-meji endowed with a stout body from top to bottom. He then proclaimed that anyone born during his time should be called the plump and stout crown (Adenimi).
The significance of this egocentric eulogy can only be appreciated by taking another look at the signs of each of the OLODUS mentioned above:

Ogbe	Iwori	Idi	Obara	Okonron	Oyeku
,	"	,	"	"	"
,	,	"	"	"	"
,	,	"	"	"	"
,	"	,	"	,	"

CHAPTER XV
IWORI-MEJI

While in heaven, iwori-meji was the most senior OLODU (apostle) of Orunmila. He was very proficient in Ifa art and practices. He brought up-several heavenly priests and he also had many surrogates working for him. He was however very conceited which explains why he eventually lost seniority to Ejiogbe and Oyeku-meji, who were otherwise very junior to him in heaven. He did a lot of works in heaven for which there are no accounts because he did not allow his followers in heaven to come to earth, who would have revealed his heavenly works on earth. A few of his heavenly works have however been told by some of those who benefited from them.

IWORI-MEJI'S WORKS IN HEAVEN.
EJIKOKO IWORI MADE DIVINATION FOR THE SUN, MOON AND DARKNESS

His title in heven was KPAU YAKATA. He made divination for the sun, the Moon and Darkness when they were coming to the world. In Yoruba they are called Ojo for Sun, Oshukpa a for Moon and Okuku for Darkness. he advised the three brothers to make sacrifice as follows:—
SUN — to make sacrifice with a bundle of brooms, white cloth, white cock and a white hen.
MOON — to make sacrifice with red cloth, a brown cock and a brown hen.
DARKNESS — to make sacrifice with black cloth, a black cock and a black hen.

He advised them to make the sacifice so that the people of the world might honour and respect them, but more especially so that people might not look contemptiously at them on the face. More importantly, the sacrifice was meant to give them power and energy which would make them inidspensable, wherever they went. The moon said that he was too handsome and popular to worry about any sacrifice. The Darkness said he was already endowed with adequate features to command respect and fear anywhere he went. He too refused to make any sacrifice. The Sun was the only one who made sacrifice. The Moon had however earlier made sacrifice for love which is why people rejoice at the sight of the new moon.

After his sacrifice, the Sun was given the bundle of brooms with which he made sacrifice to hold in his hand always with the advice that he should point the broom at the face of anyone who dared to stare at him on the face. That broom is the rays of the sun which dazzles the eyes of anyone who tries to look directly at the face of the Sun. He is nonetheless admired, because the heat he generates is used for a variety of purposes throughout the planetary system.

No one cares very much about darkness and it is not used for any tangible purpose because he made no sacrifice. For the same reason, the moon is merely admired but is neither dreaded like the sun, nor used for any productive purpose.

Iwori Meji made divination for Akun (the Coral Bead)

Before leaving heaven, the Bead also went to Iwori-meji for divination. He however directed three of his surrogates to make the divination for the Bead. They were:—
AFUN YIN YIN
AKE YIN YIN and
OYIN YIN KE BI ALA.

They made divination for the Coral bead (Akun in Yoruba and Ivie in Bini) who was called Olomo Akeriwaye in heaven. They advised him to make sacrifice so that he might live forever on earth as an instrument of adornment and nobility and in order to be handled with respect and dignity. He was to make sacrifice with a he-goat, a rat, a fish, a white hen, a white pigeon, white cloth and white thread. He made the sacrifice before coming to the world where he was easily received with jubilation. Since coming to earth, he has come to command the respect of all and sundry to his day. He is associated with regal aristocracy and ceremonial adornment.

He Also made divination for the Lead.

In heaven, two awos who were working for Iwori-meji, made diviniation for the lead (Oje in Yoruba and Oze in Bini), when he was being commonised as useless, in heaven. The two awos were:—
Kaun gere awo Ile Aran, and
Afosile awo ode kanran Musi, adifa fun oje mini mini nigba ti gbogbo orun fi oju imere wo oje.
Since he had a maleable physique he was told that he would not live long when he got to earth. He was regarded as a fay who would die as soon as he got to the earth.
At divination, the awos told him to make sacrifice with a duck, a cock, and vulture. He did the sacrifice and came to the world where he lived so long that he outlived all those who expected him to die young.
That is why a poem was composed in praise of his longevity which is song by awos to this day:
Ugun-ugun kii ku Lewe; Kange;
Maadagba maadarigbo kange — meaning
The vulture dies not in infancy,
I will live to a ripe old age, because,
Neither the lead rots, nor
the brass goes rusty.

When Iwori-meji comes out of divination or at Ugbodu for a sickly person, this special sacrifice (ono Ifa) should be prepared for him so that he might live long.

This work is said to be the last done by Ejikoko iwori before he came to the world. He composed the following poem before finally coming to the world:—
Ejikoko Iwori
Alade teeju momi koo, womi ire
Bo omode baa teju, moma ri owo,
Bo omode baa teju, aamofa;
Eji koko Iwori
Alade Teeju momi ko wo omi ire;
Eji koko Iwori
Jengen Jengen Jengen
Awaade olode Igbodo.

Ejikoko Iwori made Divination for the Lion, the Cow and the Buffalo

The Lion, the Cow and the Buffalo were born of the same father, who was king of the animals of heaven. When he left for the world, it became necessary for one of his children to replace him as the king of animals. The Lion meanwhile ran to their father's diviner, Ejikoko Iwori for divination. He was advised to make sacrifice as follows:—
    (i)   To throw ten pieces of elephant meat to the river;
    (ii)   To serve his head with a pigeon and a kolanut; and
    (iii) To give a he-goat, filter and beads to Esu.

He did the sacrifice without any delay and was assured that he would eventually take his father's title. Meanwhile, the cow being the eldest of the three brothers did not bother to go for divination since the law of primogeniture in heaven, entitled him to take his father's crown. He was meanwhile crowned the king of animals.

Soon afterwards, the cow's wife went to the river and saw a big lump of meat and picked it up. As she was going home with it, Esu transformed the meat into fresh elephant meat with blood oozing out of it. At the same time, Esu drew the attention of the lion to the piece of meat on top of the water pot which the cow's wife was carrying home from the river and persuaded him to trail the woman right up to her house. Soon afterwards, the cow's wife, now a queen, was publicly accused by the lion of stealing his meat. Since stealing is punishable by death in heaven, the cow knew what the consequences were and quickly abdicated the throne and escaped to earth with his wife.

Following the sudden disappearance of King Cow from the throne, the buffalo was next invited to become the king. Since he never expected to become king, he too entered the throne without bothering to go for any divination. Right from the outset, he was a very ferocious king. Whenever two or more animals appealed to him for settlement of mutual disputes, he would horn the complainant and respondant to death. His flock then began to run away from him.

When the lion saw that the buffalo had been crowned king, he went back to ask Ejikoko Iwori why his prediction that he would become king had not come true. Ejikoko Iwori advised him to exercise patience, but that if he wanted the prediction to manifest quickly, he should arrange to have his own Ifa, after which he would surely become king within a period of three months. The Lion got his own Ifa and it was Iwori-meji that appeared for him at Ugbodu.

Meanwhile, the community of animals who were perplexed by the aggressive and destructive reign of the buffalo also went to Ejikoko Iwori for divination on what to do to end the Buffalo's reign of terror.

He advised them that they would only have peace and tranquility if they succeeded in returning to their fold, the three children of the forest that had earlier been banished by king Buffalo.
They were:—
    (i)   Oten — omo Ilara
    (ii)   Ogoro — omo olode;
    (iii) Oju — omo ijarere.

He also advised them that their rightful king was still hiding inside a rocky cave in the forest. He gave them a full description of the place and the animals quickly went there for him. When they got to the cave, they saw the lion and had him thoroughly beaten up for hiding away instead of joining them to combat the menace of the buffalo.

Thereafter, they assembled an army and drove out the buffalo from the throne and he too escaped to earth. It was after the expulsion of the buffalo that the lion was brought in to the town in triumphal procession with a cloth tied to his neck.

Meanwhile, they went for OTEN who insisted on being carried on someone's shoulder. Ogoro also insisted on being brought home on someone's head, while Oju was carried back home in someone's hand because they left the town helter skelter.

The lion had been on the throne for four days without uttering a word. He was scared of being beaten again like they did to him in the cave.

As the lion was being beaten, he told them where his late father kept all his instruments of authority including his diabolical wands. With that he was formally proclaimed king and all the animals went on their knees to greet him traditionally.

Iwori-meji Leaves heaven for Earth

While in heaven Iwori-meji was the most senior OLODU of Orumila. It was procrastination and complacency that brought him to the third position when he got to earth. When Orunmila returned from his first and only trip to earth, he invited his sixteen children to accompany the children of other divinities to earth to found a permanent abode there. On second thought he proposed that they should go one after the other instead of leaving in one fell swoop, Iwori-meji was the first to come out to say that he was so useful in heaven that it was not yet time for him to leave. Besides, he remarked, "a good general does not send his best soldiers first into battle." He then proposed that Omonighorogbo who became Ejiogbe on earth, should be the first to go. In a mood to flatter Ejiogbe, he described him as being the only OLODU — sociable enough to interact effectively with the other divinites, and that he would be a better ambassador of the Orunmila kindred. Ejiogbe volunteered to lead the way since he had a good reason to go to earth.

As we have already discovered under Ejiogbe he was made the king. of the Day as soon as he got to the earth because he got there in broad day light.

When Ejiogbe did not report back his findings on earth, it was also Iwori who proposed to Orunmila that Oyeku-Meji should next go to earth. As we have already discovered under Oyeku-meji, he was born by night and was eventually crowned the king of the night.

When he began to hear news of how life was flourishing on earth, Iwori-meji decided to follow his two brothers. As soon as he decided to come to the world, the following Awos made divination for him:—

Akaka ra ka, Moni tiika,
Owara wiri, oju egun
Iba afo demi, mu akpoko, — Akpowa mo mu ko.
Strong persons make others strong.
A divine shrine is always shrouded in mysteries.
My father told me to carry the bag of success on my neck, and so,
I will not surrender the bag of prosperity to anyone.
These are the names of the three awos who made divination for Iwori-meji before he left heaven for the world.

They advised him to give a he-goat to Esu and a cock to his head or whatever he knew he would eat. He gave the he-goat to Esu, a pigeon to his head and a ram to Ifa. He also went to Olodumare (The Almighty God) for clearance and blessing. As he was leaving the divine palace, he asked God for Akpominijekun (mystery bag) which he was given. Thereafter he set out for the world.

The Birth of Iwori-Meji

His father was a pauper while his mother was a divine priestess. The mother was called Jetti (the untidy one) and his father was called AKO-OKO. While in the womb, he attracted gifts and benevolence from all and sundry to his parents. While his mother carried him in the womb, she was not often allowed to pay either for services rendered to her, or for goods she bought from people. She was often told that the child in her womb was a great Ifa priest who deserved to be respected.

On the day he was born, he cried in front of the father's house but the cry echoed at the back of the house. He was often left on his own because of the mystery surrounding his life. He often strayed into the bush where he used all kinds of foliage to rub his head. He had a chequered up-bringing because his parents could not altogether make ends meet.

Even as a boy, he was already a seer. He would often tell people about their problems. On one occasion, he told his parents to serve their heads mutually so that they might prosper. The father was to use a hen to serve the mother's head, while the mother was to use a cock to serve his father's head. After that sacrifice, their lot improved dramatically.

Iwori-meji contests for Seniority on Earth

On getting to the world, he discovered that his two younger brothers, Ejiogbe and Oyeku-meji, who got to earth before him had respectively been crowned kings of the Day and Night. From the outset he was determined to establish his heavenly seniority on earth over his two brothers. Even his marking sign:—
```
 ||   ||
 I    I
 I    I
 ||   ||
```
two in and two out, were designed to challenge the authorities of Ogbe and Oyeku. On their part they were equally determined to impose their earthly authority over Iwori.

One afternoon, Iwori was sitting in front of his house when he saw a large procession approaching. He saw every-body bowing in reverence to the man on the horse at the head of the procession. When the procession got to where Iwori was sitting he saw that it was Ejiogbe to whom all that reverence was being made. When he saw Ejiogbe he did not kneel down to greet him like everyone else was doing. He merely shook his own horse tail (Oroke) to greet Ejiogbe as awos are wont to do. He did not see why he had to kneel down to greet his junior brother, although there is nothing in the tradition which exempts the elder brother of a king from kneeling down to greet him.

Ejiogbe then stopped the procession and ordered that if Iwori knew he was too big to greet him like anyone else, he should in future lock himself in-doors throughout the day, if he could not see himself as coming under the authority of the king of the day. Iwori-meji then retired inside his house in anger.

At nightfall, he came out of the house to move around. As he came to the road junction near his house, he again saw another procession at the head of which was Oyeku-meji with dazzling lights that were as bright as the rays of the sun. Again, rather than go on his knees to greet Oyeku-meji like everyone else was doing, he only waved his horse tail at him. Once more, Oyeku-meji told him that if he could not subject himself to the authority of the king of the Night, he should refrain from leaving his house at night. He then retired home.

He was thus effectively banned from leaving his house by day or by night. In that situation, he could not even leave his house to fetch his daily bread.

When Esu saw that Iwori's condition was becoming untenable, he transfigured into a chief and went to Iwori to advise him to invite his two brothers to a rendezvous to settle their scores. The benevolence of Esu was in return for the he-goat which Ejikoko Iwori gave him before leaving heaven.

Iwori accepted the advice of the chief and invited Ogbe and Oyeku to meet him at the foot of the palm tree where the divinities climbed down from heaven, and through which Orunmila himself returned to heaven. They eventually met at that point to discuss their problems. Both Ogbe and Oyeku insisted on holding on to their terrestrial superiority over Iwori. It was finally agreed that Iwori should occupy the third position. He only accepted the decision reluctantly. In fact, it is revealed that he went back to the heavenly awos who advised him to give a ram to his Ifa to enable him to command as much authority as his two brothers. He did the sacrifice in heaven before returning to the world. The special significance of this part of the life of Iwori is that when it comes out at Ugbodu, the person must be a third child in his family. He must either have reincarnated previously or he must have died soon after birth, and been born again through the same parents. In this connection, I should like to reveal that I have a child who was given his own Ifa soon after he was born when he was at the point of death. It was revealed to me by Ifa priests eight years ago before I knew anything about Ifa, that the child did not wish to live because he lost his seniority. They asked me whether I had lost a child earlier. It was then I remembered that the first children delivered by his mother were a pair of twins both males. The first to land of the two children died five days after birth at the General Hospital in Benin City in the Bendel State of Nigeria. Two years later, his mother had another male child. The next child birth was also a male and it was this child for whom Ifa had to be prepared. He became well after the completion of the ceremony. His Ifa is Iwori-Meji

How Iwori-meji excelled his Brothers eventually

Back to the life history of Iwori. Several years later, the awos who made divination for Iwori in heaven decided to visit the world's nobilities with a proclamation that whoever was able to disclose their names would be made rich. That proclamation added that whoever they visited, that did not know their names would be sent back to heaven for retreat.

They began visiting the reigning monarchs, and those who could not reveal their names were forced to return to their ancestors in heaven — and all their earthly belongings were confiscated and packed in a mysterious bag that was neither full nor weighty. At that time most of the reigning kings died one after the other in mysterious circumstances.

After dealing with the kings, their next point of call was the home of Iwori-meji who was serving his head when they arrived. Before then, appalled at how death had been striking at the reigning monarchs, Iwori consulted his Ifa, who told him to quickly give a he-goat to Esu in order to survive the test that was soon coming to him. He was told to add Akara, Eko, a gourd of palm wine and three cudgels to the sacrifice to Esu. He was also to serve his head with a guinea fowl after making the sacrifice to Esu. He made the sacrifice to Esu without any delay.

After receiving his offerings, Esu built a small kiosk on the free space near the entrance to Iwori's house. On the fateful day when the heavenly knights were to visit Iwori, Esu arranged freshly prepared Eko, Akara and palm wine in multiple units, at the kiosk. Thereafter, he (Esu) waited there for any intruder.

Shortly afterwards, as the heavenly knights were passing by, ESU invited them to a feast, where they dined and wined inside the kiosk to their hearts' content. As the feasting progressed, Esu asked them what was the object of their mission to the world, when they had so much to do in heaven.

In reply, they told Esu that they were bound for Iwori-meji's house to give him the test of his life. If he succeeded in knowing their names, they would make him a wealthy man. If he failed, they would make him return to heaven. Esu lied to them that Iwori was a very wicked man and that he would be happy to see him die because he was too conceited. Esu however persuaded them to tell him their names so that after they had killed Iwori, he would at least know the identities of the men who finally succeeded in eliminating the wicked man from the face of the earth.

The eldest of the three of them took one of the three cudgels inside the kiosk and beat his legs with it saying:—
Unokare, Akaka ra ka moni tii ka — which he said was his name.
The next one similarly used the second cudgel and pronounced his name as: Owara wiri oju egun.
The last one took the third cudgel and used it on his leg disclosing his name as:— Ibara fo demi — mu akpokpo. Esu assured them that the wicked man would have to go to heaven to be able to know their names.

As soon as they left the kiosk, Esu transfigured into another person and entered Iwori's house through the back entrance and quickly alerted him to the approach of the killer-knights from heaven. Esu then gave him their names in order of seniority. Thereafter, Esu sat down with Iwori-meji to await the arrival of the heavenly knights.

Not long afterwards, they arrived. As soon as they appeared in his house, Iwori embraced them by mentioning their names with an air of familiarity, one after the other while shaking hands intimately with them. This was how he did it:—
Akaka raka Moni tiika — Ojure ree
Owara wiri oju Egun — Odojo meta
Ibarafo demi mu akpoko — Ojure re — Ekerubo
He then motioned them to sit down while he went inside his room to bring them kolanuts, after thanking them profusely for coming to help him serve his head.

As soon as Iwori went inside, Esu asked the visitors whether they were awos and they answered affirmatively. Meanwhile they hung their mysterious bag of treasures on a nail by the side of the wall of the sitting room.
When Esu saw that they had hung the bag, he told them that three days earlier, a diviner had told Iwori that three awos from an unknown land would visit him as he was serving his head. The diviner advised Iwori to use the three awos to serve his Ifa so that he might prosper. With that they took to their heels in fright, leaving behind the bag of treasures.

When Iwori came out of the room with the kolanuts, Esu told him that the visitors had left. He however told Esu to go and call them back. Esu hailed at them to return to collect their bag. But they replied that as a compensation for knowing their names, they left the bag behind for the benefit of Iwori-meji. Esu then told Iwori that the visitors had run away and had no wish to return. Esu drew Iwori's attention to the bag they left behind disclosing that it was a bag of wealth left behind to enrich him. At first, the bag gave the appearance of oozing out fresh blood but when they brought it down, it was seen to contain all kinds of items of wealth — money, brass, human beings and animals of all descriptions in multiples of several hundreds.

Iwori-meji then thanked Esu, with another strong he-goat. Thereafter he invited all the awos including his two brothers for an elaborate feast — at the end of which he sang in praise of the heavenly awos and there was rejoicing and merriment.

Thus, although Iwori-meji lost the battle for seniority to his two elder brothers on earth, he became exceedingly more prosperous than the two of them. If Iwori-meji comes out at Ugbodu, the initiate will surely become very prosperous later in life provided he does not abandon his Ifa and keeps in close touch with Esu through frequent sacrifices.

How Iwori-meji became a strong Ifa priest.

Having become wealthy, he began to incur the envy of everyone else. He then went for divination to an awo called Atari Ogbigbo mu arayen bi oje (the beak or nib on the mouth of a tiokam is as strong as lead metal). The awo advised him to make sacrifice with a strong ram to the elders of the Night and a he-goat to Esu. He did the two sacrifices.

After the sacrifice, the elders of the night worked on him for seven nights to make him a strong and invincible man. On the seventh night, they gave him four eyes with which to see in the night.

Simultaneously, Esu also invited the strong men of day light to prepare him for seven days. On the seventh day, they gave Iwori four eyes with which to see whatever happens in the day. That is why he is regarded as the strong OLODU of the day and the night — which eventually made him more powerful than the kings of the day (Ejiogbe) and the Night (Oyeku).

The later Works of Iwori

As soon as he became strong and wealthy, he was surrounded by many subordinates, who were trained by him in Ifa art and practice. Having imparted his knowledge to surrogates, they assisted him in making divination for whoever came to him for succour.

The first of his surrogates was Okiti to berebere maye — who made divination for Oni Iwori Eyo when his fortune was about to be transformed from penury to prosperity. He advised Oni Iwori eyo to make sacrifice with plenty of corn and beans because he was going to prosper before the end of that year. He was to add for the sacrifice, a white cock, and a white pigeon. He made the sacrifice.

After doing the the sacrifice, the Ifa priest divided the corn and the beans into two portions each, giving him one portion to carry with him to wherever he went. At the same time he was advised to move about from place to place. In consonance with the advice of the priests, Oni Iwori eyo began to travel about until one day he came to a place where the birds of the forest were holding a conference.

On getting to the meeting place, the birds demanded food from him and he gave them corn. When they finished eating the corn, they asked for more food and he poured the beans down for them. After eating the beans, they asked whether he had anything left and he replied that he had nothing more to offer.

In a gesture of gratitude, the birds assured him that he would become a wealthy man before that year ran out. A bird called Aluko (Awe in Bini) plucked two of its feathers and gave to him, while the parrot also plucked two of his red feathers for him. Another bird called Okin, the peacock, also plucked two feathers and gave to him. Thereafter, he proceeded on his journey.

Not long afterwards, he met Ogun, the great warrior returning from battle with 200 captives in his front and 200 captives to his rear, all carrying the spoils of war. When he met the convoy, he stopped to greet Ogun, but told Ogun that in spite of his bellicose looks, he lacked dignity and nobility. Esu quickly inspired Ogun to demand from Oniwori eyo to show him how to avail himself of dignity and nobility. Oniwori eyo then ordered all of Ogun's followers to close their eyes and they did. He quickly inserted two feathers of Aluko (red in colour) on the head of Ogun. Thereafter, he asked Ogun's followers to see the new look of their Lord and master. When they saw the two red feathers on Ogun's head, all his followers exclaimed, Ogun Yee! which to this day is the traditional greeting to Ogun. When Ogun asked his followers to comment on his new look, they all confirmed that he looked noble and honourable. Ogun wears red feathers to this day to complete his regalia.

Ogun then surrendered the 200 captives in his front together with what they carried to Oniwori eyo as compensation. Oniwori Eyo then proceeded on his journey. He next came to the palace of the Olofen, who was sitting on his throne. Once more he told the king that although he was looking very prosperous, his looks lacked majesty and nobility. When the king asked Oniwori Eyo to demonstrate what majesty and nobility meant, he inserted the feathers of Okin on Olofen's crown. He told the palace audience to comment on the new look of the king and they all hailed, Aba Iyeoo! They all confirmed that he looked majestic.

Olofen then gave a part of his kingdom to Oniwori-Eyo to administer and he continued on his journey. He next came to where Orisa-nla was sitting on his divine throne. Once again, he told Orisa-Nla that although he had authority over the entire universe, his appearance lacked dignity and majesty. When Orisa Nla told him to demonstrate how to look honourable and majestic, he told all the divinities present to close their eyes and Oniwori eyo inserted the two parrot's feathers on the head of Orisa Nla.

When everybody opened their eyes to the new look of Orisa Nla, they all shouted, Baa Taa Laa oo! Orisa felt so contented that he gave Oniworieyo ten units each of all treasurable valuables on earth.

At the end of his tour, Oniwori-eyo became a very wealthy man, richer than any body around.

He made divinalion for an only child:

Agbonmota lo otun, agbonmota loori — were the two followers of Iwori who made divination for Omokon or Okonbi an only daughter of her parents. They warned her to refrain from the habit of going out alone by day and in the night.

She was advised to serve her head with a cock and to offer a he-goat to Esu. She was also to collect all eatables and tie them in a rafia bag (oke in Yoruba and Ebo in Bini) including Ekuru (Emieki in Bini) and a small chicken for sacrifice in the heart of the forest — to her enemies (Erhee in Bini and Ota in Yoruba). She was also to offer a cock to Sango. She did the sacrifice to Esu and was about to leave home with the sacrificial rafia bag to make the forest sacrifice when her father instructed her to prepare food for him.

Before she completed the cooking of her father's food, all the market women had left for the market and the road had become desolate and lonesome. That was the setting in which she left home alone to deposit the sacrifice, and for the market, to buy the remaining materials for her sacrifice. On getting to the heart of the forest, she settled down to pray with the sacrificial bag. Instantly, one man came out from the forest. He was the notorious forest bandit who had terrorized people in that stretch of the forest, for a long time.

When the bandit called her, she began to tremble. The bandit was about to murder her when he was stopped by Esu who meanwhile took over his mind with more conciliatory thoughts. The bandit dropped his matchet and told her to go first to buy him some articles from the market. He gave her money to buy him a cock from the market, showing her the route to take on her journey to and from the market, and warning her to return unaccompanied.

On getting to the market, she bought her own cock for sacrifice to Sango as well as the cock ordered by the bandit. While she was in the market a strong gale-force wind began to blow followed by heavy rainstorm. The strong wind uprooted a big tree in the vicinity of where the bandit lived in the forest and it smashed his hut killing him outright.

When the rain subsided, the girl set out to return to the forest to deliver the cock to the bandit. When she got to the spot where the bandit directed her to wait for him, she hailed on him to let him know that she had returned. There was no response. She however saw the signs of a fallen tree. She followed the foot-path until she came to find the bandit dead under the fallen tree. She then used the bandit's cock to serve her head on the spot.

When she lifted herself up, she saw all the loot of the man's banditary over the years. She then collected what she could of the valuable treasures and went home. On getting home she narrated her experience and discovery to her father, who immediately accompanied her to the forest to collect the remaining valuables.

Meanwhile, she served Sango with the cock she bought from the market. Thereafter she went with 2 goats, cloths and neck-beads to thank the Ifa priests who made divination for her, adding a bag of money and plenty of yams. This experience translated her into prosperity thereafter.

When this Odu appears at divination the person should be advised not to move alone in quiet moments in order to avoid the risk of falling victim to marauders, who might kill him unless he makes the sacrifice recommended above.

He made divination for Orare:

The third of the followers of Iwori-meji was Aro Ni Ikpin who made divination for Orare, a pauper who was suffering below the starvation line. Having suffered penury for a long time, his guardian angel appeared to him one night and advised him to go to Orunmila for consultation. He then went to Eji-Iwori who asked Aronikpin to make divination for him. He was advised to strive to make arrangements to have his own Orunmila. He was also told to give he-goat to ESU and to rear a wretched dog after making all the sacrifices. He went about to look for money with which to do the things he was asked to do.

The tradition of the town at the time was that when the King died, all male adults in the town would each buy a dog and tie it up at a road junction. Koriko, the lion would them come from heaven to take away one of the dogs. Meanwhile, the Oba of the town died and every male adult began to tie up their dogs at the various road junctions of the town. Orare followed the example of others and also tied up his wretched dog at a road junction. He only did it to satisfy the custom of his people because he was so sure that the heavenly visitor would not be interested in his miserable dog.

When Koriko eventually visited the town, he only took away Orare's dog. Next morning everybody else found his dog where they were tied except Orare whose dog had been take away by Koriko.

The custom of the place was that the person whose dog was taken away had to be crowned as the next king of the town. When the King-makers finally verified that it was Orare's dog which was taken away he was invited to the secret conclave and prepared for the coronation. He was subsequently crowned as the new king.

After the coronation, he prepared an elaborate thanksgiving feast in which there was general merriment and he sang in praise of the awo who made divination for him.

He made divinalion for Kiniun:

The fourth follower of Ejiwori was Alatushe kiite Atushe Arare Kuu — who made divination for Kiniun (Dinosaur) when the other bigger animals were trying to deprive him of his father's land. He was advised at divination to make sacrifice with a ram, a goat and a he-goat.

After the sacrifice the priest advised him to go to the disputed land and encircle it with his urine. Thereafter, he was to stand on the middle of the land and shout a proclamation asserting his title to the land. He was to stay there and watch subsequent developments.

He actually did as he was told and after encircling the land with his urine, he stood at the middle and shouted that anyone who felt justified to contest the ownership of his father's land should meet him for combat. Since the other contestants challenging his title had been looking for Kiniun for a long time they went into the bush determined to kill him. Anyone who crossed the urine circle fell down and died instantly. When the others saw what was happening, they ran away abandoning Kiniun to inherit his father's land in peace. That is why Kiniun is described as Eni tomu ito gba uyi owo eron Koogbo. When it comes out of divination for anyone competing for the ownership of anything which rightly belongs to him, he should be told to make a similar sacrifice and he will surely win the contest.

Advice to the sons of Iwori-meji

At the height of his prosperity, an Ifa priest visited Iwori-meji. The priest was called Eni aja baawa ni aja banlo — meaning:— the dog returns home with the person with whom he went for an outing. He gave Iwori-meji the following advice in the form of a poem:—

    Ifa teju mo mi,
    Koo womi ririe,
    Eji koko Iwori,
    Okpe teju mo mi rire
    Eji koko Iwori.
    My ifa has taken good care of me,
    I will also take good care of my Ifa,
    The divine palm tree should protect me
    as I will also serve Orunmila with all my heart.

When Iwori-meji comes out for a new initiate into the Ifa religion at Ugbodu, the person should be advised to serve Orunmila whole-heartedly because Orunmila will also take good care of him always.

CHAPTER XVI
EDI-MEJI

Edimeji is one of the strongest Olodu in the Ifa family. He is very aggressive and pugnacious. While in heaven, he was better known for his bellicosity than for priesthood. He was nonethe-less a proficient Ifa priest. On account of his various out door activities in heaven, he did not do much of Ifa practise. Instead, that part of his work was mainly done by surrogates. For instance, when ODE (Exterior or OUTSIDE) went to him for divination when his fortunes were flagging, it was one of Idimeji's assistants who helped him.

IDIMEJI HELPED ODE (outside) TO REGAIN PROSPERITY

The surrogate was called EWURE ABORI KPETEKI LOON DIFA FUN ODE NIJOTIUWA ODE SUN. Ode's three wives had deserted him when he became too poor to satisfy them materially. The names of his three wives were:
  (1)   Ire or play (Iku in Bini)
  (2)   Oyin or Pleasure (Oyenmwen in Bini)
  (3)   Ujo or Dance (Iku-owe or Ugbemwen in Bini)

It was the active support and cooperation of his three wives that gave ODE his identity. When they left him he became very dull. It goes without saying that Outside only becomes attractive and interesting when there are outdoor plays, pleasantries, music and dancing. People go outside to play and dance. Pleasure is mainly manifested by people's expressions outside their homes.

To get his wives back, the Ifa priest advised ODE to make sacrifice with one goat and to slaughter a second goat for a feast in his house. He was to cook yam on the fire and was assured that while the yam was cooking on the fire, his wives would return to him one after the other. He did the sacrifice as advised.

After making the sacrifice, he prepared a pot of yam and put it on the fire. The invitees to the feast were wining and dining on the meat when Esu went out to meet ODE's wives. When Esu got to Ire, he gossipped to her that it was a mistake to have left the husband merely because his fortunes suffered a temporary eclipse. He remarked that since eclipses were transient and ephemeral, ODE was already back in prosperity in a big way — so much that people were always feasting in his house daily. Esu added that at that moment one of such elaborate feasts was in progress. Esu visited the other two women and told them the same story.

The wives then decided to go and verify the story where-upon they found the yam cooking on fire and they joined hands to prepare the food. Thereafter, they all agreed to stay with ODE for good. With the return of his wives ODE's prosperity blossomed once more. When Idimeji comes out of divination for a person whose fortunes are flagging, the Ifa priest will tell him to make a feast with two goats, one through Ifa to feast the elders of the night and the other to make a feast to the people around him and his prosperity will surely return to him.

How the Groundnut came to multiply

Shediye Kimi bae joko loon difa fun Ekpa, tiolo run ebe obigba omo.

He made divination for the groundnut when she left heaven to produce 200 children on earth. Ekpa or groundnut had no offsprings and was anxious to procreate. She went to Idimeji who advised her after divination to make sacrifice with a hen, cock, rat, fish and one bag of money. She did the sacrifice after which she was taken to the farm to be washed. She subsequently gave birth to 200 children and the groundnut kindred became very prosperous.

IDIMEJI MADE DIVINATION FOR THE MALE SPERM AND THE FEMALE MENSTRUATION

It will be recalled that at the beginning of time, plants and animals did not procreate as we know it today. Following the creation of men and women, they merely lived together without knowing how to procreate. We have already seen a synopsis of how Esu re-positioned the female pelvis from the forehead to between the woman's legs. The woman did not know what to do with her pelvis and the man did not know what his penis was meant for beside respiration. The sperm and menstruation who had separate identities then went for divination in the home of Idi-meji where they met his servants called:—

Ogan ofori so siki
Ofese so yeghe
Ofi agbede gbede meji son lebe
Ibo efun obale de rumu rumu

Awon lo difa fun ATO (or Ekuu in Bini) Abufun ASE (or Ehe in Bini). Spermatozoa and Menstruation were both anxious to know how to procreate. God had created them leaving them to use their own intelligence to contrive how to procreate. They were both advised to make sacrifice with a goat. The sperm was told to add a chalk, white cock, white cloth, white pigeon and okro. Menstruation on the other hand was to add red cock, and can wood — to her own sacrifice. They produced all the sacrificial materials and the Ifa priests used them to prepare medicine for them to eat.

Thereafter, the sperm was told to go and live with man while menstruation was advised to visit the woman and stay with her for five days after every thirty days. That is how we became the children of the sperm and menstruation through the instrumentalities of man and woman.

This is the kind of medicine that an Ifa priest will prepare for anyone who is anxious to procreate.

IDIMEJI AS A PROMINENT FIGHTER

As already stated above, Idi-meji was famous or notorious in heaven more for his pugnacity than for his Ifa practice. His daily chore consisted of challenging the stronger divinities in heaven to combat and almost invariably, he was always victorious.

He was in the habit of going ouside his house every morning to shout Loogban-o! One day, when he shouted Loogbaan-oo! the King of Death himself came out to challenge Idimeji to a wrestling contest. In a sarcastic and contemptious response, Idimeji told the king of Death that he was not in the habit of wrestling with one-headed beings because he would not have the opportunity of demonstrating the superiority of his strength to them. He insited that he only accepted challenge from creatures with more than one head.

As soon as the news got round that Idimeji would only wrestle with people carrying more than one head, a divinity with two heads came out to meet him. As soon as he engaged the challenger, he plucked off one of his two heads leaving him with one. Explaining his objective, he declared that no one had a right to carry more than one head and he was determined to reduce all inhabitants of heaven to single-headed creatures.

The next day, the divinity with three heads came out to challenge Idimeji and he plucked off his two extra heads, leaving him with one. The process continued until he came across the nine-headed divinity. The nine-headed divinity was the first to come out in the morning to challenge Idimeji by also shouting Loogban-oo!

When Idimeji engaged him, he quickly plucked out the divinity's eight extra heads. No sooner did his opponent fall to the ground than he was up again to re-engage Idimeji for a second contest.

Meanwhile, Ajala otherwise known as Agbede-Ogun who is the head moulder in heaven rejoiced that as long as Idi was in heaven he would have plenty of work to do. He was at the venue of the wrestling contests, When Ajala saw that the contest was becoming stiff, he made an oxymoron to Idi by leading him with an expression that Ajala knew how to cast all parts of the body save the vertebral column. That was a hint to Idi to attack his opponent by the vertebral column.

Idi immediately got the message, and instantly threw up his opponent lifting him on the vertebral column and he fell to the ground. After defeating his opponent, Idi went home with the wives and properties of all those he vanquished as was the custom in heaven. The last divinity he defeated was the Alara of heaven.

On getting home, Idi invited all the awos of heaven and told them to reveal the name of Alara's wife, the last woman he inherited from his contests. Her real name was Bola wun mi — meaning my favourite wife. To proclaim her name the literary way would connote a desire to seduce the woman which would get the person revealing her name into trouble with Idi. Anyone who mentioned her name that way was immediately challenged to another spear (Okparere in Yoruba) (Osogan in Bini) pinning contest on a stony floor.

All those who went through this ordeal failed and Idi seized all their belongings in the process, until it came to the turn of Oligharabafe, who had been advised at divination to offer a fowl to his head and prepare it with Eko. He had been advised to reserve the hand of the fowl for his first visitor on the morning following the sacrifice to his head.

On the other hand, he was to prepare another sacrifice to Esu with Okro pudding, made up of corn comb, and other slippery objects. He was advised also to insist that he would only fight on top of an Ifa tray called Akpako.

On the morning of Oligharabafe's contest with Idi, the latter sent his three children called Iboru, Iboye and Ibosise to visit Oligharabafe, and to invite him to visit him because he was very ill. When the boys got to Oligharabafe's, he told them to inform their father that he would visit him as soon as he collected some leaves from the bush for his treatment.

As the boys were about to leave, he remembered the hand of the fowl he had been advised to give to whoever was his first visitor that morning. He quickly called back the boys and invited them to eat something before returning home. They ate Eko and the fowl's hand. After eating, the eldest of Idi's three sons remarked to his other two brothers that no one kills a host after enjoying his hospitality. In other words, the law in heaven was that no one should kill a person after eating his food. With that, they resolved to reveal all their father's secrets to Oligharabafe to save him from the machinations of their father. They taught him the correct way to pronounce Bolawunmi's name, as well as the point on the stone floor at which to pin the Okparere or spear to the ground of their father's private chamber, that is, at the water drain (Uroramen in Bini or Oriole in Yoruba) at which point a frog was used for sacrifice every morning. They also told him how to position his Akpako, advising him that as soon as their father stopped, he should proclaim that he had fallen. With that the boys left for home.

When Oligharabafe got to Idi's house, he complained about his illness, but told him that before doing anything to heal him, he should first reveal the name of his wife as a testimony to his prowess. Oligharabafe quickly asked him, Is it not the former wife of Alara called Bolawo kpe Uwa jewon — awo (that is, the only woman who enticed the Ifa priest). Idi became annoyed and immediately challenged Oligharabafe to a fight on the seventh day. Oligharabafe quickly replied that there was no point waiting for seven days because he was ready for the contest there and then without any further preparation. Idi however insisted that since he was not well enough for any instant contest they should hold it in abeyance until the seventh day. It was a deal and with that, Oligharabafe brought out the medicines he prepared for Idi, gave them to him, telling him how to use them and left for home. Before leaving, Oligharabafe warned Idi that the name of Bolawumi actually meant that if he failed to return her to Alara, he would lose his own life on account of her seduction.

On the seventh day, Oligharabafe returned to Idi's house for the contest. As soon as the contest started, Idi sat on the Akpako of Oligharabafe, which made it difficult for the latter to operate. Not knowing what to do next, Oligharabafe brought out his divination instrument and sounded it and he was told to quickly offer a he-goat to Esu, which he did frying the meat and putting it in front of Idi who was then hungry from his sitting on the Ifa tray. He was also advised to use a pigeon for sacrifice which he roasted and dubbed it with palm oil after which he tied it to a string hanging from the roof on where Idi was sitting. The oil from the pigeon was dropping on Idi's head. When he looked up he saw the roasted pigeon.

When Idi lifted himself up to reach for the meat, Oligharabafe quickly pulled his Akpako clear of Idi. Idi then saw the attractive he-goat meat in front of him. As he got up to take out of it to eat, his opponent finally removed his Akpako. As soon as Idi discovered that Oligharabafe had succeeded in pulling off the Akpako, he conceded that his opponent had passed all the tests, but that there was a final one to go. He invited him to pin his spear on the floor of his inner chamber. Oligharabafe quickly saw the water drain and he hit the spear there and it stuck to the ground, a feat which no one before him had accomplished.

At the end of the contest, Idi exclaimed that his work in heaven had been completed, having met someone as strong, intelligent and skillful, as himself. He then decided that it was time to leave heaven for earth, like all his three other fellow OLODUS — had done before him.

When Idimeji comes out at Ugbodu, the person should be advised to make sacrifice so that he might not suffer from the problem of children. When it comes out of divination, the person should be told to beware of a contest over a woman. He should be told to offer he-goat to Esu, in order to succeed in the inevitable contest. He should also make sacrifice to his head and to Ogun.

When it comes out of Okpele divination, the person should be told that he is preparing for a journey which he should refrain from undertaking. But if he must go, he should serve Ogun before embarking on it. He will also be invited for settlement talks which he should not undertake without serving Ogun first.

IDI-MEJI LEAVES FOR EARTH

Idi was so conceited that he never bothered to do any prior divination before embarking on his exploits. For one thing, he did not see why he had to go for divination with inferior Ifa priests or divinities. For another, he was always sure that his skill and strength would see him through all challenges. When he concluded that it was time to leave heaven for earth, he decided only to travel with his two main instruments of power and authority — tunder-stone and a blast furnace. These are instruments used by the thunder divinity (Sango) and the metal divinity (Ogun). Both instruments were embedded inside his head.

When his followers saw him leaving for earth without any prior preparations, some of them gathered together and reminded him that he never had a wife of his own choice while in heaven. They told him that by the same token he was going to go through life on earth without a wife of his own unless he made sacrifice with a he-goat to Esu and a guinea fowl to his guardian angel. He retorted that if no one was able to subdue him in heaven who was it on earth who could withstand him or stand in his way. He vowed that he was going to accomplish on earth similar feats like he recorded in heaven. They told him to remember the disruptive influence of all the other divinities whom he had disgraced in heaven. He would be powerless to subdue them on earth, since they got there before him.

Among his surrogates who gave him the warning were:—
Abimi Lorigi — Omo igi ni mi,
Edo okpe ni monje
Edo oke ni mo mu
Okuro mi ogbigbo

He was born on earth to a father who was an Ogun Priest, and a mother who was a Sango priestess. He came out of the womb with a tunder stone and a blast furnace which were preserved for him to use when he grew up. At the age of ten, he was already fighting with adolescents who were several years older than himself. No one could ever touch the ground with his back. He became so ferocious that every one was afraid of him. He was nicknamed the invincible one.

Meanwhile, he had gone to keep the wands he brought from heaven at a secret place where he retreated to use them from time to time. One day, he saw his father preparing to serve his head with a dog. He told the father it was forbidden to serve the head with a dog. He took him to where he kept his blast furnace and slaughtered the dog there. When the people present challenged his action, he told them to go to the spot where he slaughtered the dog and verify whether they would not find a live goat there. The dog had been transfigured into a live goat and it was brought to his father to serve his head with it.

On a second occasion, his mother was preparing to serve her head with a female sheep. Once again, he told her that it was forbidden to serve the head with an ewe. He took the ewe from her to where he kept his tunder stone and slaughtered it there. He was again challenged by the elders around and he told them to go to where he slaughtered the ewe whether they would not find palm oil and a cock there. The people collected the oil and the cock and the mother offered them to her head — while he directed her to drink the oil.

At that stage, he told the parents that he came from heaven to remind them of their patron-divinities, Ogun and Sango which they had ignored. He then gave the blast furnace to his father to use to perform all acts of manufacturing with iron and steel and gave the tunder stone to his mother for use in her assignment as a Sango priestess. He taught his father how to serve Ogun and his mother how to serve Sango. This re-discovery of their paths of destiny immediately transformed them into a famous and prosperous couple. It was Idi who taught the world how to serve Ogun and Sango. It is infact believed that he was the first ODU who brought the service of the two divinities to mankind. Thereafter he left his parent's home and wandered into the heart of the world. Wherever he went, no one could subdue him. But he was so much dreaded that no woman agreed to marry him nor did any man agree to live with him.

When he discovered that he had become effectively ostracized, he left all towns and villages of human habitation and built an abode for himself in the heart of the forest. As soon as he began to live in the forest, he was written off as a mad man.

In his new abode, he planted kola trees, walnut plants and pear trees. They soon grew up and began to bear fruits. One night, his guardian angel appeared to him in a dream and told him that the reason he was suffering so much deprivation was on account of the sacrifices he refused to make in heaven. The angel told him that although it was getting late because he was then an old man, he should nonetheless make the sacrifice.

Not knowing who was talking to him, he decided next morning to consult his Ikin divination and it was his own Ifa that appeared. He realised that it was his guardian angel who appeared to him during the night. From the proceeds of the sale of his fruits, he was able to buy a he-goat for Esu and a guinea fowl for his Ifa. At last, albeit belatedly, he did the sacrifice.

After performing the sacrifice he again sounded his Ifa who told him that something strong was going to happen in the town nearby and that he would have to play a decisive role. Meanwhile, the eldest daughter of the Oba was having a difficult labour. All the Ifa priests and the priests of other divinities had tried and failed to make her deliver the baby. When there was no other awo around to be invited, Esu entered the mind of one of the Oba's counsellors, who instantly reminded the Oba that Idi could be invited to try his hand at the problem.

Idi was instantly invited. On getting to the palace he brought out his divinition bag (Akpo minijekun) and brought out some leaves from it. He prepared the leaves and added his Iyerosun, (divination powder). After preparing the leaves he repeated the following incantation, which Ifa priests use to this day to deliver women in difficult labour:—

Awo laafi rabe taafi dae loko gbaa (3 times)
Edon a moju ganranwu (3 times)
Oruko taankpe oko (3 times)
Ila abenukpa ka (3 times)
Oruko taankpe obo (3 times)
Ala arisa no ti gbe omo olomode sinu (3 times)
Etu omo olomo bo ogboro orite eje waye

While he was repeating the incantation he was using the leaves to wash the woman's abdomen, after making her to drink out of it. As soon as he mentioned the last stanza of the poem, the child together with its placenta came out at the same time.

The only reason why I have chosen to bring out this incantation like

I did not do in other instances, is to illustrate the significance of incantations generally. It will be remembered that it was Idi in heaven who made it possible for the man's penis and woman's pelvis to bring forth children. On earth, he merely reminded the vagina that it was only appointed as a passage for taking in a child and bringing it out of the womb. The whole essence of incantation is to remind the subject of his heavenly name and his earthly role and thereafter it can be conjured to behave as desired.

As soon as the woman brought forth the child, all the palace chiefs began to marvel that the man who was written off for a lunatic had such geat powers. His worth was at last appreciated, and only after he had made sacrifice. To compensate him, the Oba gave him a gift of money as well as a man and a woman. Since he was already too old to mate, he told the man and the woman to live with him as man and wife for the rest of his life.

Once his worth was recognised, his abode was frequented by people who had all sorts of problems and he was able to help all of them. He was eventually given a title by the Oba and told to transfer his abode to the town of Ife. In a warming up ceremony in his new abode, he sang in praise of his awos in heaven lamenting for ignoring their advice. In the song he advised people to make prescribed sacrifices to avoid suffering his kind of fate — because he had planted cash crops which others were going to reap since he was leaving no one behind on earth to reap his heritage. Idi is known to have performed very few assignments thereafter before he returned to heaven.

Idi Cures the Cripple and the Blind man

Having settled down at last, Idi soon got some auxiliaries who were assisting him in his divination works. Among such people were:—
Dimi Dimi Barakata,
Oron gbinrin gbinrin,
Okuku gbinrin,
Agada bule are re je,
fo un ba koje.
Together they made divination for the blind man and a cripple who were very poor. They went to Idimeji to help them and he told them to give a he-goat to Esu. The cripple had previously sighted the skull of a he-goat somewhere. Since he did not imagine how they could afford to buy a live goat, he crawled to collect the skull where he had seen one previously.

They subsequently offered the he-goat's skull to Esu with a promise to bring him a live he-goat if and when they prospered enough to afford one. Meanwhile, they continued to live in penury. In a mood to end their sufferings they hatched a plan to commit mutual suicide. One day, they set out for the river. The blind, with a stick in hand carried the cripple on his shoulder to lead the way to end the worthless life by harakiri.

On getting to the river, the cripple suggested that the blind man should first jump into the river. The blind man refused on the ground that he could not see his way to the river. He then suggested that the cripple should jump first into the river so that the splash of his impact would make him know the direction from which to dive into the river.

With that suggestion the cripple crawled and collected a mud image built by ants (Ulelefe in Bini) moved to the embankment of the river, made his last wish bidding farewell to his friend and threw the mud image into the river, thus hoping to decieve his blind friend. The blind man called on the cripple several times but there was no response. So, he assumed that he had drowned.

After lamenting that he was going to die in poverty and deprivation, thus suffering to the end, he began to hit the ground with his stick towards the direction in which the cripple is assumed to have jettisoned into the river. On getting there he used his walking stick to hit continuously hard on the ground. When he felt the presence of an obstacle on his way, he continued hitting that spot, not knowing that he was in fact hitting the legs of the cripple whose hitherto numb legs instantly regained life. The former cripple was now able to stand on his feet. As the blind man was hitting the ground towards the river, he was shouting that a man about to die must make a last ditch effort (In Bini — Okpia te wu, To zighaza). While the cripple was getting up, he shouted that the blind man was trying to kill him and as soon as he was on his feet, he slapped the blind man, who also instantly regained his sight.

As they were blaming each other, they went into open embrace and began to rejoice. They both walked home for the first time, completely healed and looked for money to buy a he-goat which they offered to Esu without any delay. Eventually, they both went to thank the old man Idi for the efficacious divination he made for them.

The Healing of the Blind and the Hernia Afflicted

Oyin ferere miofe, made divination for Idimeji when a new child was born in his house. He invited Arukuku Taaku, awo ono Alara and Arukuku taaku, awo ono Ijero. The Awo of the Alara had hernia while the Awo of Ijero was blind. Idi invited the two of them to participate in the divination for the naming ceremony of the new child.

The Awo of Ijero (Adeve) was the first to arrive and he proceeded at once to make Ikin divination for the child. As the Awo of Alara (Aro) was coming, he heard the sound of Ikin divination and he immediately declared outside before entering the house that the Awo who was divining without waiting for him had hernia. The Adeve on hearing the proclamation of the in-coming awo, said that the awo who declared his own problem was himself blind on one eye.

The Adeve asked the awo outside what he was to do to cure his hernia He was told to serve his late father with a ram. In reply the partially-blind awo asked the awo inside what he was to do to heal his blind eye. He was told to serve his head with a cock.

The one-eyed awo went back home without seeing his colleague. The Adeve also abandoned his divinational assignment and went to his house to serve his father. As he was serving his father with the ram, the animal kicked one of its hind limbs and it hit the awo's hernia and all the pus in his testacles got burst and began to ooze out. He instantly fainted and was taken to his bed to rest without completing the sacrifice. By the time he woke up the hernia was gone.

When the one eyed awo also got home, he quickly arranged to serve his head with a cock. As he was praying to his head with the cock, it shot out one of its toes and it hit his bad eye, and amidst severe pain, he regained the use of the blind eye.

From their respective blind houses, each of them, after being cured of his affliction, decided to go and thank Idimeji in his house. The two awos met for the first time as they were crossing the bridge just before getting to Idi's place. After formal introduction, they embraced each other, and together, decided to go to Idimeji to complete the divination for the new

child.
    On getting there they both thanked Orunmila and themselves for the miracle.

CHAPTER XVII
OBARA-MEJI

```
I    I  I
I I  I I
I I  I I
I I  I I
```

Confusion and misunderstanding began with this fifth OLODU of the Ifa genealogical corpus. With the first four OLODUS, (Ogbe, Oyeku, Iwori and Idi), whether their marking signs are turned upwards or downwards, they will retain their identities. It was with Obara that turning their signs downward began to give a different nomenclature. If the marking of Obara is turned upside down, it becomes Okonron. So it is with the remaining eleven Olodus of Orunmila.

It was therefore Obarameji who ordained that before giving food to Orunmila, the offeror has got to beg him to accept the food. Whether the food is a rat, fish, hen or goat, the offerors will have to beg Orunmila on their knees before he can accept any food offered by them. That is why it is said that it is not difficult to beg for favour from one's patron divinity.

Obarameji was famous for his concern about the poverty of God's creatures. People had deluded themselves with the feeble and defeatist philosophy that there was virtue in material poverty. He demonstrated that a creature's destiny was his own choice and that whether or not a person stayed poor was the measure of his personal effort. For instance, when the coconut was leaving heaven for the earth with her other sister, the royal palm, they both went for divination with an awo called Jeemfi di hee. The name of Obarameji in heaven was Jeemfidihee. He made divination for them and advised them to make the prescribed sacrifice. On getting to the world both sisters became married to Ode (that is outside). The coconut produced a lot of fruits which made her the favourite of all people. On the other hand, the Royal palm, although more beautiful than her sister, coconut, remained an object of barren decoration to her husband, lacking in any significance to anyone else.

He also made divination for the Frog when she was coming to the world. He advised the frog to make the same sacrifice prescribed for the palm sisters. She did it, and she began to multiply as soon as she got to earth. After helping several others in heaven, he saw a lot of poverty on earth and he decided to come to the world to bring prosperity to it.

First, he went for divination to an ifa Priest called Urore — koo laaagba, gbogbo won lo maada wenke wenke. Urore advised him to make sacrifice with four pigeons and a white piece of cloth so that prosperity and wealth might accompany him to benefit the world.

The rough Passage of Prosperity to the world

When the king of Death heard that one awo was leaving in the company of wealth and prosperity for earth, he decided to stop whoever it was. Not knowing exactly who it was, he decided to put all the awos in heaven to the test under pain of death. He had fourteen of his counsellors with him.

Meanwhile, the king of death wore his wife's garment, that is, illness, because the wife of Death is illness. He became so ill that his body even
*See the table of Seniorities.

began to emit a very offensive odour. He also prepared a number of kolanuts, which were actually eggs and kegs of wine containing sheep's urine, for entertaining his invitees. He then invited the heavenly awos one after the other to come and cure him. He gave each of them seven days within which to cure him, failing which they would not return home. As soon as any visiting awo arrived, Death would give him the kolanut to break as a testimony to his prowess. Most of them failed in the kola breaking test and were instantly put in chains. The few who passed the kolanut test by revealing what it actually was, an egg, could not survive the actual healing test because the more they tried to administer medicine to the king of Death, the more indisposed he looked. He already had several heavenly awos in his cell, when it came to the turn of Obarameji.

When Obarameji received the king of Death's invitation, he (otherwise called Jeemfidi Hee or let me sit quietly and inoffensively, as he was called in heaven,) decided to consult his Ifa, who advised him to offer a he-goat to Esu and a goat to his guardian angel. He quickly performed the sacrifices. When he was leaving for Death's place, he wore his magic necklace (Ude), which was his main instrument of authority — ASE. He had also been told to give a ladder each to his guardian angel and to Esu, which he did.

When he got to Death's house, he knocked at the door, but before opening the door for him, he was told to reveal the number of people in the room within, and what they were doing at that instant. He quickly looked into the crystal ball of his necklace and revealed that there were fourteen of them in the room, each holding a wine cup from which he was drinking. With that he was cleared to enter the room with his back to the door. The door then opened and he entered.

Eventually, the king of Death appeared looking seriously ill. As soon as he took his seat, Death ordered that kolanut and wine be given to him. When the kolanut was served, Jeemfidi hee told the others that kolanuts had arrived and he told them to break them.

Using a special incantation in which he invoked them by their heavenly names, he conjured the kolanut and the wine that if they were actually wine and kolanut as God created them, they should stay as such, otherwise they should before his eyes, change into their true and real identities. Instantly, all the poisonous concoctions contained in the wine immediately surfaced and the sheep's urine base was at the bottom. At the same time, the kolanuts turned into eggs. He then protested to the king of Death for treating him so inhospitably. Death apologized to him and appeased him by bringing him proper kolanuts and wine. Death however appealed to him that in spite of his initial upset, to nonetheless assist in curing him of his ailment. He replied by saying that he had to eat and drink first, because he was hungry from his long journey.

As Obarameji was being served with food, Esu transfigured into a yaws-afflicted boy and stood by the gate. Before eating the food, he brought out his okpele divination instrument and his own Ifa appeared. That made him to wonder whether the food was wholesome and safe. He then invited the yaws boy to eat out of the food. The boy swallowed up the whole meal and its container. In return, the boy told Obarameji to dispose of the clay pot which was actually the container with which his yaws was normally treated. As he went out to dispose of the pot, the boy advised him to consent to cure the king of Death.

When he got back to Death's chamber he volunteered to do his utmost to heal him. He also agreed not to return to his house if he failed to accomplish the task within seven days. On his part, Obarameji stated that since there was no debit without a corresponding credit, he wanted to know the reward that awaited him if he succeeded in curing the ageless king of Death of his ailment and Death promised to surrender half of his heavenly belongings to him, if he succeeded. By the same token, the yawsed boy also asked Obara what he would do for him if he succeeded in helping him and Obara promised to give him half of whatever he got as a reward.

The King of Death was in the habit of removing his sick dress at night whenever he went to bed only to put it on again first thing in the morning. On that first night, as soon as he went to bed, Esu used the ladder with which Obara made sacrifice to climb into Death's bedroom. As Esu was doing that, he conjured Death to sleep soundly away. As soon as Death fell heavily asleep, Esu, as the yawsed boy, led Obara to climb up the ladder to see how hail and healthy the old man looked and particularly how smooth his body was without his sick garment.

On the next morning, Death invited Obara to begin the work of curing him. In response, Obara collected all available leaves and added Iyerosun, his divination powder, and prepared them for Death to bath with for 7 days. Death however did not bath with the preparations. Obara was meanwhile always giving the lion's share of any food given to him to the yawsed boy.

On the 6th day, the king of Death told Obara that he was not getting any better and that on the contrary, he had been having sleepless nights. On that night, Esu again conjured Death to a heavy honey dose of slumber and he catapulted Obara and the yawsed boy through the invisible ladder into Death's bed room. When they got into the room, the yawsed boy told Obara to carry the pot containing Death's sick garment. Once outside, Esu conjured the way to the river to be cleared of all living creatures, because it is forbidden for any living being to see that pot. Thereafter, they proceeded to take the pot to the river into which it was jettisoned. On their return from the river, they both went back to sleep.

Shortly afterwards, it was dawn and the fateful day had arrived. As soon as it was broad daylight, a crowd of heavenly host had gathered to witness the fate of Obarameji. Meanwhile, Death had his bath and reached out for the pot containing his sick garment, but it was no where to be found. On failing to find his sick garment, Death decided to lock up himself in the room. After waiting in vain for the king of Death to emerge from the room, Obara sent for him because he was anxious to know what his fate was going to be. After knocking several times at the door of Death's bedroom, the old man got dressed and came out. He took his seat on the throne with his body shining radiantly and transparently looking hail and healthy. Obara then asked Death to announce the result of his efforts and he confirmed that his treatment had given him a clean bill of health.

Death then went inside to bring out all treasures in twos to give to Obara. The yawsed boy advised Obara to scream because the king of Death had gone back on his words. Obara accordingly cried out and his cry was amplified and echoed by Esu, which sound, made the very grounds of heaven to quake. The incident shook the king of Death and he then went into the room to enclose half of all his belongings in a casket of kolanuts and brought it out. Before he came out, the yawsed boy had advised Obara that he should only accept a casket of kolanuts from the king of Death.

Eventually, Death came out with two containers — a brass box containing rubbish and a casket of kolanuts and asked Obara to choose one of the two. In consonance with the advice of the yawsed boy, Obara chose the casket of kolanuts and left for home. Meanwhile Esu had transfigured into an old man and was waiting for Obara on the way. Obara searched in vain for the yaws-boy and when he could not find him, he left some of the gifts to his own guardian angel and continued on his journey.

Before getting to his house, he met an old man in a make-shift hut which was not on that spot when he was going on his mission. The old man told Obara to show him the reward of his mission. He began to wonder whether it was Esu at his game again. To disabuse his misgivings, he brought out his ASE and conjured the old man to transform into his real self. The old man instantly transformed first into the yawsed boy and next into Esu in his full regalia. Obara then thanked him for all the assistance he rendered to him during his impossible mission. He brought out the casket of kolanuts and told him to take whatever proportion he wanted from it. In reply, Esu told him to take him along to wherever he was going and to be giving him a part of what ever he ate as he did generously to him during his exploits.

On getting home, Obarameji gave another he-goat to Esu and a goat to his guardian angel. He then invited his friends for a thanksgiving feast, being the only awo who succeeded in frustrating the treacherous machinations of the king of Death. For that reason when Obarameji comes out of divination for a person and death is seen to be knocking at his door, he should be advised to make the same sacrifice that Obara made before leaving for the test of Death.

At that stage, Obarameji decided that it was time to leave for earth. Before leaving heaven, he sent for his Ifa priests to make divination for him. The awos were called:—
Wosemi kpelembe kpelembe
Oromi mimi mimi
Lake Ori Udi koko ni kpa eron
Lembe lembe aabe be
Ouni mo ju oloja titu rin rin rin.

He was told that to succeed in carrying prosperity to the world he should make sacrifices with a goat to his Ifa, adding a casket of kolanut — and to give a he-goat to Esu. He did the sacrifice and left for earth.

He was born of a father who only had the left hand, whilst the mother was blind on one eye. In spite of their physical deficiency, his parents had plenty of enemies. It was Obarameji who introduced dreams to the world because while in the womb, he was always revealing impending dangers to his parents. While in the womb, the elders of the night saw that a child was going to be born who would bring prosperity to earth and they were determined to make him still-born.

One night, he told his father in a dream to prepare one medicine in a soap worth 35K to be bathing with in order to ward off the onslaught of the elders of the night. He told the father in the dream that as soon as the leaves were collected, he should leave them overnight on the shrine of Esu. He was to grind them the following morning and mix them with soap for them to be bathing with.

Obarameji was eventually delivered safely and they had no more problems from the elders of the night. When he was born, the parents approached an Ifa priest for birth day divination. The Awo was called:
Afenju Omo
Omo are kii kon fene fene
Kpobi gbite gbite ya alumen
Ite onaye magba.
Nio ni gbe ite orun.

Obarameji was the only child of his parents. He quickly grew up to be very rascally. He was always telling fortunes that made nonsense of all the elderly awos of Ife and they were not happy with him. At a very early age, he was always attending the meetings of the elders where he often stole the show. There was a meeting of elderly awos held every seventeen days in the palace of the king of Ife. The game of ayo was often played after the meeting, but the game often ended with the death of one of the kings' children.

At the first meeting attended by Obarameji he had a lot to drink and after getting drunk, he boasted that at the next meeting he would reveal the names of those who were responsible for the periodic deaths of the king's children. There was one high chief called Oshin who was stealthily performing all the attrocities. After the proclamation of the young Obarameji, the meeting dispersed on the note that if he failed to carry out his promise, he would be executed.

Convinced that Obarameji could not reveal their names, the consiprators hatched out a plan of how to kill him. They sat by the bush path to hatch out their plan, and Obarameji's mother, who they did not know, was returning from the farm, overheard the men firming up their nefarious plan against her son. After hearing the details of the plan she ran home to consult their Ifa priests (named above) on how to save the life of her only son.

The mother was advised to prepare three pounded yams and three pots of soup and to send them to the bank of the river. She was to wear a bead on her waist when going to the river, where she was to have her bath. While having her bath, she would discover what to do in order to save the son's life.

She got home and did as she was told. On getting to the river, she deposited the pounded yam and the soup on the embankment and went into the river to have her bath. While she was bathing, a man called Okpolo came to the river and greeted her. The man quickly had a bath in the river and went out in a hurry. When the woman asked him why he was in a hurry, he told her that he was hurrying to attend the day's meeting at the palace of the king. She invited him to eat out of the food she left on the shore before leaving. Since no food was normally served at the long meetings in the king's palace (which explains why they were killing his children) Okpolo was only too happy to eat before leaving for the meeting.

While eating, he remarked that an important event was going to take place on that day at the king's conference because they were going to kill the loquacious and presumptuous Obarameji, since he would not know the section of the ayo players who were responsible for the deaths of the king's children, as he boasted. He ended by disclosing to the woman that he, Okpolo was in fact one of the conspirators because the king was so stingy that he was never serving any food or refreshments at the long meetings.

The next man to come along was Obuko, who behaved in much the same way. After eating the pounded yam, he told the woman the details of their mission for that day, adding that he was one of those killing the king's children, because of his stinginess. He also disclosed that as one of the conspirators, they were bent on killing the garrulous and boastful Obarameji at the conference, since he would never know their names. He then introduced himself to the woman as Obuko — Omo lubebere tube — and that the others were:— Agbo — omujojoguole and Okpolo — ami sosu run. He ended by confirming that they were the three plotters who were killing the children of the Olofen after playing the ayo game. He further disclosed that Obarameji had boastfully promised to reveal the name of Oshin as the sole conspirator whereas Oshin was in fact not going to take the chair at the conference on that day — and that the senior son of Oshin called AREMO was going to occupy his father's place at the day's meeting while Oshin was going to sit at the side. He finally disclosed that a special seat was going to be prepared for Obarameji under which would be a hole covered with a mat. The indiscreet Obuko even went on to disclose that the only way Obarameji could avoid the fate awaiting him was by coming with a dog and a parcel of eko and akara. If he threw the eko and akara on the mat beneath the chair reserved for him, his dog would go for them. In her own remarks, the woman emphasised that it would be good riddance for Obarameji to die because the town would be a more peaceful place without him. With that Obuko left for the king's palace.

Agbo, was the last to come to the river. He too went through the same revelation ritual after eating the pounded yam and confirmed what Okpolo and Obuko had disclosed before him. He also revealed why and how they proposed to kill Obarameji. After eating his share of the pounded yam Agbo left for the conference.

Soon afterwards, Obarameji's mother left for home to brief her husband and the son about what transpired at the river. She quickly went through the sequence of events telling Obarameji what to do. He was to go with his dog called Boghoye aje — ejobi. She advised him to throw the eko and akara under the chair prepared for him and to call on the dog to fetch them. If the dog fell into the hole he should get up and ask for the person called Obuko. As soon as the person identified himself, he should order that he should be offered as sacrifice to Esu.

He should next ask for the person called Agbo and if he identified himself, he should order that he should be offered as sacrifice to the public shrine of the town's forebears.

Finally, he should ask for the person called Okpolo and as soon as he identified himself, he should order that an arrow be pierced through his mouth and anus and he be offered for sacrifice to the ground divinity (Oriole).

When asked why the three men were to be killed, he should disclose that those were the conspirators responsible for the death of the children of the Olofen, after playing ayo game with him. After that episode, he should order the man on the throne to vacate it because he was an impostor — and that he should give way to his father Oshin, who at that time would be smoking from a long pipe called Ekitibe — by the side of the hall. When Obarameji was leaving for the conference, he wore his father's gown called gbariyee and his cap called Labagaden. He went with his dog called Boghoye atoju ma oko. On getting to the main outer entrance to the town hall, the spectators began to sing his praise with cries of Obarameji afenju — omo.

When he got inside the hall, he was quickly directed to occupy the chair set aside for him. At that stage, he stood still, brought out his parcels of Eko and Akara and threw them under the chair earmarked for him, directing his dog to go for them. The dog went straight for them but it fell right through the mat covering into the deep hole laden with hooks and thorns below.

Reversing the order in which he was to carry out the day's assignments, he began by ordering the man sitting on the throne to vacate it at once, and give way to Chief Oshin, his father. The man on the throne quickly vacated it and his father moved up to occupy the seat.

He then called out for the man called Obuko and ordered him to get up and identify himself. He also asked the men called Okpolo and Agbo to get up and identify themselves. They all got up accordingly. Obarameji directed that Obuko should be sacrificed to Esu, Agbo to the shrine of the public forefathers and Okpolo to mother earth (Oriole).

When Oshin asked Obarameji for the offence committed by the three men, he reminded him of his vow at the previous meeting to reveal the conspirators who were responsible for the deaths of Olofen's children, after playing the game of Ayo with him. He confirmed that the three men were the culprits. After saying that, the three men were accordingly used for sacrifice. The culprits were actually the he-goat, the Ram, and the Frog.

The whole conference then rose up in a thunderous applause and ovation to Obarameji. He was carried shoulder high in open procession outside. Before he left home, Obarameji's parents had vowed to commit suicide if their only son lost his life in his encounter. As soon as his father heard shouts, he concluded that his son was dead and he took his own life. When the mother saw the son being carried shoulder high at the head of a triumphal procession, she removed her head from the rope into which she had hung her head preparatory to suicide. She then used the rope (Oja or Oza) to thank her own mother. That is the rope that people use to tie the shrine of their departed mothers in parts of Yoruba land and Benin to this day.

That is why it is said that it was Obarameji's mother who saved him from the cold hands of death.

When Obarameji comes out at Ugbodu during Ifa initiation ceremony, the person should be told that if his father is still alive, the father's end is at hand. The person should be told to forbid wine drinking entirely. He should also avoid sharing out of the legacy of a deceased person. Three days after coming out of Ugbodu, he should immediately prepare the Esu shrine for his Ifa. Thereafter, he should buy a guinea fowl for his mother — if alive — to serve her head for him. If she is already late, he should use it to serve his mother's shrine, or on his left big toe. He should also serve his own head with two guinea fowls. Later, he should prepare shrines to the Divinities of Ogun and Eziza for himself.

If Obarameji comes out from Ikin divination, the person should be advised to serve his head quickly with a pigeon or a fowl. If it comes out for a pregnant woman, she can be told in all certainty that she will deliver a set of twins.

When Obarameji comes out of Okpele divination, the person should be told to serve Ogun and Eziza each with a cock. He should be advised not to enter into any thrift contribution (Esusu) with anybody. He should also beware of permanently joining any clubs or meetings — lest his untimely death will source from there.

Obarameji's encounter with enemies

After that incident, Obarameji naturally became very famous. His fame and popularity soon began to evoke envy and enimity. He was soon to realise that success breeds envy, and envy evokes animosity which begets enimity. Generally, people do not fall in love with those who excel them.

The more elderly Divine priests from whom Obara appeared to have stolen the show lost no time in plotting his downfall. Meanwhile, Obarameji's guardian angel appeared to him in a dream and gave him a preview of the machinations of the plotters. When he woke up, he invited two awos to make divination for him. Their names were:—

Oni bara, ola bara, Eshishi bara
Eeku ookii ku so otin
Eye bara, kii ku si asi (Uho in Bini)
1.   The fly which does not get greedy, never dies inside a wine container, and

2. The fly which flies high up in the air, and who is not tempted by the baits on the low ground, does not get caught in a gum trap.

They advised Obarameji to make sacrifice with a cock and a hen. He made the sacrifice which explains why he triumphed over his enemies, after they had tried on earth and failed, and they also reported him to the elders of heaven. Meanwhile, an itinerant Ifa priest was visiting Ife and he stopped by the house of Obarameji, who extended elaborate hospitality to the visitor. The name of the awo was Eroke Ule Abiditirigi. When the man made the libation divination, he warned Obara that a messenger was being sent from heaven to fetch him. He was advised to give a he-goat to ESU and a goat to Ifa. Not only did the awo do the sacrifices for Obara, he also did traditional clearance (Ono Ifa in Yoruba and Odiha in Bini) for him. He prepared the relevant medicine for him to be taking every day.

Five days later, a tiokam came from heaven to arrest Obarameji. When the tiokam flew on top of Obara's house, he called on him to prepare to go to heaven. In an incantational reply, Obara told him that his father had told him before his death, that he was leaving for heaven to answer the early call that would have taken him (Obara) away from this world — and that his father also said that he was not to leave the world until a tree called Aro in Yoruba and Uruaro in Bini, produced leaves, and until the roots of a Parasite plant called Ose in Bini and Afuma in Yoruba (which grows on top of trees) touched the ground — and until Elaa shed its leaves. Obarameji collected the tree plants and gave them to the tiokam to give to the king of Death, who sent for him in heaven.

When the tiokam delivered the message in heaven to the king of Death, he ordained that Obarameji would have to get lost on earth never to know his way back to heaven. That is why Obarameji is said to have lived on earth for about 260 years and in the end he had to beg God to accept him back into heaven. If the children of Obarameji are able to prepare this Ono Ifa, they must live to a ripe old age.

OBARAMEJI TURNS BLACK INTO WHITE

The last major test undergone by Obarameji before seeing the limelight occured when his fellow awos cajoled him to get drunk at a party in the king's palace. This explains why the children of Obarameji are forbidden to drink any alcohol whatsoever. After getting drunk he began to make pronouncements which he could not live up to. Among the proclamations he made in his state of drunkeness was that he could serve the Olofen's head whereas it was forbidden for any Awo to do so. He also boasted that he could wash a black cloth to become white. The proclamations of Obarameji were quickly reported to the king who invited him to perform the feats in seven days time, failing which he would be executed.

On getting home he told his mother what transpired at the king's palace. His mother cried out in disgust, for daring to make such empty boasts, which no one else had done previously. He explained that he was drunk when he made the proclamations. The only person that used to serve the head of Olofin was a man called Okete. There was also a man called Aro, who alone was capable of washing black into white.

Obarameji's mother went to befriend the two of them. On the seventh day, the Olofen brought out a ten yard piece of black cloth and gave it to Obara to clean it in the river to become white. Before getting to the river, his mother was already waiting for him. The king sent messengers to accompany him to verify the operation. When the party arrived, Obara's mother was singing to invoke Aro to appear. When the Aro fish heard the song, he moved to where Obarameji was washing the black cloth, seized it from him, swallowed it and vomitted it out and it was snow white.

As soon as Obara saw that the cloth had turned white, he brought it out drip-dry and showed it to the two witnesses sent by the king to verify the washing operation. They all trooped back to the palace and everyone including the king was astonished by the miracle performed by Obarameji.

The next operation was the ceremony of serving the Olofin's head. The man who used to serve Olofen's head annually, was called Ewu-okete. He had a tradition of going for his own divination and sacrifice before performing Olofin's annual sacrifice to his head. On this particular year, he had gone for divination and was told to offer a he-goat to Esu. He failed to do the sacrifice.

When the time came for him to serve Olofin's head as usual, the cermony failed to manifest. The climax of the festival was invariably for the cloth with which the ceremony was done to turn into white. In view of the sacrifice which Ewu-Okete refused to make to Esu, the black cloth refused to change its colour to white.

It was clear from then on that the festival was a failure and the sacrifice to the head did not manifest. Normally the festival of Olofin's head was invariably followed by peace, prosperity and progress both for king and kingdom. But after the abortive ceremony of the head for that particular year, things began to get difficult for king and country. That was the year in which the king's children were dying after playing Ayo with his visitors. There were no rains and food and cash crops got burnt. There were several cases of still-births and abortive pregnancies. This was the state of affairs at Ife, when it was time for another festival. While the search was on for a new person to serve Olofin's head Obarameji boasted he could do it.

Before doing anything about it, the mother went for divination and she was told to give a he-goat to Esu which was quickly done. Subsequently, she invited Ewu-Okete to teach her son the incantation with which to serve Olofin's head.

Woni ki oba wa bori olofen
Kori Olofen fin
Ki Obara bo aya olofen
Kaya olofen gba
Ko fowo kan ala
Ko di dudu
Obara bori Olofen
Ori Olofen fin
Obara boaya olofen
Aya Olofen gba
Obara fowokan ala
Ala didun dun

When the time came for serving the King's head, Obara did it without a hitch ending up by touching the white cloth he brought from the river (Ala) and with the invisible help of Esu, as soon as Obara touched it, it quickly turned to black. That was enough to indicate that the bad days were over. The ensuing year proved to be very prosperous for the king and the country. Obara was also amply rewarded.

OBARA SHOWS INGRATITUDE TO THE MOTHER

After seeing Obara through all these trials and tribulations, he accused the mother of being a flirt. The mother became so annoyed that she concluded that it was time to return to her ancestors. Before giving up her life, she proclaimed that from then on, the hand with which Okete served Olofen's head should be used for digging the earth, which is what the rabbit does to this day. She also proclaimed that the white cloth which the Aro fish produced should henceforth be used for wrapping human corpse. This part of Obarameji is used to cause havoc at the shrine of Esu when there is justification for it. It is not possible to go into the details of it in this book.

OBARAMEJI WINS A CHIEFTANCY TITLE

Following the Death of his mother he had to learn to take care of himself. He had stopped drinking and so was no longer in a position to make statements and proclamations that landed him in trouble. He had learnt from his mother the virtues of divination and sacrifice. When he therefore discovered that in spite of all his achievements, he was still very poor, he resolved to get to the bottom of his problems. He then invited an Awo called Ishe toon shemi ko ni sha Alarin ni Ogun (There is no poverty that does not have an end). He was advised to make sacrifice to his Ifa with a goat, kolanut, melon and his covering cloth, and to make a feast of pounded yam with the meat of the goat. He was also to give a he-goat to Esu. The awo also advised him that he was not to go anywhere on the day he was to make the sacrifice.

Meanwhile, the king sent for him, among other awos, to come to his palace for a special divination contest on that day. The awo told him to make the sacrifice on that day but not to answer the King's invitation. He then made the sacrifice to his Ifa, but could not find a kolanut cask and melon (Elegede or Kakamisi in Yoruba and Eyen in Bini). He also gave a he-goat to Esu.

When the other Awos came to call him to answer the king's invitation, he declined to accompany them because he was making a special sacrifice to his Ifa.

When the awos got to the king's palace he told each of them to reveal the contents of a room which he had locked up in the palace. One after the other the awos tried but could not reveal the contents of the room. It then came to the turn of an awo called Oguega who revealed that the room contained 201 persons. That was the correct answer. The king then went inside and gave a gift of one cask of kola and one melon to each of the awos. He also sent Obarameji's share to him in spite of his absence.

The awos had spent a long time in Olofen's palace without having any food or drink as a result of which they were already very hungry. On their way home, they decided to call on Obarameji, who, meanwhile, had set his feast table with fresh pounded yam and the goat meat. As if the feast was earmarked for them, they all sat down and ate and drank to their hearts' content. When Obarameji asked what Olofen gave them, they all replied that they were given kolanut and melon — and also gave him his own share — which he was very happy about, because they were the two materials remaining to complete the sacrifice to his Ifa.

When the others asked him why he was so happy with such ostensibly worthless gifts, he replied that they were the staple materials used for making sacrifice to his own guardian angel.

With that remark, all the awos surrendered their own gifts of kola and melon to him, so he could have a good stock of them. Before taking leave of him, they informed him that Olofen wanted all of them to visit him once more in eight days time.

After the awos left, he served his head and his Ifa with some of the melon and kola casks. But when he cut them open with a knife, he discovered that far from containing kolanuts and melon seeds, each of them was stuffed with all kinds of treasures ranging from money to beads etc. From the jewels he collected from the casks, he was able to sew a beaded gown, a beaded pair of shoes and a beaded hat for himself and a beaded dress for a horse, which he bought meanwhile for his own use.

On the eighth day when they had to see Olofen again, he made sure that he was the last person to arrive at the palace. Before the meeting, Olofen had decorated a throne similar to his own meant for seating the best dressed man on that occasion. As the awos began to arrive, none of them had the courage to occupy the special throne, beside the king. They all took their seats by the side of the hall. When Oguega, the victor at the last contest, got to the hall in his tattered dress, he took his seat on the floor, which is where his divination is done (on the floor) to this day.

Finally, Obarameji arrived with a retinue of pages accompanying him. After offering the traditional greetings to the Olofin, he looked round and saw the decorated throne beside the king, and went straight to sit on it.

As soon as they were all seated, Olofin asked them what they did with the melon (Elegede or Eyen) and the kola cask (Obiala in Yoruba and Ohievbee in Bini) which he gave to each of them after the last meeting. One after the other, they all replied that since they were not given to eating such things, they presented them to Obarameji whose staple food they were. Olofin then understood how Obarameji came by his regal dress.

The king then brought out his instrument of authority (Ase) and told Oguega that in spite of being the winner of the test he gave them eight days before, it was his stupidity that kept him in the poverty that made him sit on the floor. He then cursed that Oguega would always languish in poverty and rags. He finally ordained that Obarameji would always tower above his colleagues and thrive on thrones and prosperity.

HOW OBARAMEJI ENDURED IN HIS PROSPERITY

Having obtained all he wished for and more, one day, Obarameji received a visitor called Efun yemi abori bebele, who advised him to make sacrifice so that his new found prosperity might endure to the end of his life. He was told to make sacrifice with a cow, having black, brown and white colours and one goat of the same colours, to his Ifa. He was also to offer one he-goat with the same colours to Esu. He did the sacrifices. That is why Obarameji lived for so long in affluence until all his children also became very old. The grey hair on his head and body turned to be as white as cotton and his wealth sustained to the end of his life. This is the last major special sacrifice (Ono Ifa or Odiha) which every person born at Ugbodu by Obarameji, must do in order to have long life in prosperity.

THE LAST MAJOR MIRACLE PERFORMED BY OBARAMEJI

There were three bogeys from heaven which terrorised all the sixteen main towns of Yoruba land. They were called:—
1. Obuko omo Iubebe — The He-goat
2. Ejo omoni rongo — The Snake
3. Ekuku Ale, Omonimene — The Pigeon.

Ota loon ba aye ati orun jaa — They were sent to ravage the earth by the king of Witches in heaven. They caused the Death of so many men and women in various places and there was pandamonium all around. The three heavenly plunderers took their victims in mysterious circumstances and always seemed to be picking on important personalities adjudged to be the useful citizens of the towns. Incidentally, they seemed to have been given the principal assignment of bringing Obarameji back to heaven.

When they finally set out on Obarameji's trail, his own guardian angel appeared to him in a dream and warned him of imminent danger of death. Although he did not worry unduly about death, he was nonetheless still enjoying his hard-earned prosperity. He then decided to sound his Ifa through an Ikin divination. His domestic surrogates called Uroke and Oroke told him to quickly make sacrifice with a cock, a rabbit and mashed yam (Obobo in Bini Eewo in Yoruba) which sacrifice he was to carry by himself to a road junction. He was also to give a he-goat to Esu. He did the sacrifices promptly.

As he was carrying the sacrificial offering to the road junction, Esu got up and told the three evil messengers from heaven, that Obarameji, who they had been searching for, was at the road junction. The three men quickly rose up to meet Obarameji. While Obarameji was offering prayers, after depositing the sacrifice at the position, Esu also warned him of the approach of the evil killers from heaven. With that warning Obarameji quickly took to his heels and ran into the safety of his house.

Incidentally, Obuko omo olubebe forbade cock, Ejo omoni rongon forbade marshed yam (obobo), while Ekuku ale omoni mene forbade rabbit. Those were the very materials with which Obarameji made sacrifice at the road junction. When the three evil men got to the road junction, Esu again appeared to them, telling them the food on the ground was the feast which Obarameji was sending to the 200 divinities (Ihenuri in Bini and Ugba Orumole in Yoruba). Esu convinced them to eat it because Obara had to abandon the food, when he saw them approaching.

After eating the food, they remained determined to pursue Obarameji right to his house to engage him there. Meanwhile, on their way to Obarameji's house, the poison in the forbidden food had begun to react on them. On their approach to Obarameji's house, they began to drop dead one after the other. All this happened in the night.

The following morning, Obarameji came out only to discover that the three evil men were dead on the approach to his house. He then sent messages to all the sixteen monarchs of the towns that had long been under seige by the heavenly terrorists. As soon as they were all assembled in the palace of the Olofin, Obarameji told them how he procured the death of the evil men and they all rejoiced and thanked Orunmila profusely for protecting them from the menace.

CHAPTER XVIII
OKONRON — MEJI

```
I I    I I
I I    I I
I I    I I
 I      I
```

Okonron-meji performed a few important works in heaven before leaving for earth. He was called Okonron kon loun, Okonron kon Nihin. — He made divination for Araba (Obadan in Bini) and Iroko (Uloko in Bini), before they left for the world. Araba and Iroko were always cats and dogs and never saw eye to eye on any issue. At that time, Iroko was so powerful and strong that everybody dreaded him.

The diviner advised both of them to pay homage to Esu with a he-goat, a cock, an axe and a cutlass. Araba made the sacrifice but Iroko refused to do it because he considered himself strong enough to be invulnerable.

After feasting on the offerings made to him, Esu went to advise human beings how strong Iroko was for making doors. Before then, the Iroko tree looked so ferocious that no one dared to think of attacking him in any way. For one thing he is physically very strong and huge and for another, his house is the meeting ground of the elders of the night.

The intervention of Esu was to destroy the myth shrouding Iroko's image and to make him look as ordinary as any other tree. Esu even offered to lead human beings to the home of Iroko, giving them an axe with which to mow him down. The people were at first reluctant to use the axe on Iroko, but with the encouragement given to them by Esu, they made an onslaught on him.

The fall of Iroko was so great that the echo reverberated throughout the forest. When Araba heard the fall, he wondered what was happening and he was told that the great Iroko had fallen to the axe of human attack. Realising that Iroko's fate was the result of his refusal to make sacrifice, Araba congratulated himself for abiding by the advice of Okonron-meji. Araba then sang in praise of the diviner who made divination for him to overcome the menace of Iroko who was otherwise a thorn in this flesh.

When this ODU comes out of divination, the enquirer should be told that he or she has a strong and tall enemy who is seeking his or her downfall. To overcome the problems posed by the enemy, he should be told to make sacrifice with a he-goat, a cock, an axe and a cutlass to Esu.

He made divination for the Ant (Erira)

Okonron-meji also made divination for the ant before he left heaven for earth. The ant was so small that he wondered how he was going to be able to work for a living on earth. He then went to Okonronmeji, otherwise known as Okon feere and Eji feere. He told the ant that he would be given governance over all the food in the home if he could make sacrifice. He was told to make sacrifice with 2 pigeons, 2 rats and 2 fishes, in order to gain everlasting control over all household materials in the world. He made the sacrifice and left for earth.

This situation explains why the ant treads and feeds freely on all household food and materials to this day. They move freely about in the house unhindered and what to eat is never a problem to them. That is the manifestation of the sacrifice they made in heaven.

He made divination for the tree family

The last major work associated with Okonron-meji before leaving for earth was performed on his behalf by one of his followers called Efunfun Lele (the wind). At that time, all the trees were preparing to come to the World. Before leaving, they went to Okonron-meji for what to do in order to have a successful mission to the world. Since Okonronmeji was himself also arranging to leave for the world, he was busy making his own preparations. He then asked one of his subordinates called Efunfun Lele to divine for the trees. Efunfun Lele accordingly divined for all of them advising them to make sacrifice to Esu with a he-goat, to serve their heads with cock, pigeon, and kolanuts, and to serve Ogun with a cock, a tortoise, a keg of wine and roasted yam, and to serve Sango with a cock, bitter-kola and wine.

All the other trees refused to make the sacrifice with the exception of Agbon (Urua in Bini) or Royal palm. Thereafter they all left for the world.

Many years later, after they had all flourished on earth, news reached heaven that there was too much wickedness on earth. The divinities commissioned Sango to go the world to find out what was happening. Efunfun Lele (the wind) who made divination for the trees, was told to accompany Sango on his mission to earth.

On getting to the world, the heavenly commissioners discovered that many trees had been contaminated by the wicked ways of the world. One after the other the thunder and the gale force wind destroyed all the trees. When they got to the abode of the Royal Palm or Urua, he began to sing in praise of the diviner who made divination for him in heaven, recalling the sacrifice he had made and thanking him for his success on earth. The royal palm was therefore the only tree whose life was spared. That is why to this day, the Agbon (Urua) is the only tree that is insured against any attack from thunder and gales.

Okonronmeji leaves Heaven for the World

Realising that his colleagues had left for earth, he too decided to obtain clearance from God to emigrate from heaven. He went to a diviner (Awo) called Asokon deji who advised him to make sacrifice before going to receive his instruments of authority (ASE) from God. He was told to make sacrifice with a rat, a fish, a hen, a goat, a he-goat and a pigeon. He accordingly made the sacrifice and went to the divine palace to make his wishes for earth.

His original plan was to travel in the company of the gourd and the clay pot, but the awo told him to travel alone by a different route.

On his way to the world, he came across a farm. On the edge of the farm was a trap which caught an antelope that was beginning to decompose. He removed the antelope from the trap and butchered it, and set about to prepare fire in the farm to dry the antelope's meat.

As he was arranging the meat on the drier, the owner of the farm came and challenged him. He however explained that he did it out of magnanimity to prevent the meat from total decomposition. When the farmer realised the kind gesture of Okonronmeji, he thanked him and gave him one hand of the antelope, which is the part of any animal which the Ifa priest who slaughters an animal for sacrifice, takes to this day. That is why Okonronmeji is described as the Ifa who was given the free hand to prosper in life.

For this reason, the children of Okonronmeji are advised to take to farming because he came through the farm. When he was subsequently born in the world, he grew up to be a farmer but he was initially very unfortunate. He was mainly planting yams and corn, but his harvest were often devoured by animals. He decided to go for divination, where he was told to make a gown for himself having pockets all over it, stuffing them with kola nuts and bitter kola. He was to annoint his body with a chicken and to hold a walking stick called okparere in Yoruba or Osogan in Bini. He was also to collect materials from the top of two hills close to each other, as well as from the two gable ends of the house, all to be used to invoke Esu to drive away the intruding animals from his farm. He did the sacrifice accordingly.

After being appeased, Esu planted invisible traps round Okonron's farm which caught the animals one after the other. Having rid it of the intruding animals, his farm was left to flourish. He also made plenty of money from selling the meat of the intruding animals caught in the traps prepared by Esu.

With the money so realised, he decided to get married. After marriage, his wife did not have a child for a long time. However, one night the wife dreamt and saw Okonronmeji dancing about the town with a multitude following him.

She decided to go for divination to find out the significance of the dream. The Awo told her to prepare two sticks with sharp pointed ends and to get a parcel of spicy pepper (Otawewe in Yoruba and Akpoko in Bini). They were to be used to make sacrifice to Esu beseeching him to transform her hard luck to good fortune. She quickly made the sacrifice and things began to change for the better in all facets of human endeavour.

But the woman still did not become pregnant. Little did he know that the woman was a destructive and ruthless witch. These facts were subsequently revealed to him in a dream by his guardian angel who disclosed that he (the guardian angel) was responsible for making it impossible for his wife to have a child. The guardian angel told him in a poem that:

    A snake begets a snake.
    Like a witch begets a witch
    From its mother's womb
    The snake inherits the venom sac
    Just as the witch sucks
    Witchcraft from the mother's bowels.

The woman eventually left him, and soon afterwards, his parents also died. When this ODU comes out of Ikin divination, the enquirer should be asked whether there is a deceased member of his or her family who has not yet been given a final burial. He or she should also be asked whether there is a woman in their family who is not having any child. If the man has a childless wife, he should be told that the woman will surely leave him because his marriage to her was not sanctioned by his guardian angel.

After the loss of his wife and parents, he decided to change abode temporarily and he went to an Ifa priest called Kponrikpon Abidi Tirigi for divination. He was told to make sacrifice in order to avoid getting lost in the forest. He was told to give a he-goat to Esu and a pig to his Ifa and to hold 16 packets of Eko and Akara for his journey. He was also to travel with 2 dogs.

He did the sacrifice and left Ilaye Ule, his permanent abode for Ilaye Oko where he sought to retreat temporarily. Before then, but unknown to him, the journey between the two places had been a tortuous nightmare. Those travelling between the two places rather mysteriously never got to their destination and no one knew exactly what happened to them.

Half way on his journey to Ilaye Oko, his two dogs were hungry and he gave them part of the Eko and Akara to eat. As the two dogs were eating, a mysterious boa constrictor emerged from nowhere, pounced on the two dogs and swallowed them up.

Having swallowed the two dogs the boa became helpless and Okonronmeji got a strong stick and killed it. He left the serpent there and went to Ilaye Oko. When he told them what he had experienced. It was then the people realised that it was the boa constrictor that was swallowing up travellers between the two towns.

The people followed him to the spot to butcher the boa. He only took the small stone found in the boa's stomach (Iyin Osunmale) and the oil, leaving the meat for the town's people.

That singular experience launched him into fame and popularity as an Ifa priest. While in the town he was given several women in marriage.

Okonronmeji became the Head Chief of Ilaye Oko

On getting to Ilaye Oko, he soon developed a close association with the elderly diviners of the town, for doing for the town what they could not do after several years of trying. One of such awo was called Ojikutu Ogbede Sorun — Orin gbere gbere Kaaye. The man advised him to make sacrifice with a he-goat for Esu, a goat for Ifa, a Rabbit for the night and a cock for his head because he was likely to receive an elevation. He was told to beat a drum and dance outside his house. The occasion was the eve of the appointment of the Head Chief of the Town. Being a visitor, he never aspired to the headship of the town, but he made the sacrifices all the same.

After making the sacrifice, he got people to beat the gong and drums, gave Uroke to his wives and they all danced till day break. All the divine priests in the town came up to participate in the dancing.

Early the next morning, it was concluded that he was to be the next Head Chief of Ilaye Oko and there was general merriment and rejoicing.

Thereafter he recruited a number of subordinate Ifa priests, who practiced the Ifa Art in his name.

He made divination for Akpon to be able to bring peace to Ife when it was in turmoil

Once upon a time, Ife was experiencing a severe famine. There was a long drought and all the rain makers around had tried in vain to procure rainfall. Meanwhile, they heard of Okonronmeji and sent for him. He was otherwise a farmer and not vast in the Ifa art. Before answering the invitation, he went for divination and he was told to make sacrifice before leaving for Ife.

On getting to Ife, he actually saw the devastation already caused by the drought. Having got his share of the sacrifices, Esu, who was responsible for the difficulties, quickly unscrewed the rain plug from the sky and from the very evening of his arrival after merely using Iye-rosun and the appropriate incantation, the rain began to fall. It rained continuously for three days and the people of Ife began to rejoice in praise of Okonronmeji, who performed the miracle. The incantation used by Okonronmeji was that:

The battle of the heat never conquers the spoon and the spoon never breaks inside the soup.

The Salavation of Akeriwaye

Two of his subordinate priests were Shekutu Molagua, Ojo okpa akiko Iyere Re Ododi, who made divination for the mother of Akeriwaye when enemies were wishing death to the girl. The mother was told to make sacrifice with 2 cocks and she quickly did it. The cocks were used to make sacrifice to Ogun and Esu. Meanwhile, Akeriwaye was asleep one night, when an evil spirit came to her in the form of a snake to enter the room where she was sleeping. As the snake was about to enter through the door, Esu quickly released the iron bar supporting the door and it fell on the snake crushing it to death. The sound of the fall of the heavy iron object, woke up the mother and when she saw what happened, she went on her knees and sang in praise of Okonronmeji who made sacrifice for her.

When this ODU comes out of divination normally (that is if it is Ure) the person will be told that his or her mother had just made sacrifice for him or her and that it has now manifested.

If it comes out abnormally (that is as Ayeo) the person should be advised to tell the mother to make sacrifice for him or her against imminent danger or death.

The ill-fated coronation of Adeguoye

Eti Lawo moruge. Ita aare nije ata ono, were the Ifa priests who made divination for Adeguoye, the only son of the king. Adeguoye was born when his father was already very old. The Ifa priests advised Adeguoye soon after the death of his father to make sacrifice to the elders of the night with a goat and to offer a he-goat to Esu, so that he might live through the coronation ceremonies. Being a young man, he did not appreciate the significance of sacrificial offerings. He therefore could not understand why he had to make the sacrifice for what was merely a traditional ceremony.

Meanwhile, after the burial of his father, the kingmakers invited him to arrange to succeed to the throne. The ceremony was to commence with a retreat into seclusion in a secret conclave for fourteen days.

One night, the witches, who will not normally strike without giving their prospective victim advance warning, visited him and rubbed his body with their hands. The next morning he became ill. In spite of his indisposition, he still was not convinced that he should perform the sacrifice. His mother who would have been the only one to advise him was already too old to do anything. On the seventh day in the conclave, he died, but his death was not formally announced. Under the cover of a curfew (ORO) his corpse was borne to the house and the coronation ceremony was completed post-humously by his infant son, who was made the king.

When this ODU comes out of divination for a person who is planning to take up a new appointment, he should be told that there is success awaiting him but that death stands between him and the achievement of success. He should therefore make a sacrifice to the elders of the night and to Esu in order to remove the danger of death from his way.

CHAPTER XIX
IROSUN — MEJI

```
I   I
I   I

I I   I I
I I   I I
```

Very little is known of the heavenly works of Irosunmeji. He is associated with two main works and one minor one in heaven.

(1) He made divination for all the divinities before they left heaven for the earth

In heaven, he was called Akpejo Uku, that is, the man who can alter the course of death. He advised the 200 divinities before leaving heaven that on getting to the earth, they should refrain from laying down inflexible rules and regulations because — rigid laws breed avoidance and evasion. He told them to seek the support of Esu by offering a he-goat to him. They refused to do it, because they all traditionally despised the trickster divinity. Orunmila was the only one who gave a he-goat to Esu. Thereafter, all the divinities left for the earth.

As soon as they settled down on earth, the first decree they enacted was that as soon as any of them grew grey hairs, that divinity should return to heaven.

In consonance with the decree, whoever had grey hairs died in turn. Eventually, it was Orunmila's turn to have grey hairs. As soon as grey hairs became prevalent on his head, the other divinities reminded him that it was his turn to die. He agreed with them that it was indeed time for him to return home to heaven.

Meanwhile, he sounded his Ifa, who advised him to make sacrifice with a he-goat to Esu. He was also to grind dried water yam mixed with ashes and tie the powder in a bag, made from the raffia palm, to the main entrance to his house. Thereafter, he was to serve Ifa with a pig and to feast all the remaining divinities with it. He made all the sacrifices and preparations as he was advised.

Then came the day of the feast which was supposed to be the send-off party for him before leaving for heaven. Traditionally, it is forbidden to enter the house of any of the divinities with a cap on the head. As soon as any of them got to the entrance of Orunmila's house, he had to remove his cap and at that point, Esu would rub the visitor's hair with the powder inside the bag at the entrance and he would go instantly grey. He would place his cap back on his head after crossing the entrance. That ritual was done to each of the visiting divinities, but unknown to them all.

As soon as the feast was over, they all asked Orunmila when he was going to die. He replied that he had completed his arrangements to die that very night because he was very pleased to participate in the mass death that was about to take place. They wondered what he meant by mass death, since he was the only known divinity slated to die. He then explained that since he was not the only one who had got grey hairs, he concluded that all of them would have to die simultaneously. He told them to remove their caps from their heads and they all discovered to their amazement that everyone in the chamber had gone completely grey.

In the face of the ensuing perplexity they quickly passed a unanimous resolution that from then on, only those who where old enough to die, should die. The resolution emphasised that the appearance of grey hairs on anyone's head should no longer constitute the yardstick for measuring the time of death.

That was how Orunmila changed the morbid decree of the divinities because if that law had persisted, no one would have been living for more than 40 to 50 years on earth.

He made divination for the Crocodile

While in heaven, the crocodile was often a helpless creature. He only had his mouth with which to eat, talk, and defend himself. As he prepared to come to the world, he went to Orunmila for divination on what to do to live happily on earth. He was advised to make a sacrifice with an iron saw and a he-goat for Esu. After the sacrifice was made, he was given a second mouth which was his tail made from the sacrificial iron saw. With the second mouth, he was to defend himself and to fight for his food. But he was warned not to be ungrateful to his diviner.

That is why on getting to the earth, the crocodile being an amphibian, would use his tail to beat up and weaken his victim, and then use his real mouth to drag the victim into the water. The crocodile can swallow anything but not the seeds of Orunmila (Ikin). The day he swallows Ikin, he will surely die.

He made divination for the Fish and the Rat for them to multiply

He made divination for the Rat and the Fish with the following incantation when they were coming to earth:
Ejeji Laasun Lere, Ejeji Laasun,
Eji Lomo Eku sun Loko, Odeta,
Eji Lomo Eja sun Lomi, Odeta.
Males and Females mate to multiply
Two Rats must mate on land to beget a third rat
Two Fishes must mate in water to beget a third fish.
They wanted to find out what to do in order to multiply while on earth. He told them to make sacrifice with a hen, a pack of yams, a gourd of water, a fermented melon, (Ubobo ogiri in Yoruba and Evbarie in Bini), and all the condiments used for preparing soup.

He used the materials to serve his Ifa, beseeching him to bless their offerers with children. He also prepared vegetables for them to make soup with for their consumption, with parts of the sacrificial fowl especially the gizzards. The soup was to be consumed by them as well as their husbands. Soon afterwards, both the rat and the fish became pregnant and delivered within three months and they soon multiplied by leaps and bounds.

If this ODU comes out for a woman who is anxious to have a child, the proper leaves are collected to prepare a soup with the gizzard of the hen used for making sacrifice to Ifa, and she will surely become pregnant.

Irosun-meji — comes to the World

The Ifa priests who made divination for him before leaving heaven were called:
Ariro sowo gini gini moko,
Irawo bese leyin eran,
Oju imo kirawo matu eron se.
He was advised to make sacrifice with a cock and a tortoise to the misfortune divinity (Elenini or Idobo) and a he-goat to Esu. He was also told

to give a guinea fowl to his guardian angel. He refused to do any of the sacrifices. He then came to the world where he was practising Ifa art. When he grew up, he was so poor that he could not afford to marry let alone have a child. The hardship became so severe on him that out of frustration, he decided to throw his Ifa seeds away. Meanwhile, he had a dream in which his guardian angel appeared to him telling him that he was the one responsible for his problems because he had stubbornly refused to make the sacrifice prescribed for him. When he woke up in the morning, he decided to sound his Ifa and it was only then he realised that it was his guardian angel that appeared to him in the night.

He quickly arranged to do the sacrifice to his Ifa and gave a he-goat to Esu. His Ifa advised him to return to heaven to report back to God from whom he failed to obtain clearance in the first place. For his trip to heaven, he was told to go with a cock, a tortoise, a pack of yams, a gourd of water, a gourd of oil, pepper, okro and snuff. He collected all the things and packed them up in his divination bag (Akpominijekun or Agbavboko).

After travelling as far as the boundary of heaven and earth, he had to cross seven hills before getting to heaven. On getting to heaven, he went straight to the divine palace where he met the keeper of the Divine chamber — the misfortune divinity or Yeye Muwo, the mother of obstacles. He knelt down at the Divine chamber and proclaimed that he came in all humility to renew his earthly wishes. Yeye Muwo intervened that it was too early in the morning to make any wishes because there was no food in the house. From his divination bag, he immediately brought out his fire wood, water, oil, pepper, salt, okro, snuff and finally, the cock all of which the mother of obstacles demanded in turn, as her usual delaying tactics, but Irosunmeji was fully prepared.

Thereafter, Yeye muwo cleared him to make his wishes. Since it was forbidden to knee down on the bare floor, he knelt on the tortoise which he brought from earth. After making all his wishes, God blessed them with his Divine Mace. When Yeye muwo heard the sound of the mace she quickly finished her cooking, but before she could come out, Esu motioned Irosun-meji to leave quickly for earth.

When the mother of obstacles finally emerged from the kitchen, she asked God for the man who had been making his wishes and the Almighty Father replied that he had gone. When she queried why He did not ask the man to make bad and good wishes God replied that it was not His tradition to interfere when His children were making their wishes.

In spite of all the gifts he had given to Yeye muwo, she nonetheless left quickly in hot pursuit of Irosun-meji. As she was pursuing him, she sang:

Ariro sowo gini gini moko,
Irawo be sese le eyin eron,
Oju ima ki irawo ma tu eron ise,
Olo orire omomi duro demi buwo ooo

He replied with a refrain of the same song saying that he had already made sacrifice and his wishes, leaving nothing out. As he was singing he was racing along in fright.

When Yeye Muwo saw that she could not reach him, she stood still and stretched out her thumb and tore through his back with it. That is the hollow line running through the human back-bone, to this day, which is to constantly remind us that the only way we can escape the long hand of misfortune is by making sacrifice. With that mark, Yeye muwo proclaimed to Irosun meji — and ipso facto to the rest of humanity — never to remember his heavenly wishes on getting to earth since the eyes cannot see the back of the body and that before realising his wishes, he would have to grope in darkness for a long time and experience a lot of hardship in the process.

The pain of the injury made Irosun meji unconscious and he lapsed into a trance of utter-darkness. When he woke up, he found himself on his bed on earth. He had forgotten everything that happened before then. He however went about his business and prospered long afterwards.

The state of darkness is symbolised by the length of time that Ifa stays in palm oil before being brought to life. It also symbolises the gestation period we spend in the womb, during which we lose all recollections of what we plan to do on earth.

Irosun-meji made divination for the earthworm

The first work he did on getting back to earth was for a very beautiful woman who had been married to the Rain in heaven, a man called Ojo dudu bolojo ra le lede orun. He made divination for her and advised her to make sacrifice with a parcel of ashes, salt, the dried branches of palm tree, dried leaves, adding a he-goat for Esu. He also told her not to abandon her husband in order to avoid physical disability that could cripple her. She neither made the sacrifice nor heeded his advice not to divorce the husband. As soon as she met a more handsome man called Orun (sunshine) on earth, she despised her former husband on the grounds that his abode was too filthy, wet, and cold for comfort. She heaved a sigh of relief on meeting Sunshine saying that she had at last met the right husband. In defiance of the advice of Irosunmeji, she began to live with Sunshine, her new husband.

Not long afterwards, the home of Sunshine began to get heated up. The weather became very hot and dry. She was not used to intense heat, which made her very uncomfortable. Meanwhile, she began to avoid her new husband and left his house to look for a cooler abode. When Sunshine realised that she was giving up on him, he prepared a fire wand and with it visited her in her hide-out. When he was leaving, he told her to escort him which she agreed to do.

When they got to a very dry spot, he asked her whether anyone at home would over-hear a cry from that spot. She replied that the place was not within ear-shot. She became afraid not knowing what was going to happen next. He queried why she had left him and was ignoring him. She replied that his house had gotten too hot for her because she was not used to over-heated surroundings.

He then brought out his fire wand and set the dry leaves on the ground ablaze. The fire soon spread and surrounded her. As she was about to be consumed by the fire, she remembered her former husband in heaven (Rain). She begged Rain to save her from the fire unleashed on her by Sunshine with the following poem:—

Ojoo Arata Ojo
Uno kpikpa beleje o
Ojo Arata ojo
Ojo dudu bolojo
Ojo Arata ojo.

When Rain overheard her cry in heaven, he was moved with sympathy for her, and almost immediately, the rain started falling and soon extinguished the fire gutting her. The rainfall provided immediate relief and she began to rejoice.

However, in view of the sacrifice which she refused to make to Esu, she was not altogether free from danger. As she moved to return home, she did not know that there was a hole in the ground containing some burning wood inside the ground which the rain could not reach. She fell with her two feet and hands into the fire hole and her limbs got burnt. With that she lost her limbs and became crippled.

That is how the earthworm came into being and she began to crawl on her abdomen from that day. That explains why the earthworm disappears into the earth in search of wet grounds during the dry season and only happily crawls about during the rains. Thus the saying goes that a woman never appreciates a good husband until she has had cause to try a second one.

Irosun-meji begins a new life on earth

Having forgotten his wishes in heaven, he did not exactly find life easy initially. He was to grope for sometime before finding his bearings in spite of the sacrifices he had made. That was due to the effect of the curse of the mother of obstacles. He became an ubiquitous traveller moving from one town to the other for his Ifa art and practice.

During one of his travels, he married a woman called Moromokpe (Imiomotie in Bini) who was in the habit of flirting about whenever he was away from home. She however became pregnant, and during labour for delivery, she could not deliver the child. After trying everything he knew, he became perplexed. At that point, another Ifa priest called Adawara se wara, came to visit him. He was famous for making divinations and predictions that manifested instantly. When he made divination on why the woman had a difficult labour, he revealed that she had committed adultery after becoming pregnant and that she would not deliver unless she confessed her misdeeds. When the woman was questioned closely, she confessed to having affairs with two men after and during her pregnancy. After the confession she delivered the child safely.

On the 7th day, Irosunmeji again visited Adawara se wara for a Naming ceremony divination. He disclosed that he had a good child but advised that sacrifice would have to be made with a cock and a he-goat in order to minimse the problems the child was bound to encounter in life. The child was named Ifamude (Ihasainbo in Bini). As the child grew up, he prepared a boomerang (Ekpede) for himself. The Ifa priest had warned that the child should be told never to go into the forest on Sabbath days, in order to obviate the risk of seeing his guardian angel in the forest. His mother was also called Deyi.

One day, his father was away to the farm, while his mother went to the market leaving him alone in the house. Out of rascality, he climbed through the roof of the house and hid himself holding his boomerang. To his utter amazement, the goats in the house came out in different dresses belonging to his mother. Almost in unison the goats began to sing.

Uja bele bele ta ko ko
Deyi Lo oja
Eran wule ogbedo kpashe ba
Eye wule egbedo kpa seye
Uja bele bele ta ko ko.

The significance of the song is that the goats were complaining that Irosun-meji and his wife Deyi were so niggardly that they could not afford to offer any of the several goats and fowls they had in the house to their fore-bears.

Ifamude was so stunned by the incident that he quickly came down, took the father's gun at the shrine of Ogun and shot the singing goat. The remaining goats ran into the bush with Deyi's clothes which they had on.

When Deyi came back from the market, she discovered that all the goats had disappeared with all her clothes. When she saw the dead goat that could not run away, she enquired from the son what had happened and Ifamude narrated the events to her. He explained that the reason he could not pursue the goats into the forest was because it was a sabbath day when he was forbidden to enter the forest.

When the husband returned from the farm he too was told what had happened and he thanked his forefathers for sparing the life of his son in the circumstances in which he found himself. Almost immediately he got one grey coloured goat, two hens and a fish, to make sacrifice to their forebears.

When this ODU comes out of divination the subject should be told to beware of the risk of robbery and theft against him.

The benevolence of Irosun-meji

Irosun-meji was always prepared to assist anyone in difficulty. One of the beneficiaries of his benevolence was a hunter called ODE who approached him for assistance in collecting from the forest the animals he had shot in his hunting expedition. He obliged without reservation. Another was the farmer called Ogbe who also approached him for help in harvesting his crops from the farm. He also obliged without qualms. Not only did he help the hunter in collecting his game from the forest, he also helped to roast and butcher them.

While he was roasting the games, fire accidentally burnt his eyes and gave him a permanent disfigurement. Soon afterwards, while he was harvesting crops for the farmer, the rays of the sun dazzled his eyes and made them red. These two accidents blurred and affected his sight. In spite of this inconvenience, the hunter and the farmer clearly repaid him with crass ingratitude.

The two of them went to meet his lover and queried her for continuing to befriend a man who could hardly see. They wondered whether she could not get a complete man to marry.

During his subsequent visit to his lover, she began to cold-shoulder him, and finally told him that she was no longer in a position to marry him because of his occular defects. She however disclosed to him that his friends ODE and Ogbe had come to scandalise him before her.

He then appealed to his guardian angel and his head to rid him of the affliction that brought the defect to his appearance. The following night, someone appeared to him in a dream and told him to make sacrifice with a goat and some leaves with which he was to wash his head and eyes for seven days. He was to be washing his head into the water drain (Uroramen in Bini) of his house.

At the end of the head and eyes washing operation, the defects to his eyes had disappeared and he was as handsome and as presentable as ever. He then went back to the lover who was so happy to find him with his new looks. Soon afterwards they got married and became happy and prosperous ever after.

Meanwhile, he decided to deliver a curse on his ungrateful friends in the following incantation:
Ino loma kpanju ode
Orun loma kpanju ogbe

It meant that forever after, the hunter will be identified by the redness of his eyes while the farmer will always be beaten by the rays of the sun before he can derive any benefit from his farm. He lived to be very prosperous and famous.

He made divination for Airowosebo and queen mother of the Benin throne

Arigala rigala made divination for Airowosebo, the man who was too poor to afford the sacrifice prescribed for him in order to prosper in life. Airowosebo in turn made divination for the wife of the Oba of Benin when she was anxious to have a son. At that point in time, the woman had just commenced her menstruation. As soon as she entered the house of Airowosebo, he told her that she was having her monthly period, and that if she made sacrifice, she would become pregnant the following month and would bring forth a male child who would ascend to the throne of Benin. She was told to make sacrifice with a he-goat, a cock, a duck, a hen and 16 cowries. She quickly made the sacrifice.

True to the prediction of Airowosebo she became pregnant soon afterwards, and subsequently gave birth to a male child who was being groomed to become the next Oba of Benin. When his father joined his ancestors, the crown prince became the Oba of Benin.

All these years Airowosebo still could not earn enough money to make the sacrifice which stood between him and prosperity. One day, Airowosebo was passing by the Oba's palace in Benin and the Queen mother saw him in the distance. She quickly ran up to him and greeted him reverently on her knees — a most unusual occurence in Benin City to see the mother of the Oba greet anyone on her knees.

When the Oba saw his mother greeting one wretched looking subject on her knees, he sent for his mother and the man. He queried the mother for paying such unregal respects to a commoner who was demonstrably a pauper. The mother however explained that far from being a pauper, he was in fact the man who had made it possible for her to have him when his late father had no male child.

The Oba then turned to Airowosobe and asked him why he was incapable of helping himself, if he truly had the power to help others to prosper in life. He explained that he was wretched because he could not afford to perform the sacrifice prescribed for him to make decades previously by Arigala rigala. Asked what the sacrifice involved, he disclosed that it was a rat and the meat of a pig. The oba asked him whether he believed that making a sacrifice with these two animals would truly solve his problems, and he confirmed that it would do so.

Under pain of the death penalty, the oba decided to help him on the condition that he became visibly prosperous after the sacrifice. He was then given a special accommodation in the royal guest house at the Ogbe quarters of Benin City. The Oba then ordered for 200 rats and a live bush pig, which were assembled before sunset on that very day. Of course the word of the Benin monarch was law at the time. In those days there were no domestic pigs in the Benin Empire, so, a wild pig had to be fetched from the forest.

Airowosebo took only one of the rats added kolanut to it to serve his late father. There was one tree of life (Akoko in Yoruba and Ikhinmwin in Bini) in the rear court-yard of the royal guest house. He tied the pig to the tree awaiting sacrifice, the next day. That night, it rained heavily, and the pig dug up the grounds surrounding the tree. As it dug into the earth, the pig unwittingly unearthed pots of treasure apparently buried there by a departed king. After digging up the treasure pots, the pig cut the rope with which it was fastened, broke loose, and ran back into the forest.

Next morning, Airowosebo came out to inspect the pig only to discover that it had escaped, leaving behind the pots of treasure it had unearthed. The pots contained plenty of money, beads, clothes etc. He removed all the treasures into his house. He then used some of the beads to make a beaded dress, shoe, cap and neck lace for himself. He sold some of the rest and used the proceeds to buy himself a horse.

Four days after the sacrifice, he got himself dressed up in his new beaded outfit and rode on the horse to the palace to demonstrate to the oba that his sacrifice had manifested. On seeing him, the oba congratulated him and proclaimed him a proficient Ifa priest. He was then appointed as the Royal Diviner and he lived in affluence and influence ever after in the Benin kingdom.

How Irosunmeji got popularity with kingship

His association with the king of Benin brought him popularity in all the neighbouring towns and villages throughout the kingdom. He was on a divination round on one occasion when he met an Ifa priest called Adayooko, who made divination for Irosunmeji otherwise called Eleko Odere. He was told to make sacrifice with 7 rats, 7 fishes, 7 cocks, 7 hens, 1 he-goat, 1 pig, 1 goat and 3 dogs. He made the sacrifice adding N5.00.

After the sacrifice, all the obas from far and near began to send gifts to him on account of the services he rendered to them. Among the gift offerings he had were human slaves, cows, goats, money etc. That was how his prosperity became boundless.

He made divination for Olowu of Owu

Yeri Yeri, Afasho didu bora, was his nickname when he went to make divination for the Olowu of Owu. He advised the Olowu to make sacrifice in order to have power and influence. He was told to make two sacrifices one with a Ram, and the other with cow's meat, a goat, a pig, a dog, a tortoise, a duck, and a rabbit, in order to avoid having problems from a yellow woman. He made the first sacrifice but refused to make the second one — although he also made sacrifice with the cow's meat.

Meanwhile, the Armed Forces of Oyo launched an attack on Owu — an event which was a regular feature in the relationship between the two kingdoms at the time. The attacking forces from Oyo were surrounded by the Owu army and they were all taken captives. The king of Oyo then went for divination and was told to make the kind of sacrifice that the Olowu refused to make including 201 eggs, 45 rabbits and 41 gourds of oil. The king of Oyo quickly made the sacrifice.

There was one yellow woman in the town of Owu who was so powerful that her wishes were law, but had fallen out with the Olowu of Owu. The woman who felt slighted, quickly decided to make the Olowu realise how high was the price of offending her. She prepared a concoction of wine and can-wood and threw it into the power house of the Olowu of Owu, while he was asleep. The woman was in fact a witch and was only able to perform that operation psychically.

At that point, the troops from Oyo attacked Owu, and in the process massacred the entire Owu army, and took the Olowu himself captive.

When the Olowu was brought as a war prisoner before the king of Oyo, the latter agreed to let him return home to his domain. The Olowu, otherwise a very proud king, replied that he had no home to return to. He then pronounced an incantation for self immolation and he died instantly. The yellow woman, who was also captured, was used to make sacrifice to the fore-bears.

He made divination for the Eko and Akara sellers of Odere

There were two women in the town of Odere. One prepared Eko (porridge) for sale while the other prepared akara (Bean Buns) for sale. When their trade began to decline, they both decided to approach Irosunmeji for divination. At that time, he had three Ifa priests lodging with him namely Adarooko, Adaroodo and Ada toro Iyangan. They were the ones who made divination for the two women in the home of Irosunmeji.

After divination, the three Ifa priests told the women that their trade would flourish if they could make sacrifice. The Eko producer was told to make sacrifice with a hen, 2 pigeons and one snail, while the Akara producer was told to make sacrifice with a cock, 2 pigeons and one snail. They both made the sacrifices.

Thereafter, their trade became very prosperous and the two items became complementary foods, and from then on, people scarcely took Eko without akara. Alakara was a fair skinned woman while the Eleko was very pale in colour (almost white).

If danger (Aye O) is indicated at divination, the sacrifice is made with a brown or red cock, a red cloth which the person already has in the house, and pepper. Flames of fire extinguished with water are used to wash the person's face, in order to avoid a catastrophe that could make the person weep.

If it comes out normally (URE) he should be told that a light skinned woman would be coming his way, to whom he would eventually get married, and whose first born would be a baby boy. He should however be advised to make sacrifice with a goat.

If on the other hand it comes out for a person anxious to have children, a sheep is offered to Ifa and the person will surely begin to have children.

Ifa-Alaaye, takes the crown of Odere

At this stage of his life Irosunmeji had become very prosperous and his popularity had spread to the four winds. Meanwhile he had a number of other Ifa priests serving under him. One of such awos was called Ojikutu kutu gbede.

One morning Ifa Alaaye came for divination. The Awo made divination for him and told him to make sacrifice quickly because of an up-coming contest. He advised him to make sacrifice with 7 cudgells, so as to win a crown that was lurking around him. He was also to make sacrifice with 7 he-goats, one goat, one pig, one ram and his own wearing apparel, in order to survive an imminent battle. He did the sacrifice but only with 3 he-goats to Esu.

Meanwhile, it was time to choose a new King for the town of Odere, where Irosunmeji lived. The favourite choice was Ifa-Alaaye, but all eyes meanwhile turned to a man called Ogunlana. Ifa Alaaye came back to ask Irosunmeji why his name was not being mentioned in connection with the contest. He sounded Ifa and it revealed that Esu was still expecting four more he-goats from him, and to add a drum to the sacrifice. He quickly completed the sacrifice.

The following night, Esu got up and beat the drum round the town singing, Ogun dee, aya jamagere giri giri. It was a song heralding the approach of war, and the people of Odere all hid themselves in their houses. That night Ogunlana, the favoured candidate for the Kingship lost his senior wife and his eldest son. The ensuing grief and melancholy made him to lose interest in the contest for the kingship. There was also so much confusion and devastation in the town that all those who favoured Ogunlana for the contest were either dead, bereaved or mourning.

When the actual contest fell due, it was only Ifa Alaaye who was left and he got the crown and rejoiced exceedingly. He went to thank Irosunmeji with plenty of gifts in appreciation for the divination and sacrifice made for him.

The last Test for Irosun-meji

He was now a successful man revered by kings and commoners alike. He was also very prosperous. One morning, one of his domestic priests called Eyindede Eso ilu, made the traditional morning divination for him and revealed that he should make sacrifice so that his influence and popularity might not nose-dive into a bottomless precipice. He was advised to make sacrifice with a cow, a he-goat, 3 pads (Osuka in Yoruba and Ukoki in Bini) and 3 cudgells. He did the sacrifice.

Three years after the sacrifice, the king of death dug a mysterious trench stretching from heaven to the house where the children of Irosunmeji resided. The ground divinity (Ebora ile in Yoruba or Erinmwin Oto in Bini) revealed to Eji-Olorun in a dream that there was a bottomless grave under his house which could only be closed with a cow. He quickly offered the cow to the ground. Soon afterwards, there was an influenza epidemic which ravaged the town. All the children of Irosunmeji were also afflicted, but they all survived the epidemic. He then rejoiced and lived to a ripe old age before returning to heaven.

CHAPTER XX
OWANRIN — MEJI

```
I I    I I
I I    I I
 I      I
 I      I
```

The most important work done in heaven by Owanrinmeji was the divination he did for two brothers, Fefe and Ale (the wind and the ground,) when they were coming to the world. He advised them to make sacrifice in order to command the respect of all and sundry on earth. They were both told to make sacrifice with a palm frond, a parrot's feather and a sheep to their guardian angels and to give a he-goat each to Esu. ALE was very calm, patient and a very good listener. He quickly did the sacrifices. Fefe was on the other hand, very swift, rascally and full of alacrity. He was so conceited that he did not consider it necessary to make any sacrifice. They both left for the earth at the same time. On getting to the boundary of heaven and earth, they parted ways.

Ale was very successful on earth, where he became the sheet-anchor of God's living creatures. They had been told in heaven that they would live for ever if they did the sacrifice. Since it was Ale alone that made the sacrifice, it turned out that every plant and animal coming to the world had first to pay respect to him by touching its or his head on the ground for Ale. Fefe on the other hand could not live a settled life on earth. His habitation was ephemeral because he took to shuttling between heaven and earth. That is why the ground has a stable and permanent existence on earth, while the wind is not only invisible but has no known existence. His presence can only be felt but not seen.

Owanrinmeji Prepares to come to the world

On seeing that most of his elder brothers in heaven had left, he too decided that it was time to come and see what the earth was like. Those who came before him had given a situation report on what things were like on earth. He was so scared by the hard luck stories told by the others, that he decided that before coming to the earth, he had to fortify himself.

He approached an Ifa priest in heaven called Oshukpa, omo alasho Arankije, who made divination for him. He was advised to make sacrifice with 3 rats, 3 fishes, 3 goats, 3 he-goats, 3 cocks and 2 dogs as follows:
2 he-goats to Esu Obadara
1 he-goat to Esu — Jelu
1 goat to Orisa
1 goat to Ifa
1 goat for Sarah
1 dog for Ogun
1 dog for Obalifon
1 cock to Uja Atikiriji
1 cock to Osonyin
1 cock to Enimity

He was told that he was going to come across three trials while on earth and that these sacrifices were necessary in order to survive them. He was told that he would lead a prosperous life, but that Death would always be on his trail with a cudgel. Also on his life chart, was the risk of a very long and incapacitating illness. At the rear of the two trials would be the welcome air of prosperity and wealth. He made all the sacrifices.

On account of the elaborate sacrifice he made to Esu, he began to see the good effects of it even before he departed for earth. As soon as Esu ate his he-goat, he removed the skull of the dog given to Ogun and put it at the entrance to the house of the King of Death. Meanwhile, Ogun was searching for the skull of the dog he had eaten and traced it to the house of the King of Death, who at the time was away on his daily chores to the earth in search of food.

Ogun eventually saw the King of Death somewhere on earth and apprehended him. Needless to say that Ogun is stronger and more vicious than Death. Ogun accused Death of stealing and ingratitude, saying that he was not satisfied with the human meat he fetched for him through accidents every day but had also began to lust for his own (Ogun's) favourite food, the dog.

Knowing that he was helpless in a combat with Ogun, Death disappeared as he is wont to do. Ogun on the other hand, does not have the capacity to disappear. He however ran swiftly back to heaven to meet Death in his house.

When Ogun met Death in his house, he began to attack him with his matchet. Death, who is a fat and tall divinity, finding the punishment too much for him, cried out for all the dogs in heaven to be assembled. His followers collected 201 dogs and roasted seven of them right away for Ogun, who had meanwhile destroyed many lives and properties in heaven.

While Ogun was punishing Death, his wife, the Sickness divinity, was injured in the stampede and could not follow Owanrinemji to earth, as she had planned to do. It was during the furore in heaven that Owanrinmeji sneaked out of heaven on his journey to earth.

When the dust settled and Ogun had left Death in peace, Ariku and Aje (Long life and Prosperity) had the chance to accompany Owanrinmeji to the world. It is significant to observe how the elaborate sacrifices made by Owanrinmeji began to manifest themselves, by diverting the attention of the obstacles that would have disturbed him on earth. That is why the children and followers of Owanarinmeji are endowed with wealth, long life and prosperity, provided they are able to make the same sacrifice that he made before he left heaven for the earth.

Owanrinmeji ties the hands of his enemies

Just before leaving heaven, he met other Ifa priests called:
Oronkpon Tolo Tolo
Iri arimo nirin biri biri biri
Ojo kpa agbalagba Ninu oko
Ode le eerasho mu bura.

They advised him to make sacrifice in order to avoid being the victim of a conspiracy while on earth. He was to give another he-goat to Esu on the very eve of his departure. Thereafter, he made the feast with a grey coloured goat to the elderly Awos of heaven and they all gave him their blessing, promising him eternal support while on earth.

Finally, he went to God for blessing and clearance with a piece of white cloth, a big white chalk, a parrot's feather and two white kolanuts. God received the offering; and gave him His good wishes, thus clearing him formally to go to earth.

He came out of the town of Oyo and took to his art as an Ifa Priest — whilst also trading on the side-line. He was initially successful in both vocations, but his prosperity soon began to evoke envy from the more elderly Ifa priests.

The elders soon began to plot against him. They did a collective divination on what to do to dwarf the popularity of Owanrinmeji. They finally decided to go to him for divination on what to do to destory him. He told them to make sacrifice with a goat to his Ifa and a he-goat to Esu. Meanwhile Esu warned him that the sacrifice was being made against him and he reassured Esu that he had seen it during divination for them and that he knew what to do to checkmate their machinations. They did not return for the sacrifices.

Meanwhile, it was time for the annual festival of one of the deities in the town. The conspirators invited Owanrinmeji to accompany them to the ceremonies. They had dug a hole in the ground on the route to the venue of the ceremony, that is, the shrine of the deity. They expected him to take that route while they took a different route. It was customary for visitors to the shrine to come and go by different routes.

After their conspiracy had unfolded itself to him, Owanarinmeji told them that he was forbidden to visit any other shrine, other than Orunmila's but they retorted by threatening to expel him from the town if he failed to be present at the ceremony, because it was a civic obligation of all the inhabitants of Oyo.

With that threat, he decided to consult Ifa on what to do and his Ifa asked for sacrifice to him with a grey coloured goat, and a he-goat for Esu. He did the sacrifices after which he set out for the journey to the shrine, where all visitors were required to stay for fourteen days. It was customary for all of them to go in groups, but to return home severally.

On the fourteenth day, all the ceremonies were over and it was time to disperse. The conspirators told Owanrinmeji that being a neophyte, he should lead the way on the return journey home. This was how they hoped to lure him to fall into the hole they had camouflaged on the path.

As he approached the location of the concealed hole, Esu transformed the skull of the he-goat with which he made sacrifice, into an obstacle on the ground. He hit his foot against the stud installed by Esu, jumped over the hole, and continued safely on his journey home. People rejoiced with him when he arrived safely home.

Meanwhile, Esu covered the hole dug by the conspirators and prepared another one just outside the main gate to the shrine. After Owanrinmeji had long left, the conspirators decided to leave one after the other.

Without having cause to suspect the presence of another hole just outside the shrine gate, Esu had installed the he-goat's skull as a stud on the immediate approach to the hole. The first conspirator knocked his feet against the stud installed by Esu and he fell right into the hole. Esu then prepared the stud and the hole for the next conspirator, until all of them were safely inside the bottom-less grave dug by Esu.

Once the last conspirator was in the hole Esu sealed it up as if nothing had previously been there. That was how all the conspirators disappeared out of sight without the slightest indication of what happened to them. From that day, it was ordained by Orunmila that whoever goes to seek salvation from a holy shrine must do so with a clean heart, because the wicked ones may not return alive.

Soon afterwards, there was complete pandemonium in Oyo as many families began to look for their missing husbands, sons and relatives. The town decided to go for mass divination. They again went to Owanrinmeji, who after divination revealed that the King of Death had sent messengers from heaven to abduct all those returning from the shrine, who had wicked intentions. He disclosed to them that it was on account of that vision he had told them before they left for the shrine to offer a goat to his Ifa to appease the King of Death and a he-goat to Esu, to ward off the danger, but they did not return to perform the sacrifice. He also advised that to be able to buy the lives of those who were by then, too scared to leave the shrine, the sacrifice still, had to be made. The sacrifices were quickly done and it was only then that Esu cleared the way for the remaining celebrants to return safely home.

When the blizzard was all over, Owanrinmeji made a large feast at which he rejoiced with a song in praise of the priests who made divination for him in heaven; thus;

The elders of Oyo were told to make sacrifice,
But they ignored it.
I was told to make a similar sacrifice,
I listened and did the sacrifice.
I missed my steps and survived,
Because I made sacrifice.
Others missed their steps and died,
because they failed to make sacrifice.
Those who make sacrifice,
unfailingly receive salvation.

Owanrinmeji's experience as a trader

His first trial as an Ifa priest shook him so much that he thought he should give up the practice and take on a less contentious vocation. He was astonished by the enimity that success and achievement engendered in the Ifa art and practice and decided to limit his activities to trading with the following poem:

Gbi kodo Legunmaja
Gba aghen mu bo ri
Uma sho Lugobodo
Jogun fe maya
Ja ayo jere tumodon

He was trading with the water divinity, but not having made adequate preparations before embarking on it, his effort failed woefully and he lost all his money and became heavily indebted. He then approached the parrot for assistance, but the parrot told him that he too was in debt up to his neck. The parrot proposed that since no one ever agreed to give financial assistance to debtors, they should begin by both practising the Ifa art. They decided to leave Oyo for another town where they were not known.

Owanrinmeji had one good luck soap which did not help him in his trade. But when he gave it to others to use, it was quite efficacious and those who used it came back to express their gratitude with plenty of gifts. His partnership with the parrot paid off and together they succeeded in assisting several people to flourish in their trading activities. That is why the saying goes that a doctor can cure others but not himself.

Owanrin-meji tries his hands at farming

He was a successful farmer. Compared to his experience in trading, he recorded an impressive harvest. One year, he had a prolific yam harvest and as the yams were being barned, he had a disagreement with his mother. When he shared the yam barn between his two wives and his mother, the latter complained about the size of the barn allocated to the wives. He had two wives; who unknown to him, were both witches. His mother had often accused him of giving more attention to his wives than to the mother who brought him to the world. The sharing of the yam barn rekindled the grievances of the mother and she again complained bitterly. In the ensuing scuffle, he pushed his mother who burst into tears accusing him of beating her. She left the farm and cried all the way home.

When she got to the town, she met the elders holding a meeting at the town hall. They asked her why she was weeping and she explained that her son had beaten her up in the farm on account of his wives. Among the elders at the town hall were some of Owanrinmeji's deadliest enemies who also belonged to the witch cult. They had previously sought in vain to find fault with him as an excuse for condemning him in the witch club. Normally, the rule of the club is that no victim is punished without the benefit of a fair trial and conviction.

In fact it is well known that no matter however much witches may hate a person, they do not strike until the person has been tried and found guilty. For as long as the person cannot be charged and convicted, they will not touch him. In this case, his own mother had provided a prima facie case against him. Unknown to him, his two wives had long teamed up with his enemies in the witch-club to destroy him, but he had refrained from providing them any justification for doing so.

Following the public complaint levelled against him by his mother — which explains why it is important for people to resist the urge to ventilate their domestic grievances in public, for fear that some evil minded listener may amplify it in the witch-world — the matter was tabled at the next meeting of witches.

During the deliberations, his two wives corroborated the allegation of his mother and he was summarily tried and convicted, albeit, in absentia, because he was not a witch himself. He was slated to be killed. That night however, his Ifa gave him in his dream an esoteric picture of his trial and conviction. Frightened by the dream, he asked Ifa the following morning, whether the dream signalled the approach of danger and it was so confirmed. He was told to give a he-goat to Esu immediately and to refrain from going to the farm on Sabbath days until further notice — to avoid falling victim to a treacherous conspiracy. He made the sacrifice.

Meanwhile, one of his wives proposed that they should go to the farm on the next Sabbath day because there were no foodstuffs at home. That was the day he was proposing to make the sacrifice. He told the wife that he was not in a position to leave the house on that day because he was going to make a sacrifice. When that plot faltered, his enemies immediately resorted to another strategy. They invited and told him that since he often went to the forest to fetch leaves for his Ifa practice, he should be initiated into the secret cult (ORO) of the forest. He agreed to get intitiated and he was told to come along with a cock, white chalk, a parrot's feather and aligator pepper, into the forest for the initiation ceremony. He was to be led blindfolded into the shrine of the ORO cult. He immediately sounded Ifa for advice and he was told to give another he-goat to Esu, who would foil the morbid plot being hatched against him. He did the sacrifice and told the town's elders that he was ready for the initiation ceremony to the ORO cult.

On the appointed day, the Chief priest of the cult led him in a nocturnal procession from the town towards the forest shrine, amid a town-wide curfew. As soon as they left the town's precincts, they told him to stop and his blindfold was removed. They told him to stretch out his hands to touch the sky. He replied that the hands of a child could not stretch out to touch the sky. Next, they told him to clench his fist and put it into the mouth of a gourd. He again replied that the fist of an adult could not enter the mouth of a gourd.

He was then told that any neophyte to the cult, who failed to perform the two feats, never returned home alive. He was instantly pushed forward apparently to be sacrificed to the shrine. Meanwhile, Esu was poised to intervene, having installed an invisible obstacle on the ground against which he hit his foot — injuring himself — and he disappeared into invisibility. He miraculously found himself in his house.

While he was nursing the injury he sustained, the men at the shrine trailed him to his house where they met his mother and asked her for his whereabouts. She told them that he was indisposed. They pushed her over and ordered her to produce her son because she was the one who precipitated the mayhem against the son by complaining at the town hall that he had beaten her up in the farm. They told her that as a result of her accusation, the son had been slated for ritual execution.

She then knelt down to beg them not to execute her son because she had forgiven him. In the light of her passionate pleading, they told her to get the son to produce a goat to be slaughtered at the town hall for a feast to the town's elders. After the feast, they still insisted that Owanrinmeji should be properly initiated to the Forest Cult since he had seen part of the secrets of the shrine. The ceremony was subsequently completed without any incident and they gave him one parrot's feather to wear from time to time, as a staff of membership.

Eventually, they disclosed to him that his two wives were the culprits who instigated the cult of witches against him, although the catalyst was his mother's complaint. Nonetheless, it was his mother who also pleaded for his life. The witches then took one of his wives in lieu of himself and the woman subsequently died in her sleep. He eventually did away with the second wife.

When this ODU comes out during Ifa's initiation ceremony, the person is warned never to ill-treat his mother and to beware of his first two wives, if he is married, or his first two marriages because the women are likely to be witches. He should also be advised not to allow himself to be initiated into any secret cult, unless he makes the requisite sacrifice.

Owanrinmeji Takes a New Wife

> Suru La fi wa owo
> Eni to fe kpa eja lodo, kpelu awon ni lati
> fi suru kpelu e.
> The search for honest money requires patience.
> Catching fish with a net also involves a lot of patience.

These are the names of the two Awos who made divination for the princess of Ado (Omo ewi Ado) when she was going to commence the trading business. She was told that she was the wife of Orunmila, who alone would help her to succeed in the business.

Meanwhile, Owanrinmeji visited the palace. He was attracted to the princess and asked the Ewi of Ado (the girl's father) to give her to him in marriage. The Oba responded that he would raise no objection if his daughter agreed to marry him. The Oba offered to give Owanrinmeji a chieftaincy title if he succeeded in making his daughter's trading business to flourish. Owanrinmeji however promised to help the girl, but declined the offer of a chieftaincy title.

At that point, the Ewi invited his daughter to sound her on the marital proposition of Owanrinmeji. When the princess was asked if she would agree to marry Owanrinmeji, she readily confirmed that she was interested in him and would agree to be his wife. There were several other admirers in the town who had been having their eyes on the princess. As soon as the news went round that the Oba had betrothed his daughter to Owanrinmeji, they reacted by deciding to stop paying homage and respects to the Oba.

On getting home, Owanrinmeji asked Ifa how to make the princess succeed in her trading business. Orunmila advised him to make sacrifice with 16 pigeons, 16 ducks, 16 guinea fowls, 16 bags of money, 16 pieces of cloth, 16 parcels of soap and a he-goat to Esu.

Owanrinmeji began the sacrifice by giving a he-goat to Esu. He collected the relevant leaves from the bush and used four each of the things prescribed for the sacrifice to prepare a soap dish. He left the 12 remaining pigeons to be reared at home. He gave the soap to the princess to be used for bathing.

The following day, she travelled to Oja Ajigbo mekon. Before arriving at the market Esu had collected all the valuable wares onto a central stall in the market. Having done that, Esu also went round with a bell in hand, announcing throughout the market that the princess of Ado had beautiful and durable wares for sale. She sold all the merchandise at supernormal profit and those who could not buy from her wares beseeched her to come with more wares on the next market day.

That was how her business flourished until she eventually became richer than her father. She was a lovely wife to Owanrinmeji and they had several children between them.

Owanrinmeji checkmates the machinations of his enemies

He soon began to wonder whether there was justification for all the problems he was getting from his enemies. He therefore decided to go for divination on what to do about it. He went to an Ifa priest called Alakpata Abiye gongonron, to find out what to do to tie the hands of his enemies. He was advised to make sacrifice with 3 rats, 3 fishes, one goat, one he-goat, 10 snails and cow meat. He was to use the jaw bones and the tongue of the cow, and the relevant leaves were to be added, for preparing an ASE with the incantation that the cry of a cow does not assemble a conference of human beings. This is the Ase with which Owanrinmeji neutralised the evil plans of his enemies and it is one of the important preparations for the children of Owanrinmeji.

Owanrinmeji on the threshold of Prosperity

Among the awos who visited him during the feast that went with the sacrifice made with the cow was a powerful priest called Osomusore Abira fiun. When the feast was over, it was that awo who split the last kolanut (Obitayen). After throwing the kolanut on the ground, he told Owanrinmeji that there was going to be a heavy rainfall which was bringing wealth to him from heaven, because his prosperity was still outside.

He was advised to make yet another sacrifice with one pig, one pigeon, 8 eggs, 2 hens and one cock. He again made the sacrifice to the night, Ogun and Esu. One month after making the sacrifice, a very heavy rain fell. Thereafter the pregnancy of his wife which had not developed for several months, suddenly matured and she delivered shortly afterwards. The rain fell throughout the night, and in the morning, three persons came through the rain to visit him.

The visitors complained of being hungry. He told his wife to arrange for pounded yam to be prepared for them. Later that afternoon, Owanrinmeji went out to visit his friends, but before he returned home, one of the three visitors died. The next day, another one of the visitors died and the third one also died on the fourth day. He buried each of them.

However, the visitors had come to Owanrinmeji's house with loads of treasures, which were left behind in the house, after their deaths. One of them had a luggage of beads, the second had a load of clothes, while the third had a load of money. It was clear thereafter that the expected gifts from heaven had arrived, but Owanrinmeji did not know about the parcels.

It transpired that the visitors had been in the rain for five days, during which no one agreed to give them shelter. Following the deaths of the visitors, he invited the awo who made the divination for him to perform another divination on the significance of these events. Without any previous knowledge of the facts, the Awo told him that he had three parcels of money, beads and clothes in his house. That was how he knew that the parcels existed in his house. He quickly organised a search and found the parcels in the room occupied by the strange visitors. He then thanked the Awo who made divination and sacrifice for him and gave him a share of the gifts amidst general rejoicing. That was how prosperity came to him.

Owanrinmeji becomes famous through his son

Owanrinmeji had a singular dislike for the chieftaincy institution. He had on a number of occasions stoutly rejected offers of chieftaincy titles. Since the conferment of titles was the high-water mark of prosperity and popularity at the time, he was relatively socially unknown. His marriage to a princess however, brought him to the threshold of societal luminance.

Meanwhile, an itinerant Ifa priest paid a routine visit to the home of Owanrinmeji. As was the tradition, the visitor had to make divination for him. The visitor was called Aiya Oshuru gongon gagbon. He told Owanrinmeji that his son was going to become the Olowu of Owu. He was told to avoid becoming temperamental and to persevere so that his son's fortune might not be shattered. He was advised to make sacrifice with 2 dogs, 3 he-goats, 3 goats, 3 pigs, 8 rats, 8 fishes, and 8 snails. He made the sacrifice. Ultimately, the son became the Olowu of Owu.

Subsequently, he travelled to Owu. The Olowu of Owu had meanwhile, made divination on what to do to prosper to the end of his life. He was told to make sacrifice to the head of his mother with a goat and a pig so that his mother might not upset his prosperity. He got the goat but could not get a pig to buy. The mother took the goat but did not serve her head with it. Instead, she bought a hen to serve her head. The next day, she stealthily took the goat to the market, sold it, and kept the money.

Subsequently, the Olowu succeeded in getting a pig. He quickly took the pig to his mother to serve her head, but the mother retorted that no one served the head in broad day-light but by night. With that, the Olowu returned to his palace in the hope that his mother would serve her head with the pig at night time. The mother again did not serve her head with the pig. Instead, she used a dog which she slaughtered to use for preparing a meal for her husband.

She served the food to her husband in the night, when it would be difficult to recognise the dog meat. As her husband sat down to eat the

food, the son's wife told him not to eat it because she felt the smell of a dog in the food. Remembering the warning he had been given not to lose his temper in the face of provocation, he ignored the wife's action, wondering what her intentions were.

The following morning his wife (Olowu's mother) invited her husband to empty the container with which she had passed human waste in the night. He refused to do it with the explanation that although he gladly did it for her when she was a bride, he did not think he should repeat it when they were both already old. He then accused her of provoking him the previous evening by trying to feed him with dog's meat, which he would have eaten but for the vigilance of his daughter-in-law. His wife retorted by calling him the son of a dog. This annoyed him so exceedingly that he did not have the peace of mind to perform what he came to do for his son.

Nonetheless, he told his son to bring his divination instrument (Ikin) as a result of which he told the son that he was required to serve his (the father's) head with an elephant, a buffalo, and a tiger. He quickly ordered all the hunters of Owu to go into the forest to fetch these animals. Before noon they returned with the young ones of the three animals. Owanrinmeji extracted some blood from the skins of the three young animals and released all three of them to return to the forest.

With the blood so extracted, he prepared a medicine for his son to mark on his body. On arrival at Owu, Owanrinmeji had observed that his son, the Olowu, did not prostrate to greet him, as tradition demanded. All the same he did for his son what he had to do, in spite of the embarrassment he got from mother and son.

As he was preparing to return home, he brought out his divine instrument of authority (ASE) and proclaimed that from then on, the pure citizens of Owu would always prosper but that their prosperity would only get to the evening of their lives after receiving from their wives and children the kind of treatment he got at Owu. It is believed that as a result of this curse pronounced by Owanrinmeji, the wealthy and successful sons and daughters of Owu may find it difficult to live to a ripe old age without making the special Ifa sacrifice for revoking the curse.

It is also believed that this curse is responsible for the fact that the Alake of Abeokuta, who was the son of the daughter of the Olowu, has since become more influential than the Olowu of Owu. It was the crown of Olowu that was subsequently given to the Alake of Abeokuta which, explains why the Olowu is said to have had no crown.

The Last major work of Owanrinmeji — He saved the favourite wife of Olofen from the evil machinations of her mates

The king of Ife had many wives but one of them held the key to his heart. This naturally evoked the envy and hatred of her mates. They succeeded in using diabolical means to render her barren. That was why the king invited Owanrinmeji to come to his palace at Ife to help his favourite wife to have a child. The woman was called Eninikpola.

On getting to Ife, he made divination for the woman, advising her to make sacrifice with a dog and a cock to Ogun and a he-goat to Esu. She was advised not to allow anyone to see the animals before the sacrifice was made.

With the excitement of making the sacrifice, she forgot the aspect of secrecy associated with the sacrifice. After buying the sacrificial animals, she kept them in the open courtyard of the palace harem. Meanwhile, the king's tiger disappeared and was nowhere to be found. A proclamation

had gone out for the tiger to be returned live to the palace.
It was at that point that she made her sacrifice. As was the tradition, the heads of the sacrificial victims had to be left on the shrine of the divinity served. After offering the sacrifices to Ogun and Esu, the heads of the he-goat, dog and cock were left on the two shrines. All these things were done to the full knowledge of her mates.

Later that night, the mates arranged to obtain the head of a freshly slaughtered tiger and deposited it on the Ogun shrine, thus preparing the grounds for accusing Eninikpola of using the king's tiger for ritual sacrifice.

Next morning, after seeing the head of the tiger on Ogun's shrine, the mates went to report to the king that someone had used his missing tiger to make sacrifice. He asked from all the women of the harem and all the accusations pointed to his favourite wife. He then invited her for questioning; accusing her of killing his tiger and warning her that the penalty was death. She was quickly bound in chains.

Meanwhile, Esu had transfigured into a do-gooder who removed the tiger's head from the shrine, replacing it with the dog's head. During the ensuing adjudication, Esu influenced one of the Olofin's counsellors to propose to the king that before condemning the woman, the offence should be verified and the tiger's head produced. Agreeing with the plausibility of the suggestion, the king appointed two persons to go to the Ogun shrine and come back with whatever they saw there. They brought in the severed heads of the dog and the cock.

At the sight of what they brought, Eninikpola confirmed that those were the heads of the dog and the cock with which she made sacrifice to Ogun. When asked what was the purpose of the sacrifice she made, she explained that it was made to enable her have a child.

She was instantly unchained. An investigation was conducted to find out the origin of the Tiger's head allegation and the woman who contrived the conspiracy was summarily executed.

At the end of that month, Eninikpola became pregnant and subsequently gave birth to a male child. She eventually rejoiced and thanked Owanrinmeji for solving her problem.

He makes divination for two wives of the same husband

Akiriboto had two wives, who had a quarrel, A few days after the quarrel, the child of the junior wife (Iyawo) became ill. As the child was about to die, they went for divination to Owanrinmeji, who asked a visting Awo to make divination for them. The Awo was called:
Akitikpa Odigba mu Uroko — The rope held Iroko
Uroko Odigba mu Akitipa — The Iroko held the rope.

He asked the senior wife (Iyaale) to narrate how she discussed the dispute between herself and her mate with a friend on her way to the market.

She quickly recalled that one market day, after a misunderstanding with Iyawo, she decided to go to the market with a friend. After telling her friend how Iyawo offended her, the friend advised her to forgive the young woman because she was still too inexperienced to appreciate the enormity of her actions.

The Awo told her that the witches were incidentally, holding a meeting on top of the Iroko tree by the side of the market road at the time she was narrating the story to her friend. It was before she got home from the trip to the market that her mate's child became ill, because the witches had intervened in the matter.

The Awo told them to make sacrifice to the night with a rabbit to be dug out at the foot of the Iroko tree on the way to the market. He advised them to go to the foot of the Iroko tree where they would find a small hill, which had a rabbit in a hole by its side. He advised them to dig for the rabbit, kill it and use it for the sacrifice. They actually did as they were told and they killed the rabbit and used it for the sacrifice. Soon afterwards, the sick child became well.

When this ODU comes out of divination for a woman, she should be advised to refrain from narrating her domestic quarrels, especially with her mate, on the way to the market. If it comes out for a sick child, it is clear that the sickness was caused by a quarrel his mother had with her mate. They should be advised to make sacrifice with a rabbit to the elders of the night.

CHAPTER XXI
OGUNDA-MEJI
EJI-OKO
OGUNDA JA MEJI

```
 I      I
 I      I
 I      I
 I I    I I
```

Ogunda meji was one of the most powerful diviners both in heaven and on earth. He is reputed to have combined the strength of Ogun and the intelligence of Orunmila in his work. He was the one who revealed the story of the second attempt made by the divinities to inhabit the earth. Obara bodi, one of the disciples of Orunmila will later reveal the details of the first attempt to inhabit the earth and how it was founded.

Ogun, the iron divinity and the most senior of the divinities created by God, was also physically the strongest of all the 200 divinities. He is often referred to as the Path — finder, because he led the second reconnaisance mission from heaven to the earth. We are told by Ogunda-meji that it was on account of the physical attributes of Ogun that God appointed him to blaze the trail for the second habitation of the earth. He is known to be self-centred and conceited and scarcely ever consults anyone else for advice. He relies almost exclusively on his manufacturing skills and physical strength. That explains why he never bothered to go for divination or to consult anyone else when he was nominated by God to undertake the task of establishing a habitation on earth. As soon as he received the marching orders from God, he proceeded almost immediately. God gave him 400 men and women to accompany him on the mission. On getting to the earth, it took no time before he discovered the consequences of not making adequate preparations before departing from heaven.

His mortal followers soon became hungry and demanded food to eat. Since they did not come to the world with any food-stuffs, he could only advise them to cut sticks from the surrounding forest, to eat. The process of feeding on sticks gave them no satisfaction and very soon many of his followers began to die of starvation. Apprehensive of losing all his followers to death by starvation, he decided to return to heaven to report mission impossible to the Almighty Father.

God next invited Olokun, the water divinity to lead a second mission to earth. He too is equally proud and full of self-confidence. He was also given 200 men and 200 women to accompany him on his mission. He neither did any consultation nor divination with the heavenly elders before leaving for the earth. On getting there, he too had no clue on how to feed his followers. He only asked them to drink water when they became hungry. Since water could not feed them effectively, they began to die of starvation. Soon afterwards, he too returned with his surviving followers to heaven to report the failure of his mission.

God then invited Orunmila accompanied by 200 men and 200 women to found a habitation on earth. Orunmila pondered whether he could succeed on a mission which had defied the efforts of more senior and stronger divinities like Ogun and Olokun. God persuaded him to try his utmost, because it was necessary to depopulate heaven by establishing a satellite habitation on earth. His faithful servant Okpele advised Orunmila not to decline the assignment because with adequate preparations, he was convinced that success awaited him.

With the coaxing words of his favuorite Okpele, Orunmila agreed to embark on the mission but appealed to God to grant him the indulgence to prepare for a few days before setting out. Orunmila approached the elderly diviners of heaven to assist him in planning for his mission. They assured him that he would succeed in founding a living on earth. Ogunda-Meji, one of his own children asked him for six cowries and advised him to collect one each of all the known plant and animal foodstuffs in heaven for the mission. He also advised him to give a he-goat to Esu and to appeal to Esu to follow him to earth on the mission.

After making all the sacrifices prescribed for him to make, he went for final clearance from God. Before leaving he begged God to allow Ule, (Owa in Bini) the Dwelling divinity, to go with him. But God told him that it was not His divine intention to dispatch two divinities to earth at the same time since He intended to send them one after the other. God however assured Orunmila that if he succeeded on earth, he should dispatch his servant Okpele to return to heaven to fetch Ule (Owa) to assist him. He then left for earth.

As soon as Orunmila set out, Esu went to tell Ogun that Orunmila was travelling to earth through the route which he (Ogun) established. Ogun immediately went to block the route with a thick forest. When Orunmila's party came to the forest, they did not know what to do next. He sent the rat to find a path through the forest. Before the rat returned, Ogun appeared to Orunmila and queried him for daring to proceed to earth without informing him. He however explained that he had sent Esu to inform him and when Ogun remembered that it was Esu who actually came to alert him, he quickly cleared the forest for Orunmila to proceed on his journey. Before leaving him, Ogun told Orunmila that the only other obligation he owed him was to feed his followers with the sticks as he did and Orunmila promised to do so.

Meanwhile, Esu also went to report to Olokun that Orunmila was on his way to earth to succeed where he failed. Olokun reacted by causing a wide river to block Orunmila's advance. When Orunmila came to the bank of the river, he dispatched a fish to find a passage through the river. While waiting for the fish to return, Olokun appeared to him and queried why he dared to embark on a trip to earth without obtaining clearance from him.

Orunmila explained that far from slighting Olokun, he had in fact dispatched Esu to inform him of his mission to earth. When Olokun realised that Esu had in fact came to him he cleared the water for Orunmila to proceed on his journey. He however warned Orunmila that he was under divine obligation to feed his followers like he (Olokun) did, with water. Orunmila promised to abide by Olokun's advice. With no more obstacles in his way, Orunmila proceeded on his journey to the earth.

On getting to the world, he quickly advised all his male followers to clear the bush and to construct temporary huts roofed with mats (Aghen). When that assignment was completed, they brought out the crops and seeds he brought with him for his followers to plant in the bush they had cleared. At dusk, they all retired to sleep in their respective huts. Esu, who had been given a he-goat before the mission left heaven, went to work on the planted seeds and the animals. When they woke up at sunrise; they discovered that all the crops had not only germinated, but had brought forth fruits, ready for harvesting. These included yams, plantain, maize, vegetables, fruits etc etc. At the same time, all the livestock they brought from heaven had multiplied over night. That was the first miracle performed by Orunmila on earth, as a direct manifestation of the sacrifices he made before leaving heaven.

When his followers then asked for food before embarking on the day's chores, he told them in deference to Ogun's injunction, to cut sticks from the surrounding bushes to eat. They did as they were told. After chewing the sticks for a long time, he told them to drink water as he was enjoined to do by Olokun. The process of abiding by the instructions given to him by Ogun and Olokun, is carried out to this day by all humanity, through the routine of beginning the day with the chewing of sticks or brushing of the teeth and rinsing of the mouth with water.

Having deferred to the wishes of his elders, Orunmila told his people to feed themselves on the plants and animals that abounded in the settlement. They had succeeded in setting the stage for a permanent habitation on earth. Satisfied that nothing then stood in their way to succeed on earth, Okpele next proposed to Orunmila that it was time to send him to inform God that the earth was already adequately habitable enough for Ule to join him. Orunmila agreed, but told him that he should first invite Esu to join him on earth before asking for Ule. Having previously promised to join him as soon as he was invited, Esu readily agreed to accompany Okpele to earth.

Before arriving, Orunmila asked his followers to build a hut for Esu at the entrance to the settlement. As soon as Esu settled down in his quarters, Orunmila sent a he-goat to him. He was very happy to feed on his usual staple food, which he thought would not be available on earth.

When Okpele came to check whether Esu was alright, the latter told him to beg Orunmila to forgive him on account of the initial difficulties he created for him before he left heaven by inciting Ogun and Olokun against him. Orunmila forgave him and implored Esu to stay on earth to be his listening post, promising to feed him always.

After waiting in vain for Orunmila to fail and to return to heaven with his followers, Olokun decided in heaven to return to earth to find out how the mission was faring. When Olokun got to the earth, he met Esu who told him that Orunmila had succeeded in making the earth habitable. When Olokun got to Orunmila, he asked for forgiveness on account of the initial obstacles he created for him. Orunmila told him that the apology was not necessary because success is not gratifying without initial difficulties. Orunmila however told Olokun to agree to live with him on earth. He agreed to do so but insisted that he would have to go to heaven to request the Almighty Father to permit him to come back with his followers. Olokun got to heaven and God cleared him to return to earth with his followers.

When Ogun heard that Olokun had left to join Orunmila on earth, he too decided to go and see things for himself. When Okpele saw Ogun leaving heaven for the earth, he alerted Orunmila who immediately instructed his followers to give another he-goat to Esu to avoid any clash between Esu and Ogun. By the time Ogun arrived, Esu was still eating his he-goat and was too busy to annoy Ogun. He merely motioned Ogun to proceed to where Orunmila lived. As soon as Orunmila saw Ogun, he went on his knees to greet him, being his eldest brother.

Ogun retorted by apologising to Orunmila for the ihitial difficulties he created for him. Once again, Orunmila explained that the apology was scarcely necessary because without that teething problem, he would probably have had no clue on how to feed his followers. Orunmila then persuaded Ogun to stay with him on earth, because without him (Ogun) it was impossible for any technology to develop on earth. Orunmila explained that he only knew how to make divination but not how to invent or manufacture. Feeling flattered, Ogun readily agreed to return to heaven to obtain clearance from God to come back with his followers to earth. Ogun eventually come back with his followers.

It was at that stage that Orunmila finally sent Okpele to fetch Ule from heaven. When Okpele narrated Orunmila's message to God, the Almighty Father instantly invited Ule to proceed to earth to join Orunmila. Esu was again the first agent that Ule met on getting to the earth. Esu directed him to meet Orunmila in his hut. Far from challenging Ule like he did Olokun and Ogun, Esu prayed for Ule that he would forever be more successful than all his elder brothers and without him, no one would have full satisfaction on earth.

That was because he was characteristically patient and inoffensive. When Ule met Orunmila, he paid respects to him for making it possible for him to come and join him on earth.

Orunmila retorted by proclaiming with his instrument of authority (ASE) that:—
  (i) Whatever respect was given to him, should always be extended to Ule;
  (ii) Olokun would always reside in water in view of the river he used to block his approach to earth, but that he should be the dispenser of wealth and prosperity to mankind.
  (iii) Ogun should always be used to perform great achievements but that he himself would always restlessly work night and day and have no peace of mind.

He then told the three of them to go their separate ways. The three of them left Orunmila's chambers. They had scarcely moved away from Orunmila's apartment when Ule suddenly dropped dead. As soon as he dropped dead, his corpse vanished out of sight and in its place a constellation of houses, halls, and dwelling apartments appeared on the ground. Thus, Ule had transfigured into respectable dwelling houses for all the existing and future inhabitants of the earth to live in.

Orunmila instantly left his mat-roofed hut and went to stay in the best palatial apartment provided for him by Ule. Ogun was annoyed and refused to stay in any of the apartments provided by Ule. He then built his own ramshackled house called Izegede which is where he stays to this day.

Olokun also felt challenged and turned into water to constitute the oceans, seas and rivers of this earth. The men and women brought to the earth by Orunmila, Olokun and Ogun soon began to intermarry and multiply to spread to the four winds of this earth. It is important to remember that the off-springs and subsequent reincarnations of the followers that initially came with Orunmila, Ogun, Olokun and other divinities to the earth, became the priests and children of these divinities, to this day and to eternity. Those who veer away from the flocks, or who are not privileged to discover their kindred, are the men and women who run into all kinds of difficulties on earth.

At that stage, Okpele left for heaven but told Orunmila to look for him after sometime on the way to the farm. He eventually turned into a tree whose fruits are used to this day to prepare the Okpele divination instruments. Okpele told Orunmila how to use the seeds he would bring forth for Divination.

The Heavenly works of Ogundameji:

In heaven he was called Eji-oko. He made divination for the tiger with this incantation — Onoshe muroko nijo to onlo oko ode — when the tiger wanted to commence hunting. He advised the tiger to make the following sacrifices; to give he-goat to Esu, and to serve Ifa with hen, fish and rat, so that he might be able to hunt successfully. The sacrifice was necessary to avoid hunting in vain, or suffering a set-back called — (Amubo in Yoruba and Osobonomasunu in Bini). He refused to make the sacrifice.

The following day, he left for the forest to hunt. The tiger has two idiosyncrasies. When any heavy object falls behind him, he instinctively runs away in fright. Secondly, when he jumps over any animal he has killed, he is forbidden to eat the animal. On getting to the forest, he saw an antelope and he killed it by drinking its blood. As soon as he released the antelope to fall to the ground, he heard the sound of a tree-branch which fell behind him. Out of fright, he jumped over the antelope and instantly abandoned it.

Next, he killed a black antelope called Edu in Yoruba and Oguonziran in Bini. Once again, the heavy bunch of a ripe fruit dropped from the tree behind him and he jumped over the prey, leaving it behind him. By this time, the tiger was becoming tired and hungry not having eaten anything since morning. As the sun was about to set, he was preparing to leave for home when he saw a deer. He again succeeded in killing the deer but just before reaching for it, a bunch of palm fruits fell to the ground behind him and he again jumped over the deer and he had to abandon it. He became hopelessly frustrated and left for home. Esu was obviously responsible for his unusual misfortune.

On his way home he sighted a rabbit and pursued it until the rabbit entered its hole. As the rabbit was entering the hole, the tiger held on to its tail and began to drag it. But the rabbit stuck its nails to the hole so firmly that the tiger only succeeded in unskinning the exposed lower end of the rabbit's tail. The rabbit then pulled free into the safety of its hole. That is why the lower end of the rabbit's tail is white to his day, which distinguishes it from other mammals of its size. This last incident got the tiger to draw a correlation between his failure to make sacrifice and his abortive hunting expedition.

On getting home, he reported his fruitless venture. To determine the veracity of his story a search party went into the forest and actually saw and brought home the three animals killed by the tiger. The animals were brought to Ogunda meji. It was then that he went to Ogunda meji to make the sacrifices.

After performing the sacrifices he went to the forest the next day and killed a deer which he brought home without any incident. From then on, the tiger became a skillful hunter and he went to express his gratitude to Ogunda meji.

He made Divination for the Boa:

After creating the various species of the snake family God distributed weapons to each of them in the form of poison but forgot to give any to the boa, who is called Oka in Yoruba and Aru in Bini. The boa began to starve because he lacked the weapons with which to fetch food to eat. He then went to Ogunda meji for divination to advise him on what to do to overcome his difficulties. The Arrow was one of the surrogate priests living with Ogunda meji and it was the Arrow who made divination for the boa. The Arrow's full name was Okofi doo, Oko reyin ya bo olooko — Odafa fun Oka, elewu-obobo meaning — The Arrow with which the boa kills an animal returns to its stomach. The boa was described as the velvet skinned reptile.

The Awo advised him to make sacrifice with three tiny arrows, kolanuts, and a hen. He brought the materials the next day and the Awo used the hen to serve Ifa for him. With the blood of the hen, leaves and iyerosun, the Awo prepared a medicinal portion for him to swallow. He was also advised to go with the kolanuts and serve his head with it by the roadside. He was to abandon the parcel of kolanuts at a conspicuous place by the roadside and to conceal himself in the bush nearby to watch for anyone who will pinch the kolanuts. He was to hold on to the three arrows. He was advised against the risk of uncontrollable temper, which explains why the boa remains the most patient snake to this day.

That day coincided with the day that God was going to attend the meeting of the divinities which traditionally began with the breaking of kolanuts. God forgot to hold any kolanuts when he left home. He was accompanied by his favourite servant, the rabbit who held his divine bag (Akpominijekun or Agbavboko).

When God saw the parcel on the road, He asked the rabbit to pick it up. He was relieved to see that it contained kolanuts which he forgot to take from home. As the kolanut was being put in the divine bag, the boa came forward and wondered why God should also take his food when he had forgotten to give him any poison. He complained that he had been starving because he lacked the weapons with which to fight his food.

God immediately sympathised with him and explained that he did not forget him. He told the rabbit to bring out whatever remained in the divine bag, and he came out with an ASE. The boa had explained that Orunmila prepared three arrows for him and God took the arrows from him and blessed them. After blessing them God directed the boa to open his mouth to swallow them. After swallowing the three arrows, God told him that whenever he saw any victim, the arrows would automatically come out to his nostrils and he should shoot them at the victim. He was not to run after the victim but to wait on the spot, for it to return to him. He should then swallow the victim and the arrow would return to his stomach for subsequent use.

Before leaving the boa, God introduced the rabbit to him and warned him never to use his weapons on the rabbit. When God arrived at the venue of the conference, he discovered that they had left the divine bag behind at the spot where he gave weapons to the boa. God was reluctant to despatch the rabbit to fetch the bag, for fear that the hungry boa might be tempted to use the newly acquired weapons on him. But the rabbit assured God that he would discreetly collect the bag without provoking the boa.

When the rabbit got there, he started teasing the boa. He accused him of being lazy for remaining on one spot, when he was supposed to move around in search of food. The rabbit teased the boa so tantalizingly that he even began to drag the boa's tail; which the latter forbids. Overcome with temper, the arrows in his stomach moved to his nostrils and he struck them home to hit the rabbit, who then quickly removed the divine bag and ran back to meet God at the conference.

When the rabbit got back to God, he reported that he had been attacked by the boa. God told the rabbit that he must have provoked the boa to incur his wrath and advised the rabbit that true to his proclamation, he (the rabbit) should return to the boa to die. The rabbit struggled back to that spot and died as soon as he got there and the boa swallowed him up. This incident reassured the boa that the weapon given to him by God was effective indeed. He then became very happy.

At the end of the meeting, God had to carry his bag home by Himself. On getting to the spot where the boa lay, he saw the boa who instantly prostrated to thank the Almightly Father for the assistance given to him. God however queried him for contravening his order not to attack the rabbit, his servant, and the boa explained how he was provoked by the rabbit. God told him that he was prepared to forgive him on that occasion because he acted on provcation.

God however proclaimed that from then on, the boa himself would die on the very day he attacked and killed any rabbit. God then appointed the squirrel to be chronicling the location of the boa as a means of warning animals that the boa was around. As soon as God left, a swarm of squirrels surrounded the boa and began to shout at him with the words:

Okaa reeoo — Elewu Obobo
Waa wooo — Elewu Obobo

Since that day, the squirrel has become the bitterest enemy of the boa.

He made Divination for ODE

Ode is the Yoruba word for the exterior, that is, outside courtyard of the house. There was a time in heaven when there was famine and everywhere became dull. People became too hungry to engage in outside chores, and ODE was very ill. He managed to go to Ogunda meji for divination and he was advised to make sacrifice with 200 baskets of pepper, and ginger seeds, (Ighere in Yoruba or Oziza in Bini), 200 seeds of aligator pepper and a cock. He was also advised to give he-goat to Esu. The 200 baskets of pepper were set on fire and people ran out of their houses to fetch fresh air outside. Life soon began to bubble again outside and the people began to sing and dance.

Eji-Oko Seduces the wife of Death:

It was one of his followers called Ala boun boun lofo kpiriri kparara, who made divination for Eji-Oko when he unknowingly seduced Epipayemi, the fair complexioned wife of the King of Death. Ala boun boun was infact the wasp, who warned Ejioko to avoid having anything to do with a yellow woman who was going to be the Queen of Death. He was however advised to give a he-goat to Esu which he refused to do because he had no intention of having anything to do with a yellow woman or the King of Death.

Not long afterwards, the King of Death sent his wife Epipayemi with a bag of money to buy a he-goat for him from the market of Oja-Ajigbomekon Akira. At the same time, Eji-Oko, had, on second thought, resolved to make the sacrifice and set out for the market to buy himself a he-goat for an offering to Esu.

When Epipayemi got to the market, she bought the he-goat and a number of cooking condiments, and kept them in her stall to look for other things in the market.

Meanwhile, Eji-oko got to the market and discovered that the only he-goat in the market was the one tied up at the stall of Epipayemi. He held on to the he-goat with the determination that he would buy it from whoever owned it. Soon afterwards, Epipayemi arrived at her stall to meet a man holding on to her he-goat. She was irresistably beautiful. She told Eji-oko that she owned the he-goat because her husband, the King of Death, had sent her to buy it from the market.

Inspite of this disclosure, Eji-oko forcibly took the he-goat from her and left with it for home. Indomitably, the woman held on to its rope and struggled along with Eji-oko until they got to his house. On getting to his house, he used the he-goat to offer sacrifice to Esu and professed love to Epipayemi. It was now nightfall and it had become too late for Epipayemi to return home.

She had no option but to spend the night with Eji-oko who made love to her during the night. She however warned him of the consequences of his action because she was sure that Ejioko could not withstand the wrath of her husband.

The following morning when Epipayemi failed to return home, Death began to enquire from people who went to the market the previous day, why his wife failed to return home. They explained to him that they saw her struggling over a he-goat with one dark complexioned man believed to be one of the children of Orunmila.

Death then sent two messengers to Eji-oko to warn him that for seducing his wife, he was coming in seven days time to deal with him.

It was at that point that he remembered what the wasp told him at divination about the risk of seducing the wife of the King of Death. Knowing that he was helpless in the face of the punishment awaiting him, he decided to resign himself to it. He began to lament and stopped eating any food.

On the fifth day, Osonyin, a brother divinity of Orunmila decided to visit Eji-oko. On getting to Ejioko's house, he met him in recluse awaiting death. Osonyin told him to pluck up courage and to brace up. He volunteered to go and confront Death.

Osonyin asked Ejioko for the dress with which he used to transfigure, as well as his divination wand (Uroke) and his cap. He wore the dress and the cap, holding the wand in his hand. When Osonyin arrived at the home of Death, he quickly recognised the house because it was scrubbed daily with human blood.

On entering the house, he sat down in the sitting room and demanded to see the King of Death because he had come to pay him a visit. When Death was given the description of the visitor, he knew it was Eji-oko that sent Osonyin to come and try him. In anger, Death gave instructions for the visitor to be apprehended, executed and slaughtered into tiny pieces. The followers of Death got Osonyin thoroughly beaten and butchered into tiny bits and pieces. On Death's orders, the pieces of Osonyin's corpse were scattered at the road junction.

By the time his executioners got back to the house Osonyin was sitting down complacently waiting for them. As soon as they saw him, he insisted that they should not waste his time because he came to see the King of Death. Gripped with fright and amazement, the messengers reported to Death that the visitor was back in the house before them after they had killed and chopped him into pieces. Death ordered them to kill him again and throw his pieces into the river to feed the fishes.

Once more, they killed and chopped his corpse into very tiny bits and jettisoned it into the river. When they returned home to report mission accomplished, they met Osonyin again in the sitting room this time fuming why it was so difficult to see the King of Death. He queried whether the ferrocious Death was afraid of seeing a junior divinity.

When they reported his mysterious resurrection to Death, he told them to chop him up once more, cook the pieces thoroughly and throw them into the incinerator to be burnt into ashes. They did as they were directed, but before they got back to the house, Osonyin was once again waiting for them in the sitting room raging that he was going to gate-crash on Death if he continued to refuse to see him.

Not knowing what next to do to him, Death sent his messengers to ask Osonyin to tell his brother that he had surrendered Epipayemi to him in peace. When they narrated the message to Osonyin, he roared that if he was not to create an uproar in heaven, Death should be told to send one of his messengers to accompany him to deliver the message to his brother. Death immediately conceded and sent one of his bodyguards to accompany Osonyin to carry the message to Ejioko.

Osonyin also sent a message to Death insisting that he should bring him kolanuts. The kolanuts were quickly sent to him but Osonyin insisted that Death should have come out to split them by himself. Death eventually came out to split the kolanuts giving a piece to Osonyin, while he ate one piece himself. Osonyin went home with the remaining pieces after thanking Death for his befitting hospitality.

Back home, Ejioko was short of words with which to express his gratitude to Osonyin for his unparalleled achievement. Ejioko then invited the wasp who made divination for him to sing in praise of him amidst wining and dining.

Ala boun boun lofo kpiriri kparara and Osonyin added the refrain:
Esemi luku kpaa, Odidi mode luku kpaa Odidimode meaning;
It was not myself that Death killed but the mud image of me that Death killed because Osonyin often disappeared when the executioners of Death were killing him. With that, Ejioko held on to Epipayemi as his wife.

Ejioko's second wife:

He made divination for the cock and the parrot when they were both looking for wives to marry. He advised them to give a he-goat to Esu so that the habit of passing excreta in their bed-rooms would not deprive them of the honour of marrying respectable wives. They both argued that the sacrifice was unnecessary since it was their tradition to pass wastes wherever they slept.

There was also a beautiful maiden who went to him for divination on how to get a responsible husband to marry. She was advised to make sacrifice to avoid the misfortune of engaging in two abortive marriages before settling down in a third one. She thought that it was unnecessary to make the sacrifice because her good looks and native intelligence were enough to see her through any difficulties.

Not long afterwards she met the cock who was very good looking. She fell at once for him and agreed to marry him. She moved into his house without any delay. Thus, a couple who both refused to make sacrifice, had married in defiance of the advice of the Ifa priest. The following morning the bride discovered that her husband had littered their bed with excrements. The woman was thoroughly disgusted. People immediately began to ridicule her for marrying a husband who discharged excreta on his bed. She could not withstand the embarrassment, and so, left the cock as quickly as she married him.

A little later, she met the parrot, another very handsome person. She fell in love with him immediately and agreed to marry him. When she prepared the first meal, the parrot told her that they would have to eat their meals separately. She was curious to find out why the husband imposed such an embargo on her. When she prepared corn for the parrot, he only ate the soft nucleus of the corn and abandoned the rest. The leftovers littered the whole room.

On a second occasion after serving him a meal, she went to hide to watch the parrot's eating habits. She saw that he was eating with his feet and scattering the remnants of the food around him. When she later confronted the parrot to ask him why he was scattering his food around him, the parrot replied that life was so short that it was not his habit to eat the roughage of any food. Asked why he ate with his feet, he explained that it was the custom of his people so to do. Once again, she considered the situation too much for her and for the second time, she left the parrot. The prediction of the Ifa priest had so quickly manifested.

At that stage, she decided to go again for divination — and she was told to give he-goat to Esu and a ram to her father's Ifa. She gave he-goat to Esu but could not afford to buy a ram for Ifa. She had been told that to settle down, she would have to marry an Ifa priest.

At the same time, Ejioko dreamt that he was going to marry a second wife. He consulted Ifa, and his own ODU came out. He invited his surrogates, Uroke and Orofa to interpret the significance for him. They told him that a woman was coming to him and that she was a princess. He was told to give he-goat to Esu and a ram to Ifa. He made the sacrifices the following day.

At the same time, the Princess left her father's house for an unknown destination to consult two Awos called Elemo Ugo and Osoro Ugomugo. She left home with a bag containing Eko, Akara, Ekuru, and Adun. Just before she got to the town of Itoko where Ejioko lived, she felt like easing herself. Unknown to her, she passed excreta on top of a patient boa which was lying on the ground and the leaf with which she cleaned her anus fell on a snail close by. After easing herself, she continued on her journey. The two Awos had gone to visit Ejioko.

As she got to the town of Itoko, she heard Awos making divination and hitting the ground with the divine knife, (Aja in Yoruba and Aza in Bini), and chanting incantational songs. She brought out her bag to eat out of the food inside it. As she began to eat, Esu stretched his hands towards her and all the food she was eating got stuck in her throat. As she was beginning to choke, she ran for help into Ejioko's house. When she got inside, she beckoned for water. They gave her water with Ifa's water cup and Esu quickly released his hands from her throat and she was instantly relieved. She was then motioned to take her seat. Feeling relieved, she greeted Ifa by bowing her head to the ground.

They made divination for her and told her that she was a princess. They also told her that she had had two abortive marriages and was preparing for a third one. She was told that her father had his own Ifa, to which she was previously advised at divination to offer a ram, but had failed to do it. They told her that she did a sacrifice to Esu but not to Ifa and she confirmed their revelations. They however insisted that she still had to serve Ifa with a ram before she could settle down.

She was also told that she passed human waste in the bush by the roadside just before she arrived at Itoko town. They disclosed that the sickness she suffered before coming into the house was because Orunmila was already annoyed with her for passing excrement on the boa that was going to be used to serve him, and covering the snail with which he was going to cool down her life, with the leaves she used to clean her anus. She did not know about these disclosures but offered to go and show the Awos the spot where she eased herself.

When they got to the place, they all saw that the boa was still lying under the excreta she discharged and further off a snail lay under the leaves she used to clean her anus. The two things were brought home to be used to serve Ifa. Before the food used for the sacrifice was cooked, it was already dark. The princess was given pounded yam to eat. She later joined Ejioko to serve his head with the boa. She spent the night with Ejioko. Soon afterwards she missed her menstruation and became pregnant. She gave birth to a female child who was named Ayo.

When this ODU comes out for a spinster at divination, she should be told to make sacrifice lest she would marry two husbands before settling down with a third one. If she is already married she should be told that she is either in a third husband's house or is preparing to leave for it, but should make sacrifice.

Ejioko escapes from Heaven to the earth:

When he finally made up his mind to escape to the world, he did not come like the others through the womb. He ran off from heaven to the earth with his possessions. He went for divination to an Ifa priest called Olori ire Oyinkpin nigba kara ofun orisa loorun. He was preparing to go to God to collect the flag of his guardian angel. He was told to make sacrifice with a pig, a goat, a sheep, a ram, a male cow, one male tortoise and one female tortoise, one duck and one drake. After making the sacrifice, he left for the divine palace of God.

He got to the palace when God was having his breakfast. It is forbidden for anyone to see God when eating and Ejioko did not know that God was having his meal. God passed a small flag of Ejioko's guardian angel to him, but he ignored the small one and preferred to steal the bigger flag he saw there, and left. The one he picked belonged to a King's angel.

As soon as he collected the larger flag, he quickly embarked on the long journey to earth. He was already climbing the sixth hill leading to earth, when God realised that Ejioko had left with the wrong flag. God sent a messenger to call him back.

Before the messenger could reach him, he had already entered the world. The messenger went back to report to God that Ejioko had escaped into the world, thus, he was left to prosper immensely on earth. Before leaving heaven, he had been warned by the Awos not to allow himself to become temperamental. He was advised that for him to prosper he should learn to be patient and even — tempered, to avoid the risk of being surrounded by evil-minded people.

He makes divination for Oyi:

As soon as he got to the world, the first person he worked for was a woman called Oyi. Abemale Ekokan, Aboju regun regun, adifa fan oyi tolo ile igba. The woman had married several husbands without having any children. When she was preparing to marry an Ifa priest called Igba, she met Ejioko who made divination for her. He advised her to make sacrifice with 20 rats, 20 fishes, 1 pigeon, 1 he-goat, one cock and a hen. The eggs found in the bowels of the hen were used to prepare medicine for her. She was the daughter of Orisa Nla of Itakpa.

She did the sacrifice and left for a town where she met an Ifa priest called Igba and married him. She became pregnant the following month. She gave birth to a set of twins. On the whole, she had two sets of twins. After producing four children for Igba, she left him, leaving the children behind to find another husband because the man felt he had had enough children.

She again went for divination and was told to make sacrifice with a pair of 20 different things. She made the sacrifice and left for the town of Ewi-Ado where she got married to a man at Oke Ila, who had no wife.

She soon became pregnant and delivered three sets of twins during this second marriage. When the man proposed that they had had enough children, she again deserted him in search of another husband.

Once more, she went for divination and she was told to make sacrifice with a pair of 40 different materials. After performing the sacrifice, she travelled to Ijero where she got married in a village called Ikoro, about three miles from the town of Ijero. She had four sets of twins for the new husband at Ikoro. She was fair in complexion, but none of her children had taken her complexion.

Meanwhile one of the four children she had for the first husband persuaded his father to go with him in search of his mother. At the same time, the Ikoro husband told her that he was not interested in having more children. She insisted that she wanted more children and when the husband would not budge, she left him for Ijebu.

At Ijebu she again went for divination and made sacrifice. Thereafter she met another husband for whom she had six sets of twins. Once more a quarrel ensued when the man refused to mate with her for fear of having more children. All the man's other wives had left him because they did not have children. As soon as they saw Oyi having children for him, they all came back to him.

But Oyi was on the move again, this time to Abeokuta. As she was getting to Abeokuta, she met a hunter who was returning from the forest with 5 different animals. She overheard the hunter lamenting in tears that even though he had killed five animals in the forest, he had no wife in the house who would prepare the meat. Oyi instantly agreed to go with him to his home. When the husband made divination for his new found wife, he was told that the woman would leave him if he took on a second wife. With that warning, the man did not contemplate having another wife because Oyi had seven sets of twins for him even in her old age. She was now very old and lived in Abeokuta to the end of her life. When it comes out of divination for a barren woman, she should be told to make sacrifice but that she would have many children for several husbands.

Ejioko settles down on earth:

Soon after arriving on earth, he decided to go for divination with three Awos called Ugun sorire sorire Okpari, Akala Igbo sorire sorire, ogbijojoso-run, mede sorire. When he got to their house, he met Alamiyo, the Head Hunter of Itoko who also came for divination.

Both the hunter and Ogunda meji were advised to make sacrifice against the problem of ingratitude from the beneficiaries of their generosity. Ogundameji was advised to give a black goat to his Ifa and a he-goat to Esu. He did the sacrifice. On the other hand, the hunter was told to offer he-goat to Esu and to serve Ogun with dog, tortoise and cock. He did not do the sacrifice.

The hunter was very proficient in his profession, which explains why he did not consider it necessary to perform any sacrifice. Several years later, the hunter had a dream which frightened him and he went for divination. He was again reminded of the sacrifice he had earlier been advised to make. He insisted that he did not need the assistance of any sacrifice. The next Awos he approached were called Orire sumi sisee and Mada bo la tise orire, won difa fun Alamiyo tiishe Olori ode nile Illa Orangun. He was himself called Alamiyo and he was the head of the hunters in the town of Illa Orangun. They warned him that if he did not perform the sacrifice, his kindness and benevolence would shorten his life. This time, he was told to give 3 he-goats to Esu, a goat to Orunmila, a goat to his head, a dog, cock, tortoise to Ogun and 6 eggs and a rabbit to the elders of the night. He still did not perform any of the sacrifices.

Meanwhile, he left home on a hunting expedition with his hunting instrument, a boomerang (Ekpede in Bini or Akatapo in Yoruba). At nightfall he got to the town of Ipogun. The people of Ipogun had for long had one menancing problem caused by a mysterious bird which used to come to the town and leave a trail of human deaths behind it. The bird is called Agbe in Yoruba or Ukhiokhio in Bini. Whenever it shouted "kpogun" three times it would leave and soon afterwards 20 persons would die in the town. The bird had defied the skill of the best known hunters around. On the last occasion they offered a he-goat to Esu who assured them that the hunter who would kill the bird was going to travel by himself to the town.

When Alamiyo woke up the next morning, he was invited by the Head Chief of the town, and told about the problem of the mysterious bird. As they sat outside the Chief's house discussing the matter, the bird once again emerged. It shouted "Pogun" once, but before shouting the second time, Alamiyo took aim and shot it dead. The news soon spread around and it brought general relief and rejoicing to the town.

While people were still rejoicing, Esu went round to incite the young men of the town to protest to the elders to expel Alamiyo from the town on the ground that a hunter who was able to kill such a mysterious bird with one shot would not spare the whole town if anyone dared to offend him in future. The head Chief appreciated the objections raised by the youths and submitted to their wishes, by expelling Alamiyo from the town of Ipogun, which he had just delivered from a long standing calamity.

Perplexed by the turn of events, Alamiyo went to the next town called Iyinta where he was again invited to solve an age old problem of a mysterious bird that used to bring mass deaths to the town. The bird, called Aluko in Yoruba and Awe in Bini, used to visit the town periodically. As soon as it came into the town, it would stand at the entrance to the town and shout "Pogbon" three times after which thirty persons would die. As he was being told about the endemic calamity, the bird arrived and took position on the tree of life (Akoko or Ikhinmwin) at the entrance to the town. Alamiyo waited for the bird to shout "Pogbon" two times before taking aim. He shot the bird and it fell to the ground, dead. Once again, the whole town rejoiced and sang in praise of the hunter who performed the miraculous feat.

Soon afterwards however, Esu again instigated the people of the town against him and he was driven out of the town. He was already beginning to pay the price of his stubborness.

He travelled next to the town of Iye, where he was greeted with relief and expectancy because they had heard what he did in the two places he had previously visited. He was assured that they were not going to repay him with the kind of ingratitude shown to him in the earlier places he visited. They told him of a deer (Agbonrin in Yoruba and Erhue in Bini) which used to visit the town from time to time to stand on top of a hill to shout "Palura", which led to the death of 40 persons and the destruction of several buildings. Not long afterwards, the deer took position on the hill and as soon as it opened its mouth to shout "Palura", it was shot dead by Alamiyo.

He intended to settle down in the town of Iye, but while the rejoicing was in progress, Esu generated the rumour that Alamiyo was the one who used to send the deer to the town, which explained why he was the only hunter who succeeded in getting rid of it. As if that incitement was not enough, Esu turned into a visitor from Ilu Ipogun and Iyinta and asked them whether he shot the deer without looking at it and if the arrow returned to him. They confirmed that the same thing happened at Iye. He asked whether it was not possible for such a man to destroy a whole population from one spot. With that the visitor/Esu started a war song with which they expelled him from the town of Iye — Kuode jere, kuode jere, kuode jere.

After being expelled from the town of Iye, he decided to hide his boomerang in order to conceal his profession. He was also a diviner. He then took to practising Awo art which he also did very well. This time, he sneaked quietly into the town of Ijesha. But he was not recognised although he succeeded in getting married to the daughter of the Owa of Ijesha. The princess had four children for him. His wife had just had the fourth child when war broke out between Oyo and Ijesha. The invading army of Oyo was dealing a devastating blow on the people of Ijesha. The Owa of Ijesha assembled his people and told them to engage in mass divination on how to check the menace of the invading Army.

At the gathering, Esu transfigured into a visiting Ifa priest, who disclosed to the populace of Ijesha that present in their midst, but unknown to them, was the famous hunter of Itoko who performed wonders in Ipogun, Iyinta and Iye. The man announced that the hunter had concealed his profession and identity since coming to Ijesha on account of the ingratitude shown to him in those places. The Esu-turned-Awo also announced that the man with "Iyo" suffixing his name and married to a princess, was the only one who, with his mysterious weapon, could check the advance of the Oyo troops. As all eyes turned to the direction of Alamiyo, the visitor added that the man himself had one problem, which followed him all the way from heaven and had since persisted on earth. He had stubbornly refused to make the sacrifice prescribed for him. If he succeeded in doing it, he would become the most famous person in Ijesha. If he continued to refuse to do it, he would end up committing suicide by burying himself alive.

With these revelations Alamiyo got up and the visiting Awo told him, after he agreed that he had always failed to make the sacrifices, that the sacrifice had multiplied. He was then required to give 3 he-goats to Esu, a goat to Ifa, a goat to his head, 2 dogs, 2 tortoises and 2 cocks to Ogun, and a rabbit, hen, and eggs to the elders of the night.

Alamiyo then in tears said that he had done so much favour to humanity, and had been repaid with so much ingratitude, that he did not consider himself to be under any obligation to continue to be charitable to anyone. At this stage, the women of the town who had lost many of their husbands to the war, volunteered to contribute money to buy the materials for the sacrifice. The sacrifices were instantly made, and on the following morning, he brought out his boomerang from where he had kept it, brushed it, closed his eyes and shot three arrows in the direction of the invading army. Each shot killed 200 Oyo soldiers and the three arrows returned to him. When the Oyo army saw how their strength was being depleted by an unseen attacker they panicked and took to their heels in fright. Peace returned immediately to Ilesha. Soon afterwards the King of Ilesha died and since he had only one daughter, Alamiyo who was the husband of the only princess, was crowned the Owa of Ibokun Ijesha. He was the one who gave the name of Ibokun to Ilesha — meaning, where one became tired of doing favours. He finally rejoiced and sang in praise of his Awos. His reign was very peaceful and prosperous.

Ogunda-meji cures the barreness of Olofen's wives:

The king of Ife was worried that his three wives had been pregnant for long but could not deliver. He had sought the assistance of all the Ifa priests around to no avail. Meanwhile, he heard of an Ifa priest called Ogundameji who was living alone in a village on the Ijesha road called Ilu-Ogun. He was forced to retreat to the village when he was declared persona non grata in the town of Itoko where he had lived since coming to the world. His success as an Ifa priest had been acclaimed all around but it also incured him the enmity of the more elderly Awos who lived at Itoko before him.

He had earlier prepared a good luck soap for the King of Ife which he used commonly with his three hunters. The soap helped his hunters to return from the forest with good games, but could not help his wives to be delivered of their pregnancies.

His three hunters were called:
(1) Orisi Taasi
(2) Oriisi Taasi and
(3) Atama Taasi.

One day, the three of them went to the forest on a hunting expedition. The first hunter shot an elephant in the forest and it came to the town to die at the courtyard of the King. When the elephant was butchered, a live human child was found inside its stomach wearing a crown on its head and beads on its limbs.

The second hunter shot a buffalo in the forest and it came to the palace to die on the same spot. When it was butchered, a closed wooden plate with two compartments having 16 Ifa seeds on either side, was found inside its bowels.

The third hunter shot a deer in the forest that also came to die on the same spot. When it was butchered, its stomach produced a calabash containing one magic wand (ASE).

The king was obviously puzzled. He wondered what message was borne by these strange developments. The king brought out his own Ifa and he sounded it and Ogunda meji was the Odu that appeared. At that point he sent messages to all the Awos in his domain to come and interpret the significance of these events and the ODU that appeared.

They all tried but failed to interpret the meaning of the strange occurrences. As they all failed one after the other, they were chained and imprisoned in the palace cell. All the known Ifa priests in the kingdom had been similarly treated and there was none left. The king then remembered the Awo who prepared the good luck soap for him, although no one seemed to remember about him. However some people reported that the only remaining Awo in the kingdom was Ogunda-meji who was living in seclusion on the Ijesha road, in a village called Ilu Ogun. The king quickly ordered that the man should be brought to the palace without any delay.

That coincided with the day Ogundameji was serving his head. As the messengers were crossing the river to meet Ogundameji, they met the three grown up princesses of Ife, washing their clothes in the river. The girls had grown to marriageable age but had vowed that they would only marry the man or the men who succeeded in knowing their names. They were only known as, and called, princesses. The two royal messengers greeted them and continued on their journey.

On getting to Ogundameji's village, they discovered that he had just served his head and the soup and pounded yam were being prepared. They delivered the royal message that the king wanted him at Ife immediately. Soon afterwards, they got up to return to Ife, but their host insisted that they must eat out of the pounded yam before leaving. They sat down to enjoy the meal to their heart's content. After eating, he gave them fresh palm wine to drink and finally gave them kolanuts as a sign of respect.

After enjoying his hospitality, they resolved to tell him why he was invited by the King, so that he might not end up in chains like all the other Awos invited before him. First, they gave him the names of the three daughters of the King who had vowed only to marry the man who knew their names. They told him that if he wanted to marry new wives, he could have the three girls by pronouncing their names as:— (1) Iboru (2) Iboye and (3) Ibosise. This incident explains why Orunmila does not forbid marrying more than one wife from the same house or family.

Next, they disclosed what the King wanted him to do which was to interpret the significance of the strange discoveries in the bowels of the three animals killed by the three royal hunters on the same day. Since they themselves did not know the meaning, he was forewarned to prepare to unravel the puzzle which had defied the competence of all the Awos throughout the kingdom of Ife, and who were already imprisoned in chains. They warned him to keep their confidence. He thanked them for telling him as much as they did and begged them to tell the king that he was serving his head, but would turn up the following day.

As soon as they left, he brought out his divination seeds and consulted Ifa. He was told to give a he-goat to Esu and to travel with kolanuts and ripe plantain for his journey. He was also advised to be generous to anyone he came across on the way because the solution to the puzzles would be given to him on the way to Ife. He did as he was told.

He left for Ife very early the next morning. As soon as he entered the last stretch of forest before Ife, he met at old woman sitting by the side of the road. The woman was looking wretched and hungry. She called him and begged for food because she had not eaten for the past three days. He gave her roasted ripe plantain and water from his bag. After eating and drinking, he gave her kolanut to keep with her, as well as the rest of the ripe plantain in his bag. The old woman thanked him. As he was about to take leave of the old woman, she asked him where he was going and he replied that he had been invited for a mission to the king's palace at Ife.

The woman told him that victory and success awaited him at Ife. She told him that he was invited to Ife to:
(1) Reveal why Olofen's three wives who had been pregnant for a long time had still not delivered;
(2) The significance of the Elephant, Buffalo and Deer which were shot respectively by Orisi Tasi, Oriisi Taasi, and Atama Taasi, but which came to die at the palace courtyard;
(3) The message borne by the three mysterious objects found in the bowels of the three animals; and
(4) If he chose to marry new wives, to reveal the names of the three grown up daughters of Olofen.

She warned him that the first feat he would perform at the palace would be to get rid of an old witch who often sat at the entrance to the king's palace and who had the power to blot out the memory and knowledge of all the Awos coming to the palace, which explained why the other Awos invited before him had failed. The old woman advised him to order the execution of that woman before stepping into the palace because she was responsible for all the misfortunes besetting the kingdom.

His next performance would be to order the release of all the imprisoned Awos and to proclaim that it was forbidden to bind any Awo in chain or jail, because any town where an Awo was put in chains would always be in turmoil. Thereafter, he was to enter the palace. The first people to receive him would be the King's three daughters. They would greet him on their knees and he should reply by calling them by their names, Iboru, Iboye and Ibosise.

As soon as he met the Olofen, he would request him to interpret the ODU-IFA which was on the Ifa tray and to tell him why his three pregnant wives had not delivered for more than three years. He should begin by revealing to the King that his three wives were not pregnant at all. One of them had an ant-heap, (Odidimade in Yoruba and Ulelefe in Bini) in her stomach. The second one had an ant-hill in her stomach, while the third one had water yam in her stomach.

He should then move to disclose the incident of the animals and the strange finds in their stomachs. He was to do it by saying that the King had three hunters, who he permitted to use for hunting, the soap he was expected to use exclusively. It was the successful use of the soap for hunting that made the King of the forest to stock his wives wombs with these materials since he preferred forest animals to human children. He was next to say that the elephants, buffalo and deer which came to die in his courtyard, after being shot in the forest, was the last warning from the king of the forest, that enough was enough.

Finally he was to interpret the contents of the animals' bowels as follows:
(a) The live human child, wearing a crown and beads, found in the stomach of the elephant was a message that the time was approaching when he would no longer have elders in his domain to counsel him except young people;
(b) The significance of the Ifa plate found in the stomach of the buffalo was a message from God that Orunmila is the divinity he should always consult to reveal the future to him; and
(c) The calabash with Ase found in the stomach of the deer meant that no Oba would again reign in his kingdom who would be as famous as the Olofen.

As he prostrated to thank the old woman, he could not see her again. She had evaporated into thin air. He then proceeded on the journey and soon got to the palace.

When he got to the palace, the sequence of events was slightly reversed. The three girls were outside the palace walls spreading their clothes to dry. As soon as he saw them he greeted them with a familiar air by calling on their names one after the other. He greeted them one by one with good morning Iboru, good morning Iboye and good morning Ibosise. They quickly left the clothes they were spreading outside and embraced him with the words that at last they had got a husband. They immediately offered themselves to him in marriage and when he told them that he had an assignment in the King's palace, they told him that they were the King's daughters and would follow him to proclaim him to their father as their husband.

When he arrived at the entrance to Olofen's palace, he stood outside and told the Oba to come out. He proclaimed that the elderly woman who sat at the entrance should be cudgelled to death at once, because she was singularly responsible for all the misfortunes besetting King and kingdom in recent times. The woman was instantly beaten to death and dragged away.

Thereafter, he walked with the King into the inner chamber of the palace, where the Olofen showed him the ODU-IFA that appeared at divination, which happened to be his own Ifa. He then told the Olofen that he had sixteen Awos locked up in the palace cell for not being able to translate the ODU. He told him that it was not due to lack of skill on the part of the Awos, but the result of the evil spell cast upon them by the witch-woman who had just been executed. She sat at the entrance to blacken out all the knowledge, memory and soothsaying ability of any Awo that walked passed her. That is why those Awos forgot what to say when they got into the palace. He told the King that it was forbidden to lock up an Ifa priest and that he should release them at once.

The king immediately ordered that all the Awos should be unchained and brought to the outer chamber of the palace. Thereafter, he looked again at the Odu-Ifa on the floor and asked for the Royal hunters called:—

(i) Orisi Taasi, who had recently shot an elephant in the forest that came to die in the palace courtyard, and carrying a human child, wearing a crown on its head, and beads on its limbs. When the hunter emerged to identify himself, he turned to the Olofen and told him that the significance of that event was that unless he made sacrifice, the time was imminent when all the elders of his domain would die in turns leaving him to be surrounded by youngsters.

(ii) Oriisi Taasi — who on the same day shot a buffalo in the forest that came to the palace courtyard to die on the same spot and carrying an Ifa plate with 32 seeds in its stomach. He turned to the King and told him that it was a message from Orunmila that he should always consult Ifa to solve all his problems. By divining with those seeds, he would always find the solution to all his problems.

(iii) Atama Atasi — who also shot a deer in the forest that came to the palace to die on the same spot and carrying one ASE moulding (Oghoriboje in Yoruba and Ekhuae in Bini). Still addressing the king, he said that it meant that no other king after him would match his fame, influence and authority.

He then queried the King for allowing the good luck soap prepared for him to be used for hunting by his three hunters. He added that the King of the Forest sent the three animals to warn him to stop plundering them with medicine. He exclaimed whether the King did not know that it was because he preferred animals to children that his wives had ceased having children, and even the three who were pregnant had their foeti turned into an ant-heap, an ant-hill and water yam. He disclosed that as soon as he stopped using the soap for hunting, his wives would give birth to normal human children.

Ogunda meji was given a standing ovation and carried shoulder high in a procession round the town. He was proclaimed the most proficient Ifa priest that Ife had seen in recent times. Back in the palace, he told the King that for peace to return to Ife, he had to appease the imprisoned Awos by compensating each of them with a goat. The King agreed without qualms. In appreciation for their salvation, all the Awos surrendered their goats to Ogunda meji, but he declined to accept them. He told them to serve their Ifa with it but after killing the goat, they were to say that it was he, Ogunda meji, who killed the goat and not they. That has become the Ifa tradition to this day, whereby, after slaughtering any animal to Orunmila, the person slaughtering it will say, Eesemi lookpaa, Ogunda jameji loonkpa, and touch the slaughtered offering with the knife.

Meanwhile, the king decided to thank Ogunda meji with a song:
Ojudu loon shawo Alara
Ota Legbeje loon shawo Ijero,
Okon shosho ata mode loon daun looni,

Okpe — mo dami dami dami, orere, oo
   Orere dami dami dami orereoo
   dami dami dami orere dami dami dami orere
Dami lowo uku,
   orere dami dami dami oo orere
Dami lowo ojojo,
   Orere dami dami dami orere,
Igbese orun mi, ose arin

The King rewarded him with plenty of gifts in addition to betrothing his three daughters who had proclaimed him their husband. He was also made the Baalogun of Ife, the next Chieftaincy, title to the King.

He makes divination for Aguofenia (the trench hunter)

The trench hunter used to dig massive pits for catching animals. When any animal fell into the burrowed pit, it would not be able to climb out. The next day, he would come and catch the victim. It was a prolific business for him and he used to make divination and sacrifice on it every year. The pit is called Ofen in yoruba and and Uye in Bini.

On this particular year, he went to Ogunda meji to divine for him in order to have a successful hunting year. He was asked to give a he-goat to Esu, but to release the first two catches after the sacrifice and to kill the third catch. He made the sacrifice and excavated the pit for the next hunting year. The first victim was the boa (Oka or Aru) which he took out and set free. After being released, the boa looked back and promised to return the good turn one day. Aguofenia wondered how a boa could ever be of use to him.

The following day, the pit caught a rabbit which he again released. The rabbit also looked back after being set free and promised to return the good turn some day. He told the rabbit to go his way because he could not imagine how the rabbit could be of any use to him.

The next day, the pit caught a bush cat, (Ogbo or Abon). Instead of killing it as he was advised to do, he released it because he expected something bigger. After that the pit did not catch anything else. Meanwhile, he began to suffer deprivation.

After some time, the rabbit visited Aguofenia and found his house bare and replete with penury. The rabbit decided to help him by boring a hole from Aguofenia's house to the King's treasury inside the palace. Through the hole, the rabbit was able to empty the King's treasury into Aguofenia's house. Very soon he became very wealthy and his home began to boom with affluence.

The bush cat, Ogbo, who was released by Aguofenia instead of being killed as he was advised to do, also visited him. Ogbo asked him how he came by his new found prosperity and he betrayed his benefactor by disclosing that the miracle was performed by the rabbit. Ogbo quickly went to report the incident to the King who summoned Aguofenia to his palace for explanation. The King had observed the robbery in his treasury and he was now sure that Aguofenia was the culprit.

After interviewing Aguofenia, who denied the charge, the king promised to confront him with witnesses in seven days time, during which Ogbo was to be presented to confirm his allegations. Aguofenia cried home in distress, knowing that the inescapable penalty was death. On his way home he met the boa who told him not to worry because the situation presented the opportunity for him to return the good turn earlier done to him.

On the seventh day, Ogbo, himself a wine tapper, wanted to collect some wine from the bush before going to the palace. The boa had meanwhile taken position, by concealing his tail on the path which Ogbo was going to tread to the palm tree. As soon as Ogbo stepped on the boa's tail, the latter shot his arrows at him instantly. When he begged the boa to release his arrows from his body he said it was too late since Ogbo knew that it was forbidden for anyone to touch his tail. He still went to collect his wine and hurried home to prepare for the palace court session.

He had his bath, dressed up, and left for the palace. As he was going, the poison contained in the boa's arrows overcame him and he moved aimlessly to give up the ghost at the spot where the boa shot him.

Meanwhile, the palace court was seated and all eyes were on the watch for Ogbo to emerge. After waiting in vain for a long time, someone came later to report that Ogbo dropped dead on his way to the palace. The King then concluded that the ancestors and divinities had delivered their own judgement and he was prepared to abide by their decision. He remarked that Ogbo died because he must have lied. Aguofenla was then acquitted and discharged. It was at that stage that Aguofenla sang in praise of Ogundameji, the rabbit and the boa. In his eulogy he proclaimed that sacrifice manifested for those who performed them, but that no one should ignore the advice of a diviner, like he did by failing to kill Ogbo the third victim of his pit trap. He went on:—

Who could ever have believed that an ant could assist the elephant.
That the earth worm could save the boa constrictor from the jaws of death.
The rabbit and the boa were his life long benefactors.
Indeed one good turn deserves another.
As one bad turn begets another.

He also made divination for 2 fish catchers:
How Ogundameji got the sobriquet of Ogunda-Ja-Meji

There were two friends who were partners in the fish pond business. One of them called Oni had the fish pond while the other called Ooni had the catcher or bale for catching the fish.
Oni Nubu, Enugha
OoniNugba, Enubu
They both went for divination to Ogundameji and he advised them to give a he-goat to Esu. They did it. Thereafter, they went to the pond, but caught only one large fish. Oni the pond owner insisted on taking the fish because he owned the pond. Ooni the bale owner argued that without his instrument, they would not have caught the fish. He too insisted that he was entitled to keep the fish. A quarrel ensured. At the same time, Ogunda meji was alerted by Esu to go to the direction of the pond. He met the two friends fighting and he was able to settle the matter for them by declaring that they were both entitled to a share of the catch.

He then used a cutlass to split the fish into two equal halves from head to tail, giving one half to each of them. They were both satisfied. That is where he got his nickname of Ogunda ja eja meji or in short, Ogunda ja Meji, that is, Ogunda who split a fish into two equal halves.

His Surrogates take over Divination for the crown prince of Benin Kingdom:

At this stage of his life, Ogundameji decided that it was time to retire from active practice. He had become so prosperous and famous that he had several surrogate Awos working for him. After the fish pond incident he decided that he would only divine for the king thereafter. If anyone else came to him, he directed his followers to divine for him. These subordinates were however equally proficient in Ifa art and practice.

Among such surrogates were the following:
Abe kekere mu loode lyango;
Epon olude wole dere dere dere;
Taa bi ta Awo omode
Irele bi irele, Awo agba lagba
Abugbegbe sorun Awo ajero kin Osa;
Ajaa ku, omu ori lugbogbo;
Adiye ku, oko ose meji si eyin tioriwo tioriwo;
Awon lo difa fun Aganmurere;
Tiinshe omo oye oba ado ajuwaleke;
The small knife is used for all minor chores;
The big testicles that stretch to the ground;
The young Ifa priest is as sharp as pepper;
Patience and calmness are the attributes of the experienced Ifa priest;
The priest with a head tumour is the diviner for Alara;
The priest with neck tumour is the diviner for Ajero;
The dead dog laid its head on the cudgel used for whipping it to death;
The dying hen used its two feet to dig behind it.

These are the surrogate Awos of Ogunda meji who made divination for Aganmurere the heir to the throne of the Benin Kingdom where the King adorns himself with beads. They advised the heir apparent to serve Ogun with a dog, a cock and a tortoise on account of an imminent war. He was also told to serve the ground divinity with a sheep, and to serve his guardian angel with a white goat, in order to have a peaceful reign.

Meanwhile, the people of Taakpa, a province of the Benin kingdom, rebelled against the throne of Benin. Aganmurere led the invading troops that subdued the people of Taakpa. The Bini troops were victorious and Aganmurere subsequently ascended to the throne of his father and became the Orongun or Orogbua of Ado.

He had a reasonably peaceful reign because no war was fought on the Benin soil during his reign. He was also credited with expanding the Edo empire to Eko, Isidahome (or Dahomey) Iga or Ga in the old Gold Coast, and the West of the Congo, Itogo etc. He was also reported to have brought salt to Benin from Isidahome for the first time.

Later in his life, he invited Ogunda meji and his surrogates to Ado where he expressed his gratitude with elaborate gifts to them.

He helps the people of Oyo in their war with Ilesha:

One day, while living in Oyo, he had a dream which frightened him. He invited three of his surrogates to make divination on the dream:
(1) Ekun lu uki Oyo
(2) Ooki lu uki Ijesha
(3) Aikiki le eruse ale ano Looyo oohun.
Odafafun Orunmila, Uku elegidigbe gidide.
(1) Ekun is the traditional greeting at Oyo;
(2) Ooki is the traditional greeting of Ijesha;
(3) A greeting reflecting a bad deed done the previous day does not give joy.

These are the names of the surrogates who made divination for

Ogunda meji when, like the sword of damocles, the danger of mass death was hanging over the world. The King of Death had slated the strong men of the earth for a ruthless kind of mass destruction. The three Awos advised Ogunda meji to make sacrifice with a whole bush goat (Edu in Yoruba and Oguonziran in Bini) cock and 5k in 201 places. He was also advised to give he-goat to Esu. He was to use the skin of the bush goat to make a large drum and to give a cock to Ogun.

Subsequently, war broke out between Oyo and Ijesha, which caused a 24 hour curfew to be imposed in Oyo. No one was allowed to go out. It however became necessary to make divination for the Alaafin of Oyo, but no one dared to go out. Esu went to Ogunda meji in his capacity as one of the royal diviners and told him to go to the palace to divine for the King. He was too scared to go but Esu persuaded him to beat the drum he had just made from the skin of the bush goat right up to the palace.

Singing with the names of the Awos who made divination for him, he sang and drummed to the palace. By the time he got to the palace, hostilities had ended with the withdrawal of the invading Ijesha Army. Peace and tranquility then returned to Oyo.

Ogunda-Meji leaves for Heaven:

Just like he came to the world without passing through the female womb, he left for heaven at a ripe old age without passing through the grave. As already indicated, the King of Death had contrived a ruthless scheme for eliminating the strong Awos on earth. They were invited to heaven one after the other to come and cure the King of Death who was "ill". Following the end of the Ijesha-Oyo war, he had a dream in which he found himself in heaven but could not return to the earth. He invited two of his most proficient surrogates called:

Uroke mi lawo ligonrin, and
Oroke milawo le eturuye

to make divination to interpret the dream. They told him that the King of Death was sending a message to him to come to heaven to divine for him. They told him that the task he was going to be invited to perform was a tedious and arduous one, but that since no task was impossible for Orunmila, he would survive it if he made adequate preparations. He was told to give one he-goat to Esu at home and also to give a small he-goat including Akara, Eko, Ewo (Obobo in Bini) water and cotton wool, to Esu in the forest. He was to perform the second forest sacrifice on his way to heaven. He made the first sacrifice at home and got prepared for his trip to heaven to meet the King of Death. The following day, he was visited by two men dressed in the uniform of the knights of heaven. He did not know how they got to his house. He just found them in his sitting room. They told him that he was required by the King of Death to come and cure him in heaven. He offered to entertain them but they refused because they were under orders not to eat or drink from anyone they visited. He asked them how he was going to travel to heaven and they told him that he was supposed to know what to do. With that, they disappeared out of sight.

To travel to heaven, he had to wear his mystical garment with which he could disappear. As soon as he got fully prepared, he went into his mystery room and instantly, he found himself on the last gate to heaven.

Before entering heaven, he went into the forest to make the second sacrifice. As he settled down at a spot in the forest to make the sacrifice, he saw an old woman with her limbs stuck to the ground, and her eyes oozing out offensive liquid as if at the point of death. Other people used to see her and pass her by, but he stopped to help her. He got her hands and feet released from the bolt with which they were fastened to the ground, and brought out the cotton wool for his sacrifice to clean her eyes. Seeing that the woman was obviously hungry, he gave her the Eko and Akara to eat and the water to drink. The woman asked him for the he-goat in his pocket and he gave it to her.

He then continued on his journey satisfied that he had served the Esu of the forest. Before getting to the house of the King of death, he met a beautiful girl who asked him whether he recognised her. She asked him whether he did not see an old woman in the forest. The girl lied that the woman was her mother, but it was infact herself, now transfigured into this good-looking girl. She asked him where he was going and he replied that he was going to answer an invitation from the King of Death. She disclosed that she was the mother of the King of Death and he was startled.

She told him that the King of Death was not ill at all and that he merely wanted to destroy all the proficient Awos on earth, because they were draining his source of food supply by saving human beings from dying. She added that she was going to help him on account of the good turn he did to people including herself.

She disclosed that every morning, the King of Death was in the habit of putting on his wife's garment, that is, the sickness dress (Sickness being the King of Death's wife) which would make him look as if he was about to die. The garment was usually tied to the back of his leg. Several Doctors had previously been invited to cure him but they had all failed. None of them was able to survive the preliminary trial by which Death tested their capabilities. They were required to stick a spear (Okpaorere in Yoruba and Osogan in Bini) on the floor of the inner chamber of the King of Death. Unknown to them, the floor was lined with stones. When the spear could not stick to the ground the Awos were tied up for execution. She disclosed that thirty Awos from earth had already been tied up that way.

She advised him that to be able to stick the spear to the floor, he had to strike it at the mouth of the water drain of the inner chamber, which was the only soft spot in the room. He would recognise the place by the presence of a giant frog on that spot. He should not be afraid of hitting the frog, because it would disappear as soon as he aimed to strike. If he did not see the frog, he would meet one old woman sitting and spinning cotton wool, with her foot covering the soft spot. He should not be afraid of hitting her foot, because she would remove it as he took aim.

Finally, she gave him the following warnings:
(i) He was not to split the evil kolanut to be presented to him before seeing the King of Death;
(ii) He was to insist on seeing the King of Death unaccompanied;
(iii) He was to demand the release of the 30 Awos in chains before accepting any reward; and
(iv) He was not to accept any physical gifts because the heavenly police would not allow him to take them away. She then gave him a small calabash from her head which he could knock on the ground to take whatever was given to him. He should use the calabash to disappear back to his house.

He thus realised the manifestation of the sacrifice he had made, otherwise there was no way he could have come by this vital information. Before the girl disappeared, she promised that she would always come to his rescue at critical moments during his exploit.

Without much apprehension therefore, he proceeded to the house of the King of Death where he was welcomed by the knights of the Death squad. As soon as he introduced himself, they told him that the tradition was for him to stick a spear to the ground before taking his seat. He was directed to the inner chamber where drums were beating and he began to dance to the tune of the music with the spear in hand. He danced round the room and without any warning, he startled the old woman sitting near the water drain and by reflex action she removed her foot from the mouth of the drain and he stuck the spear right on that spot and it held on to the floor. He won the applause and praise of all those who were present.

He was then given a kolanut to welcome him. He remembered the girl's warning and insisted that before enjoying any entertainment, he had first to see who invited him to perform the task for which he was invited. He demanded to see the King of Death alone.

He was then allowed to see the King of Death alone. Death recognised him as the man who seduced his wife several years before, and praised him for getting away with it. He prayed him also to cure him of his seemingly incurable ailment. Ogunda meji laughed hilariously and greeted the King of Death. He told him that he was aware that he had to pay the debt he owed to death in the end, but that he was not going to do so on the King of Death's terms. He settled down to serious business and told Death that he was only feigning illness by wearing his wife's garment and that nothing was wrong with him.

Ogunda meji then knelt down to unfasten the garment from the heels of the King of Death and with that, he removed the sickness garment and Death looked hail and hearty. Ogundameji threatened to burn the garment, but Death refused on the ground that it truly belonged to his wife. But the King of Death warned him not to give his secret away to anyone in heaven.

Thereafter, Ogundameji came to the outer-chamber with the King of Death having apparently cured him. He was again praised and applauded by the heavenly host as the king of Death took his seat on the throne.

Before taking his seat, Ogunda meji knocked his head and there was a loud roar which shook the grounds of heaven and everybody begged him to soften up. He then demanded the immediate release of all the 30 Awos who were put in chains before him. Knowing what Ogunda meji was capable of doing, Death quickly ordered the release of the 30 Awos from earth, but since they refused to make sacrifice before leaving earth, they could not longer return to earth.

Death gave him several gifts knowing that it was impossible for him to take them away from heaven. After completing arrangements for his return home, he surrounded himself with the gifts he was given and brought out the calabash the girl gave to him. He sprinkled its content on all the gifts and he told them, including the 30 Awos to prepare for home. With that incantation they all disappeared and were instantly at the sitting room of Ogunda meji's house on earth.

All the Awos thanked him and promised always to remember him in whatever they did. Some accounts have it that Ogunda meji did not return from heaven because he preferred to remain there. The account which was given to the writer is that he returned to earth but died a normal death soon afterwards.

Before finally leaving the earth, he told his children that they should always do favours, although they would always be repaid with ingratitude. He advised them not to allow that problem to deter them from humanitarian behaviour, because as long as they could operate as loyal disciples of Orunmila, benevolence would always bring them salvation and prosperity. He added that ingratitude done to them by their beneficiaries them multiple rewards, from the Almighty God.

His last words on his death bed are contained in the following poem:
Oroo (a plant without leaves) was so benevolent;
That it was left with no leaves;
But it is the only plant that survives all climatic conditions.
Igeregere or Afuma (a plant that grows on other trees) was so benevolent;
That it has no roots on the ground;
But it was crowned the King of all plants.
The ground does so much favour to the world,
That his significance is not even appreciated;
But he is the final inheritor of the universe,
The sun is so benevolent;
That he is cursed and praised by his beneficiaries;
But he lives forever.
His children would always be more prosperous;
Than those who show them ingratitude.
Just as a thief can never prosper;
As much as the victim of his theft.

Finally, he told his children not to take to hunting of any kind as a profession, be it for animals, birds and reptiles in the forest, or for fishes in the water. With those words of advice, he lapsed into the great beyond.

CHAPTER XXII
OSAMEJI

```
I I   I I
I     I
I     I
I     I
```

Not much is known about the work of Osameji in heaven. It is said that he made divination for the white man when he was coming to the world. He is said to have advised the white man in the following poem:
   Oyi Odade owo
   Oyi Owewu okun
   Oyi rogun — Oyi bogun
   Oyi rogbon — Oyi bogbon
      Adifa fun Oyibo nigbati oyibo maa gunle sikole aye.

The white man was advised to make sacrifice in order to be able to create, invent, develop and achieve great heights — and to command universal honour and respect. He made the sacrifice.

When this ODU comes out of divination, the person will be told that he will give birth to a child who will command the respect of all and sundry.

When a woman called Ogodo yaya was leaving heaven, she went to the Awos listed above to make divination for her in order to be able to have a child who will change the course of events in the world. She was advised to make sacrifice with cotton, rat, fish, cock and hen. She made the sacrifice and came to the world. On getting to the world, she did not have children, so she went to two Awos on earth called Ukporo bayi and Aila baayi. She was told to make sacrifice with a rat, fish, cock and hen. She did the sacrifice after which she began to have children.

Later, she wanted to have more children and again went for divination. She was told to make sacrifice with 40 eggs and a he-goat to Esu. After making the sacrifice a child was born with a pale skin and curly hair. Afraid of the kind of child she had, she ran to the Awos who made divination for her to explain what it meant. They told her that since she left heaven with a wish to give birth to a child who would alter the face of the earth, her wishes had manifested and she was told that the child was going to begin a new generation of white men on earth. That is how the white race came into existence.

When this ODU comes out of divination for a woman, she will be told that after having several children, she would give birth to an Albino. That is why it is said that the black man came to the world before the white man, although the white man was the one who changed the course of events on earth.

He made divination for the cotton plant:

The cotton plant also went to Osameji in heaven for divination when it was coming to the world. At that time, the people of the world were only wearing leaves. The cotton was told to make sacrifice because it vowed to come to the world to provide clothing for humanity. It was told to make sacrifice with a he-goat to Esu adding plenty of white chalk. The cotton was otherwise brown in colour, but when it produced children on earth, the children were surrounded by white hair (or wool) to which Esu changed the white chalk with which the cotton made sacrifice.

It was also Esu who advised mankind to spin and weave the cotton into clothing for wearing instead of wearing leaves.

Osameji prepares to come to the world:

When Osameji discovered that most of the divinities had left for earth, he decided to go and see what the place was like. He went to three Awos called:
Age eni je, ee mo odun
Ala ra ra ije eemaagbe
Ogbologbo ekutele, Eeje erin ogini ninu ule.
Whatever bites one does not know when the year ends.
He who buys cooked food to eat does not bother to know the farmer who produced it.
The big domestic rat does not allow the cat to stay at home.
Osameji was advised to make sacrifice because he was going to practise his Ifa art in the midst of witches. He was told to give he-goat to Esu, a guinea to his Ifa and pigeon to his head. He did not perform the sacrifice as he was in a hurry to come to the world.

Although he was one of the sixteen children of Orunmila who decided to come to the world at about the same time, he did not find the way to the world in time, because of the he-goat he failed to give to Esu. His guardian angel could not guide him because he also made no sacrifice to him. His Head did not come to his rescue either, because he offered no sacrifice to it. He was therefore wandering on the way until he came to the last river in heaven before crossing to the world. At the bank of the river, he met the mother of witches, Iyami Osoronga who had been there for a long time because no one else agreed to help her to cross the river. She too was coming to the world but was too feeble to cross the tiny thread bridge over the river. The bridge is called Ekoko Bridge.

Iyami Osoronga begged him to back her through the river, but he explained that the bridge would not take two passengers at a time. She then proposed to him that he should open his mouth so she could get into it. He agreed and she took a position inside his stomach. When he got to the earth end of the bridge, he told her to come out, but she refused on the ground that his stomach provided a suitable abode for her. His problems with witchcraft had begun. When she refused to disembark, he thought he could bluff her by saying that she would die of hunger inside his stomach, but she said that she would not die for as long as he had a liver, a heart and intestines, because those were her favourite meals.

He realised what problem he was up against, when the woman bit his liver. He then brought out his divination instruments and sounded Ifa on how to get out of the impasse. He was told by Ifa to make instant sacrifice with a goat, a bottle of oil and white cloth, which he brought out quickly from his Akpo minijekun.

He quickly cooked the liver, heart and intestines of the goat and told Iyami that food was ready for her. When she smelt the inviting scent of the food, she came out of his stomach. She however told him that it was forbidden for her to eat in full view of anyone. He then made a tent with the white cloth and she went under the tent to enjoy the meal. As she was eating Osameji ran away and quickly found a womb to enter to come to the world.

As soon as Iyami finished eating, she looked round for Osameji but he was nowhere to be found. She began to shout his name Osasa, Osasa, Osasa, which is the cry of the witches to this day. She is still looking for Osameji up till now.

The birth of Osameji.

Osameji ran into the womb of the first woman he came across as he was running away from Iyami Osoronga. Little did he know that he was merely running from the frying pan to the fire, because the woman who was to become his mother was a member of the cult of Iyami Osoronga.

He came to the rescue of a husband whose wife had completed arrangements for offering him as a sacrifice to the elders of the night. When he was born, he was always crying out late at night but no one knew what was responsible for his nocturnal cries. The father was a layman who had no knowledge of what was going on. As soon as he cried out in the night the parents would wake up to pacify him. It was only the mother who knew the secret of why the child was always crying out at night.

The child used to cry to intercept the ritual process of sacrificing the father for a feast in the witch cult. That process continued until the child was old enough to speak. Subsequently, as soon as he grew up to be able to talk, instead of merely crying in the night, he would shout the word Iyami Osoronga, which would instantly wake up the mother and she would thus abruptly depart from the night's ritual ceremony of trying to sacrifice the husband. This used to happen on a particular day of every week.

One night, the witches subpoenaed the mother to explain why she used to leave their meeting abruptly whenever she was praying with the goat (she used to turn the husband into a goat before trying to kill him, because the witches do not kill human beings without first turning them into animals). She explained that it was her son who coincidentally used to shout the name of the witch-mother (Iyami Osoronga) at that point of the proceedings. She was instructed to come with her son to the next meeting which was the General Assembly meeting and feasting day. All the witches had contributed money to serve their heads on that night.

When that day arrived they served the heads of all their members one after the other. When they got to where Osameji was sitting they also served his head but he did not eat out of the goat used for serving their heads because he did not contribute towards the cost of buying it, since he had not been initiated into the cult.

Next morning he woke up and went to his father to advise him to serve his head with a goat because of a dream he had. He told him to do it so that he might get well because he had been ill for a long time. The father accepted the advice of the small boy and bought a goat to serve his head. After making the sacrifice, Osameji asked his mother to provide an open clay pot and plenty of oil. He collected parts of the goat and all the uneaten remains of the goat's meat and put them in the pot adding oil and salt as well as sand from the ground (represented today by Iyerosun). He then went to deposit the pot at the incinerator (Otitan in Yoruba and Otiku in Bini). That was the first offering by any human being to the elders of the night and is also how offerings are made to them to this day. After the sacrifice they all went to sleep but by the next morning his mother did not wake up. From then on his father became well. Things became clear to him after the death of his mother and eventually he told the father that his mother was all along responsible for his indisposition, and narrated how he used to see her in his dreams.

It is for this singular reason that some Ifa priests refer to Osameji as a witch, but he never was. From then on people began to respect him. Anyone who wanted to serve his head always invited Osameji to perform the sacrifice for him or her. He was able to hold meetings with the witches right from the time his mother touched his head with the wand that made it possible for him to accompany her to the meeting of witches. He was from then on able to hold meetings with them but could not eat with them because he was not formally initiated. To this day, it is possible with the aid of similar preparations, for a novice to hold meetings with witches, without being formally initiated into their cult.

Esu finally gets his he-goat from Osameji.

His first performance as an Ifa priest was to deliver a pregnant woman. Esu had all along been waiting for him to begin his ministry before holding him to ransome for his he-goat. As soon as he grew up to be a man, he got married to a young, beautiful girl who was also a witch. The house he lived in was also inhabited by witches. The entire town in which he lived was a witch-infested place. Esu pushed him to the place as a punishment for stubbornly refusing to give him a he-goat. When he got to the town he discovered that everybody had gone out of the town to the farm, so he waited until the following day throughout which the town was still desolate but for one pregnant woman who was in labour. As the only person around, he helped the woman to deliver the child.

Not having eaten any food since the previous day he was now very hungry and as he tried to find something in the house to eat, he moved to the overhead food storage counter where he inadvertently dropped an egg which broke into pieces. The next object he touched instantly changed the pigmentation of his two hands to albino white. This incident scared him so much that he ran into the bush.

When the town's inhabitants returned from the farm the newly delivered woman told them of a visitor who came to the town. As soon as they heard of his arrival they began to search for him as he was sure to become the next sacrificial victim in the cult of witchcraft. Meanwhile, he met a hunter in the forest who told him that the town he came to settle in was totally inhabited by witches. He also told him that the people were searching for him at that instant and that his life was in danger. To ward off the danger, he was required to give a he-goat to Esu immediately.

He then provided a he-goat from his divination bag and gave it to Esu. After sacrificing the he-goat, the hunter got leaves from the forest and washed Osameji's head with them. Osameji did not know from where the man got the water and the pot with which to wash the leaves. It was then he realised that Esu had probably transfigured into the hunter. The hunter washed his two hands with the substance as well as his entire body. Instantly, his two hands regained their normal pigmentation.

Meanwhile, the newly delivered child who spoke from the day it was born, narrated how Osameji came to the town and how he got the colour of his two hands changed. With that mark of indentification the people thought it would be easy to apprehend him whenever they eventually caught up with him, but after the washing the hunter gave him, his whole body became darker than ever before.

As he tried to escape from the area, Esu told him not to abscond because it was necessary to belie the information given about him to the people by the newborn child, lest the witches would pursue him wherever he went until they killed him. Esu emphasised that he was already a target and that once the witches marked anyone down for execution, there was no escape, except through checkmate and sacrifice. With that he agreed to follow Esu to the town.

When he got to the town, the woman indentified him as the man who dropped the egg and fouled their medicine. When they asked him, he denied it. They told him to stretch out his two hands which they were told had turned white from the medicine he touched. They discovered that his two hands had the same colour as the rest of his body, as dark as charcoal. The people then turned to the woman to explain how she knew that it was the stranger who committed the offence and she disclosed that it was her day old child that told her.

Since it was clear that the woman had lied, they accused her of crass ingratitude for trying to destroy the man who came to her aid in the procurement of a safe delivery at a time when nobody was at home. The elders quickly returned a verdict of death by execution on the woman and her child. Osameji pleaded in vain for them to spare the lives of the two, but they told him not to waste his words, because there was nothing like forgiveness in their own tradition. The mother and child were executed because it was forbidden under pain of death for anyone to lie in the town.

To thank Osameji for the assistance he rendered in their absence, they rewarded him with gifts made up of a man, a woman and a goat — all witches. On getting home, he offered the goat to Ifa and gave another he-goat to express his gratitude to Esu for coming to his rescue at a critical moment. He then did a feast in praise of Orunmila.

The Witches Discover the truth:

During the next meeting of the witches they discovered that it was Esu who helped Osameji to falsify the account of the story given to them by the executed woman and child. They then decided that Osameji was to die before the end of that year. He saw it in his dream and he decided to approach the following Awos for Divination:

Ajibola ni sawo ki maaki, meeki
Opolo mi ko yongidi le wa
Akidara mi Ata mode
Ojo ko ba mo ni run, Oni moni dede.

When they sounded Ifa for him, his own ODU came out. They told him that death was in store for him before that year ran out and that nothing could be done to stop it. After this sordid news, he went into recluse and began to weep. When his wife saw that the end of her husband was at hand, she packed her belongings out of his house and left.

On getting to the market place she met two Ifa priests called Oleu ken bi aja and Olurin kurin oma erukunse soro soro. They asked whether she was not Osameji's wife and she confirmed but added that the witches had passed a death sentence on her husband and that it had been confirmed at divination that he was going to die before the year ran out, and that it was on account of the hopelessness of the situation that she was leaving.

They persuaded her to return with them to the house and she did. They assured her that they were convinced there was going to be a remedy because Orunmila does not surrender to impossibilities. They met Osameji still crying his eyes out. When he told them the ODU that came out, they wondered why he was crying because the meaning of it was that, that was the year that prosperity was coming his way, if he could make the necessary sacrifice. They told him that he was going to have a new child that year, build his own house and have plenty of money provided he could give:

(I) He-goat to Esu;
(II) Pig to Ifa and
(III) Pigeon to Olokun.

He quickly brought the things out and they helped him to make the sacrifice. He compensated the visitors and they left for home.

At the end of that month his wife missed her menstruation and she became pregnant. Not long afterwards his popularity soared and his work became very prolific and money came to him from all directions. As soon as he felt that he had enough money, he built his own house. After completing his house, his wife delivered. He entered the New Year with unprecedented affluence and contentment.

To express his gratitude to the divinities that brought him prosperity he gave a pig and a goat to Ifa, a he-goat to Esu and cock and pigeon to Olokun. For the feasting, he invited the two sets of Awos who made divination for him and after the wining and dining, he sang in praise of the Awos and the divinities and everyone rejoiced with him for surviving his difficulties.

Osameji makes divination for sixteen Obas:

Ofuu fuu Lere Oodo giri, odule alara Isa omo ojibolu. Owole saka saka, Owole soko soko.

The ubiquitous wanderer, or wind, who does what he likes and means what he does, was the nickname of Osameji.

He went to the palace of Alara, a very strong Oba who was famous for destroying strong Awos at will. He told Alara that Death had completed arrangements to bury someone in his house and that that fate was earmarked for him, the Alara, because the night elders had tried and condemned him to death and that nothing was going to save him except sacrifice with a goat, a hen, a rabbit and the stem of plantain. Alara Isa refused to take the young Awo seriously. Seeing that his advice was ignored, Osameji left the palace.

He also went to the Ajero, Olowo of Owo, the Illa of Orangun, the Owa Obokun of Ijesa, the Ewi of Ado, Oba Ado Ajuwaleke and the rest of the sixteen Obas of the known world at the time. One after the other they all ignored him. They did not know much about witches and their influence over the world and so did not know what credence and weight to give to the advice of Osameji. He felt he was under divine obligation to alert the Obas of their imminent demise and he had done his duty. He then returned home. On getting home he too went to his Awos for divination and he was told that Death was also on his trail and that a grave had been prepared by the elders of the night in his house. He was also told to make sacrifice with a goat, a hen, a rabbit and the stem of plantain prepared as a coffin. He quickly did the sacrifice.

One month later the sudden death of the Alara Isa was announced and one after the other all the sixteen Obas he had forewarned, joined their ancestors. When the agents of the night who were consuming the Obas, got to the house of Osameji, they saw that he had built fortifications round himself and they left him unscathed. They feasted on the feast he had prepared for them through the sacrifice he had made, but since they had prepared a grave in his house, they buried the skull of the goat and the coffin of plantain stem inside it, and left his house. He lived to a ripe old age.

Osameji is accused of being a witch:

One night, he dreamt that he was arraigned before the conference of the divinities and accused of an undisclosed offence. The following morning he went to an Awo called Asare Lo, Awa Ajoyo, for divination. He was told to make sacrifice with a ram, 10 snails, a rabbit and a fish to Ifa so that someone might not level a false accusation against him. He did the sacrifice.

Meanwhile there was confusion among the 16 OLODUS of Orunmila when Orongun-meji accused Osameji of being the witch who was killing the children of Eji-Elemere. The accusation created so much furore that the sixteen Olodus convened a conference to resolve the matter. They discovered that the children of Eji-Elemere were being killed by his wives. Osameji was then victorious and Orangun-meji was told to apologise to him for lying against him.

Osameji discovers the cause of his problems:

He was becoming worried as to why he was just solving one problem after the other. He went to an Awo called Esi Saara, Esi Jasan, who told him to give a he-goat to Esu and a pig to Ifa and eight eggs and a castrated he-goat to the elders of the night. He made the sacrifice.

Soon after the sacrifice, his senior wife fell flat on her face one night and began to confess how she had been fermenting one problem after the other for him through witchcraft. The woman confessed everything she had done and promised that from then on he was not going to have any more problems and that he would be enjoying perpetual bliss for the rest of his life. The woman then begged him for forgiveness and he readily forgave her. Thereafter, Osameji did not have any more problems from witches.

Osameji finally settles his score with witchcraft with a concordat:

He was the one who brought them to the world and he was the one who saved them from total extinction from the face of the earth. The matter originally concerned Orisa Nla who, as God's own representative on earth, was the head of all the divinities, including the witch community.

Orisa had two lakes at the back of his house. One of them used to dry up during the dry season whilst the other provided year-round water supply. The two lakes were used commonly by all and sundry. But Orisa's wives were jesting at him for allowing witches, among others, to make use of his lake. He reacted by making the all-season lake exclusive for the use of his household, whilst allowing the witches to use the one that dried up in the dry season.

Knowing that their lake could not provide them with water during the hot season, the witches went for divination on what to do to ensure year-round water supply from their lake. They were advised to give a he-goat to Esu. After Esu had eaten his he-goat, he dived into Orisa Nla's exclusive lake, removed the stone with which the spring of the lake was dyked and transferred it to the witches' lake. The effect of the stone was to stop the water from flowing underground. Assured that their lake would no longer dry up, they appointed two birds to watch over it against intruders. The birds were called Ikaare (Akpalakperan in Bini) and Otuutu (Erimohi in Bini).

When the dry season came Orisa Nla's lake quickly dried up, while that of the witches remained filled with water. The witches gave the two birds the call sign with which to alert them if any intruder came to fetch water from their lake. When Orisa Nla's household became short of water, they went to the witches' lake. The birds allowed them to fetch water but the wives also went into the lake to have their baths. It was at that stage that the birds began to give the call signs to their principals.

Ikaare was the first to announce "Aya Orisa weee" and Otuutu shouted "Aya Orisa ponmi tu tu tu tu". With that, the intruders realised that there were guards watching the lake. They quickly took to their heels and ran home.

When the witches came, they asked the guards who the intruders were and they reported that they were members of Orisa Nla's household. They swore to punish Orisa Nla for contravening the proclamation he made by himself, by allowing his family to use their lake.

The witches marching song was:
Eni Asoro, omo eronko aafobo oniyan,
To Orisa Taayare, Aarije, Aarimu.
Pandemonium is let loose today
All the birds of the forest will
speak like human beings.
We shall comsume Orisa Nla and
his wives this day.

When Orisa Nla heard the witches' war song from the distance, he escaped from his house to take refuge with Ogun. Ogun got prepared to do battle with the invaders and sat in front of his house waiting for the witches to arrive. As soon as they arrived at Ogun's gate, he threw up his matchet and it sparked fire. But they swallowed Ogun up with his fighting instruments — and Orisa Nla escaped through the back door. He took refuge in Sango's place and the same fate befell him. Orisa Nla ran to the homes of all the other divinities but they were all swallowed up by the invading witches.

Orisa Nla finally ran to Orunmila's house and he prepared a hiding place on his shrine for him to hide. He made Orisa Nla to hide under the shrine and he covered him up with a white cloth with his head protruding through the white cloth. That is today signified by the elevation protruding under a white covering on the shrine of Orunmila. It is called Orite.

Osameji then brought out his divination tray (Akpako) and prepared the divination powder and the markings of his own Ifa and with Uroke, he blew it over his house shouting Ero, Ero, Ero, (that is peace, peace, peace,): When the witches got to the road junction close to his house they lost their bearings and were confused. But they sent their two path-finders to direct their advance to wherever Orisa Nla was. The two scouts found Orunmila in front of his house and they told him that they had traced Orisa Nla's footsteps to his house. He confirmed that he was infact keeping him, but appealed to them that he was already so pale and lifeless that if they killed him in that condition, there would be no flesh in him. He convinced them to give him seven days to fatten him up before killing him. He then offered to share out of Orisa Nla's meat.

He spoke to them with an incantation which is forbidden to be mentioned or spoken because it evokes havoc. The summation of it is that he conjured them to accept whatever explanation he gave them for keeping Orisa Nla. Under the influence of the incantation they agreed and retreated to base.

The following morning Osameji made divination and he was told to give a black hen to Ifa and a he-goat to Esu. He quickly did it knowing that the witches would shorten the length of the ensuing days and nights. He was also told to prepare a feast with rabbits for the witches and to prepare palm wine poisoned with Iyerosun and the incantation which could not be mentioned above.

He also prepared a fenced-in enclosure in front of his house and got a kind of adhesive gum, called aare in Yoruba, and Uho in Bini, to daub the fence. He prepared sixteen wooden seats, also daubed with the gum, and positioned them within the reception enclosure.

Not long afterwards the appointed day arrived and on that day, Osameji prepared the feast and placed the food and drinks within the reception enclosure. As soon as the witches arrived, they took their seats and began eating and drinking. After eating and drinking they told Osameji to produce Orisa Nla and before he could respond one of them sighted Orisa Nla within Orunmila's shrine from where he peeped to see the invaders. The one who saw him shouted that Orisa Nla was under Orunmila's shrine. As they moved to attack, Esu had glued them firmly to their seats and they were helpless. As they tried to roll the seats the glue on the fence held up their wings. They were totally over-powered.

At that point, Osameji gave his Ifa knife (Aza) to Orisa Nla and he held on to the Uroke and they began to destroy the witches one after the other. When they had destroyed all of them, they heaved a sigh of relief. They did not know that one of them managed to crawl to take refuge under Orunmila's shrine, the same place where Orisa Nla had hidden before the attack.

As they were killing them they were singing:
"Ota mi po yee
Okon kon nu uku saan paa yeye.
My attackers are many.
I will kill them one after
the other."

When Orisa sighted the one hiding under the shrine of Orunmila, he wanted to kill him as well, but Osameji stopped him on the grounds that he could not destroy anyone who took refuge under his Ifa shrine just as his (Orisa Nla's) life was spared after hiding under the same shrine.

They then brought out the witch who was a woman and removed the glue from her body. When they examined her closely they discovered that she was pregnant. Osameji then remarked that it was forbidden to knowingly kill a pregnant woman. In Bini it is said "Aigbozi gbeken".

Orisa Nla insisted that if the woman was allowed to survive, she would produce more witches that would attempt to destroy the world like the first generation of witches tried to do. It is strongly believed that if that woman had been killed that night, it would have meant the end of the genealogy of witchcraft on the face of the earth. Orisa Nla however suggested that she should be made to take an oath not to destroy innocent persons on earth.

Osameji then proposed to Orisa Nla that the ground was the only divinity capable of destroying the witches if they misbehaved, since the ground is the only force that supervenes all other earthly forces and agencies. He dug a hole on the ground and filled it with all eatable items of food with kolanut put on top of it. They then made her to swear on the ground to kill her or any of her off-springs from generation to generation if they ever killed any of God's or Orunmila's children without just cause. She took the oath and ate the kolanut on top of the heap.

She however asked them to let her know how she was to feed if she could not kill any of God's or Orunmila's children. Orisa Nla replied that if he or any of his children offended them or their matter was brought to them, he would atone for the offence by killing an animal, be it ram, goat, fowl, etc and spill the blood outside the house. That is a signal that the offender has atoned to them for the offence committed. They should then leave him alone. That is the significance of the sarah which children of God make to this day. It is a sign that the offering is from a child of God and the witches will accept it and grant the offerer's wishes.

On the other hand Osameji told her that if she saw any food prepared in a pot and deposited at a road juction, by the wayside or on top of an incinerator, she should know that it is from Orunmila's child and she should accept the food and leave the offerer alone. This is the Etutu (Izobo in Bini) that Orunmila often advises his followers to make to the night when they are in trouble with the witches. That is why the Iyerosun markings of Osameji are often marked on the divination tray when offerings are being made to the night.

The incantation, which cannot be mentioned here, and which Ifa priests repeat when making an offering to the night, is to remind them that the offerer belongs to Orunmila and that they should remember the oath they administered to their mother on the fateful day.

The significance of this revelation is that no other divinity is able to withstand the witches when they decide to fight. They can always subdue all of them, with the exception of God and Orunmila, due to the way they handled them on that fateful night. Anyone who believes that charms and other diabolical preparations can subdue witchcraft is merely deceiving himself, unless they transgress the concordat which their mother entered into on that night and which saved them from total extinction.

CHAPTER XXIII
ETURA — MEJI

Lahila llala hu. That is the call sign of Otumeji — because he was the one in heaven who made divination for Baba Imole, before he left heaven for this world. He went for divination to Otumeji who in heaven was called Eni Baba laaba.

Eni a ba la aba, Eeni abaa laaba,
Eni aba la baa lanpe ni baba, adifa fun Imole
abewu gereje tiojokosi ibikon tio maakere aye je — meaning:—

The person you meet once, meet again, and meet later as an elder in a town, is called an old man. That was the name of the Awo (Otumeji) who made divination for the head of the Imoles to enable them inherit the prosperity of the earth with minimal effort, from a sedentary position. Baba Imole, was told to make sacrifice with 4 hens, 4 cocks, 4 pigeons and 4 snails, and he made the sacrifice.

When he got to the world, he struggled for a long time before he was able to realise his destiny, but when he finally met Otumeji again on earth, he made the same sacrifice for him in the cave and told him that his flock was going to multiply but that the reward of his sacrifice would be reaped by his descendants and followers. He was told that money would always come to them with very little or no effort. Those who wanted to know the truth about God would always come to him for the message.

He made divination for the Groundnut:

When the groundnut was coming to the world, it was Otumeji, who made divination for her. The groundnut was anxious to have plenty of children on earth so that her kindred might enjoy everlasting popularity on earth. But she was told to make sacrifice so that after having so many children, her brothers and sisters might not turn round to destroy them. She was advised to serve Ifa with a Ram and Esu with a he-goat. She refused to do it, and left for the world without performing any sacrifice.

On getting to the world, she was indeed very productive becauce she gave birth to several children at a time. Meanwhile, Esu informed the rabbit who had also just had her own children and was looking for food with which to feed them, that the groundnut had just had children, but hid her young ones underground. Esu also drew the attention of the hedgehog (Okhaen in Bini or Urare in Yoruba), and the hare (Ekun in Yoruba or Orere in Bini) to the nutrient value of the groundnut's children. Following upon the advice of Esu, they all began to feed on the children of the groundnut. When she discovered that she was running out of children, she went to an Awo called Jemi Sudi for divination. The Awo also advised her to serve Ifa with a ram and Esu with He-goat. After the sacrificies, Esu went to the farmer to advise him to set traps round his farm in order to catch the intruding animals who were ravaging his farm. The farmer accordingly encircled his farm with traps which caught several of the intruding animals. When the animals saw that the groundnut had been effectively fortified, they gave up the farm, and the groundnuts and her children were left to thrive and survive to become profitable cash crops for humanity. The seeds of the groundnuts also survived to keep their generation flourishing to this day. The groundnut later went to thank Orunmila for helping her to survive the onslaught of her relations.

He made Divination for the white man when he was anxious to know how to manufacture a live human being:

The most important work done in heaven by Otumeji is the revelation of how the white man attempted to learn from God how to produce a human being. The white man had become so vast on earth in the field of inventions that he thought he should crown his achievements by going to God to teach him how to manufacture a human being. When he got to heaven, he approached an Awo called Ayegbe kooshe gbere gede, "No mirror can be wide enough to see the length of a whole year". Kafiriron kadun — (loon difa fun oyibo tooma ko ushe ona omo lowo orisa.). The white man was advised to give he-goat to Esu but he refused to do it because he did not believe in making fettish sacrifices.

Without making the sacrifice he went to the palace of God and asked to be taught how to produce a human being. Since God never refuses any request made to him, he told the white man to fetch mud for the work, which he did. God has a large mirror in his workshop which he looks at when moulding any object. He examines the reflection of the object from the mirror and he must pass it as perfect before confirming it as being fit for existence.

With the mud fetched by the white man, He moulded the image of a human being and the white man watched him. After moulding the human image, God left it to dry and meanwhile moved to his inner chamber to attend to other callers.

As soon as God left, Esu came into the workshop in the shape of a heavenly police and asked the white man whether he could not replicate the image prepared by God. The visitor confirmed that he could. Esu then told him to leave for home with the image, because it would speak after drying up.

With that piece of deceptive advice, the white man left with the human image. When he however got home the image could not speak after drying up. That is why the white man is unable to cast any speaking image to this day. It was on account of the sacrifice which the white man refused to make. When Otumeji comes out of divination for someone anxious to do something, he should he advised to exercise lots of patience so he might get to the bottom of the matter.

He made divination for Truth and Falsehood:

With the following poem he advised Truth and Falsehood in heaven when they were quarrelling;
 Oso gegege — obeke
Odewu gereje gereje, ofi iboka mole
Eni toba yole da ohun were were
Aamayo Oluware she.
I threw a missile;
And it hit a trickster;
Who made a long dress;
To conceal his treachery.
Whoever hides to practice;
Wickedness against others;

Will have evil endangering him openly.

Truth and Falsehood were arguing between themselves. Truth argued that he was more powerful than Falsehood. On the other hand Falsehood argued that he was stronger than the Truth.

Otumeji told them that the power of falsehood is transient and ephemeral and that Truth, although slow and weak, overcomes Falsehood in the end. He then sang:—
Lojokon, Lojokon;
Alekpo sika Lojokon;
No matter how powerful wickedness is;
Righteousness overcomes wickedness in the end.

Otumeji leaves heaven for the World:

There were two friends in heaven who agreed to leave for earth at the same time. Ori Ala (who was called Otumeji on earth) and Ori Atosi. They went for divination with two Awos called Odogbo kon Areyi and Odogbo kon Oro orun. They were both advised to make sacrifice with a ram each to their guardian angels. The ram was to be used to feast the divinities. They were also advised to make sacrifice with he-goat to Esu, including, a cutlass and pap (Ogiri). Ori Ala made the sacrifice, but Ori Atosi refused to make any sacrifice. He insisted that as soon as God cleared one to go to the world, it was a waste of valuable money and effort to make any additional sacrifice to lower divinities. They both left for the world.

After they grew up on earth, they turned out to be bosom friends. Their profession was to fetch firewood for sale. One day, Otumeji insisted that they should both go for divination to find out how to prosper in their trade. His friend, who was named Alaroye on earth, argued that it was an exercise in futility to waste the valuable money they earned from the sale of wood on divination. They went to an Awo called Peremu sheke for divination. Otumeji collected all his savings which amounted to 65K and dragged his friend to accompany him for divination. Each of them had a matchet with which they fetched fire wood in the bush and a cock to wake them up in the morning to prepare for their daily chores.

At divination, each of them was told to make sacrifice with a cutlass, a cock, and the cloth in which he travelled to the bush. Alaroye jested that the Awo wanted to deprive them of their only possessions and insisted that he was never going to make such a self-depriving sacrifice.

When Otumeji got home, he decided that he was going back to the Awo to make the sacrifice. He collected his only cutlass, his only and favourite cock and the apparel (Etalugbo in Bini and Bamte in Yoruba) leaving only his pant on him. He also went with all the money left with him at home.

He was also told to add the pad with which he used to carry fire wood from the forest and to the market.

The Awo made the sacrifice by burning the pad and the cloth and left the cutlass on the Esu shrine. Through an incantation, the Awo told Esu that Otumeji had made the sacrifice with all the instruments with which he pursued a vocation that ran counter to his destiny and begged Esu to prepare his feet to tread on the right path of his destiny. He then slaughtered the cock on the Esu shrine. After the sacrifice, Otumeji came home empty handed, without the slightest idea of what to do next.

The following morning, Alaroye came to him for the day's round to the bush to fetch fire wood. When they got to the bush, Otumeji collected firewood with his hands because he had no cutlass to use. His friend fetched better fire wood with the cutlass which he refused to use for sacrifice.

It was time to fetch a rope with which to tie his fire wood. He appealed to his friend to lend him his cutlass for that purpose but Alaroye refused to oblige, on the grounds that if he had not surrendered his cutlass, he would not have gone aborrowing. His friend completed his own task and left for home, leaving Otumeji to 'roast in his own juice'.

After his friend left him, he used his teeth to cut a rope to tie his firewood. As he was cutting the rope with his teeth, he saw one giant tortoise, carried it, and used the rope to tie it up. He then went to fetch another rope with which to tie up his fire wood. As he drew the second rope, he saw yet another tortoise and again tied it up. He tied up the first tortoise within his pack of wood and tied the second tortoise on top of the luggage. He then carried the firewood home with one tortoise clearly visible on top of the luggage, while the other tortoise was concealed inside the fire wood bundle. By the time he left for home, it was already dark and he was very hungry.

Back in heaven, the daughter of Olokun, the water divinity, was having a difficult labour and had been told that they needed a tortoise with which to make sacrifice in order for her to have a safe delivery. Olokun had sent errands to the market of Oja ajigbomekon to fetch a tortoise at all cost. That market was commonly attended by the inhabitants of heaven and earth. At the same time, the wife of Ala, the divinity of prosperity, was also ill in heaven and at the point of death. Ala was told at divination to make sacrifice with a tortoise so that his wife might get well. He too, had sent a messenger to the market to fetch a tortoise at all cost. The heavenly messengers had scanned the entire market all day to buy any available tortoise, but could not get any to buy. When they got back to heaven to report the failure of their mission, they appealed to God for divine assistance, who despatched the heavenly police to take positions at the boundry between heaven and earth and to crystal-gaze into any location where tortoises existed. Esu had meanwhile caused all living tortoises to bury themselves beneath the ground and they were all eclipsed into invisibility.

That was the point at which Otumeji was returning from the bush with a tortoise on top of his load of fire wood. From the positions they occupied, the heavenly police saw Otumeji walking home with a tortoise on top of his load. They telescoped the distance and in no time they accosted Otumeji and offered to buy his tortoise. The bargain fo the tortoise then began. The bargain had reached the point at which they were prepared to pay 200 men 200 women, 200 bags of money, 200 bundles of clothing, 200 bushells of beads, 200 goats, 200 rams, 200 cows, etc., when Esu emerged in the shape of a neutral hunter. He advised the heavenly messengers to return home to bring the prizes they had offered so he might convince the seller to agree.

Olokun's representatives were the first to return and they were given the first tortoise in exchange for the prizes they brought. Esu then asked Otumeji whether he had any other tortoise to sell and he replied that he had one left inside his load of fire wood. As soon as Olokun's representatives left, Esu advised him to hide their prizes in a hut nearby. Thereafter, they took position to await the arrival of Ala's representatives. Soon afterwards, Ala's representatives arrived with their prize offerings which they gladly and hurriedly paid and collected the second tortoise, rejoicing that they had beaten Olokun's representatives to it. With the departure of the celestial messengers, Otumeji took all the things to the hut and the human prizes were quickly made to build an abode for their new master. Esu however advised him to go and sell his fire wood and to eat with the proceeds. He sold it for 65K and Esu told him to use the money to buy his usual food to eat. That was the last of his fire wood trade.

His life was instantly transformed from penury to affluence and he easily became the richest man around. He now had a new settlement to himself with plenty of wives, servants and tradesman at his beck and call.

One day, his friend realised that he had not been seeing Otumeji in the bush for a long time. He decided to go and look for him. He arrived at his gate with his pad and cutlass. He saw an air of prosperity all around, with massive buildings dotted all over the settlement. He was confused. His first inclination when he did not see Otumeji's usual hut was to think that he had probably been dispossessed by wealthier occupants. As he was wandering around, the gate men challenged him, and he explained that he was looking for his business partner, Otumeji. For daring to mention their Lord's name, the gatemen began to molest him. He however insisted that the man was his friend and they took him inside to meet their master.

When he saw Otumeji, he could not recognise him. He however insisted that he was looking for his friend with whom he used to trade in firewood. Otumeji asked him whether he would recognise the man if he saw him. With that Otumeji began to shed tears and identified himself. He disclosed that it was the day he abandoned him in the forest after refusing to lend him the use of his cutlass that he discovered his new-found wealth. Otumeji reminded him that his prosperity was the outcome of the sacrifice he made. He also asked him whether he was ready to make his own sacrifice and he replied affirmatively but nagged that he had no money for it.

At that stage, Otumeji gave him money with which to make his sacrifice and collected 5 men, 5 women, five goats, five bags of money etc for thanksgiving to the Awo who made divination and sacrifice for him and begged him to make the overdue sacrifice for his friend. He also gave Esu five he-goats to thank him for the assistance he rendered to him.

After the sacrifice, Otumeji brought him home to give him a house to live in with his own retinue of followers. They both lived together and prospered immensely every after. They remained very close to Peremu sheke, the Awo who made divination and sacrifice for them.

Otumeji opened the way for wealth to come to the world:

It is significant to emphasize that it was Esu who caused the illnesses of the daughter of Olokun and the wife of Ala. He was also responsible for concealing all the available tortoises in heaven and on earth. He contrived the subterfuges to create a favourable atmosphere for helping Otumeji.

When the heavenly Police returned to heaven, they reported to God the high cost of buying a single tortoise from earth. God wondered that it was probably on account of the prevailing poverty on earth that they had become so extortionate. God then ordered the treasury keeper in heaven to open the treasure gates for money to leave for earth. A constellation of money then left for earth.

Once more, Esu went to Otumeji and told him that money was coming in large armies to the earth, but that they would only enter the home of a host who was able to decorate his home with what they ate and liked. Esu advised Otumeji to spread a white cloth in front of his house and to keep plenty of mashed yam (Ewo in Yoruba and Obobo in Bini) to throw round his house.

After alerting Otumeji to the approach of the heavenly visitors, Esu went to meet the host of money on the way, and warned them that the people of the world were too untidy to provide suitable accommodation for them. He told them that there was only one man called Otumeji who was capable of giving them befitting hospitality.

Without stopping at any other place, they trooped to Otumeji's house where they actually found a familiar atmosphere for them to thrive. That was how Otumeji became the most wealthy person in the known world at the time. When Otumeji comes out of divination for a poor man, he should be told to have his own Ifa and to make the necessary sacrifice after which his fortunes would doubtlessly blossom.

The origin of Coup d'etat against Seniority/Authority

The next revelation of Otumeji is how it came about that both the young and the old have some sort of authority. Traditionally, seniority of age was the test of wisdom and authority. A young person was not allowed to, and dared not, interfere when the elders were deliberating. Otumeji has told us how the tradition was altered to make it possible for junior persons to contest for position and influence, with their elders. He tells us that when the young person (Youth) and the elderly person (Elder) were going to ask for ASE from God, they went for divination to three Awos called:

OTIN LOTIN EJO — Soft sweet drink
OBILOBI UWA — Noble kolanuts
EMULEMU ARA JONJO — Alcoholic wine.
Loon difa fun Omode ipapo;
Abufun agbalagba Ipapo.

They were both advised to make sacrifice, after which they left for heaven.

When they got to heaven, God told them to return after seven days with 201 cowries each. That was before Esu closed the route leading from heaven to earth, the details of which we shall see in later books. It was still possible at the time to travel back and forth between heaven and earth. The Elder had no difficulty in collecting 201 cowries. Youth could only raise 50 cowries. On the appointed day, they both set out separately for heaven.

Meanwhile Youth met Elder on the way and offered to assist in carrying the load of cowries, for the Elder, who was grateful for the kind gesture. Youth however told Elder that he could not travel at his slow pace. Youth therefore travelled at a faster pace but promised to wait for Elder at the gates of heaven. Youth moved very fast and soon got to heaven.

Before getting to heaven, Youth tied up his 50 cowries together with Elder's 201 cowries in a single parcel and left with it straight for the divine palace of God. On getting to the Palace, he surrendered the parcel of 251 cowries as if it was his own prize for a higher authority. God however told him to await the arrival of Elder.

When the Elder subsequently arrived, he thanked the Youth for assisting him in carrying his parcel and for waiting for him. But when he demanded his cowries from the Youth, the latter denied ever relieving him of the burden and insisted that the whole parcel belonged to him. He infact accused the Elder of attempting to rob him of his parcel. The ensuing argument attracted the intervention of God who asked how much each of them brought. The young man explained that he left home with 251 cowries because he was anxious to have a stronger authority. When the parcel was counted, it actually contained 251 cowries. God then decided that the cowries belonged to the Younger man and He gave him the ASE.

This incident explains why the Youth are able to seize authority and the reins of power from their elders in various communities of human beings to this day. Before that, one had to attain the status of an elder before aspiring to any height of authority. That is why younger persons participate in governance to this day, by seizing power from their elders in the world. That is not the situation in heaven where the Elders still enjoy supremacy.

When it comes out of divination, the person should be advised not to allow anybody to carry his bag for him if he is travelling, lest he runs the risk of losing it. The Ifa priest who is responsible for this revelation, Chief Omoruyi Edokpayi, confirmed that it manifested wonderfully for a man who once came to him for divination.

Awo Omoruyi Edokpayi once visited another Awo called Adeniyi, who was making divination for a Muslim (Alfa) priest called Yesuful Adeniran, of Usi in the Ekiti area of Ondo State of Nigeria. Edokpayi is from Benin City, whilst Adeniran was from Usi in Ekiti and Adeniyi was from Imesi in Ekiti.

When Edokpayi got to Adeniyi's house, he met the ODU of Otumeji on the Ifa tray and as it is the tradition in Ifism, the host asked Edokpayi to interpret the Ifa on the tray.

Edokpayi told Yesufu to make sacrifice with a tortoise, cudgel and cutlass, in order to avoid losing his money or his life during a proposed trip. Yesufu made the sacrifice before leaving for the trip to the town of Igbomina in Kwara State.

His alfa work was very lucrative and he realised a net gain of N600.00 from the payments made by his clients. He then gave the money to his host to keep for him pending the date of his departure. Thereafter, he made some additional money which he kept by himself.

Meanwhile, his host who was indebted to several creditors spent Yesufu's N600.00 to defray part of his indebtedness. After Yesufu had announced the date of his departure, the host began to wonder how he was going to get the money to return to his guest. Eventually, since there was nothing he could do to raise the money, he decided that the only solution was to matchet Yesufu to death in his sleep.

By the eve of his departure, his host had firmed up his morbid plans. That night, he kept pacing the corridor adjoining the guest room in which Yesufu stayed. But Yesufu was engaged in special prayers until very late that night. At about 2 a.m. the host's patience ran out and he decided that sleeping or not, it was time to carry out his nefarious design.

He then moved stealthily into the room with matchet in hand to butcher Yesufu from behind. Just before he raised his hand up to strike, he fell flat on his face and his fall attracted all members of the household including the astonished Yesufu himself. Esu and intervened on account of the sacrifice made by Yesufu.

The host later explained the circumstances which led him to such a desperate decision and appealed to Yesufu to forgive him, but at the same time to thank God for stopping him from carrying out his plan. Yesufu forgave his host and told him to forget about the money.

He left for home the following morning and went to narrate the incident to Awo Edokpayi.

This practical real life diversion was brought in to illustate how close the interpretation of the Ifa ODU corpus can be to perfect exactitude.

Otumeji goes to Imodina to help the Imoles

It is revealed that Otumeji travelled to Imodina and that he was the one who taught the Alufas, the art they practice to this day. Before leaving, he went for divination to a group of Awos called:

Ru Ru Ru Laha
Ru Ru Ru Lohun
OO holoo lo hun
Agbada mofi Odo
Odo ni fi lu agbada.
Awon loon difa fun Otumeji nijotofe
Ko awon Alufa jade ni nu Odu ale.

These are the Awos who made divination for Otumeji when he was going to bring out the Imoles from the cave.

He was advised to make sacrifice with he-goat to Esu because of the Ifa gospel he was going to preach in an unknown land (Ilu Aimon). After travelling for a long time, he was beginning to wonder whether he had any clear idea of where he was going. When he could not answer the question of where he was bound for, he decided that it was time for him to go back. He was accompanied by sixteen Awos including those mentioned above and several members of his domestic staff. They had taken enough food to last them for three months, but the stock was running out.

That night, Orunmila appeared to him and told him that people were already waiting for him at the place where he was going. He told him that he would have to travel for about three hundred days and 300 nights before getting to the place. He assured him that he would have a lot of work to do both on the way and at the place. Orunmila assured him that he was never going to be in want of what to eat during his journey.

Meanwhile, he had passed through all the forest belts and was beginning to come to hilly and sandy territory. It was also beginning to get much hotter. His party was beginning to get bored and they sat down by the side of a very big rock to rest. As they were resting, they heard voices as if they were those of people, living underneath the earth. Otumeji quickly organised a tour of the rock and saw an opening — as well as footsteps leading into and out of it. He decided to sit by the hole to see the kind of people who would move into or out of it. Not long afterwards, he saw some people coming out of what looked like a cave. The people were surprised to see him because they had thought that they were the only inhabitants of the world around. He did not understand their language and they did not understand his own, but somehow, they were able to communicate with one another. It was clear that Otumeji and his followers wanted food and the cave men were quite happy to oblige.

After providing them with food, Otumeji decided to perform a divination and he quickly discovered that they had a problem. He asked for their leader and after identifying himself, he demonstrated to him that the reason he brought his followers into the cave was because he was a eunuch. The men confirmed his story. This problem is often associated with all the Ugbodu children of Otumeji. The Onoifa has to be prepared for them on the Esu shrine with a he-goat, after which their problems will be over.

He told the man that it was because of the pap (Akamu) which he used to drink that he developed the impotence. He told him to give up taking pap. He also pointed to the next man and told him that he was complaining of lack of money. When he asked them the name of the place, they told him it was a village on the town of Imodina.

He told the second man that the reason for his financial problem was because he had abandoned the divinity (Shango) that followed him to the world. Thereafter the people wondered with what force and power

Orunmila was able to make these revelations. To prove the power to them, be began to teach them his own art of divination. Before they could attain perfection, they all had to leave to fight a war and their leader who was called Momodu led them into battle, leaving only the mother of their leader behind in the cave. Unknown to Otumeji, no one was left to look after the aged mother as he too went out on his divination exploits. Thirtyone days after the departure of the Imoles for war, Otumeji returned to the cave only to discover that the mother of Momodu had died of starvation.

On the wall of the cave the woman marked 31 strokes indicating that she starved for 31 days, before giving-up the ghost. However Otumeji preserved the corpse of the woman in a special drier.

Meanwhile, Outmeji had started making his own farm which produced a very good harvest. As soon as Momodu and his followers returned from the battle field, they ravaged all the farms around including that of Otumeji. He then made divination on how to save his farm and he was told to make sacrifice to Esu with a he-goat, a cock, a chain and a matchet. He quickly made the sacrifice.

Following the return of Momodu, he discovered the death of his mother, and after seeing the mother's markings on the wall, he realised that the helpless woman had starved to death. Almost immediately he proclaimed that all his followers should starve for 31 days to mourn the death of his mother. He also proclaimed that the sacrifice of starving for 31 days in commemoration of his Mother's death should become an annual obligation.

It is strongly believed that the tutelage given to the Imoles by Otumeji explains the close similarity between Ifa divination and the Alfa divination. The markings are the same although the names are different. They also go in multiples of sixteen.

After the sacrifice made by Otumeji to Esu, the latter got set to work for the food he had been given. When the followers of Momodu returned to Otumeji's farm to ravage it once more, Esu had used the chain with which he made sacrifice to set an invisible trap round the farm. As soon as they made an impact on the farm the trap jettisoned and captured seven of them, who disappeared into the sky. The remaining seven fell to the ground. From then on the seven began to pray with their hands and faces turned to the direction of the sky to beg God to bring back their seven colleagues who dissappered into the sky.

Otumeji goes to Imeka.

After the death of his mother, Momodu moved to nearb Imeka to settle down, and he was soon followed by Otumeji who now had a large retinue following him. When Otumeji got to Imeka he met Momodu who told him that he had been trying to solve the following three problems for the people of Imeka:
- (i) To rid the town's environs of a dinosaur (locally called keneun) which was terrorising the lives of the people from the caves and rocks around;
- (ii) To solve the problem of barrenness then prevalent in the place; and
- (iii) To reduce the height of the rock, which was hanging over the town as a cliff.

Otumeji had one container called Ado which contained his instrument of authority. With it he could make and unmake. In the first instance he brought out part of the content of the wand and ordered all the rocks surrounding the town of Imeka to crush into a wilderness and instantly all the rocks came crumbling down and at the same time, all the dinosaurs were crushed to death. That is how the generation of dinosaurs became extinct in Imeka and rock crumbled into rubble.

As soon as Otumeji performed the feats of reducing the height of the rock and eliminating the bogey of the dinosaurs, one girl instinctively went on her knees and bowed her head to the ground to thank him. Others in the town followed suit, and from then on this girl became one of the followers of Otumeji. Otumeji told Momodu that before solving the third problem of barrenness, he would like to see the King of the town.

He was told that it was only possible to see the King once a year. At this point, Otumeji told one of his followers to bring out a pebble which he had brought all the way from Ife. As soon as he put the pebble on the ground, it multiplied into 200 pebbles. When the by-standers saw the miracle, they flocked around Otumeji and his followers. In no time, a crowd had gathered. He told each of them to pick one of the 200 pebbles and throw it in the direction of the King's palace. He told them that the operation was necessary in order to get their King to come out. As he threw the pebbles the wind carried them to drop on the roof of the King's residence. When the sound of the pebbles dropping on his roof became unbearable, the King decided to come out himself to verify what was happening. When the King came out, he saw Otumeji and his followers and the king was quickly briefed on the wonders already done by the visitors.

The King also confirmed to him that their major problem in the country was one of childlessness. Otumeji asked him what reward he would give him if he succeeded in solving the problem. He promised that he and his people would from generation to generation continue to sing the praise of Orunmila. At that stage, Otumeji also asked the King to throw one of the pebbles in the direction of his palace as the others had previously done before him. Otumeji also asked one of his followers to strike Momodu with a cudgel which he had with him. After striking Momodu, Otumeji asked him whether the effect was painful and he confirmed that it was indeed painful.

Otumeji then asked him why he went to hide Amina, the wife of Audu his second-in-command. Momodu confessed that he did so because he loved the woman. At that point, Audu, who was present at the time, brought out his dagger and stabbed him. Momodu was fatally injured, but Otumeji brought out a coco-yam and gave it to Momodu to eat and the stab wound healed immediately. Otumeji however directed Audu to the cave where his wife was hidden and he went there and met his wife and they embraced. The wife quickly went on her knees to beg for forgiveness with the explanation that she had been told that he was lost in combat during the War. The husband told her that it was one strange visitor who directed him to where she was hidden. When she was told of the wonderful work already done by the visitor, she offered to meet him to help her to have a child.

They both went to meet Otumeji who told her to rejoice because she was going to get pregnant and that her first child would be a girl. The woman asked how she would express her gratitude to Orunmila if his prediction manifested. The following month, Amina bcame pregnant after Otumeji had left Imeka in continuation of his tour. She later gave birth to a child whom they named Ifatumo, meaning Ifa is sufficient to depend on, which was later corrupted to Fatima. As soon as Amina became pregnant, all the other women in Imeka started getting pregnant. But Otumeji told the King of Imeka that the divinities were not happy with the manner in which Momodu hid Audu's wife and that before any woman under his kingdom would become pregnant, she had to be concealed from public view in a like manner. Anybody therefore who wanted his wife to become pregnant had to hide her from public view. This is how the convention of wearing veils by women starrted in Imeka. From that time all visitors to Imeka were required to throw stones as Otumeji directed the Imoles to do, at the foot of the rock that once hung as a cliff over the town.

Otumeji is said to have lived in the land of Aimon for over twelve years. Much as his followers preferred to spend the rest of their lives there, the custom and tradition of the area were far too alien to Otumeji to conduce to his staying permanently. That is why it is said in Ifism that Orunmila liked the people of Imeka, but since it was a land where position and wealth carried greater influence than age, he preferred to return home to Ife. He was particularly disturbed by the assumption which underscored the norms and mores of life in the entire area, which gave pride of place to abject porverty and mayhem as tests of righteousness. As a wealthy man himself, he wanted everyone to be comfortable in life since no one in heaven wishes for a life of deprivation and penury in the court of destiny. The divinities were sent to the world to live in peace with one another as they do in heaven and to abhor violence and discord. He returned to heaven soon after getting back to Ife.

CHAPTER XXIV
IRETE MEJI
EJI — EDE
EJI — ELEMERE

One of the important works done by Ejiede in heaven was that he made divination for the Pigeon and the Swamp before they left heaven. He also made divination for the dried palm fruits chaff, (Ironyin, Imon — Edin in Bini). He was called Ugbakun and or Ugba, yeke, yeke, yeke, Odifafun, kpakpa kuuru, (or Eyele) Abufun ERE (Swamp) ati Ironyin (Palm fruit chaff). He adivsed all three of them to make sacrifice in order to live peacefully and healthily on earth. They were to make sacrifice with one egg, their wearing apparel, Eka, Eko and Ewo (or Obobo). Only the Pigeon and the Palm fruit chaff made the sacrifice as they were directed.

The Swamp (Ere in Yoruba) or (Ekhuoro in Bini) refused to make the sacrifice. Thereafter they left for the world. On getting to the world the Pigeon lived a very peaceful and healthy life, and each time she flew out, she would always shout, Ugbakun, ugbakun, difa fuun, kpakpa kuuru, Ounyon, Ifani, Okureyin, Okureyin, Okureyin, That is the triumphant cry of the Pigeon to this day, in which she is thanking Orunmila for making divination and sacrifice for her, which made her to stay healthy and that progress lies ahead.

On the other hand the palm fruit chaff (Ironyin or Imon edin in Bini) also became dry and well, whilst the Swamp who refused to make sacrifice remains sick and wet to this day.

When this Odu comes out of divination, the divinee should be advised to collect his used clothes preferably black, adding Pigeon, egg, eko, eka, and Ewo (or Obobo) for sacrifice in order to become well, if he happens to be indisposed at the time. All the materials for the sacrifice will be wrapped up in the black apparel and the parcel is used to rub his body from head to toe and buried in the swamp of the river and he will become surely well.

Eji Elemere reveals how Orunmila fought the battle for prosperity on behalf of his followers:

After God had completed his creative work, He decided to create the tree of prosperity called, EGE (IGI EGE in Yoruba) or (Erhan Uwa in Bini) in other words, the tree of wealth. To protect the tree, God appointed the Boa, the Ram, and the cock to act as the custodians. As soon as the tree of wealth grew up, all the two hundred divinities (Ugba Orumole in Yoruba or Ihenuri in Bini) tried in vain to pluck prosperity from the tree. They all failed because they did not bother to discover the secret of harvesting its fruits. It was the turn of Orunmila to make an effort. But before daring the tree, he decided to go for divination from the following Ifa Priests:

Akponmi, Owo Ule eja,
Okpajiba, Owo Ule Okparo,
Alugbogbo, kuuku ni shegun,
Ogugu lutu, meaning:—

1. The person who bales out water from the river, demolishes the home of the fish.
2. Only a patient man can succeed in killing a small animal called Okhuokhua who builds two hundred houses but lives in one of them.
3. It is a strong headed missile that destroys evil.

These were the three Ifa Priests who made divination for Orunmila before he attempted to climb the tree of wealth (EGE).

He was told first to destroy his house in heaven before he could bring his prosperity to the world. He was advised to build a house with special leaves (Ebe ahe in Bini) on the shrine of Esu and for the Awos to destroy it with a he-goat. That is why when this Odu comes out of divination the person can be asked whether he is building a house, and if he so confirms, he will be advised to suspend the construction of the house for sometime.

After performing this initial sacrifice, he went to yet another Ifa Priest called Ogbolugbo Odo, Odon Oun Iodon Orun run, otherwise known as (Agogo lila, aberun, yamunya, awon loon difa fun Orunmila nigbati, Oyagun ege Igi agunla.) He was told to make sacrifice with plenty of corn, plenty pieces of yam and plenty of rats. He was to make the sacrifice to Esu with a he-goat and a ladder, and was to go with some of the sacrificial materials in a bag when going to the foot of the tree of wealth.

On getting to the precinct of the tree, the Boa snake was the first to charge for attack. As he was told to do, he quickly threw a rat to the Boa who instantly swallowed it. The cock then flapped it's wings in preparation to crow, but he quickly threw plenty of corn at it and it settled down to eat the food. With these moves, the threats from the Boa and the cock were abated. The Ram next dug in for attack. Once more he threw the pieces of yam at the Ram and it began to eat, so with his bag on his side, Orunmila climbed the tree with a ladder installed by Esu and he plucked all the fruits on top of the tree.

Having eaten all the corn he wanted to eat, the cock looked around for Orunmila and saw him on top of the tree of wealth. He then flapped his wings and crowed saying; Orunmila gegoo or. That is the crow of the cock to this day, and it means that Orunmila was the first to climb the tree of wealth. In reply, Orunmila sang, Okege, Igi agula, ifa gege, Igi oola, logun, Okege, Igi agula.

When this Odu comes out during initiation at Ugbodu, the initiate should be made to plant three trees as follows:—
 (i) A cock to plant Ege tree called (Isa in Bini).
 (ii) The head of a Boa to plant (Ebe Alaho in Bini).
 (iii) The Ram to plant Ukpogun-kperegun, and the stone removed from the bed of a flowing river is used to prepare Esu for him.

This is the secret of how Orunmila is able to make his children rich and prosperous.

Eji Elemere comes to the world:

After acquiring the secret of prosperity, Eji Elemere decided it was time to come to the world. He went to two Ifa priests called Eji wewewe, Ogbojo, and Ojo giiri, oun gbati ba owuro. These were the two Awos who made divination for him. They advised him to make sacrifice to avoid problems in having children in the world. He was told to serve his Ifa with a goat and to give a he-goat to Esu. He quickly did the sacrifice and left for the world.

On getting to the world, he came to a town called Oke mesi where he practised Ifa art. He was prosperous but he did not have a child. He later married a wife who gave birth to a daughter. He however remained anxious to have more children. One day he decided to consult his Ifa on why he was not able to have a male child, as he was otherwise so prosperous that he used to make elaborate sacrifices during his Annual Ifa festival. He used to invite all the Awos around to participate in his annual festivals.

After the divination, his Ifa told him to make sacrifice with a whole deer (Agbonrin in Yoruba or Erhue in Bini). Not being a hunter, he travelled to the nearby village of Udo where he used to practice his Ifa art, as his base. When he got to the village, he met a woman called Kporoye who was married but childless and came for divination on what to do to have a child. He made divination for her and assured her that she would have a child, if she could make sacrifice with a hen and a rabbit. The woman quickly provided the rabbit and the hen for the sacrifice. Eji-ede used the hen to make sacrifice to Ifa and prepared the rabbit for offering to the elders of the night. He told her to deposit the sacrifice near a dug out pit in the night.

After performing the sacrifice for her, he left for the forest to fetch some leaves for his work. We went with his mesmeric chrystal mirror. As he was fetching the leaves, he saw a deer in the distance through his mirror and he conjured it to come to where he was so he could catch it. It was a very big deer. The animal obeyed his command and he gripped it. As soon as the deer realised that it was in danger, it began to struggle with its captor. In the struggle that ensued, they both fell into a deep pit. Inside the ditch, they met a long snake who had also fallen victim to the pit. Once inside the pit, he was able to kill the deer with a stick, but could not bring it out to the surface. He shouted for help but no one over-heard him, so he had to spend the night inside the pit.

The following morning, he looked at his mirror, and saw a group of young children on their way to the forest to check their traps and he then sang to them:

Omonde Udo,
Moya gbamila,
Atano, abo,
Aaritije, aaritimu,
Ela minu Olofin yi,
Ela minu Olofin yi Orunmila,
Ela minu Olofin yii ooo.

When the children heard his song which was an SOS call, they went to the ditch to peep at him. They wondered what they could do to help him out of the pit, so they left in frustration. It was time for the adults to go to their farms. When he saw them through his mirror he again sang.

Agba Udo moya gbamila
Agba Udo moya gbamila

His song attracted the men and they came to the pit to peep at him. When they saw him, they jeered, questioning why a Doctor who was capable of saving others was so helpless to save himself from the pit. They ridiculed him with the words that he was always asking them to make sacrifices with hens, goats, and he-goats, and without making any effort to rescue him, they left.

Next, it was time for the women to go to the market. After seeing them through his mirror, he sang to them.

Obinrin Udo moya gbamila
Obinrin Udo moya gbamila

When they heard his cry for help, they went to look at him in the pit and recognised him. They also challenged him that if he was as proficient, as he claimed to be, he should not need the help of others to come out of the pit. They too ridiculed him with all the meat and money he had taken from them in the past and also left without lending a helping hand.

Next Kporoye whom he had advised to deposit her sacrifice near a pit was coming to lodge her sacrifice. He saw her through the mirror. After depositing the sacrifice she turned to go back when he sang from the pit.

Kporoye Omon abalu
Udu Omun
Ekpo jere Otikpa
Imon gba mila etc etc etc.

When she heard the song she returned to the pit and saw him inside it. She asked how he got there and he explained that he fell into the pit while trying to catch the deer with which he was required to make sacrifice. He appealed to her to help him out of the pit. She complained that she had nothing with which to help him out. He then advised her to remove her head-tie and drop it into the pit while holding fast to one end of it. When she stretched the head tie down it did not get anywhere down the depth of the pit. He then conjured the head tie to lengthen itself down and it obeyed his command until he held on to it. He first tied the head-tie to the paw of the dead deer. The woman wondered whether she could pull him and the deer out, but he insisted that he could not come out without the deer. He then sang the following song:—

Bami gbe bara
Gbegbe leyin
Mole gbegbe

(This is the song used by Ifa priests to move Ifa from one position to another).

As they were about to come out fully from the pit, the paw of the deer to which the head tie was fastened severed from its body and the rest of the body fell back into the pit. At the same time, Kporoye fell flat on her back and the cloth she wore pulled out of her body and she became naked.

The sight of the naked woman was too much for Ejiede to resist. He instantly pounced on the woman who reminded him that it was forbidden to make love on the empty ground. He then pulled back and plucked enough Ahe leaves for a makeshift bed and then properly proceeded to make love to her. Annoyed that Ejiede took advantage of her, after lending him a helping hand, she intimated that she had just completed her menstruation. In reply he told her not to worry because she was going to become pregnant following that incident and that she would give birth to a male child.

Before they parted, the woman however insisted on having the means of locating him in case his prediction came true. He informed the woman that he was from a place called Okemesi. His house was scrubbed with black dyestuff. He added that there was a dried human corpse at the entrance of his house and that there was a tree at the main entrance to his compound which was famous for producing crown seeds from its top, beads from its stem, and corals from its root. The tree was called Okporo, kporo. After giving him this information, they went their separate ways.

On getting home, Ejiede used the severed paw of the deer to serve his Ifa. On her part, Kporoye missed her period at the end of that month and became pregnant. She was the daughter of the Oba of Ijero. She was at that time also married to the Oba of Illa where she lived. It was difficult for anyone to believe that she could again become pregnant because she was past child bearing age. But in the fullness of time, she gave birth to a male child who was the carbon copy of Eji Elemere. The husband was so happy that Kporoye had given him a child that he gave her the privilege of giving him a name. She named the child Olomo (Nonyamon in Bini).

The child began to grow and as he attained the age of reasoning, she told him how he was born. To the astonishment of his age mates, he was in the habit of singing the kind of songs that his father whom he had never met used to sing. He was also in the habit of picking leaves all about as his father used to do and his play mates were always ridiculing him for mimicking the Ifa priest who once came to the town. When he got home on one occasion he asked his mother who his real father was, in the light of what people were telling him outside. The mother insisted that he was still too young to be told the full story. When he however persistently demanded to know the truth, she narrated the story of how she was pregnated and gave him the description of his father's house in the town of Okemesi and of how she met the father.

On knowing the story of his birth, he insisted that the mother should at once take him to his father. The woman had no choice but to obey his command. The following morning, he set out on the journey to Okemesi to look for Ejielemere. The journey to the town, involved the risk of going through a forest that was territorised by three bandits. One of the bandits lived in Ado-Ekiti, where Kporoye's father was the Oba. The second bandit came from Okemesi where Ejielemere lived. The third one was from Illa where Kporoye was married. The names of the bandits were:—

(i) Ikpata Ule ado
(ii) Efifo kelo onon ijero
(iii) Amonita, amonide, ke se mi la ale ugotun.

They were the Kings of that forest.

When Mother and Son got to the forest, they were apprehended by the three bandits. One of the bandits suggested that the two captives should be killed. The other two however strongly objected to the proposal. The bandit who lived in the town from which they departed proposed that the two captives should be sold into slavery and that the proceeds should be divided equally between the three of them. The bandit living in the town where Kporoye's father lived, took her for sale into slavery, whilst the bandit living in the town where Ejielemere lived, took Olomo to be sold into slavery.

All this time, Ejielemere still had no child. At the time of his annual festival he gave money to his wife to buy him a slave for use as human sacrifice to his Ifa together with other materials and animals. When his wife got to the market, she saw Olomo who although small in stature, nonetheless, had a good body. She liked him immediately and bought him. As he was getting home with his buyer, Olomo saw the tree laden with crown beads, and coral at the entrance of the compound to which they were entering. When they got to the house, he also saw the dried human corpse tied up to the main entrance of the house, which was painted with black dyestuff. Olomo was satisfied that this was his father's house because it fitted the description given to him by his mother.

When Ejielemere saw the slave boy, he consigned him to the custody of an elderly woman who lived near him. The woman was to take care of him for the seven days preceeding the festival. Next morning, Ejielemere left for the forest to collect leaves and other instruments for the up-coming festival. The old woman gave the slave boy a heap of palm kernels to crack, and this incident explains why it is forbidden to crack palm kernels in any home where an Ifa initiation ceremony is taking place for the duration of seven days. It also explains why it is forbidden for an Ifa priest to crack palm kernel by himself.

As the boy was cracking the palm kernel, he began to sing a song which recalled the events leading to his birth, as he was told by his mother. When the old woman heard the song, she was determined to tell Ejielemere about it. When he returned from the forest, she narrated to him the song of the slave boy. The woman subsequently proposed to Ejielemere to conceal himself the following day, after pretending to have left the house to enable him listen to the boy's song.

The next morning he left the house under the guise of going to the forest with his bag to fetch leaves. He however returned to the house through the back door. Meanwhile, the boy was given another portion of palm kernels to crack and as he sat down to crack the palm kernels, he again began to sing:

My name is Olomo.
My mother's name is Kporoye;
Daughter of Ajero kin osa;
In the land of Ijero;
Married to Ewi of Ado.
My mother Kporoye told me;
The story of how the quest for a child;
Brought her for divination to Udo;
Where she met an Ifa priest;
Who made divination and sacrifice for her.
As she went to deposit;
The sacrifice near the pit;
She heard a distant cry for help.
From within the pit.
Behold, it was the Ifa priest;
Who made the sacrifice for her;
Who was inside the pit.
As she helped him;
To get out of the pit;
She fell to the ground;
And her feminine glory was exposed.
The Ifa priest;
Who could not resist;
The urge of nature;
Fell on her;
And made love to her.
My mother Kporoye;
Has not seen the Ifa priest since then.
But true to his prediction;
That the fortuitous event would bring forth a male child;
I was born to Kporoye;
In her old age;
At a time when no one;
Expected her to bring forth a child.
Although my mother's husband;
The Oba of Ale Ugotun;
Accepted me as his child;
The blood of my real father;
Runs through my veins.
And the fact that I went about;
Singing songs and collecting leaves;

Like my father was said;
To be in the habit of doing;
Made my play mates;
To call me funny nick-names.
One day, I confronted my mother Kporoye;
To tell me the true story of my birth.
She told me that my father;
Comes from the land of Okemesi;
And that at the entrance to his house;
There is a money bearing tree.
The branches and folliage;
Of the tree bear crowns.
The stem bears beads;
And the roots bear corals.
At the entrance of the house;
Is the dried corpse of a human body.
After hearing the story;
I insisted on coming to see my father.
On our way to Okemesi;
We were apprehended by three bandits;
And sold separately into slavery.
I lamented that I would never;
See my father again.
Even if I die as a slave;
I can now rest assured;
That I have come at last;
To the land and the house of my father.
The description given by my mother;
Assures me that the house;
To which I was finally sold into slavery;
And where I now crack this palm kernel;
Is indeed the abode of my father.
Ejielemere of Okemesi;
If I die in six days time;
It would no longer be in vain;
Because I have come to die;
On the bosom of my father.

    As Ejiede listened to the pathetic song of the slave boy, he was in tears, and he wondered whether the boy was the product of the love he made perchance to a woman near the pit into which he fell many years before, whilst in search of a deer with which to make sacrifice in order to have a child. He then left for his apartment where he asked for the boy to be brought to him to re-echo the song to which he had just eavesdropped. He ordered the boy under pain of instant death to sing the song once more. While on his knees, the boy again sang the song, this time in tears. After hearing the refrain of the song, Ejielemere decided to test the veracity of his story. He caused a strong burn-fire to be prepared. As the flames of the fire were stretching into the sky above, he told the boy after rubbing him with his divination powder to walk into the flames. He conjured the fire to consume the boy if he was telling a false story, but to rub his body with the chalk of victory if he was truly his son. Without any hesitation whatsoever, the boy walked into the burning flames, and danced and sang inside the fire until it was completely extinguished.

    Inspite of that miraculous feat, Ejielemere was still not satisfied. He had also prepared a giant pot of boiling water into which he threw the boy in a similar ritual. While inside the pot of boiling water, the boy began to sing.

    Omi are domi tutu.
That is "hot water has turned icy cool',
while he was dancing inside the pot of boiling water.

Finally he called on his father to remove him from the pot because he was getting chilly. His father now embraced him, and found that his body was as cool as ice. He exclaimed pleasantly that he had got a son at last, and he embraced him as his true son. Subsequently the day of the Festival dawned, and all the Awos from places around had assembled. Before then Ejielemere had given a he-goat to Esu, who then influenced the traditional executioner at the ceremony. When the time came for offering the sacrificial victims, the goats, rams, hens etc had been slaughtered. When it came to the time, for offering the human sacrifice the boy had been tied up awaiting execution. But the executioner under the influence of Esu, who knew that the boy was infact Orunmila's son, blunted the blade of the knife so it could not cut the neck of the victim. The executioner surrendered saying that Ifa had refused to accept the victim. He then untied the boy, stood him up and challenged the Awos to look at him side by side with the host, Ejielemere to see whether there was no keen resemblance between them. The Awos identified and acquiesced in the keeness of the resemblance. The Awos then agreed that the boy should be set free to the father at once.

Meanwhile the divinity called Egi whose role it was to carry the skulls of all the beheaded victims to heaven arrived to perform his duty. The Awos then sang to him.

    Egi mogbori eku.
Ori eku lomagba,
Mama gborie nio.
Egi mogbo rieja,
Orie ja lomangba,
Mama gborienio.
Egi mogborieron
Ori eron loomangba
Mama gborienio.

The Awos were touching the heads of father and son with the skull of each animal. There-after Egi left for heaven.

At that point Ejielemere brought out his instrument of authority (Ase) and proclaimed that from that day Orunmila would no longer offer a human being as sacrifice to Ifa. That marked the end of human sacrifice in Ifism.

When the ceremony was over, Ejielemere asked his son the whereabouts of his mother Kporoye and the son narrated that the mother had been sold into slavery to her father's home town. He quickly decided to go in search of the woman to fetch her home to live with him for good.

The father of Kporoye, the Ajero of Ijero also offered human sacrifice at his annual festivals. He had also ordered for a slave to be used for sacrifice on that year. The messenger who went to the market, coincidentally also bought Kporoye for her father. When she was brought to the father's palace, she was ordered to scrub the house in preparation for the festival. The Oba had forgotten that he ever had a daughter by the name of Kporoye. As she was scrubbing the floor, she began to sing the story of her life, her father, how she left home, where she got married, who she was married to, how she had a child, and how she was apprehended by bandits and sold into slavery.

The woman who was taking care of the slave called the Oba to listen to the song of the slave woman. After hearing the song, the father called her by her name Kporoye and she answered. Thereafter the Oba called her mother to come and identify Kporoye. On seeing her they both burst into tears rejoicing at the re-appearance of a daughter they had long given up for dead. She was instantly released from bondage and dressed properly as a Princess. The Ajero also proclaimed that from that day, human beings were no longer to be used for sacrifice in his kingdom.

Meanwhile, Princess Kporoye told her parents that her next problems were how to reach the father of her son and how to find her son. At the same time, Ejielemere had left Okemesi in search of Kporoye. He got dressed in tatters and waited by the road side. On her way to the river, Kporoye saw Ejielemere and recognised him at once in spite of the tattered clothes he was wearing. On another occasion he turned into a firewood seller and Kporoye saw and recognized him again as she was returning with her slaves from the farm, but on each occasion she resisted the temptation to betray her enthusiasm.

Thereafter, Ejielemere went into the bush, prepared palm fronds and with them dressed himself up as a masquerade and he began to dance towards the direction of Ijero. When the Ajero and his household saw the masquerade he danced towards them. When Kporoye saw the masquerade she told her parents that that was Orunmila, but they disagreed with her because Orunmila was never in the habit of dressing as a masquerade. After watching him from the distance for some time, Kporoye came out to the courtyard of her father's palace to admire the masquerade. The masquerade then began to dance towards her. As he came close to her, the masquerade gripped her and escaped with her. As soon as they were out of sight he removed his mask and identified himself to Kporoye and appealed to her to return home with him.

In order to obviate the risk of being challenged on the way he dressed up Kporoye as the masquerade and followed her as the escort to his home town. When they got to his house at Okemesi, he unveiled the masquerade and Kporoye embraced her son Olomo who then went out to rejoice with his age mates to commemorate his re-union with his mother. It was days later before the people of the town realised that Ejielemere had taken a second wife. Kporoye settled down with him and had five other children in addition to Olomo. Once the family was fully re-united they lived a prosperious life ever after.

Success evoked enimity for Eji Elemere:

Eji elemere had meanwhile become very wealthy and famous and was subsequently specially appointed as one of the four royal diviners of Oyo. The other three lived in heaven and Eji elemere was the only one living on earth. The names of the other three were:—
    (i)   Okpotere — Awo Ode Omanikin
    (ii)   Otaarata Awo Imina Ale
    (iii) Agbara mija gidi gidi — Awo Ode Ilakporo.

They used to come for divination at the Olofen's palace every five days. The King had become so uneasy about the proficiency and popularity of Ejielemere, that he decided to plot his destruction. The King caused a hole to be dug on the ground of his palace into a bottomless precipice, covering the mouth of the hole with a mat spread over it. He subsequently invited Ejielemere to visit him in the palace. As soon as he arrived at the palace, he was motioned to sit on the mat spread over the bottomless hole. No sooner had he sat on the mat than he fell into the hole instantly finding himself in heaven. While in heaven, walking aimlessly about, he came across one of his heavenly Awo companions with whom he used to have the divination round at the Alaafin's palace.

The man asked him what he was doing in heaven and he replied that he came to pay the three of them a visit. All the three heavenly Awos soon got together and slaughtered a goat to feast him, and when the feast was over, he got prepared to return to earth. But his colleagues prevailed on him to spend the night with them and he agreed. Next morning, as he was set for his return journey, the Awos presented him with a goat and showed him the short circuit route to earth. He instantly found himself back in his earthly home. As soon as he got home, he feasted his friends and followers with the goat he brought from heaven.

Three days later, it was time for the next divination visit to Alaafin's palace, but on that occasion he refused to go to the palace. As soon as the three Awos from heaven turned up at the palace, they did not see Eji elemere. When they asked Alaafin why Orunmila was not present, he replied that Ejielemere had decamped from earth. The Awos however insisted that a messenger should be sent to fetch him from his house. Two messengers were sent to his house before he responded. When he finally turned up he took his usual position.Before the day's work commenced, he disclosed how he had been treated by the Alaafin four days previously. The Alaafin had no defence to the accusation, so he was instantly fined, four goats, and four casks of wine.

The King paid the fine and the day's divination was accordingly done. As the Awos rose to return to their respective homes and destinations, they chanted a song as follows:
    Okpoteere Awo Ode-omanikin
    Otaarata, Awo Imina Ale
    Agbaramija gidi
    Awo Ode Ilakporo
    Eji elemere, awo Ode Oyo
    Awa merenrin loon shawo, awa merenrin loda faatun
    Olofen
    Osheinde jomiin, jomiin,
    Osheinde jomiin, jomiin.
    meaning, we came to make divination for Alaafin but he rewarded us with ingratitude, remember that one good turn deserves another, whilst a bad turn destroys a mutual relationship.

How the he-goat became the staple food of Esu:

At the height of his prosperity, all the Awos decided to be holding meetings in the house of Eji elemere, because he used to make elaborate feasts for them. He had a palm oil mill in the forest where he produced palm oil. Aja and Obuko were his two servants. On a particular day after the morning divination, he was advised not to go to the palm oil mill on that day. It was the day of the meeting of the Awos. But his wife soon discovered there was no oil for use in preparing the day's feast. He decided to dash to the mill to fetch palm oil for the day's feast. Before he left, he warned his two servants not to tell anyone where he was going.

Before he returned from the mill, the Awos began to arrive, one after the other. When they asked his two servants the whereabouts of their master, Obuko replied that he had gone to the Palm oil mill. He had completely ignored his master's instruction not to reveal his mission to anyone. But Aja however came to the rescue of his master's image by accusing Obuko of lying. He corrected that their master had only left for the bush behind the house to fetch leaves for use in a special sacrifice for the day's meeting. Aja sneaked out through the back door of the house, with a piece of white cloth in hand to go and tell his master what had happened. Aja told him that he had been betrayed by Obuko.

Eji ede, then changed into the white cloth brought to him by the loyal Aja, telling him to return home to clean up the conference chamber. As soon as Aja left for the house, he too, returned home with some pieces of yams and dried palm fruit chaff (Ironyin in Yoruba) and (Imon edin in Bini).

On getting home he greeted his guests, but they refused to answer. He however apologised for not being at home to welcome them, but explained that he only went out to collect materials for making a special sacrifice in their collective interest. He disclosed that Ifa recommended the sacrifice as a result of the morning divination he made on that day. The sacrifice was to be made to Esu by washing the heads of all of them on the shrine of Esu with the severed head of a live he-goat. He complained that the only material remaining for the sacrifice was the he-goat. Since Obuko was himself, the he-goat, all eyes turned to his direction. Obuko was instantly apprehended and used for the sacrifice. This incident explains why:—
1. It is commonly said that it was the mouth of the he-goat that killed him.
2. From that day a he-goat became the popular instrument of sacrifice to Esu.
3. Aja or the dog is never used by Orunmila for any sacrifice on account of his avowed loyalty to his master.

When this Odu comes out of divination, the divinee should be advised to beware of his servant who is planning to betray him or lie against him.

The divination for (Yeye Olomo mefa) the mother of six children.

When a colleague of Ejiede visited him on a sabbath day, a woman who had lost three of her six children, visited him for divination. The name of the guest-Awo was Ekpukpu dedede. At a subsequent divination the woman was advised to make sacrifice because Death was still very much on her trail, and that she ran the risk of losing her remaining children to the cold hands of Death. The Ifa priest told her to make sacrifice with palm kernel oil, a sponge, soap, a comb, okro, pepper, oil, a rat, a fish and a rabbit and to give a he-goat to Esu.

The sacrifice to Esu was made and the remaining sacrifice was prepared for her to deliver by herself to the mother of Death in heaven. She carried the sacrifice to heaven at a time when it was still possible to move from earth to heaven and back. On getting to heaven, Yeye Olomo mefa met the mother of Death at home. When asked for the object of her mission, she explained that she came to heaven to beg her to assist in persuading her son, Death, not to take anymore of her children.

The mother of Death told the woman to sit down and await the return of her son who was then on a mission to the earth. As soon as she sat down, she asked the old woman whether it was not yet time for cooking food to eat. The mother of Death explained that before cooking, she had to wait for her son to arrive with his human catches, which they would cook to eat, but the old woman complained that there were no condiments at home for preparing the soup. The visitor then produced the sacrifice she brought from the earth which contained all the traditional condiments for preparing soup. Yeye Olomo mefa then set about preparing the soup for the house. As the soup was being prepared, the visitor observed that the old lady's hair was care-worn. She proposed that she could plait the hair for her but Death's mother explained that she had no soap and sponge to bath with and that there was no palm kernel oil and comb for plaiting the hair. Yeye Olomo mefa then brought out all the materials because they were among the things contained in her sacrifice. The old lady took her bath with the soap and sponge and after eating they began to plait her hair.

After plaiting the hair the old lady told her to enter the house because her son was due to arrive shortly. Not long afterwards, Death returned with one human being which was the only catch he brought from the earth. His mother quarrelled with him for coming back with only one victim after being away for such a long time. Death explained that all the others had made sacrifices and that it was the only foolish man who refused to make sacrifice that he was able to apprehend. The mother then told him to admire her new look but told him to take his meal first. After eating, the mother told him that it was a visitor from earth who came to appeal to him for help that gave her the new look and prepared the food he ate. She then explained that the woman came to solicit for the salvation of her three remaining children having lost three of them to him.

At this point, Yeye Olomo mefa came out and at the sight of Death, she began to shiver. Death re-assured her not to shiver because if he had wanted to kill her, he would have done so before returning home to heaven, having seen her long in advance. It was then she heaved a sigh of relief and mustered enough composure to explain her problems. After hearing her out, Death told her to mention the names of her three remaining children and she gave the following names:—
    (i)   Oota (stone)
    (ii)   Aale (ground)
    (iii) Abiri shoko (Olikhoro in Bini) — a soft plant that grows with short hooks all over its body and having a big tuber.

After hearing her appeal, Death promised that never again would he touch any of her three remaining children. That is why Orunmila says:—
    (i)   Ota eeku
    (ii)   Ale eerun
    (iii) Abiri shoko eerare eshi
meaning:—
    (i)   The stone does not die.
    (ii)   Ground does not fall ill.
    (iii) No year passes that does not see Abiri shoko plant.

That is why the three of them do not die because of the sacrifice made by their mother. When this Ifa comes out of divination, the person should be asked whether he or she has six children. If so, the person should be advised to make sacrifice to avoid losing three of them to death, if it has not already happened.

CHAPTER XXV
EKA — MEJI

The name of Ekameji in heaven was Ikere Iyansi. He was a very powerful Awo in heaven having many followers under him. Among such followers were, Ekpo-keun, and Eninuo keun who made divination for Utukpa. In other words, it was the small oil and the small thread that made divination for the lamp when he was going to reap the reward of a human being. The lamp was told to make sacrifice with a cock and a hen and he did it. Thereafter he was given a human slave to serve him to eternity. That is why to this day, it is a human being who refuels or rekindles a lamp when it is about to extinguish. When a lamp is about to go out, people often call on a boy or a girl to refuel or rekindle it. If there is no one around the person does it by himself, all in the service of the lamp. Important as food, air and peace are to the body, they act for themselves while on the other hand, it is only the open lamp that is often aided by human beings.

That is why when Ekameji comes out of divination the person is told to make a similar sacrifice. If the divinee is a man, he will be told that one woman is coming to marry him for free and that the woman will serve him obediently and loyally to the end of her life. If it is a woman, she will be told that she will come across a new husband who will virtually serve her as a slave and who will not think of marrying any other woman after marrying her.

He made divination for the Cat:

One of Ekameji's surrogates called Iba rere was the Ifa priest who made divination for Uno (fire). Another priest Ikelewii was the one who made divination for the cat when he was coming to the world for hunting. The Cat was told to make sacrifice with a knife and a grip scissors (Awan in Bini and Eemu in Yoruba) adding cock and pigeon. He was required to make the sacrifice so that any victim he gripped might not escape. After making the sacrifice, he came to the world. For his hunting, he developed a strategy. The fire in respect of which he made sacrifice became the sharp light inside his eye-balls. As soon as he sees a victim, he will take a position and focus the bright light on his eyes to dazzle the victim, and say Mootishebo Ikelewi and jump at the victim and hold it. That is how a cat hunts to this days.

At divination the person should be told to make sacrifice so that whatever he is aspiring to achieve might fructify.

Ekameji prepares to come to the world:

Originally, he used to be a very junior disciple (ODU) of Orunmila. He usually sat among the disciples and not with the fifteen apostles (Olodus). As he prepared to come to the world he went to an Ifa priest called Ukere, gbagburu, wamu-awo oji. He advised him to make sacrifice with a he-goat to Esu, and a ram to his Ifa. There after, Esu went to Orunmila and told him that Ikere Iyansi (Eka meji) was proficient and experienced enough to be an Olodu. That is how he became one of the sixteenth Olodus.

The way Esu did it was to tell Orisa Nla that the grey haired Odus were junior to Ekameji and Orisa Nla sanctioned him to leave the group of Odus and join the Olodus.

Ekameji leaves for earth:

Before finally leaving heaven he went to two Awos for divination and they were called Awi are, Ese Ori ejo and Ure ejo onajawa. They advised him to give another he-goat to Esu, a guinea fowl to his Ifa and a pigeon to his head, in order to avoid the danger of having insurmountable problems on earth. He did the sacrifices and left for the world, in his new capacity as one of the Olodus. On getting to the world he discovered that because of his juniority in the apostolic genealogy in the Ifa literary corpus, he was often under-minded by the Olodus, who attached little or no importance to whatever he said. He was also having problems in making ends meet. He had no wife and no child.

Meanwhile, Esu created new problems for God by disrupting His creative art and designs. As God was wont to do, he decided to go in disguise to find out what was causing His problems. The first Awo he met was Ekameji. Before making divination for him and without knowing he was the Almighty Father, Ekameji demanded one bag of money or the equivalent to 50k as divination fee. He told the divinee that Esu was responsible for disrupting his work, and that he had to offer a he-goat for sacrifice. God replied that he could not raise the money to buy a he-goat. Ekameji brought out a he-goat from his house and used it to serve Esu for the supposedly "destitute divinee", who he could not recognize as the God Almighty. He merely did the favour on humanitarian and compassionate grounds. The divinee then thanked Ekameji, and asked for the residence of the remaining senior Awos. He showed him the direction of the house where Eji Ogbe lived down town. The visitor left for Eji Ogbe's house for divination. On getting to Eji Ogbe's house, his reaction to God's request for divination was that he had no time for divination at that material time. With that rebuff, God turned back and returned to heaven.

Before he got home, Esu had let-go of his arts and designs, and things had returned to normal, having feted him. Three days later He got dressed up in his full regalia as the Almighty God and again left for earth. When Ekameji saw Him he shook and shivered. He told Ekameji not to be frightened because he came to repay the cost of the sacrifice he made for him three days before. After compensating him for the he-goat, God ordained that from then on no one should challenge whatever Ekameji said. That is how Ekameji received his instrument of authority (Ase) from God which makes it forbidden for any Ifa priest or divinities to challenge whatever he proclaims. God also told him that he would have all the prosperity he wished for while on earth. Thereafter, he had plenty of money, wives and children.

Ekameji wins a Crown:

When he got to the world, Ekameji was one of the most junior Olodus and he therefore had no crown of his own. When he discovered that all the other Olodus already has crowns, he decided to go for divination on what to do to have his own crown. He went to an Ifa priest called Efuye Miile, who advised him to make sacrifice with a rat, a cock and one tortoise. After the sacrifice had been made, he was invited by the Kng of Ife to solve a puzzle which he did successfully. To compensate him, Olofen sent him a Beaded Crown, dresses, shoes, and walking stick.

Very early the next morning, he dressed up in his new outfit, in which he looked so gorgeous as to even win the admiration of his wives. After dressing up formally in the new outfit, he decided to make a thank-you-call on the King. When he eventually emerged at the palace, his outfit angered the more senior Olodus. He was warmly received by the King, but returned home, worried about the reaction of the Olodus.

On getting home, he invited an Awo called Agbe Onide, Awo Olode Igbodo, for divination. The Awo told him to make sacrifice for long life and prosperity. He told him to give a he-goat to Esu, a dog to Ogun and a castrated he-goat including eight eggs for the elders of the night. After doing this sacrifice he had no more problems from the elderly Olodus. He ultimately lived to a ripe old age.

Poem for correcting the difficult features of Ekameji:

It is said that when Ekameji appears for anyone at an Ugbodu initiation ceremony the person is likely to experience tremendous problems in life unless he is able to get a proficient Ifa Priest to clear the inevitable obstacles for him. Orunmila was able to do it for his Son Ekameji with the following poem:—

Abimonkon nule Ooni
Aroleka abi Ikejire
Aro likaun kaun gbara
Kai bikon tiibimon meji loode
Aroo nikaani
Agbalikaka Okani mogun
Okalule Ojiji
Ojoo doja riomon eja
Okalule toromi
Ojo loja riomon eku
Oka inon ojo olojaara
Oka lule Orisa
Owe wu oje
Okalule oduro kpekpekpe
Ojo Oloja Ikin
Oduro Oshokungbeni ikin joko
Owa maawo eyin re ashetii

The English translation:—
A child was born at home;
It was interpreted as a difficult problem.
A second child was born;
It was said to be a pleasant omen.
This was a puzzle.
How does one explain the arrival;
Of fortune and misfortune in the same house.
Will misfortune allow fortune to flourish?
A sage was sought to explain the puzzle.
The wise man explained that;
The difficult child is eel or electric fish;
Which dwells in a river;
Full of ordinary harmless fishes.
That is why the electric eel;
Is the King of fishes;
And why the harmless fishes;

Plentiful as they may be;
Cannot dare the electric eel.
In like manner the mouse;
With sharp pointed nose;
Is so dreaded that it is the King of rats.
It is called Itoromi in Yoruba;
And Okhan in Bini.
That is also why the unpredictable abdomen;
Became the King of the body.
And why the lead gains prominence;
In the house of God.
Because it does not rust;
And why the Oluro became;
The King of all Ikins;
In the house of Orunmila;
Because its front and its back;
Are lined with prosperity.

When Ekameji comes out at Ugbodu, it means that the subject will have a difficult life and live in the midst of powerful enemies, who will always seek to destroy him unless all the materials mentioned above are collected for the purpose of preparing the Ono-Ifa (Odiha in Bini) to facilitate his passage through life.

CHAPTER XXVI
ETURUKPON — MEJI
OLOGBON — MEJI

```
I I    I I
I I    I I
  I      I
I I    I I
```

Eturukpon meji otherwise known as Ologbon-meji reveals how the faculty of intelligence came to the world. This revelation is contained in the names of the Awos or the Ifa Priests who were his heavenly diviners. Their names are revealed in the following poem:—
Ologbon logbon kii taa koko omi.
Omoron moron eekika yekpe Ode.
Okpitan eekpitan mun Ekiti,
Ubore jade leewa.
meaning:—
No one can be skillful enough;
To parcel water with his cloth.
No one can be intelligent enough;
To count the sand of the earth.
No sage can be vast in proverbs enough;
To reveal his own secrets through parables.

It was also Ologbon meji who revealed how Orunmila and the other divinities returned to the world. Before going into the details of these revelations, it is important to refer to some of the known works he did in heaven.

Ologbon meji made divinition for Ekun and Ifaa (the Tiger and the Bush Cat.)

For the purpose of this chapter, we shall refer to the Tiger as Ekun and to the bush Cat as Ogbo. Ogbo had a frightful dream and decided to go to Orunmila for divination. Ekun and Ogbo were born of the same parents. After divination Orunmila told Ogbo that he was required to make sacrifice to his head with a guinea fowl because his brother, Ekun, was contriving to kill him to eat. He was also advised to refrain from serving other people's heads, no matter the closeness of the relationship. Above all, he was to be very careful and vigilant of events transpiring around him. He did the sacrifice.

Ekun also went to Orunmila for divination on what to do to be able to kill his brother Ogbo for food. He was advised to give a he-goat to Esu. Although he promised before Orunmila to make the sacrifice, nonetheless he changed his mind on getting home. He argued with himself that the meat of the he-goat with which he was required to make sacrifice was richer than that of the feeble Ogbo. He therefore refused to do the sacrifice. Ekun, meanwhile, approached other animals and promised to refrain from killing any of them if they could lure Ogbo into his trap. He told them to persuade Ogbo to agree to come and serve his (Ekuns's) head, thus providing the opportunity of apprehending him. The leopard, also of the same parents with the two of them, volunteered to convince Ogbo.

Meanwhile, Ekun tied up a goat with which to serve his head. Thereafter, he rubbed his body with palm kernel oil to feign illness. When the leopard got to Ogbo's house, he told him that his brother Ekun was very ill and that the diviner had advised that only he, Ogbo, could save him by serving his head. Although he remembered the advice given to him by Orunmila not to serve anybody's head, he was reluctant to refuse to oblige his brother. He therefore set out for Ekun's house to serve his head. On getting there, he met all the other animals commiserating with Ekun. There was an atmosphere of unspeakable melancholy and it looked as if Ekun was truly at the point of death. However, on looking straight into the eyes of Ekun, Ogbo realised at once that his brother was pretending. He instantly proposed that the sacrificial victim the goat, should be slaughtered by another animal after which he would use the severed head of the goat to dub Ekun's head in accordance with tradition. His suggestion was accepted, and the Hyaena slaughtered the goat and gave the head to Ogbo. As Ogbo was praying with the goat's head in hand, he was steadily dancing backward while pointing the goat's head in the direction where Ekun lay. As he did so, he was singing. He praised Orunmila who made divination for him. Thus:—

Ologbon logbon kii shebi Ojo,
Ifa bolo bolo niitee Ekun,
Odifafun funmi Olu Ifaa.
Mogbo, moru.
Eyiin eyiin lamujo, Eyiin jo are.

As he sang, he kept dancing backwards. After taking a vantage position in the distance, he rubbed his own head with the goat's skull and ran away. When Ekun saw the unexpected turn of events, he accused the other animals surrounding him of connivance in the escape of Ogbo. He instantly pounced on and devoured some of them. Thus, Ogbo survived the evil strategem of Ekun because of the sacrifice he made, whilst the evil designs of Ekun against Ogbo failed to materialise because of the sacrifice he refused to make.

He made divination for Egherun the most beautiful Bird in heaven as well as Ugun or Vulture.

Ologbon Ologbon shoro Ologbon
Ufa yeye shoro aye
Odafa fun egherun
Abufun Ugun.
meaning:—
The sage worships wisdom;
The fox practices hunting.

These are the names of the two Awos who made divination for Egherun, when she was going to marry the Vulture. The more eligible birds had made marriage overtures to her but she turned down all of them. Ugun began to wonder how a beautiful girl could so flagrantly rebuff all eligible suitors lusting for her hands in marriage. He decided to challenge her by working out a proper strategy for blackmailing her into submission. He went to the forest to fetch a bunch of fresh palm fruits which he kept by the road side. He then went into hiding nearby to keep watch over the fruits. On her part, Egherun could never resist the temptation to pluck palm fruits wherever she found them. On that particular day, she had gone to the market. On her way back from the market, she saw the attractive palm fruits by the road side and could not resist the urge to pick from the bunch. After collecting as much palm fruits as she could conveniently carry, she was about to take off when Ugun came out to accuse her of stealing, an offence which carried the death penalty. She began to beg Ugun who not surprisingly, refused all her entreaties. She offered to pay any amount of money to atone for her crime but Ugun refused all the same.

She then asked Ugun what he wanted of her to trade off the indignity and risk of being arraigned before the elders, where the punishment for theft was death. At that point, Ugun proclaimed that the only effective atonement for the crime was to marry him.

She agreed to marry him but Ugun insisted that she had to go with him at once to his house. She had no choice but to agree. She could not live with the embarrassment of the subsequent public knowledge that the proud and indomitable Egherun had condescended at last to marry the ugly vulture, after rejecting the proposals of several more elegible admirers.

After suffering a number of sleepless nights she decided to go to Orunmila for divination. After divination, Orunmila told her to make sacrifice with two cocks which she instantly produced. One of the cocks was split open for offering as sacrifice at the road junction. She was told to deposit the cock by herself at the road junction after which she was to go into hiding close by to keep vigil over the sacrifice. Ugun had left home to go and look for food with which to feed his bride. It is common knowledge that the Vulture cannot resist the sight of dead meat. As he was returning home, he came to the road junction, where he saw the sacrificial cock. He flew to the spot and settled down to feed on it. After eating to his heart's content, he parcelled up the remnant to be sent home to his wife. As he got set to go home, Egherun came out of hiding to accuse him of stealing. When he argued that a husband could not be accused of stealing from his wife, she countered by explaining that such argument could only be admissible within the matrimonial home of a couple, and that even then it had to be verified before the grand inquisition of the elders. She insisted that she did not make the sacrifice at the road junction for him, which meant that he had stolen.

Realising that his position was hopeless, Ugun enquired to know what he was required to do to atone for the offence. In reply, Egherun explained that all he had to do was to rescind the marriage he imposed on her by duress and to proclaim publicly that she was no longer his wife. Ugun had no option but to release Egherun from the marriage bond by proclaiming that she was free to leave him and return to her house. Egherun instantly went back to Ugun's house to remove her belongings and to leave him for good.

It was from that day that the saying began:—
Mii Omon Igbatii Egherun do Ugun;
Mii Omon Igbatii Egherun ko Ugun; meaning:—
No one knew when Egherun married the Vulture and when she left him.

When this Odu comes out of divination the person will be told that he or she will marry someone under duress, but that the marriage will not last, if sacrifice is made.

He made divination for the hunter with a stubborn wife:

There lived a hunter who had a secret agreement with the elders of the night to help him in his hunting expeditions. They provided him his game on the condition that he would always allow them to drain the blood of any animal he killed. Meanwhile, his wife was anxious to find out why he usually came home with headless animals. She decided to follow him to the forest to find ot what was happening to the heads and blood of the animals he was killing. He did not know that the wife usually accompanied him to the forest.

On one occasion, the elders of the night told him to warn whoever was following him to the forest to desist from doing so. On getting home he told the wife about the warning and she pretended as if it had nothing to do with her.

On his next hunting expedition, the wife trailed him to the forest behind his back. On getting to the forest he started hunting. When he finished hunting, he went into conference with the elders of the night and they drained all the blood and emptied them into a clay pot. At that stage the elders of the night asked him whether in defiance of their instructions, he came with any spy. He denied coming with anybody. They insisted that someone came with him. They told him to keep watch. They removed the leaves with which his wife covered herself and ordered her to come out. When the hunter discovered that it was his wife, he begged them to spare her life and forgive her. They told him that there was no forgiveness in the witch world.

They called her up and told her that since she was so curious to find out what they were doing with the blood of the animals being killed by the husband, she would have to pay the price of her transgression. They collected all the blood drained from the animals shot by the husband that night and made her to drink it. After drinking the blood, she began to suffer from palsy, or issue of blood. She became so ill that the husband had no time to devote to his hunting. The night people had turned their backs on him because of the action of his wife. He later went to appease the elders of the night and after paying the fine stipulated by them, they agreed to modify the woman's punishment, by proclaiming that from then on, the woman would only see blood once a month which is the menstruation that all women have to this day.

At divination, a man should be told that he has a wife who is stronger than himself and planning to damage his business. If he makes sacrifice with a he-goat to Esu, the woman's evil plans will either be exposed or she will leave him before executing her nefarious plan.

Ologbon-meji leaves heaven for earth:

The three awos referred to at the beginning of this chapter were the ones who made divination for Ologbon-meji before he came to the earth. He was advised to make sacrifice with a duck to his Ifa, a tortoise to his head, and a he-goat to Esu. He was required to make the sacrifice because he was going to be the beneficiary of all the intellect of the divinities on getting to the world. That is how he earned the name of Ologbon-meji after making the sacrifice.

On getting to the world, he was in the service of virtually all the principal divinities. He served each of them in turns, and he was able to learn their ways and their secrets. When he attained freedom, they subjected him to several tests which he passed because he had learnt so much from them. That is why any one who is born by Eturukpon-meji at Ugbodu must procure all the main divinities in addition to Ifa hamely, Sango, Ogun, Olokun, Eziza, Sankpana, etc, etc. He became so proficient that others began to learn from him. He had plenty of children, houses, and clientele.

He seduces the wife of Ogun:

Uja (or Efae in Bini) had been married to Ogun for a long time without a child. One day, Eturukpon-meji went to the forest to fetch leaves for his work. He met a woman in the forest who, unknown to him, was Ogun's wife. The reason she could not have a child was because she was in the habit of feeding on the blood of the animals killed by the husband from the forest. She readily returned the affection of Eturukpon-meji and agreed to marry him, but insisted on remaining in the forest.

She however told him that her former husband often fed her with animal blood and meat and told him that he would continue to feed her with the same foodstuff. He however slaughterd a goat and prepared pounded yam with soup for her to eat and added Iyerosun. When he took the food to her, he sang a poem as follows:

    Alaghere, aya ose ari,
    Wa ya gbi eje oni,
    Aisode laari ibi,
    Awo onje leeyi oo.

He then concealed himself and the woman came out to collect the food. She ate the food and returned the pots to where Eturukpon-meji left the food. That was how he fed her for seven days. It was on the seventh day that she followed him home from the forest.

On getting home, she became ill. Having discovered that Ujaa had been seduced, Ogun began to curse her, and she became ill. Her new husbnd invited his Awos for divination and he was advised to go and pay a dowry on her. That is why it is necessary for any son of Orunmila to pay a dowry on a woman whom he has seduced. To pay the dowry, he was to make sarifice with a he-goat, cock, tortoise and dog. He was to prepare a hut surrounded with palm fronds, cook the meat there and leave the food for her former husband to collect in the hut. He did as he was told, on the spot where Ujaa lived temporarily in the forest.

When Ogun got there, he saw the food inside the hut and without bothering to find out who seduced his wife, he ate the food, satisfied that the seducer had paid for her.

At the end of that month, Ujaa became pregnant and had a child for the first time in her life.

How Orunmila left the World:

    Gudu Gudu Aboju gberegede,
    Ojo baba aluwe taa gudugudu,
    Ologbon logbon koota koko omi,
    Omo ran, koo mooye yekpe ile.
    Alaa raa raa, emo bibi ale gbe kpekun,
    Aje kuru jakara ni moru ko eere,
    Odifa fun Orunmila baba shawo losi,
    Igbe ri okun tinyin tinyin.
        The large-faced drum.
        The water used to bath,
        In the bathroom,
        Sprinkles on the walls and floor,
        Of the bathroom.
        No man is wise enough,
        To count the sand of the earth.
        No one travels far enough,
        To know the dimension of the earth.
        He who eats akara and moyin moyin,

Knows the sobriquet of beans.

These were the Awos who made divination for Orunmila when he was returning to heaven through the sea. As he left for the sea (Okun) his followers asked him. Now that you are leaving us for good, who shall we call our father. He told them to refer to anyone they pleased as their father. He decided to go back to heaven never to return to the world physically again. He however told them that he would send them the instruments through the tree of life (the palm tree) through which he would always talk to them.

CHAPTER XXVII
OSE — MEJI

Osegunmeji is not known to have done any spectacular work in heaven. He was only notorious for His pugnacity. He was the one who, however, revealed how money came from heaven to earth. He disclosed how an Awo called OROKUN ARO KOOSE MUNUKUN made divination for money when it was preparing to leave heaven for the earth. The same Awo also made divination for the divinities on what to do to be able to enjoy the benefits that money could bestow. The meaning of the name of the Awo is — The knee of the cripple does not bend. Each of the divinities was told to make sacrifice with 16 pigeons, 16 hens, 16 rats, 16 fishes, 16 bean buns (Akara) and 16 eko. Instead of making the sacrifice individually as they were advised to do, they decided to join hands to do a single sacrifice. Thereafter money left for the world in the form of cowries, by growing from the sky until it touched the ground.

As soon as they sighted money's impact on the ground, the divinities got together and deliberated on how to get it to their various homes for spending. Orunmila however warned them not to extract the money until they did fresh divination and sacrifice. Ogun challenged Orunmila to stay at home and do his divination and sacrifice whilst the rest of them went to excavate the money. He wondered what was the neccesity of performing divination and sacrifice before eating the food served on the table for one to eat. Orunmila accepted the challenge and told them that he neither had the intention of joining in the excavation of money at that point in time, nor of imposing his wish on the rest of them and that they were free to proceed without him.

Ogun took the hoes and diggers which he had manufactured for that purpose and left for the money heap. On getting there, he dug far into the heap of money, keeping at one side whatever he was able to extract. As he dug deeper into the heap, the top layer gave way, and the avalanche fell on Ogun and buried him alive under the debris, leaving four pieces of cowries on his chest.

Sanpana was the next to go to the heap, and he ended up the same way with 16 cowries left on his chest. All the other divinities had similar experiences including Sango and Olokun. When they did not return home, Orunmila began to ponder on what had happened to them. He decided to go and verify for himself what was holding them back. On getting there he found all of them dead and collected and tied up in separate parcels the number of cowries he found on the chest of each of them.

Thus it is said that it was avarice that sent back the first generation of divinities who inhabited the earth, to heaven. Osegunmeji therefore advises that if the quest for money is not bridled with discretion and patience, it will come in an avalanche to the seeker after it and destroy him. That is why all those who seek after money with greed and avarice get buried prematurely under the avalanche of money.

Meanwhile, Orunmila decided that there was no point in approaching money the way others did and went home without touching the heap. He chose to approach the situation with his characteristic surreptitiousness.

On getting home, he sounded Ifa who told him to make sacrifice with 2 pigeons, 2 ladders, and 4 U-bolts. Ifa told him to nail down the U-bolts on each of the four corners of the heap, and to serve the heap with the two pigeons after nailing down the U-bolts. He was told to throw mashed yam (Obobo in Bini and Ewo in Yoruba) right around the heap because pigeon and mashed yam are the staple food of money. He was told to position the ladders on the heap and begin by excavating it from the apex instead of the base.

He did as he was advised by Ifa and as he offered the sacrifice to money, he spoke an incantation telling money that no-one kills the offerer of food to him, and begged money not to kill him as he did others, having offered his food to him. Thereafter he climbed the heap with the ladder and excavated it in small units until he got everything to his house. It was from that day that Orunmila started sitting on top of money which is why his shrine is often decorated with a throne of cowries. To consult Orunmila for serious divination, the Ifa priest has to sit him first on a throne of cowries.

After getting the money heap to his house, he invited the eldest children of the dead divinities and gave each of them the number of cowries he found on the chest of their fathers respectively. It is the number of cowries which Orunmila gave to the children of the demised divinities that they use for divination to this day.

The children of Ogun use four cowries for divination, while the children of Sanpana and Sango use sixteen cowries for divination.

That is why anytime Osegunmeji comes out of divination for anyone, the person is advised to look for money with caution and discretion so that money might not destroy him.

Osemeji's activities in heaven:

He was originally one of the four eldest apostles of Orunmila which is why he is called Arugbo-Ifa (the elderly apostle of Orunmila). He was however very powerful and treacherous. For instance, his parents used to leave his junior brothers and sisters under his care whenever they were away to the farm or the market. He was however in the habit of inciting the children to fight among themselves, and the children used to sustain several injuries in the process.

Once, when his two most junior brothers, Olugbodo (Akobie) and Fefe (Ehoho) were left under his charge, he incited Fefe, the most junior, against Olugbodo, and they began to fight. In the course of the fight, Fefe used a cudgel to whip Olugbodo's legs and he became crippled which is why the latter has no legs to walk with. He then became the divinity of infants, who is served by little children to this day.

On his part, he was a never do well and when he grew up to be an adult, he was only notorious for carrying fights into the four corners of heaven. Everyone feared him. His name was Ajakadi. His parents who were worried that he would live to be a nuisance, advised him to go for divination and he went to an elderly Ifa priest who advised him to make sacrifice with a small he-goat and the vertebral bone of snake to Esu, a goat for his head, a ram for Ifa, killing the ram before offering it to Ifa. His head was to be washed with the head of the ram adding 201 leaves.

He was advised that as his head was being washed, he was to sing the following incantation:—
      Gbogborogbo ni ika she yoju ori
      Alaja lesunmare la ju orun,

Osika Awodi loni Keye miin mara,
Eleda mi, jekimi begbe jo.
The hand is longer than the head,
when stretched upwards.
The rainbow cuts the sky wholly,
and not in halves.
It is a wicked bird that tries,
to prevent other birds,
from flying in the sky.
My guardian angel
let me prosper along
with my contemporaries.

On account of his total reliance on his strength, he did not bother to do the sacrifice. He grew up to become a very strongly built man. He was an invincible wrestler. Every morning, he would go outside his house in heaven to challenge each of the divinities to a wrestling contest, in which he was invariably victorious. That is the purpose for which he was told to add the vertebral bone of a snake to the sacrifice to Esu to mellow his strength. That is also why the children of Osegun meji are advised to forbid snake's meat.

It will be recalled that when he was born, his father prepared medicine with an axe and the crown of a cock and embedded them into his head. That is why he grew up to be an invincible wrestler.

He began his wrestling contests with Ogun who he vanquished with ease. He followed that up with each of other divinities and he was victorious over all of them. But he was scarcely able to afford food to eat because all the good divinities of heaven became afraid of him.

One day, his guardian angel who was not happy at his plight was determined to do something to weaken him so that he might prosper. His guardian angel went to beg Esu with a he-goat and the vertebral bone of a snake to subdue Ajakadi. Esu ate the he-goat and worked out a strategy for dealing with him.

When it was again time for the annual wrestling contest in heaven, all the heavenly hosts were gathered, and the divinities had taken their respective positions in order of seniority. Once again, Ajakadi was the first to come out to be challenged. As usual, he stood out for a long time and no one dared to come out to challenge him. As was the tradition, if no one challenged a wrestler, he was free to challenge anyone. He pointed to the direction in which Ogun, the war divinity and the most senior and the strongest of all the divinities sat, and challenged him for the opening match.

Ogun had no option but to accept the challenge. As soon as he stepped out into the arena, Ajakadi engaged him. He quickly lifted Ogun with all his strength into the air, but as he released Ogun to drop to the ground, Esu focussed his mysterious gaze on him and miraculously, he fell to the ground first before Ogun fell on him. Even Ogun did not know how it happened that his challenger was the first to drop to the ground.

While on the ground, he called on Ogun to behead him with his sword. He lamented that not having fallen to the ground before in a wrestling contest, he could not fathom the indignity of standing on his feet again. As Ogun brought out his sword to behead him, Esu intervened and announced that if anyone dared to behead Ajakadi there would be an endless tribulation and cataclysm in the whole of heaven.

To demonstrate what he meant, Esu caused the very grounds of heaven to quake. The sky and the ground of heaven began to close up on each other and instantly, there was total darkness in heaven.

Meanwhile, God saw the confusion that was generated and shouted to enquire who was disturbing the peace of heaven. God was told that Ogun had just fallen Ajakadi, the invincible wrestler in the annual wrestling match. God immediately ordered that whatever had to be done to appease Ajakadi should be done to return tranquility to heaven. Once again, Esu intervened and announced that it was forbidden for Ajakadi to fall to the ground, and that to appease the ground on which he fell, the following atonements should be presented to him:

- 200 men
- 200 women
- 200 cows
- 200 goats
- 200 rams
- 200 dogs
- 200 bags of money, and
- 200 of every item of wealth.

The atonements were quickly produced and Esu muttered into the ears of Ajakadi that he should get up to accept the offerings. As soon as he got up, the ground and the sky moved back into place. There was light again and calm returned to the four winds of heaven.

On getting home with his newly acquired wealth, he gave a strong he-goat to Esu to thank him for coming to his rescue. He also gave the biggest of the cows and the biggest of the goats and rams to his guardian angel. It was at this stage that Osemeji realised that his wrestling days were over in heaven and that it was time he moved to earth. He however vowed that while on earth, he would continue with his wrestling contests.

OSE — MEJI leaves for the Earth:

Osemeji left heaven for earth without telling anyone. He neither made any divination nor sacrifice. He was born to aged parents who had lost the hope of having any children. He was born with grey hairs on his head and he lived to a ripe old age on earth, but only after returning to heaven to make sacrifice. We shall see later how he did it.

As he grew up, he proved to be a terror among his age mates. His parents died when he was still a boy and he lived on his own contrivances thereafter. He neither practised the Ifa vocation nor any respectable profession. He was an itinerant wrestler. But he was not living a happy life. He could scarcely afford to feed himself because he did nothing that was capable of earning him a living.

One day, he went out for his wresting contest, being the only profession he knew. He went to the palace of the Alara to challenge him to a wrestling match. He defeated the Alara in the contest, but got no reward for his victory. He then moved to Ijero where he also challenged the Ajero to a contest. He was also victorious over the Ajero but got no compensation for the achievement. He moved to Owo where he defeated the Olowo. He next moved to Benin where he defeated the Oba-Ado. He did the same with all the sixteen Obas of the known world of the time.

After his wrestling rounds, he was returning home empty-handed when he met three Ifa priests by the roadside between Ado and Ife and he was stopped by them.

The Awos were called:—
Oshe kele, Ogba Ogun
Onagbaja, Ogba Ogoji

Ekoji Otunla, Ogba agrikpa obuko, meaning:—
One who summersaulted and got 20 rewards.
One who moved forward and got 40 rewards.
One who won a he-goat after 3 days.

They told him after divination that he was starving because he was not doing the profession he was supposed to do on earth. They assured him however that he would prosper in the end from his chosen wrestling profession, but only after making sacrifice which he had to do in heaven. He did not take them seriously because he could not imagine how he was going to travel to heaven to make a sacrifice. By that time, Esu had closed the route between heaven and earth. The Awos told him that he could not expect anyone he had defeated in a wrestling contest to reward him with any gifts. He was however advised to give whatever he could afford to his late father who would save him from his plight. On getting home, he offered a cock to his father and begged him to help him to tread on the path of his destiny.

Meanwhile, his father went to his guardian angel in heaven and complained that Osemeji was not doing well on earth. His guardian angel replied that it was because he was very pugnacious. Between his father and his guardian angel, they decided to persuade the good things of heaven to go and visit Osemeji on earth.

Traditionally, as soon as the cock crows in the morning, it is a sign that all the good things of life are leaving heaven on their daily visits to the world. The group, consists of children, peace, wealth, abode, money, health and prosperity. They all leave heaven in the early hours of the morning to visit whoever can receive them on earth. They visit the quarter of heaven inhabited by the guardian angels of everyone living on earth before they leave heaven in the morning.

Osemeji's father spent that night with his son's guardian angel in heaven. In the early hours of the following morning after the cock crowed, the good things of heaven were reporting to the guardian angels that they were leaving for earth and asked whether they had any messages for their wards. Osemeji's guardian angel came out and appealed to them to visit his ward Osemeji on earth. They were all unanimous in replying that they dared not visit him because he would destroy them. They reminded his guardian angel of how pugnacious he was in heaven and the commotion he caused in heaven before escaping to the earth. They insisted that good and evil did not live together except as combatants, and that heat and coolness could not live together, just as light and darkness did not live in the same environment at the same time. As long as he insisted on antagonising and disgracing those who would have benefitted him, they would never go in his direction. With these pronouncements, the good tidings of heaven left for the earth.

Thereafter his father began to weep over the hopelessness of his sons situation. He then appealed once again to his guardian angel who disclosed that he made him to spend the night with him so that he could be a witness to what he had been experiencing since Ajakadi left for earth. His guardian angel said that he had for years been persuading the good tidings of heaven to visit Osemeji, but that they had consistently refused to do so for the reasons they had just given.

As a result of the persistent entreaties of his father, the guardian angel decided to evolve a new strategy for dealing with the situation. He told the father to return to his house and that he would see his son before the cock crowed next morning. The father did not understand the import of what the guardian angel said. As soon as Osemeji's father left, the guardian angel went to the wife of Death and gave her gifts of kolanut. It will be recalled that Sickness is the wife of the King of Death. Just as the good tidings of heaven visit the earth daily, Sickness, the wife of the King of Death, visits the world daily. Death himself does not come to the world, he sends errands.

The guardian angel of Osemeji persuaded Mrs. Death to meet his ward on earth and invite him to heaven because he had something important to do for him. The old woman agreed to deliver the message that very day.

Meanwhile on earth, Osemeji was suddenly taken ill, which was a novelty because he had never been indisposed hitherto. Towards evening of that day, the sickness became serious and he went into a coma. Since no one liked him, he did not have anyone to attend to him. In fact, people were rejoicing when they found him in a coma. Just before midnight, he gave up the ghost, and nobody even knew that he was dead because there was no one to attend to him since he had no wife and no child of his own.

As soon as life departed from him, he appeared instantly in heaven before his guardian angel, who had earlier told his father to return to his house after dusk on that day. His father was therefore present in the home of his guardian angel when Osemeji turned up in heaven. It was then his father realised what his guardian angel meant, when he said that he would see his son before the cock crowed the next morning. They both welcomed him and before the cock crowed the next morning, his guardian angel directed him to hide behind a mat he had prepared for the occasion.

Soon after the cock crowed, the good tidings of heaven were again visiting the home of each guardian angel. When they got to the gate of his guardian angel, the latter called them each by their respective names, children, fellowship, wealth, health, prosperity, money etc, and begged them once again to visit his ward Osemeji on earth because he was suffering there. Once more, they told him that they were not used to singing the same song day in and day out. They told him that his wrestler-ward was too vindictive to accord a befitting reception to any of them and that they had vowed never to go near the street where he lived on earth, let alone, to visit his house. They said in unison that it was not their custom to visit any one who would destroy them, since the man was very bellicose. They added that anyone who dared to fall down Kings and Princes and Divinities alike in wrestling contests, would crush them easily between his fingers.

His father then shouted that the man behind the mat should listen to what the agents of the fortune divinity were saying about him. He was dumb-founded behind the mat. It was only then he realised that he had been pursuing the wrong ends in life.

As soon as the hosts of beneficence passed, he came out to ask his guardian angel and his father what he was to do and he was told to make the sacrifice that he failed to make before he left heaven. He was advised to give a he-goat quickly to Esu, who would wash his head and his back to whittle down his physical and diabolical strength. He did the sacrifice at once because the goats he left behind in heaven had multiplied manifold. He also told his guardian angel to offer the biggest of his cows to the heavenly police for a feast.

Thereafter, his guardian angel told him to take a special path with which to return to earth. As soon as he set his feet on that path, he blinked his eyes on earth and instantly regained conciousness. Three days later, he became well and inspite of what had transpired in heaven, which he remembered vividly, he once more began to prepare for his wrestling rounds. Before then he brought out one of his goats and slaughtered it to his father and gave a ram to his Ifa; which is the earthly representation of his guardian angel and made a big feast with them. The people around wondered what had changed his outlook since he was not known to have made any sacrifice previously. He also gave a he-goat to Esu. Two days after that, he left for the palace of Alara. On his way, he met an old Ifa priest, who was a transfiguration of Esu and the man pretended to be a soothsayer. The old man told him that he was going on a wrestling contest, but that although he could defeat his opponents, he should pretend to fall to the ground as soon as he engaged them and that he should watch out for subsequent events, the outcome of which he would not regret. The man clearly told him that as soon as he shouted Gidigbo, Gidigbo, which is the signature tune for a wrestling match, he should pretend to fall to the ground.

He started with the palace of the Alara, where he shouted Gidigbo, Gidigbo, and the call sign brought out the Alara. As soon as they engaged each other, Osemeji threw up the Alara but he quickly fell down to the ground before the King fell on him. In consonance with the advice which the old Ifa priest (Esu) had given him, he remained fallen on the ground without getting up.

Meanwhile, Esu created an unprecedented commotion in the town. The whole town was engulfed in total darkness and the ground began to quake. The cocks began to lay eggs and the hens began to crow. The women who were pregnant began to have false labour and the animals of the forest were running helter-skelter into the town, while the domestic animals began escaping into the bush.

When Alara saw what was happening, he begged Osemeji to get up from the ground. Once again, the elderly Ifa priest that Osemeji met on the way, appeared from nowhere and intervened. The man told the Alara that it was forbidden for the son of Orunmila to fall to the ground and that for him to get up, it was necessary to appease him with 100 each of able bodied men, young and unmarried women, cows, goats, cocks, hens, bags of money etc.

Out of fright, the Alara, quickly ordered each house in the town to produce the required atonements. As soon as they were assembled, Osemeji got up and the old man prepared Iyerosun, (divination powder) and blew it into the air, and light, peace, and tranquility quickly replaced darkness, commotion and confusion. Osemeji then ordered the human gifts to carry the atonements to his house at Ife and to start building new abodes before he returned home.

The following morning, he went to the palace of the Ajero kin Osa where the same thing happened followed by similar visits to the Illa Orongun, Olowo, Ooni, Oba Ado etc, where he collected similar rewards. At the end of his mission, he became an exceedingly wealthy man and prosperity had come his way at last.

This incident marked the beginning of paying money for divination, because throwing the Okpele divination instrument on the ground signifies the fall that Osemeji had in the hands of the Kings, for which they paid atonements.

That is why when Osemeji appears at divination, the person should be advised to refrain from doing anything that involves a show of strength. He should be told that he is not prospering in life and that prosperity would not come his way unless he changed his ways to resort to caution and discretion in all his activities.

Osemeji takes to Ifa art and practice:

As soon as he became wealthy, Osemeji decided to give up wrestling. Since he knew no other profession, he decided to employ a number of indentured Ifa priests to live with him. He got some of the most proficient Awos in the world around either to live with him or to make divination visits to his place. One of such Ifa priests was Ose kele baba laro ile orunmila.

He makes divination for Akinyele of Iwere:

Akinyele was a famous chief in the town of Iwere. One night he had a dream in which he saw a man with a horn, carrying a gun on his shoulder, and guarding the gate of a house with no rooms, filled with treasure. Akinyele himself was attracted by another bystander, who advised him to try to open the house because his wealth was stored in it. As he moved to the gate of the house, the horned man aimed the gun at him, and he stopped. Try as he would to persuade the gate-keeper to let him into the house the man was indomitable. He woke up panting for breath.

The following morning, he went to the home of Ose kele, but he was told that he had been to Ife to visit Osemeji the wrestler. On getting there he told the Ifa priest about the dream and he made divination on it. He was told that good fortune and death were lurking around him, but that if he made the necessary sacrifice, the fortune would come within his reach and he would avoid premature death. He was advised to make sacrifice with 10 rats, 10 fishes, 10 pigeons, (5 hens and 5 cocks), 10 guinea fowls, 2 goats, and 3 he-goats, male and female pigs and one ram. He made the sacrifice. He was told that it was Esu he saw in the dream who was sitting on top of his fortune. He was therefore to serve Esu by spilling the blood of the he-goat, not on the shrine of Esu but at a short distance on the empty ground away from the shrine.

After the sacrifice, as Esu moved from his shrine to eat the he-goat given to him outside his base, he unwittingly got off from Akinyele's fortune on which he had been sitting, and his guardian angel dragged the fortune into the home of Akinyele. Thereafter, things began to take a better turn for him.

One night, there was a heavy gale storm and he felt like easing himself. He got up to go to the pit-latrine outside the back of his house. It was raining heavily. As he was in the latrine, he suddenly heard a big sound and as he got up to find out what was happening, he saw the roof of the latrine collapsing. He was already outside the door when a tree crushed the latrine under its falling debris. But he was already outside the latrine. He was grateful to God for sparing his life from the accident.

The following morning, he discovered that it was the ageless kolanut tree at the back of his house that had been uprooted by the gale force wind that accompanied the heavy rain of the previous night. When he went to inspect the root of the fallen tree, he saw that beneath the root of the tree lay a brass casket, which contained several beads, money and a crown, which had been buried there by his ancestors. He took the casket to his house and the contents made him exceedingly wealthy. He was able to make a beaded dress for himself and he was later crowned the King of Iwere.

True to the dream he had, he suceeded in getting his hidden fortune, and in avoiding the incidence of death. When this ODU therefore comes out of divination, the person should be advised to make sacrifice so that the obstacles be-clouding his prosperity might abate.

The hard luck story of Olokose:

Olokose was one of the Awos living with Osemeji. One day he decided to go on a tour for Ifa practice. He was to be accompanied by his wife, Omude. Before leaving, Osemeji insisted that he should ask his colleagues to make divination for him. The following Ifa priests also living with Osemeji, were assembled to divine for him.

Ojuri, koogbi, koofo,
Aje Okpo Uya maabi,
Oun tooshe gbagba to fi ile re sile,
Oun tooba tiri koofi rera,
The eye which saw,
but did not disclose.
He who persevered in suffering,
but did not nag about it.
Misfortune befell many people,
but it did not sack them from
their homes.
Whatever a man experiences,
he should bear with equanimity.

The four Awos advised Olokese to offer a he-goat to Esu before travelling, so that he might not loose all his gains from the tour and his wife to a more powerful man. He refused to perform the sacrifice because he relied on his competence and capabilities.

He left for the tour with his wife. He was otherwise a very proficient Ifa priest and wherever he went, he suceeded in impressing his hosts which earned him a lot of profit and compensation.

Finally, he came to a man called Agunfan, who was so powerful that he was an ubiquitous fighter. When he saw Olokose he engaged him in combat and seized all his belongings and his wife from him. Thereafter he expelled Olokose from the town. He then returned home empty-handed and without his wife.

When this ODU therefore appears at divination for a person who is proposing to embark on a tour, he should be told to make sacrifice against the risk of losing his property to a vindictive person without being able to fight back.

The Divination for the Olubadan of Ibadan.

The King of Ibadan had a stubborn son called Okoko maniko who was always causing trouble in his father's domain. Once upon a time, the son became ill and he was at the point of death. Having heard of the fame of Osemeji at Ife, the King sent errands to go for divination in his place. On account of the importance of the message, Osemeji assembled the following Ifa priests to do the divination:

Kii Aroju Kaa wo Igbo
Biaba de Odan ton, ofeni yio daa.
If one is patient in the forest,
one will come across a clearer ground
which will make movement easier.

They advised that a he-goat should be offered to Esu at once so that he might be saved from dying in the hands of the evil forces that were determined to take him away from the earth. The sacrifice was quickly made and before the messengers got back to Ibadan, Okokomaniko was already beginning to get better.

When this ODU therefore comes out for a sick person, he should be told to make sacrifice because of his stubborn ways. The person should be told that he has a stubborn child who does not listen to advice. He should be told also to prepare Ifa for the son if he is to live long. If the person does not already have a child, he should be told to prepare Ifa for the first son he will have.

He made divination for Olokun.

When Olokun got to the world, she was so beautiful that she did not bother to find out what her destiny was. She was suffering and men were afraid to venture near her. She then heard of Osemeji and went to him for divination.

Osemeji invited one of his Awos called Jeje jeje muje to make divination for her. She was advised to make sacrifice with a goat to her guardian angel, a he-goat to Esu, and a bag of money, and white cloth to the market place. She quickly did all the sacrifices. She was also told that the reason she could not marry and have children was because the elders of the night had their eyes on her and had enveloped her entire being with a veil that made her sight repugnant to men inspite of her beauty. To wash off the evil spell on her, the Awo told her to fetch a pot and a cock. The Awo collected leaves called Ewe Iwo (Ebe Asivbogo in Bini) to prepare for her to be bathing. She was assured that as soon as she started bathing with the pot, all her enemies would begin to die one after the other. She was taught the incantation to repeat whenever she was bathing with the pot.

Soon afterwards, the men and women she had relied on as her close confidants and associates began to die in turn. Not long after that, the Oba of the town invited her to become his wife and she agreed. She soon became pregnant, and had several children. Her trading activities became prolific and her star sprinkled wealth and prosperity on her husband and his domain.

The personal experience of Osemeji.

Osemeji had become very famous and prosperous. He was not aware that one of his wives was a witch and that she was planning to destroy his fame and wealth. He had a frightful dream one night in which he was bound in chains. He then invited two of his more proficient Awos to make divination for him. They were called Eshi Saare and Eshi joson. They told him to make sacrifice at once in order to avoid the danger of trial and imprisonment. He was told to give a he-goat to Esu, a pig to Ifa and a goat to his head.

Meanwhile, his junior wife went to the market and alerted hat sellers, hen sellers, goat sellers, cloth sellers, pig sellers, and the sellers of all imaginable wares in the market, to take proper care of their merchandise because a robber (who she gave a description that fitted the identity of her husband) was in town planning to plunder. The people of the market began to wonder where the woman came from and they were told that she came from Oke Tase in Ife where her husband lived.

The news was reported to the king of Ife who ordered the royal executioner to get prepared for the summary execution of the thief after positioning the local police to apprehend the robber as soon as he moved to plunder.

It was at that stage that Osemeji made the sacrifices to Esu, Ifa, his Head, Ogun, and the night. After the sacrifice, the woman who was, otherwise the expelled wife of Esu in heaven, from where she escaped to the world, stole a number of materials from the market and concealed them in her husband's (Osemeji's) house.

Meanwhile, the owners of the stolen wares were tracing the home of the thief with the description earlier given by the woman. Having eaten his he-goat, Esu quickly installed a mysterious veil round Osemeji's house which made it difficult for anyone to match the outward appearance of the house with the description given by the woman. The problem thus abated and not knowing that it was his wife who started it all, he continued to live with her and she gave birth to five children. After scheming several evil machinations and failing, she gave up and lived happily with the husband nonetheless.

Osemeji lived longer than any other Olodu.

The Olodus, that is, the sixteen main apostles of Orunmila, were in the habit of going to the river to wash the signs of old age from their bodies. After each such bath, they often came out looking several years younger than their ages. At one of their weekly meetings, the sixteen Olodus agreed on the date they were to go to the river for their annual cleansing session.

On getting home from the conference, Osemeji invited one of his Awos called Gere Gere Shalu Gere, to make divination for him against the upcoming trip to the river. He was advised to offer a he-goat to Esu because of the benefits awaiting him at the river. He did the sacrifice without any delay.

On the appointed day, all sixteen Olodus assembled at the river and they began to have their dives into the river in order of seniority. Each of them was required to make three dives into the river. When it was the turn of Osemeji to dive, being the fifteenth Olodu, he dived the first time and came out of the river with a dried fish on the left hand and a fresh fish on the right hand. He made a second dive and emerged with a white cloth on his left hand and a black cloth on the right. In his third and final dive, he came out with 200 cowries on his left hand and beads on the right hand.

The other Olodus accused him of playing magic, but he declined saying that he did not know how to make divination, let alone magic.

On getting home he assembled all his surrogate Awos and told them to interpret his finds in the river. They told him that the fishes indicated that he would live long enough to enjoy all the good things of life. The cloth meant that he would live in peace and concord to the end of his life, which was going to be very long. The last finds meant that he was going to live a life of prosperity and abundance. He actually lived a full life and lived longer than any other Olodu on earth.

CHAPTER XXVIII
OFUN — MEJI

Ofunmeji, who was called Orangun deyin ekun in Heaven was the most senior son of Orunmila in heaven. He was originally the first ODU to come to the world, but we shall see the circumstances in which he returned to heaven to become the last of the Olodus to come to the world. He it was, who revealed that it took six days for the Almighty God to complete his creative works, after which he rested on the seventh day. We shall read more of this story shortly. Meanwhile, let us examine some other important works associated with Ofunmeji in heaven.

Ofunmeji reveals how long it took God to complete his creative works:

Odibi reku reku lere
Odibi ridi ridi
Je aje akakpo ogun
Kobo eledare
ibi reku reku
Odibi reku reku lere
Odibi ridi ridi
Je akakpo Orunmila
Kobo eledaare
ibi reku reku
Odibi reku reku lere
Odibi ridi ridi
Je aje Ugba Erumole
Kiwonbo eleedaa won
ibi reku reku.
    The difficult problem,
    That was resolved peacefuuly,
    In the end:
was the name of the Awo who made divination for Ogun, Olokun, Orunmila, and all the other divinities. He advised them to make sacrifice to their guardian angels over a period of six days, in order to rest in peace and tranquility on the seventh day.

Orunmila asked why the sacrifice should last for seven days instead of one day. The Awo replied that it took Olodumare (God) six days to create the land, seas, atmosphere, plants, animals and humanity. The reason God created all organic and inorganic matter before creating the mankind was to provide abode for man, water for him to drink, food to eat, air to breathe and for him to settle down to a routine life in heaven from the seventh day. He disclosed that God rested on the seventh day after completing the creation of the divinosphere. He told them that in consonance with the precedent established by God at creation, it would take six days to complete the initiation ceremony of any divine priest, and he should clean the house and rest on the seventh day. It is only through this process that the sacrifice will manifest.

Orunmila asked again whether a ceremony lasting seven days will not breed arguments and confusion during the span of the ceremonies. The Awo replied that it is forbidden to have quarrel and discord during the initiation ceremony in the home of a priest. Ai koro Lule awo. Orangun deyiin ekun — eekpaa.

How the Parrot became a symbol of nobility:

It was Ofunmeji who in heaven revealed how the Parrot was transformed into an honourable bird and how it acquired its red feathers. He did so through the following poem:—
   Idemu Odide werewe,
   Oni batti anni Aje Ile eni dide ninde,
   Ayaa Ile eni dide ninde,
   Omo Ile enii dide ninde, meaning:—
      It multiplied in small measure.
      He who attains riches multiplies.
      He who has plenty of wives also multiplies.
      Just as he who has many children has multiplied.

This is the incantation with which divination was made for the Parrot, before all the divinities came to discover him not only as an instrument of decoration, but also as a symbol of authority and influence. He was advised to make sacrifice with a piece of red cloth, a red cock, black cloth, a pigeon, a hen and can-wood. He did the sacrifice in the house of Esu. Thereafter Esu invited the Parrot for a transformative operation.

Esu daubed the red cloth with can-wood and wrapped it round the tail feathers of the Parrot and blew it into his anus. At the end of the operation, all the feathers at the tail end of the Parrot's body became red. When Esu was asked for the significance of the operation, he replied by proclaiming that from then on, all the divinities would only be able to have authority and see into the future, through the use of the Parrot's red feathers. He directed them to be buying the red feathers from the Parrot for adornment and decoration. That explains why there is no divinity that does not use the red Parrot feathers to this day, being the light with which they see into the future. From then on, the Parrot became a noble bird as well as a wealthy one.

Orunmila converts the authority of all the other divinities to himself:

Ofunmeji also reveals how Orunmila succeeded in collecting and converting to his own use, all the instruments of authority (ASE) given by God to all the divinities. He does so in the following poem:—
   Okiti kpuke,
   Awo eba-ono,
   Adifafun Orunmila,
   Nigbatii Ofelogba aya gbogbo,
   Erumole lowo Ogun.

Ogun, the metal divinity, and the most senior of all divinities, was the custodian of all the ASE (Instruments of authority) given to them by the Almighty God. This meant that any of them who wanted to use his instrument of authority had to go for his own from Ogun.

Meanwhile Orunmila the wisdom divinity contrived a ploy for taking all the powers from Ogun. That was why he went for divinition to Okitikpuke, the road side soothsayer, who told him that he would succeed, if he could make sacrifice with a sheep, a pigeon, and a horse tail. He accordingly made the sacrifice.

After the sacrifice he set out on a visit to Ogun's house. On getting there he told Ogun that he came to pay him a visit. After the usual exchange of courtesies, he told his host with the following incantation that he actually came to collect all the powers of the divinities which were kept under his custody:—

An infant child does not refuse the mother's milk.
The fowl does not refuse the invitation of the corn.
The penis does not refuse the invitation of the pelvis.
One cannot ignore the bite of a snake.
No one resists the invitation of the cough.
No one ignores the bite of a scorpion.
The earth cannot refuse the rays of the sun.
The cloth does not refuse the onslought of a needle.
No one can stop the cat from mousing.
No one disobeys the call of nature.
Even you, Ogun cannot resist the sight of a dog.

As soon as he completed the recitation of the incantation, without any hesitation whatsoever, Ogun went to his safe and brought out all the ASE and sheepishly surrendered them to Orunmila. With the powers safely in his hand, Orunmila took his leave. As soon as he got home he swallowed up all the ASEs. All this time, Ogun acted as if he was in a trance. It did not occur to him to ask Orunmila why he came to collect the powers from him.

Five days later, Ogun realised that the powers were no longer in his possession. After combing his house for the whereabouts of the powers, he remembered that the only divinity who visited him during the last five days was Orunmila. He decided to visit Orunmila because he did not know how to explain the loss of the powers if any of the divinities came to ask for their own. When he got to Orunmila's house, he enquired what he came to do in his house during his last visit. More emphatically, Ogun asked Orunmila whether he was the one who came to collect the strength of all the divinities from him.

When Orunmila realised that Ogun did not have any clear recollection of what transpired when he collected the powers from him, he decided to capitalise on Ogun's temporary mental hallucination. Orunmila denied ever visiting Ogun, let alone collecting any powers from him. Rather dejectedly, Ogun walked back home helplessly. That was how Ogun lost all the powers of the divinities to Orunmila who although one of the most junior of them all, has since become more powerful than all of them. When Ogun left his house, Orunmila sang the following song:—

Shigo shigo agoton,
Mukomi ton kio to shiiyere,
Shigo shigo agoton,

That is why, on the appearance of this Odu at divination the divinee is told to make sacrifice in order to avoid the risk of loosing a treasured asset to a surrepticious schemer.

Ofunmeji leaves for earth:

In heaven, he was called Orongun deyinekun. He was said to be highly temperamental and harsh as he contemplated coming to earth. His guardian angel told him that unless he did something to soften up his temper, he was not going to have an easy time on earth. He then decided to go for divination and went to a female soothsayer who had no limbs.

She was called:— Ugbin eenowo eenose,
Ejo kodu kodu, meaning:—

The snail which has no hands and no legs.
The snake which moves on its abdomen.

She advised Orongun deyenkun to make sacrifice in order to prosper on earth because he was going to be a man of many parts provided he was able to take control of his temper. She advised him to serve his Ifa with 16 snails, which would soften him up and tone down his aggressiveness. He was also advised to serve Esu with a he-goat. He made the sacrifices and received the clearance of God and his guardian angel before he left for earth.

The birth of Ofunmeji:

He was born as the son of a King, who named him Ada-abaye. Even as a child, he had the rare gift of whatever he said coming true. He was the last born of the King, and whatever he asked for was given to him. As he grew up to be a man, he became very dictatorial, and was not in the habit of listening to any advice. His wishes were law and he insisted on having his way all the time. After the death of his father he became the King of his place. His reign was marked by extreme arbitrariness and tension. His people under-went severe stress and mental agony. When the going became too uphill for comfort, his people got together and told him defiantly that they could no longer tolerate him as their King. As if to lend manifestation to the plot being hatched against him, he too decided to abdicate from his throne. All this time, he had no wife and no child.

Ofunmeji returns to heaven:

He too was so disgusted with his inability to make it on earth that he decided to return to heaven to probe his problems. During his journey back to heaven, he met the limbless woman, who made divination for him before he left heaven but he did not recognize her because he had lost all memories of what previously transpired in heaven. Otherwise, he would not have ignored the advice given to him before leaving heaven in the first instance. He was surprised to see the unusual creature having neither hands nor legs and ran back in fright. The woman beckoned on him to move nearer and not to run away. He moved nearer to the woman reluntantly.

The most obnoxious aspect of the woman was that she was also afflicted with leprosy. On seeing her condition he exclaimed "eekpa" in astonishment. That is the traditional exclaimation to this day as soon as Ofunmeji appears at divination. The woman however begged him to make divination for her because, she suspected that he was an Ifa Priest. The woman told him that the two things she wanted most in her life were how to cure her affliction and to have a child. He then brought out his divination instrument and divined for her.

After divination, he told her that if she could make the necessary sacrifices, she would become well and also have children. She was required to make sacrifice with three goats, three hens, three pigeons, three snails, three rats, three fishes, three bitter kolas, three kolanuts, and three yards of white cloth.

It was at this stage that she asked Ofunmeji whether he realised that they were in heaven where she could not obtain these materials. Ofunmeji invited her to return with him to earth so he could make the sacrifice for her there. Thereafter he carried her on his back.

Soon afterwards, they came to the three road junction (Oritameta). Before they got to the three road junction the woman told him that in the light of her condition she was not only forbidden to live in the town but also not to travel by daylight except in the night. At that point, they met a man who was the controller of the three road junction, called Ashipa. With the assistance of the Ashipa, they cut a path into the bush and built a hut there. At the instance of the woman, the hut had no door and the only way of knowing the entrance to the hut was the point at which the tree of life (Ako Oko in Yoruba and Ikhinmwin in Bini) was planted, as well as the point at which a palm frond was tied to the hut. Before leaving her to fetch the instruments for the sacrifice, Ofunmeji asked her how he would be able to see her since the hut had no inlet. She taught him the incantation to repeat after which he was to put his back to the wall under the Palm frond and the gate would open to let him in. He was to say "Oro oyin kiimu eyon, eekpa — aikoro lule awo". Before leaving her; Ofunmeji discovered that she had only one breast. That hut was called Ile-Odi popularly know today as Iledi.

Before resuming his journey to heaven Ofunmeji visited his close confidant called Akpena who had been looking for a wife. After telling him the condition of the woman he asked whether he was prepared to marry a woman having those deformities. Surprisingly, Akpena agreed to meet with the woman. Thereafter Ofunmeji asked Akpena to collect all the materials for the sacrifice and they both returned to the hut to make the sacrifice. After the sacrifice, Ofumeji formally introduced Akpena to the woman.

Before the woman agreed to become Akpena's wife she brought out a mysterious wand on which he was made to swear an oath never to reveal her condition. She also said that if anyone else was coming to the hut to see her for any reason, he should be blind-folded to prevent him from seeing her condition. The only exception was Ofunmeji and all other Ifa Priests after him. Before anyone else saw her, the same oath had to be administered to him or her, not to reveal her condition.

Ofunmeji returns to heaven:

As soon as the sacrifice was made, the crippled woman became cured of her leprosy, and her beauty as a young and beautiful woman became noticeable. Thereafter Ofunmeji decided to resume his journey to find out the cause of all his mysterious problems. On getting to heaven he quickly headed for the home of the crippled female Ifa Priest who had previously divined for him. The woman was nowhere to be found. His guardian angel told him that the woman had since left for earth and advised him to do everything to locate her because she was the only one who could make him prosper on earth. It was then he realised that it was the woman he had just settled into the hut on earth. He quickly returned to the world.

Ofunmeji was the first of the Olodus or Apostles of Orunmila to become a king on earth because he was the first to come to earth. He fell from grace because of his dictatorial tendencies. During his second coming to the earth he became the last of the sixteen Olodus of the Ifa genealogy after Ejiogbe and others had come. That was however not until he re-established contact with the woman whose turn it was to make divination for him. After divination, the woman advised him to make a sacrifice with two pigeons, black cloth, a walking stick, mashed yam, kolanuts and cowries at the road junction, and that he would become a king again. We shall see later how the sacrifice benefitted Ofunmeji.

The Origin of the Secret fraternity:

The marriage of the crippled girl to Akpena flourished immensly. They are said to have had sixteen children between them. Little is known however of the other children with the exception of the two eldest ones, who were called Ogbo nicknamed Yaya and the next one called Oni nicknamed Yoyo. They grew up as Cats and Dogs always fighting each other. At one time they even resorted to the use of diabolical means of mutual destruction. When their parents discovered that they were running the risk of destroying each other, they took them into the hut previously inhabited by their mother and made them to swear on the mother's charm called Edan. In the oaths, they swore never to plot or do anything against each other. That was the first initiation ceremony into the Secret fraternity.

The name Ogboni is a derivation from the names of its two founders, Ogbo and Oni.

It is reputed to be the first Secret Society on earth, according to Orunmila.

Ofunmeji's second coming to the earth:

When he got to the world the second time, he took to the practice of Ifa art, specializing in the preparation of good luck charms for people. Thus, it was said of him, Ofun Iofueni Owo, Ofun Iofueni Omo, Ofun lo fueni Aya, meaning:— That Ofunmeji is responsible for providing assistance to people desirous of having the benefit of money, marriage and child birth. He was a proficient benefactor in these matters. Nonetheless, he was being despised and ridiculed by his people who saw him as having climbed down from grace to grass. He however retorted to these jibes by warning people not to tantalise him unduly becaucse he still had the means of barking and biting in the face of provocation.

In spite of his warning, several smart alecs continued to despise and tantalise him. He began to destroy those who were undermining him. As people began to feel the wrath of his reaction, they started dreading him. Meanwhile, he decided to go for divination, where he was advised to desist from his aggressive stance. The Awos who made divination for him on that occasion were:—

Afuye Omo aje
Ewon bale Iowoji
Odidere Awo agbado
Elomon biriti
Babalawo Edu.

They told him to make sacrifice for peace, prosperity, wealth and long life.

They made all the sacrifices for him and eventuallly he became so wealthy that he ended up being made the Orongun of Illa Orongun. He also lived to a ripe old age. It is said however, that his friend Akpena who married the crippled woman finally settled down in Itagbolu where the shrine exists to this day.

The Divination for Orangun and Akogun:

Obo to bo tori eku
Ekutele to soro fun toni ojo oroju
Ojona gooni ojo oroju
Adifa fun orongun. Abufun akogun.

> The monkey tied to the roof,
> Became hungry from neglect,

is the name of the awo who made divination for two brothers Orongun and Akogun when they were contesting the throne of their departed father. As they fought to the point of destroying each other, the kingmakers intervened. They decided to give the throne to their uncle. Their uncle did not last long on the throne. Following the death of their uncle, the two brothers settled their score amicably. Eventually, the Kingmakers decided to give the throne to the eldest of the two brothers, Orongun, while the junior one Akogun, was made the spokesman of the town, without whose consent, no decision of any significance, was ever taken. Orongun had a long and peaceful reign with the active support of his brother Akogun.

Divination for Aganbi, the barren woman of Ife:

> Ofun tututu bi eleji
> Amuji kutu wenu,
> Ibi Titu maa kanju
> Orunrun ale won maa nissin.

Adifa fun Aganbi ile ife nijo toon fi omi oju shubere omo tuuru tu.

> Ofun the white one,
> Was as cool as rain water.
> The Drinking water pot,
> Is washed clean every morning,
> Before refilling it.
> The cool shade need not fret,
> For lack of company,
> Because the sun,
> Will soon drive clients to him.

These were the Awos who made divination for the barren woman of Ife when all her relations abandoned her as a hard luck case because she did not have children. She was advised to make sacrifice with white cloth, white cock, white hen, corn, and honey, and to marry an Ifa priest. She made the sacrifice and eventually got married to a practicing Ifa priest.

She soon became pregnant and gave birth to a child. Her next pregnancy gave birth to a set of twins. Thereafter, all her friends and relations who had written her off, returned to rejoice with her. She became very happy and sang in praise of the Awos who made divination for her.

When this ODU comes out of divination for a person who is anxious to have a child, he should be told to exercise patience and to make sacrifice. If the subject is a man, he should be told to arrange to have his own Ifa. If a woman, she should be advised to marry a practising Ifa priest after making sacrifice.

ALL RIGHTS RESERVED

www.ingramcontent.com/pod-product-compliance
Lightning Source LLC
Chambersburg PA
CBHW061437300426
44114CB00014B/1722